THE LIFE AND MINISTRY OF WILLIAM BOOTH

THE LIFE & MINISTRY OF

WILLIAM BOOTH

Founder of

THE SALVATION ARMY

ROGER J. GREEN

Abingdon Press
Nashville

THE LIFE AND MINISTRY OF WILLIAM BOOTH
FOUNDER OF THE SALVATION ARMY

Copyright © 2005 by Abingdon Press

This book is printed on acid-free paper.

Library of Congress Cataloging-in-Publication Data

Green, Roger Joseph.
  The life and ministry of William Booth : founder of the Salvation Army / Roger J. Green.
      p. cm.
  Includes bibliographical references and index.
  ISBN 0-687-05273-4 (binding: adhesive, pbk. : alk. paper)
  1. Booth, William, 1829–1912. 2. Salvation Army. I. Title.

  BX9743.B7G74 2005
  287.9'6092—dc22

                                                        2005026520

All scripture quotations unless noted otherwise are taken from the *New Revised Standard Version of the Bible*, copyright © 1989, by the Division of Christian Education of the National Council of the Churches of Christ in the United States of America. Used by permission. All rights reserved.

Excerpts from Roger J. Green, *Catherine Booth: A Biography of the Cofounder of The Salvation Army*, copyright © 1996, published by Baker Books, a division of Baker Publishing Company. Used by permission.

05 06 07 08 09 10 11 12 13 14—10 9 8 7 6 5 4 3 2 1

MANUFACTURED IN THE UNITED STATES OF AMERICA

Dedicated, with love, to my father, Brigadier Clyde P. Green,

retired Salvation Army Officer,

and to my two brothers, David and Robert

CONTENTS

Acknowledgments ix

Foreword xiii

Introduction 1

1. Beginnings: Life from 1829 to 1849 5

2. A Follower of Wesley: Association with Methodism 21

3. Providential Meeting: William Booth and
   Catherine Mumford 37

4. Finding a Denominational Home: William Booth
   and New Connexion Methodism 51

5. Difficult Decision: Leaving New Connexion Methodism 75

6. The Road to Freedom 93

7. The Beginning of a Mission 105

8. The Evolution of a Mission and the Creation of an Army 123

9. The Army in the Public Square 139

10. Turning Points 159

11. Three Who Left 183

12. International Evangelist 197

13. England Recognizes Her Son: Honors Bestowed
    upon William Booth 213

14. Darkness and Light 223

Epilogue 233

Notes 235

Index 279

ACKNOWLEDGMENTS

My interest in William Booth has grown over the years, and the time now seemed appropriate for me to tell his story yet again. However, in the telling I am indebted to many people, and those mentioned here are only a small number indicative of my great appreciation to those who have made this book possible.

First, my thanks go to my wife, Karen, for both her patience and support while this work was in progress. Writing this book has meant many trips away from home and countless hours at the computer. I am, as usual, indebted to Karen for her constant love and support.

This book would not have been possible without the assistance of Gordon College. The College's Faculty Development Plan that includes a generous sabbatical program has made all of this possible. In addition to the generous provisions of the Faculty Development Plan, I have applied for and received many grants throughout the years that have made the research for this project possible, providing both the time and the funds to travel often to London to the British Library and The Salvation Army International Heritage Centre. However, special thanks are due to my friend and colleague Dr. Marvin R. Wilson, Harold J. Ockenga Professor of Biblical and Theological Studies at Gordon College. He has helped and encouraged me in innumerable ways as I have worked through this project and as I have sought a publisher for this biography. His familiarity with the publishing field, because of his own publishing record, has been invaluable to me. I am constantly grateful for his friendship and his support.

There are four people who wrote endorsements for this book. First, Lieutenant Colonel Marlene Chase, the editor-in-chief of Salvation Army publications in the United States, readily agreed to write an endorsement, as well as my friend of many years, Dr. Jonathan S. Raymond, the president of William and Catherine Booth College in

Winnipeg, Manitoba, Canada. I serve with both Colonel Chase and Dr. Raymond in producing The Salvation Army's theological journal entitled *Word & Deed: A Journal of Salvation Army Theology and Ministry,* and I know of their dedicated ministry of service, exemplified in teaching, in administration, and in writing.

Two of my friends from the Methodist tradition have also agreed to write endorsements of this book. First, I am indebted to Dr. George H. Freeman, General Secretary of the World Methodist Council. Dr. Freeman has been very generous in his support of the ministry of The Salvation Army, and I know of his interest in Salvation Army history and theology. Second, Dr. Paul Wesley Chilcote has kindly agreed to write an endorsement for this book. Dr. Chilcote is Professor of Historical Theology and Wesleyan Studies at Asbury Theological Seminary, Florida Campus, in Orlando. Dr. Chilcote is likewise interested in Salvation Army theology and ministry. Both Dr. Freeman and Dr. Chilcote recognize the importance of placing William Booth within the context of the Methodism in which he was nurtured and the Wesleyan theology that he readily embraced. I am privileged as a present member of The Salvation Army's International Doctrine Council to be in theological dialogue with the Methodists, and both Dr. Freeman and Dr. Chilcote are representatives in that dialogue.

General Paul A. Rader accepted my request to write the foreword to this book. He is eminently qualified to do so. As a successor to the office of William Booth, he was the General of The Salvation Army from 1994 to 1999, and he is presently the president of Asbury College. His insights into the theology and ministry of William Booth, both from his Salvation Army experience and his leadership within the broader Wesleyan tradition today, are invaluable in understanding the life of the founder of The Salvation Army. I am indeed grateful to General (Dr.) Rader for taking time out of his busy schedule to write this foreword.

Several people have shared both their resources and their time with me for this book. I mention but a few. First, Commissioner Orval Taylor, a retired Salvation Army officer, gave me a box of material that had been in his family, and from that I discovered a wealth of interesting writings, some of which I have used in this biography. Likewise, many years ago as a captain in The Salvation Army Kenneth Hodder shared with me research that he had done on Frank Smith, an officer who played an important role in the shaping of the Army's social ministry. I treasure the resources from these two Salvation Army Officer friends. Likewise, the time given to me by other Salvationist friends is greatly appreciated. Graham Cook and

Gordon Parkhill, both Salvationists at the Leigh-on-Sea Corps, took time to show me the Hadleigh Farm Colony, one of the most successful farm colonies of William Booth's social ministry, and still being operated by The Salvation Army. And Major Ray Brown of The Salvation Army in Nottingham gave of his valuable time one day in taking me to many of the sites in Nottingham connected with William Booth. I am appreciative to these and other friends for giving so generously of their time.

The research for this book was conducted in many places, but two in particular deserve mention. First, I spent countless hours in the British Library, and always found the staff extremely helpful. Second, however, most of my time was spent at The Salvation Army's International Heritage Centre in London, England. The staff there has been nothing short of remarkable in their patience with me throughout the years and during my several visits. No detail was too small, no question too obscure, and no request too problematic for the members of the staff. I am indebted to them for their care and friendship throughout these years. However, two people deserve special mention. I am grateful first to Commissioner Karen Thompson whose assistance to me has been invaluable in writing this book. Her knowledge of Salvation Army history and of the history of the Booth family is fascinating, and she was a constant help to me and a source of encouragement.

My special thanks go to Gordon Taylor. Through the many years of my researching at the International Heritage Centre, he has been an invaluable resource, and, I am pleased to say, our friendship has developed during those years. I count Gordon as a friend and colleague, and am convinced that no person knows more about Salvation Army history than Gordon Taylor. My conversations with him and Commissioner Thompson were often as illuminating and helpful as my research. Gordon's knowledge is limitless. Gordon agreed to read the manuscript of this book and helped me a great deal. Thank you, Gordon, for your work on my behalf. However, I quickly add that the blame for any errors in this book is mine and mine alone.

Finally, my thanks go to the staff of Abingdon Press. I am especially grateful to Kathy Armistead. She guided this project through to my submission of the manuscript, and I am appreciative to her for her constant encouragement.

However, whatever is in this book is finally and fully only my own. I can only pray that the reader will find in this book a helpful biography of William Booth, and will readily forgive any error or failure in this work.

FOREWORD

Catherine Booth once opined that The Salvation Army was first conceived as an idea in the mind of God. Whatever its divine provenance, it sprang to life in the passionate heart of William Booth, its founder and first General. Its theological grounding and organizational development, not to mention its remarkable missionary expansion, are owed in large measure to the giftedness of the first company of family and faithful friends whom Booth summoned to his Blood and Fire banner. Of these no contribution to the Army's success and legitimacy as a vital expression of the mission and reality of the Church was greater than that of his wife and cofounder, Catherine Booth. And it is significant that this biography was preceded by Roger Green's account of the life and ministry of the Army Mother.

The founder's family was remarkable by any measure. Both the faith and foibles of that colorful tribe are here candidly explored, and rightly so. Whatever the Army has become owes much to their dedication to its mission. But without the vision and passion of William Booth it is difficult to conceive that there ever would have been a Salvation Army. Booth was not without his faults, but in Wesleyan Holiness terms he had a heart made "perfect" in love. The zeal of the Lord consumed him. He was a visionary who dreamed of conquests for his Army that in his view could have completed the Great Commission alone. He was first a passionate evangelist. He preached with a heart torn by the plight of the poor and marginalized struggling in a stormy sea of sin and suffering, of poverty and pain.

Booth is a study in leadership. He had a genius for inspiring devotion to his cause that found expression in an almost fanatical devotion to himself. As these pages will make clear, the heroic aura that surrounded him was partly a result of his social milieu. But few have succeeded in gaining such absolute command over the lives and labors of their devotees. He was loved. In spite of his uncompromising demands on his legions and the autocratic control he insisted upon in his life and had drawn into the foundation deeds of the movement that survived him, he evoked an almost religious allegiance. Indeed, devotion to the founder and to the Lord whose Army he was born to lead, were not infrequently regarded as one and the same. The will of the founder became for his followers the will of God.

Doubtless he would have been a very different leader today. To a great extent he was a man of his times and the product of the social and historical context into which he was born. And yet his life and leadership continue to fascinate and inspire almost a century and a half later.

The appearance of this latest treatment of William Booth's life and ministry is especially timely for two particular reasons. It is only in relatively recent years that the Army as a movement has begun to understand and accept its ecclesial identity and function. Not until the most recent editions of the Army's Handbook of Doctrine has the word Church been associated with the Army as a movement or its local fellowships as churchly expressions of the Body of Christ. Its mission statement declares that the Army is an "evangelical part of the universal Christian Church." That has always been understood. But the Army has resisted identifying itself as a Church body or its local corps as "churches." It has preferred to view itself as a "continuing mission to the unconverted" with its "message based on the Bible, its ministries motivated by the love of God, and its mission to preach the Gospel of Jesus Christ and meet human need in His name without discrimination." Like Wesley before him, Booth had no brief for denominationalism. He never envisioned establishing yet another church body. Yet, partly due to the emergence of the Church Growth movement in the 1970s as well as the increasing engagement of ordinary Salvationists in the broader evangelical movement and its popular expressions, the Army began to reflect more seriously on its churchly identity and pastoral responsibility to those who find their vital connection to the Body of Christ solely through their membership in its ranks and participation in its life and mission in local corps congregations. The Army has always sat uncomfortably to standard ecclesial categories, whether as a denomination, a church, a global movement, a human service agency, or evangelistic mission. In the minds of its members it is all this and more. Commissioner Philip Needham in his seminal study on Army ecclesiology sees the movement as community in mission.

Given this search for a clearer understanding of the Army's ecclesial identity and mission, Green's careful recounting of the Booths' struggle to find a home within the Body of Christ and its denominational iterations in England of the mid-nineteenth century, is particularly helpful. Christened an Anglican; converted under Methodist influences; inspired by the American revivalists, Caughey, Finney, Palmer, and others; caught up in volatile issues of polity, practice, and political infighting among proliferating Methodist groups; and just briefly enamored of the possibilities for ministry in the reformed tradition, Booth found his destiny in the streets of East London. It was a long and painful pilgrimage, but he never strayed far from his Wesleyan loyalties. Finally his life journey led to the place and purpose providentially ordered for him and the movement he and Catherine birthed together.

In a vital sense, the Army did not begin in Mile End Waste. These turbulent years of uncertainty were years of gestation. The Army cannot be fully understood without coming to terms with the influences that played upon the Booths long before 1865 and the founding of the East London Christian Mission, which became The Salvation Army in 1878. Salvationists need to reconnect with that earlier history.

The Army was born in the flames of the second evangelical awakening that swept across England and America in the mid-nineteenth century. The Booths were prominent players in that vital movement. Green makes clear how important the issues of evangelistic practice and strategy became in the often-acrimonious power struggles within Methodism of the period. It is perhaps worth observing that the issues were not much different than those that have been precipitated by the "choir wars" in contemporary mainline churches across America. As for the Booths, their ministry would be forever marked by their immersion in the powerful spiritual movements of which they became a part. Indeed, the chronicler of awakenings in Britain and America, J. Edwin Orr, once observed that The Salvation Army was the most enduring result of the midcentury awakening in England. James Caughey, Phoebe Palmer, and others were a formative influence on William and Catherine Booth, particularly in their articulation of the Wesleyan understanding of Scriptural Holiness. Under these influences, Catherine Booth confirmed her own calling to public ministry. Given her obvious giftedness for a preaching ministry, it did not take long for William Booth to come to "settled views" on the issue. And the Army has provided what is perhaps the most outstanding demonstration of the value and validity of women's pastoral and preaching ministries ever since.

Before the Army ever came to life, the die was cast for the centrality of the penitent form or Mercy Seat as symbolizing the immediacy of God's saving and sanctifying grace available to all who believe. The accessibility of platform and pulpit to women as well as men was assured. And the centrality of what in most American centers of Army worship is known as the Holiness Table would give witness to the Army's affirmation of "the privilege of all believers to be wholly sanctified," enshrined in its doctrinal statements from the beginning, but rooted in the Holiness Revival within midcentury Methodism.

There is another reason the appearance of this biography, which so intentionally roots the Army in its Methodistic tradition, is so timely. Dr. Green has served as cochair of an historic dialogue between The Salvation Army International Doctrine Council and representatives of the Methodist World Council. The first consultation was held in London in 2003. The second at World Methodist Council headquarters in Lake Junaluska, North Carolina. Dr. Green presented a paper at the most recent meeting outlining the Wesleyan foundations of Salvation Army missiology. The consultations have probed the issues surrounding the role and leadership of women in ministry including the advantages of spousal team ministry, the doctrine of the Church in Methodist heritage, and the place of the sacraments as a means of grace. This tentative exploration of points of commonality and the distinctives of Wesleyanism has great potential for the future of the Army in the development of its own self-understanding and a reconnection with its foundations in the Methodist tradition. Roger Green's biography of William Booth will make its own vital contribution to the dialogue and its potential for energizing and informing the life and mission of both the Army and the broader Methodist community.

Dr. Roger Green brings to his task his scholarly skills and his own life-long identification with the Army, to which he continues to make an incomparable contribution as a lay Salvationist. He served on the International Spiritual Life Commission of The Salvation Army and currently holds membership on its International Doctrine Council. He presents a richly nuanced Salvationist perspective tempered by the scholar's discipline. The result is an unvarnished and insightful insider's account of William Booth, the influences that shaped his life and ministry, and his own formative influence on the movement that he launched and led for nearly half a century.

Paul A. Rader
General (Ret.)
Lexington, Kentucky
March 2005

INTRODUCTION

William Booth, the founder and first General of The Salvation Army, served Christ and his own generation. This is a story of that service told through the life, ministry, and theology of William Booth. There are other biographies of Booth. Some simply tell his story, while others are more in-depth treatments, placing him and his Army within the context of Victorian life and culture. And so it is fair to ask how this particular biography adds to our understanding of William Booth.

I am convinced that this biography, written with great appreciation for what has been written previously, will assist the reader in several ways, but there are three in particular. First, I have attempted to understand William Booth within the context of the Methodist tradition in which he was nurtured and to which, by his own admission, he owed so much. This is crucial in understanding Booth.

Second, and definitely related to the first, I wanted to place William Booth theologically within the Wesleyan tradition. One of the great faults of some of the previous biographies of Booth is that they have failed to understand that he was driven by a particular theological vision. To miss the theology of Booth, or even to deny it, is to neglect from the outset what was most important to Booth. He was a biblical Christian. And his theological vision was not merely broadly Protestant or even generically Evangelical. It was Wesleyan, and Booth's theology of redemption—including his understanding of sin, grace, salvation, holiness—can be understood only if this is taken into account. The time for treating William Booth apart from or in spite of his theological background and convictions is over. This is the moment for a renewed theological understanding of this man and his Army.

Third, I have tried to understand and explain William Booth's relationship with those around him, including his relationships with the members of his family. After the death of Catherine Booth in 1890, William had a falling out with three of his own children and their spouses. They left the Army, while the other five children remained in the Army. However, the story of the three that left is one that must be told if the reader is to understand both William Booth and the formative years of The Salvation Army. There was great personal pain and suffering in those later years, and even tragedy. William Booth allowed his greatest strength—his love for his beloved Army—to become his greatest weakness when he failed to see his love for his children as something to be equally embraced, nurtured, and cherished.

Nevertheless, in the telling of those stories as part of the full picture of William Booth, I attempt to see William Booth for the man he was, not a perfect stained glass window figure or saint. This in no way diminishes William Booth, but makes him a remarkable example of how God uses people in spite of their human failings. We do no service to William Booth or to ourselves in seeing him as more than human. Only when we see him as we see ourselves, and only when we know him as we know ourselves will we learn to appreciate him for the man that he was. And, in spite of his personal failures and frailties, he is a constant reminder of what biblical servanthood is intended to be. Even the most jaundiced observer of William Booth could never claim that he schemed and plotted and connived to get his own way. He had no hidden agenda for self-aggrandizement. He valued the truth of the central message of Christ—to love God and love our neighbor. He served his generation as an agent of that truth. He was forthright in who he was and what he believed. In this day, when the ministry of the gospel is so obscured behind the smoke of self-seeking and ego-driven preachers, when many notions of servant ministry are merely meaningless words, William Booth comes across as a genuine preacher and leader, a biblical man.

As with my other writings, I set out to steer a middle course with this biography. On the one hand I want to appeal to the general reader, to the person whose sole interest is to learn about William Booth in what I pray is a comprehensive biography. I realize that people will not go back to the older biographies of William Booth that are often voluminous, and so I have taken what is useful from those older works. On the other hand, I include material that will be of interest to the scholar who wishes to do further research on Booth or his Army. It is indeed a tragedy that many original sources—documents, letters, diaries—were destroyed as a result of the bombing of The Salvation Army's International Headquarters in London in May of 1941, and so reliance on some of the older biographies is necessary for the accuracy of those texts. Also, I mention here two rather insignificant matters, but they may be of interest to the reader. When the word *corps* is used, please understand that that is the word for the Army's local church. Also, the legal name is The Salvation Army. However, where other writers refer to [t]he Salvation Army, which frequently happens, I have decided to let that remain as is rather than correct it each time.

My research and understanding of William Booth will always be a work in progress. I make no claim to some final, complete work here. And I believe that all genuine scholarly endeavors should be understood in this light, as works along the journey. And so I look forward to my own personal continued study of Booth. I pray that this work may motivate others to begin or continue their research in this and related fields.

I realize that there are two dangers for the biographical writer. One is that the writer is too distant from the subject and therefore misses insights both great and small into the life of his or her subject. The other is that the writer is too attached to the subject and cannot be objective enough. As a lifetime lay Salvationist I probably fall into the latter category. There is a sense in which when William Booth found his destiny he found mine also. That being the case, I have attempted to be aware of the failings that this brings to my writing and have tried to rise above those. Only the reader can judge if I have succeeded.

But this is a story to be told. I can only pray that I have told it fairly and honestly, and that whatever I have told points to the glory of God.

BEGINNINGS: LIFE FROM 1829 TO 1849

Introduction

The Acting Lord Mayor of London in August 1912 was Sir John Knill. He, along with the former Lord Mayor, Sir T. Vezey Strong, stepped out of the Mansion House and stood on the portico to witness the funeral cortege of one of the last great Victorians, General William Booth, the founder of The Salvation Army. They saluted the coffin. The sun burst through the clouds that day, while thousands of Salvationists marched behind the coffin of their beloved founder and General.

In a fitting tribute by the people, the streets of London were impassable as tens of thousands of people strained to see this most unusual funeral procession. The march began at The Salvation Army's International Headquarters at Queen Victoria Street, and slowly through the crowded streets found its way to Abney Park Cemetery, Stoke Newington, where William Booth's wife, Catherine, had been buried in 1890. Booth was, according to one biographer, denied burial at Westminster Abbey, but he himself preferred to be buried next to his beloved wife. The common people and the poor from around the world were mourning the loss of this man, as were heads of state and royalty.

The wreaths at the grave awaiting the funeral procession included those from the reigning king and queen, George V and Mary, from Queen Alexandra, the queen consort of Edward VII who died in 1910, the German emperor, and the American ambassador to the Court of St. James.

William Booth died on August 20, 1912, and the next day it was announced that "the General has laid down his sword."[1] The honors that were bestowed upon him in death and the respect paid to him at this moment were not, however, always foreshadowed in his lifetime:

> The lonely evangelist who had harangued the ungodly before The Blind Beggar, had raised an Army which, when he died, occupied fifty-eight countries and had nearly sixteen thousand officers who preached the gospel in thirty-four languages. It had children's homes, inebriates' homes, maternity homes, women's industrial homes, men's industrial homes, labour bureaux (long before Labour Exchanges were started by the Government), homes for the reception of ex-prisoners, homes for lepers, farm colonies, hospitals and social institutions of every sort. All these soldiers, so widely active, and all these institutions, so diverse in their purpose, had grown out of the derided efforts of one half-educated man, with a sick wife and sickly children, who had stood alone on the Mile End Waste, banging a Bible and waving an umbrella, and begging the ungodly to repent. The measure of his triumph may, perhaps, most vividly be seen in the records of Carlisle Cathedral, where, in 1880, he was denounced by Dr. Harvey Goodwin, the Bishop. Another Bishop of Carlisle, Dr. Diggle, in 1912, preached a sermon in Dr. Goodwin's pulpit, and said, "I knew the man personally, and for many years I have observed his work, and I can only say from the bottom of my heart, that I thank God for General Booth."[2]

William Booth's Childhood

William Booth, born April 10, 1829, in Nottingham, England, was one of five children born to Samuel and Mary Booth, née Moss, and he was baptized two days later at the local Sneinton Anglican Church, St. Stephen's. He was the middle child of five, but his elder brother, Henry, died on his own second birthday.[3] William's sisters were Ann, the eldest daughter, Emma, and Mary. William was the namesake of Samuel's only child from his previous marriage to Sarah Lockitt. She died on January

13, 1819. Her son, William Booth, died at the age of twenty-four of consumption, but in 1822 had married a woman by the name of Catherine, which would most certainly prove to be one of history's little coincidences—the William Booth of this biography would, in 1855, marry Catherine Mumford.

Little is known of the background of Booth's parents, but there is no evidence that William Booth was of Jewish origin. Speculation regarding the matter arose from earlier biographers primarily because of Booth's mother's maiden name, Moss, which is a form of Moses. However, any Jewish background of William Booth is unsubstantiated.[4]

Samuel Booth had acquired some wealth by the time of his second marriage. He had been a nail manufacturer in his earlier years, and seemingly progressed as a builder, although his calling himself an architect was dubious indeed. He built inexpensive housing for those people migrating from country to town to city as the industrial revolution heated up and the population shifted. At the time of William's birth he listed himself as "gentleman."[5] "Samuel Booth was prone to overstate his fortune and to claim a gentility to which he was not entitled."[6]

Fortunes ebbed and flowed for Samuel. He had lost money in speculation over lace manufacturing by machinery, a major industry in Nottingham at the time. Family fortunes would sink even further by the time William Booth was in his early teen years. His association with his father was distant by all accounts. Samuel Booth was apparently an unloving and detached husband and father. William's reflections on his father were frequently rather bitter. Speaking to one of his biographers, Booth said, "My father was a Grab, a Get. He had been born in poverty. He determined to grow rich; and he did. He grew very rich, because he lived without God and simply worked for money; and when he lost it all, his heart broke with it, and he died miserably."[7] William Booth identified his father as "religiously blind."[8] Samuel Booth ultimately took the family into financial ruin.

Mary Moss Booth provided a more comfortable image in William Booth's early years. Her family had made money from farming in Derbyshire.[9] After her mother died and her father's second marriage proved to be an unhappy one, she was taken to an aunt and uncle who reared her. Apparently in her late teen years she inexplicably moved to Ashby-de-la-Zouch where she met Samuel "who was availing himself of the waters as a remedy for his chronic enemy, rheumatism."[10] She had the good sense to refuse Samuel's marriage proposal the first time, but finally relinquished to his pesterous demands, reluctant to marry him perhaps because of his illiteracy and his rather crude ways. Nevertheless, Samuel and Mary were married on November 2, 1824.

William Booth did not remember his mother as particularly helpful in his younger days either with his schoolwork or in matters pertaining to religion. It appears that Mary Booth had become completely "absorbed during the whole of her married life in the anxieties and disasters of her husband's speculations. She seems to have felt her poverty acutely, and to have shrunk from the world in consequence. She worked for her children, she nursed her husband in his last illness, she did all she could to avert the final catastrophe of ruin; but she was a sombre, sad, silent, and tragic figure in that threatened home. William Booth . . . speaks of his early days as 'a season of mortification and misery.' He makes it clear that his childhood was dark and unhappy."[11]

There is no doubt that William Booth's life at home was difficult, but it is impossible precisely to ascertain in what ways his mother either contributed to his unhappiness or attempted to relieve it. In any case, Booth's reflections about his mother in later life were more sanguine. He remembered her as good and patient and self-sacrificing, and he stated that he loved his mother.

> I had a good mother. . . . Home was not home to me without her. I do not remember any single act of wilful disobedience to her wishes. When my father died I was so passionately attached to my mother that I can recollect that, deeply though I felt his loss, my grief was all but forbidden by the thought that it was not my mother who had been taken from me. And yet one of the regrets that has followed me to the present hour is that I did not sufficiently value the treasure while I possessed it, and that I did not with sufficient tenderness and assiduity, at the time, attempt the impossible task of repaying the immeasurable debt I owed to that mother's love.[12]

William's mother lived until the age of eighty-four. She died on January 13, 1875.

The Booth family lived in an area of Nottingham known as Sneinton, a suburb of Nottingham at the time, but still touched by the industrialization of the city. And while Nottingham had been a city of some remarkable beauty in the eighteenth century, such was not the case when William was born at 12 Notintone Place in 1829.[13] Lacemaking machines were developed in Nottingham, and in the 1840s the industry was so well developed that Nottingham was known worldwide for lacemaking, a point demonstrated by the fact that a district of Nottingham became known as the Lace Market in the early part of the nineteenth century. However, the initial prosperity could not be sustained, and William Booth knew a Nottingham suffering from poverty and ruin, and he remembered Nottingham as "a place of sorrow."[14] He found some respite, however, in the meadows that led to the river Trent and in the woods beyond, and his boyhood enjoyment of the natural life surrounding Nottingham caused him to reflect in later life that "many of the happiest hours of my life have been spent in this city."[15]

Eventually, in 1831 the Booth family had to move from the Sneinton house to a poorer neighborhood in Bleasby due to Mr. Booth's rapidly declining fortunes and the need to seek a humbler dwelling, although they moved back to Nottingham in 1835.[16] The household continued to be controlled by an austere father and a brooding mother. William was, however, close to his three sisters, and they comforted one another during their difficult childhood years. William would do anything to help his sisters, especially during these trying times. He remained close to his sisters Emma and Mary throughout his life, although his relationship with his sister Ann was strained in later years, as will be mentioned in the next chapter.

William did have some formal education in his childhood, perhaps a sign from his father that he did not want his own lack of education to be passed to another generation. Also, Samuel Booth always wanted to keep up appearances regardless of how dismal the family finances. William would be a gentleman come what may! William went to the village school for his initial education, and then was sent to a school operated by one Mr. Sampson Biddulph, a Wesleyan local preacher. There was evidently little in the way of educational stimulation at Mr. Biddulph's school, and this became a singularly uninspiring time in William's life. In time his health broke down. Perhaps, also, William was old enough to realize the crisis at home brought about by his father's failures and the ruin into which the family was falling. By all accounts, William did read, especially poetry and novels, and perhaps the writings of Sir Walter Scott or James Fenimore Cooper helped to take his mind away from the troubles at home.

On Sundays the Booth children attended the Sneinton parish church—usually without their parents. Apparently, young William did not find much of interest either in the religious services or in the priest, whom he remembered with little appreciation. Apart from a Methodist cousin named Gregory, who occasionally spoke to William about religion coming from outside of a person—from the grace of God—William had little direct religious training either in church or in the home. His father, of course, was so preoccupied with keeping from drowning financially in this life that he was religiously deaf, and his mother, while having some religious training by the aunt and uncle who reared her, confused religion with morality. At this time in his life William was understandably absolutely indifferent to all things religious.

The inevitable crisis came to the family when William was thirteen years of age. The family was financially ruined, and Samuel was unable to pay the mortgage. William was removed from school, and, in order to help the family, was apprenticed as a pawnbroker's assistant to a Unitarian employer. Booth worked for Francis Eames, "Pawnbroker and Dealer in Silver."[17] He who had been reared with the pretense of being a gentleman's son now worked in a miserable trade in the poorest part of Nottingham. In later life "he felt such a hatred for the business that he could not bear to mention it."[18] William's introduction to this business had two results, neither intended by Samuel Booth whose only goal was to introduce his son to a trade that might be the means of making some money as readily as possible for the family.

First, William quickly became exposed to poverty and circumstances more dire, more difficult, and more threatening than his own. He encountered people every day who were, like his own family, on the brink of ruin and even beyond. He developed a special compassion for the poor, not only because he experienced poverty himself but also because he witnessed the tragic effects of poverty.

> He became deeply acquainted with the misery of other people. There had been misery enough in his own childhood, but it was a form of misery that isolated him from the world. He felt his position, and knew that his parents endeavored to hide their poverty from their neighbors, as though all the neighbors were respectable and prosperous, they alone poor and struggling. But now he learned that many other people were fighting against poverty, and he grew to know that suffering and sorrow, deprivation and shame, positive penury and positive want, drag their net in a wide sea of human misery.[19]

Second, this dismal occupation created in the young apprentice a desire to escape. He longed for a better life. He refused to see himself in this trade, in this town, tied to this misery for the remainder of his life.

He wanted something better, looked for something more fulfilling. He was restless and weary, even at this young age.

Samuel Booth died on September 23, 1843.[20] He had a deathbed repentance, having finally turned his thoughts away from money and toward religion, perhaps through the ministry of Gregory, William's Methodist cousin. In any case, William was convinced that his father died at peace with God, a thought in which William would find some comfort for the remainder of his life. When it was evident that Samuel was dying, an Anglican clergyman administered the Sacrament of the Lord's Supper, the family sang "Rock of Ages," and Samuel died peacefully.

Samuel Booth's earthly fortunes had long gone, and he left very little to his family, although his self-delusions of his station in life apparently lingered until the end. Mary Booth and her children were forced to move to a section of Nottingham called Goose Gate, and the women of the family ran a small shop selling miscellaneous household items while William continued working in the pawnbroker's shop. Life continued to be a rather miserable affair for the Booth family.

William Booth's Interest in Religion

In the midst of these circumstances, William Booth's mind turned toward religion. A middle-aged couple named Dent, apparently living in the same neighborhood as the Booths, began taking an interest in William as they saw him playing in the streets. This developing friendship was inexplicable, except to say that William reminded them of their son who had died years earlier. For a brief time William was infatuated with the Dents' younger daughter, Anne. Also, as good Methodists they were concerned for William's soul, and they started taking William to the local Wesleyan chapel, the Broad Street Wesley Chapel. William became a member of Brother Henry Carey's class, and was captivated by the preaching of a lay preacher by the name of Isaac Marsden of Doncaster, who, as one biographer speculated, "gave to William Booth his great intelligent notion of a vital religion."[21] And so his religious stirrings began, leading to a conversion experience for young William.

In the meantime, however, interest in religion could not detract William from the burden of helping to support his family. His mother and sisters were depending on him. But in 1844, at the age of fifteen, William

Booth gave his heart to God. He had been prepared for this not only by the preaching that he heard on Sunday mornings in the chapel but also by his attendance at the weekly class meetings led by Mr. Henry Carey.[22] These small groups had proved to be the strength of Methodism and were the place where the members of the class examined their lives and answered questions regarding the state of their souls. John Wesley had initiated these class meetings in the previous century as one means of ensuring the stability of the great eighteenth-century revival as well as the continuation of Methodism. Wesley wrote "that it may the more easily be discerned whether they are indeed working out their own salvation, each Society is divided into smaller companies, called Classes, according to their respective places of abode. There are about twelve persons in every class, one of whom is styled *the Leader*: it is his business: to see each person in his class once a week at the least; in order to receive what they are willing to give toward the relief of the poor; to inquire how their souls prosper; to advise, reprove, comfort, or exhort, as occasion may require."[23] Eventually, instead of meeting with each member individually throughout the week, the leader assembled members of each class weekly, and this is how the classes functioned in Booth's day. During his nurture in Methodism these class meetings became an important means of spiritual nourishment for the young convert.

William Booth, conscious of his sin and guilt and conscious also of his need for a savior, experienced a rather dramatic conversion. He became convinced that the step toward God could not be taken until his guilt was assuaged and a form of restitution made. "'In a boyish trading affair, I had managed to make a profit out of my companions, whilst giving them to suppose that what I did was all in the way of generous fellowship. As a testimony of their gratitude they had given me a silver pencil-case.' This was the sin that withheld William Booth from grace. Nothing worse than this, which would have seemed to Samuel Booth a sign of enviable astuteness, had defiled the boy's life. But it appeared to him the blackest of sins, nor could he comfort himself with the counsel of God until he had found the young fellow he had chiefly wronged and confessed his wickedness."[24] Until Booth relinquished this secret sin and was free from his guilt, he could never know God or readily receive his redemption. This was doubtless the advice and admonition of his Methodist class leader. Once the restitution was made to match William's repentance, he witnessed that the guilt of his heart was replaced by the peace of God, and he was resolved to serve God and his generation from that time forth.

William Booth had decided for God. That was certain. Where this decision would take him was as yet, however, unclear. Turning to God did not mean one less day spent in the pawnbroking business or one less moment of concern for his mother and sisters who depended on him both emotionally and financially. Turning to God did not release him from his work, nor from rubbing shoulders with people of the world. His becoming religious did, nevertheless, provide both a focus for his life and a sense of purpose—both noticeably absent in his father and certainly subdued in his passive mother. William Booth was as much driven to God as he was called by God. Nevertheless, he firmly believed that he was a sinner in need of salvation, that God had graciously provided the way of salvation through sending his Son whose death on the cross was efficacious for all who believed, and that one had to decide for God in an active step of faith. William Booth acted on the theology that he had heard from the Methodist pulpit and in the class meetings at the Broad Street Wesley Chapel, and in doing so left behind him both the torment of poverty and the elusive yearning after fortune. Now he would serve God and leave present circumstances, as well as his own future, in God's hands.

One of Booth's sustaining friendships in these days was that of William Sansom—Will, as he was called.[25] Here was a genuine friendship that lasted through the years of the Booths' declining fortunes, in spite of the fact that Will Sansom came from a family of considerably better means and cultural advantage. The refinement of Will Sansom was a contrast to the rougher nature of his friend.

The common ground that assured such a close friendship between these two boys was religion. Will Sansom, much like the newly converted William Booth, was fervently religious, and as they matured, their religious sensitivities increased. It was their religious conviction of faith demonstrated in works that moved them to assist a beggar-woman in Nottingham, a woman whom they had seen in their neighborhood countless times in a wretched condition. They found a dwelling for the woman and somehow supported her, thus preventing a cruel life and death on the streets. Here was what one biographer described as Booth's "first experiment in social work."[26]

Booth and Sansom conducted religious meetings on the streets, and led processions on Sunday evenings from street meeting to indoor meeting. Will Sansom instigated these initial evangelistic expressions. William was filled with enthusiasm for the work, but he was reticent about speaking in public. Encouraged, however, by his friends, and by

David Greenbury, an itinerant preacher from Scarborough, he stepped into the street or the makeshift pulpit in someone's cottage and began to preach.

One Sunday morning, William Booth proudly led a gang of street boys into the back entrance of the Wesley Chapel and sat with them in the front pews on the right-hand side of the pulpit, only to be chastised by the elders of the church who found this behavior offensive. Booth acquiesced to their authority.[27] Besom Jack, notorious in Nottingham for his criminal behavior, was saved during this time through the ministry of William Booth in one of David Greenbury's meetings in such an unusually dramatic conversion that it caused people to talk. Booth and Sansom were obviously stepping outside the boundaries of acceptable religious practice, and it was an immeasurable loss to William Booth when his friend died prematurely.[28]

Such exciting Christian work had to happen around his work schedule, for William Booth still had to contend with the drudgery of the pawnbroking business from early morning until early evening. The only satisfaction now, however, was that Booth's exposure to the impoverished of Nottingham only increased his fervor for saving these people for heaven even if their earthly pilgrimage proved to be continuously miserable. The drama of the gospel ministry compensated for the unrelenting toil in the shop. Booth's mission was all encompassing. He began living and working for others. And there were still his mother and sisters to support.

Booth's energies could easily have been channeled in another direction. The Chartists, an English reform movement working toward a more egalitarian society, had some support in Nottingham. These "political and intellectual heirs of Tom Paine and the English friends of the French Revolution"[29] were for the common laborers, and developed a six-point People's Charter in 1838 that made demands on behalf of the working class such as universal male suffrage and abolition of property qualifications for members of Parliament. Led by atheists, deists, and a disaffected dissenter or two, the Chartists took their cause to the streets of industrial England. There was some rioting in the streets when the charter was rejected by Parliament in 1839.

Some Chartist churches were founded, and many Chartists decided to take their protests on behalf of the workers to Sunday morning services in established churches. Such demonstrations, however, were usually without incident. Owen Chadwick wryly wrote that "at St. Paul's Cathedral a band of 500, with red ribands in their button-holes, was persuaded by a single verger to remove their hats."[30] The Chartists sometimes threatened violence, but such incidences were minimal. There was the specter of a national strike after Parliament rejected another Chartist petition in 1842. Other Chartists warmed up to millennial speculations of the 1840s and looked to the great day when all people would live forever equally before God while enjoying the riches of the millennial kingdom. However, as economic conditions improved in the late-1840s, Chartism waned.

It was during this rather revolutionary time that the Chartists came to Nottingham, a city waiting for Chartist preaching because of the number of disenfranchised working people who, like Samuel Booth, had suffered misfortune and were unable to regain any financial stability. Thousands of people were in need of government subsistence. Wages were minimal, and life for many of Nottingham's citizens was intolerable. The threat of riots in the streets meant that armed troops were everywhere. It is at least possible that William Booth witnessed public executions by hanging, and in one case may have witnessed a rag merchant who auctioned his wife, standing in submission with a rope around her neck, to the highest bidder. Booth knew poverty and he knew suffering. In later life, he wrote:

> When but a mere child the degradation and helpless misery of the poor Stockingers of my native town, wandering gaunt and hunger-stricken through the streets droning out their melancholy ditties, crowding the Union or toiling like galley slaves on relief works for a bare subsistence, kindled in my heart yearnings to help the poor which have continued to this day and which have had a powerful influence on my whole life.[31]

William Booth heard Feargus O'Connor, the militant Chartist reformer who upheld the cause through his speeches and the *Northern Star*, his newspaper, and who later became a Member of Parliament for Nottingham. But for his religious sensitivities, William Booth might have become a disciple. W. T. Stead describes Booth's sympathies with the Chartists:

> Young William Booth grew up in an atmosphere of unrest, in a hotbed of quasi-revolutionary discontent. The poverty that he saw on every side filled him with a spirit of passionate revolt against constituted authority. He was but a boy of thirteen when Feargus O'Connor visited Nottingham, but in all the thousands the great Chartist orator had no more enthusiastic disciple than William Booth. He was a Chartist—a physical force

Chartist, of course, being a boy, and therefore uncompromising. He went to their meetings, he cheered their speeches, he subscribed to the Charter, and, if need had arisen, he would have been disappointed if he could not have shouldered a pike or fired a musket.[32]

Stead's description was probably more of a reflection of his own sympathies with the Chartists, but there may be some truth in his statement. Young William, however, eventually turned not to Chartism but to religion. Nevertheless, he was an example that during these times "working class allegiance shifted between religious fervor and political activism. Methodists infiltrated the Chartist movement, in terms of both men and ideas. Chartists sought a working-class parliamentary vote and representation, ideas that reflected the sentiments of upwardly mobile Methodist workers. Due to Methodist influence, Chartists used models of love feasts and camp meetings in their endeavors."[33]

William Booth and James Caughey

John Wesley often visited Nottingham in the previous century and established a strong and enduring Methodism there—not in a denominational sense but in the form of a renewal movement within the church.[34] In Booth's day, denominational Methodism, which had been established only after Wesley's death in 1791, was beginning to grow cold. Formalism was setting into Methodism, with a concomitant neglect of the poor outside of the church doors.

During William Booth's day, several itinerant Methodist preachers came to Nottingham seeking to restore the scriptural way of salvation so often preached by the Wesleys. These included John Smith and David Greenbury, different in preaching styles, but effective in winning converts and raising up the saints in the way of holiness. It was evidently David Greenbury who urged William Booth to begin preaching, as he was "struck by Booth's earnestness, by the vigour of his personality, and by his remarkable appearance and emphatic manner. He urged upon the young man that it was his duty to speak, that he owed it to God to conquer his timidity, which was a form of selfishness."[35]

It is beyond doubt that the greatest influence upon William Booth at this time was American Methodist preacher James Caughey. Booth first heard Caughey when he visited Nottingham in 1846, two years after

Booth's conversion, and so he was not instrumental in Booth's conversion as some have assumed.[36] However, upon hearing Caughey, young William may have been convinced of Caughey's suspicions that Chartist activities brought about chaos to the social order. Booth, like Wesley before him, became politically conservative. He became a monarchist and in later life developed a rather undemocratic hierarchy in The Salvation Army. However, he had compassion for the poor, and some of these poor were challenging political conservatism in Nottingham during this time.

Other American evangelists such as Charles Grandison Finney and Phoebe Palmer would be influential upon William Booth later in his life, but James Caughey was the first of the Americans to shape Booth's thinking and character, and to give Booth a vision for revivalism in England. Norman Murdoch wrote:

> Booth was Caughey's heir. Caughey convinced Booth that converting the masses was possible through scientific, calculated means. Revivals which were planned, advertised, and prayed for would succeed. From the time they met in 1846 to his death in 1912, Booth was consumed with the idea of winning souls through mass meetings, house-to-house visitation, and personal witness. That was the legacy of James Caughey, who died in 1891 at age eighty-one, largely forgotten, despite his influence, not only on the Booths, but also on all British evangelicalism.[37]

Although born in southern Ireland, Caughey was nurtured in America in a region in upper New York State that has been called the "Burned-over District" because of the many religious revivals there.[38] He became an ordained elder with the Methodists in 1839, and developed into a successful revivalist. He first went to England in 1841, and his intended two-year stay stretched to 1847.[39] He ministered with astonishing results during those six years in Ireland and England. "In six years of campaigning . . . he counted twenty thousand conversions and nine thousand persons sanctified."[40] And although many Methodists were affiliated with Chartism, Caughey denounced Chartism and argued that the collapse of the social order would be prevented by the salvation of the lost and the sanctification of the saints, and not by political fiat.

Caughey had a commanding presence in the pulpit. Carwardine wrote,

> In the pulpit, Caughey cut an impressive figure. His commanding height, keen eyes, and strong, dark, not unattractive features gave him an

assurance and presence reinforced by his "easy" and "natural" pulpit manner, by an unshakable conviction of his utter rightness, and by a complete absence of self-doubt.... Essentially Caughey's "strange fascination" lay in his capacity for stating evangelical commonplaces in novel and arresting, yet simple, ways.[41]

Following his sermons, Caughey invited people to kneel at the Communion rail to pray. The use of the Communion rail or a mourner's bench for this particular purpose gives evidence of the growing American influence on English revivalism. Charles Grandison Finney had begun to use the Communion rail for such purposes. Caughey's prayer meetings were impassioned, but not out of control.

After about five years of Caughey's ministry without any ecclesiastical supervision, problems arose and jealousies inevitably cropped up. The leadership of the denomination had to take action.

Threat to authority caused "settled ministers" to point with envy at their itinerant brother's freedom. Caughey had come to England without an invitation and had remained for five years without any official connection to a Methodist conference. His popularity had kept him in demand even when circuit superintendents preferred that he stay away. More ominous, he had encouraged "irregular ministers," uneducated men like Booth, who might overrun the denomination.[42]

Such threats, combined with the Chartists' heated denunciation of Caughey in some cities, meant that it was time for Caughey to go home.[43] He returned to England again in July 1857 when he would continue to play an important role in the life of William Booth. It was during that visit that he baptized the Booths' second son, Ballington.

As a result of his conversion, and through his attraction to Methodists like James Caughey, William Booth was inextricably tied to Methodism. He had given his life to God, and as far as he was concerned that life would be lived out within Methodism. He was determined to allow God to help him overcome temptation and to turn his back on the allurements of worldly pleasures and gains. His father's struggles for both respectability and financial security were not going to be repeated in his life. That was now resolved. Attention to the will of God and living in the kingdom of God were now of first importance to his own vital piety.

Redemption was at the heart of Booth's maturing theological vision at this point in his life, and of this he was sure—such redemption signified not only justification by faith but holiness as well. Furthermore, redemption in the life of the believer issued in good works motivated by obedience to God and love for one's neighbor. Of this William Booth was certain. Such clarity of thought would not be deterred either by the apathy of the church or the enormity of the problems that William encountered as he continued in his daily task as a pawnbroker's assistant and witnessed in the daily pathetic struggle of the poor and impoverished.

Politics, however, was not the answer, regardless of Feargus O'Connor's persuasiveness. Religion was the answer, in spite of the constant menacing poverty even in his own life, and in spite of his continual toil to earn a meager living for himself and his family. He was a resolute Christian in spite of his circumstances.

God had found William Booth in Christ, and William Booth had turned to God in faith. The certainty of this conviction and the assurance that resulted would be the sure foundation of William Booth's life from now on. But to keep this to himself was impossible for this impetuous youth with his newly found faith. He had to share; he was called to preach!

CHAPTER TWO

A FOLLOWER OF WESLEY: ASSOCIATION WITH METHODISM

Introduction

Following his conversion, William Booth was nurtured in Wesleyan Methodism. The limits of his experience with the Methodists were in his town of Nottingham, and until the age of nineteen he knew no other world. But that was fine with William Booth. He had found his theological and social home. The gospel preached by the Methodists was his gospel, and he joined the fellowship of the Methodists. His world revolved around that local Methodist chapel. It was no small or insignificant church. It was a relatively new church, built only in 1839, had a seating capacity of twelve hundred, and was apparently an important church in the community.

William Booth and the Wesleyans

The pastor of the Wesley chapel at this time was the Reverend Samuel Dunn, the superintendent of the circuit—the ecclesiastical overseer of the other Wesleyan Methodist churches in the area of Nottingham. Dunn was stationed in the Nottingham North circuit from 1846 to 1849, and was superintendent there from 1847 to 1849. In January 1849 he began a monthly periodical, *The Wesley Banner*, a publication in support of reform within Methodism, and, as will be mentioned later in this biography, was one of the three leaders of the reform movement expelled from the Connexion at the Conference of 1849.[1] One of Booth's biographers describes Dunn as "a man of some scholarship, autocratic, hard, obstinate, and incurably radical."[2] Samuel Dunn did not make up for what William missed in his relationship with his father. This was not a warm or loving relationship, but one of an authoritarian teacher and passive student. Evidently, however, William was especially moved by the preaching of Samuel Dunn as well as by his disciplined, Methodistic approach to life.

There was drama in the Methodist preaching of the nineteenth century, and drama equally in the response to the preaching. The singing of the hymns of Charles Wesley or Isaac Watts underscored the theology of the sermons preached. The prayers of the righteous, the sanctification of believers, and the conversion of the sinners who stood to their feet and walked forward to kneel at the Communion rail to repent of their sins signaled the amen to the effectiveness of the preached Word. Sunday services at the chapel filled William and countless others with visions of scenes from the Scriptures, with a knowledge of the ministry of the Lord whom they served, and with hope for the future in spite of present difficulties and personal failures. The divine drama of each Sunday made the worshippers' rather humdrum weekly lives bearable, and the Christian fellowship enjoyed on Sundays was sustained throughout the week with class meetings and prayer meetings.

As mentioned earlier, William Booth had already had a ministry of sorts on the streets of Nottingham with his friend Will Sansom, toiling for souls during his brief leisure hours during the week while struggling to earn an income that would put bread on the table. However, in spite of his Christian activities at this time, there is an indication that this ambitious young man was still conflicted. Perhaps, after all, he did not intend to make his mark on the world in the area of religion. Rather, he dreamed of parting company with poverty forever by focusing his growing ambition within the world of business.

However, many events leading up to the nineteenth year of his life proved that year to be a dramatic turning point for the young pawnbroker and street evangelist. First, his closest friend and companion in the faith, Will Sansom, died of consumption. Booth later recounted Sansom's death:

But the unexpected blow came. He fell into consumption. His relations carried him up and down the country for change of air and scene. All was done that could be done to save his life, but in vain. The last change was to the Isle of Wight. In that lovely spot the final hope fled. I remember their bringing him home to die. He bade farewell to earth, and went triumphantly to Heaven singing—

> "And when to Jordan's flood I come,
>   Jehovah rules the tide,
>   And the waters He'll divide,
>   And the heavenly host will shout—
>   Welcome Home!"

What a trial that loss was to my young heart! It was rendered all the greater from the fact that I had to go forward all alone in face of an opposition which suddenly sprang up from the leading functionaries of the church.[3]

This was a tragedy for young William both to understand and to bear. He felt alone without Will, but nevertheless continued in his resolve to preach on the streets and conduct cottage prayer meetings. With Will gone, William was now the clear leader of the other young men who were zealously, but unofficially, preaching the faith once delivered to the saints.

It was also during this time that he came to the attention of his pastor, Dunn, whom Booth continued to admire in spite of the fact that Dunn was rather displeased when he heard that William and others had assumed the responsibility of preaching on the streets. The place and the authority of lay preaching had been a point of contention since the days of the Wesleys, and Methodists still debated the work of the "sons in the gospel" or lay preachers. Richard P. Heitzenrater notes that "Charles did not develop the same tolerance, much less enthusiasm, for lay preaching that John did."[4] The central issue with the Wesleys was the fear of appearing to separate in any way from the established church, and lay preaching posed a possible threat. While John Wesley did allow for lay preachers, he was, however, insistent upon their preparation for the ministry.[5]

Dunn obviously did not have any anxiety related to an appearance of separation from the Anglican Church. But what were Dunn's concerns? He probably had two. First, street preaching, although initiated by Whitefield and taken up by the Wesleys, still sounded a note of impropriety, and many of the more established Methodists of the nineteenth century did not condone street preaching. After several generations, Methodists had become cultured despisers of any religious exercises that appeared improper to people of good breeding and acquired tastes. Second, because Booth and Sansom began this ministry on their own initiative without any formal sanction from Dunn himself, Dunn probably saw it as a challenge to his ecclesiastical authority. William Booth should have received permission for this work, although such permission would probably not have been forthcoming.

In spite of possible confrontation, Samuel Dunn, to his credit, recognized something of the making of a minister in the young enthusiast, and asked William if he would be willing to do some preaching in villages for him. He also evidently questioned William as to whether he had any intention of training for the ministry. In fact, it is highly probable that Dunn "was urgent in his pleas that he should become a minister."[6]

At the time it was impossible for Booth to consider entering into the ministry as a full-time vocation. He would continue as a local lay preacher, but he could not think of giving up his job, which provided a meager income for the Booth family. His eldest sister, Ann, had married a man by the name of Francis Brown on January 29, 1846, and moved to London, and so whatever income Ann brought to the family was now halted. But William continued to be responsible for his mother and his two sisters still living at home, who also contributed to the family income by working in the housewares shop. William was now in his sixth year as a pawnbroker's assistant and in the absence of his employer he was responsible for running the shop, but did so for no extra income.

William's future did not appear to be bright. His prospects appeared to offer a dull daily routine, leading only to a day-to-day existence, rather than advancement. The poverty was numbing, and it became apparent to William that the business in which he was engaged held absolutely no possibilities for leading him and his family into a better life. "Definitely and decisively, it seemed, this little circle of humanity had sunk into a dark obscurity from which it was impossible that they should ever emerge."[7]

The situation worsened when William's work as a pawnbroker's assistant came to an end. Precisely why this job ended after so many years of faithful service is not clear. It is possible that Booth parted company from his Unitarian boss over a recurrent argument about working on Sundays. Saturdays were one of the busiest days in the pawnbroking business and often the work had to continue into early Sunday morning. Booth, the strict Methodist Sabbatarian, would not work one moment past midnight on Saturdays. Sunday was not a day for business as usual for William Booth. Sunday was a day for worship and for working for the Lord.

Booth was out of work for a year. No door of employment was open to him. Not even the wealthy businessmen of the chapel would offer him a temporary job, and Booth later remarked sadly that "no one took the slightest interest in me."[8] Booth later recounted that "my recollection of my boyhood and my early manhood is that I never got a helping-hand from anybody—that is, directly. I had to help myself."[9] This was particularly difficult for William, given the constant boast of wonderful Christian fellowship that people could enjoy in the company of the saints. Here was a time for members of the congregation to demonstrate that fellowship in a practical way, but no help was given. He later rather bitterly recollected that "I was connected with the Wesleyans; but they did nothing for me."[10] William roamed the streets of Nottingham for that year looking for work, but to no avail. His widowed mother and his two sisters barely managed to sustain the family with their earnings.

William Booth Moves to London

In desperation, William Booth moved to London. He had no grand vision for saving the lost of London or bringing redemption to the masses. He moved to London to find work. He could not have imagined how inextricably connected his life would become with that great metropolis and with its people. He entered London in complete obscurity in the twentieth year of his life, and at the time of his first arrival no one took notice—he had little money, no friends, and no prospects. He knew only his sister Ann and her thoroughly unlikable husband, and it was to their house in London that he moved. He had been close to Ann. She had been a Christian, like William, and had even ministered on the streets of Nottingham with him.

Ann's husband, Francis Brown, was a different sort altogether. He was an avowed agnostic who ridiculed religion, a materialist, and an alcoholic. His corrupting influence upon Booth's sister was noticeable, and William Booth was downcast after seeing the state of his sister and brother-in-law. Neither he nor his form of religion was welcomed in that house. He was put out of the house. He was friendless and lonely—and still out of work.[11] The following are Booth's own impressions about his coming to London for the first time:

The sensations of a newcomer to London from the country are always somewhat disagreeable, if he comes to work. The immensity of the city must especially strike him as he crosses it for the first time and passes through its different areas. The general turnout into a few great thoroughfares, on Saturday nights especially, gives a sensation of enormous bulk. The manifest poverty of so many in the most populous streets must appeal to any heart. The language of the drinking crowds must needs give a rather worse than a true impression of all.

The crowding pressure and activity of so many must almost oppress one not accustomed to it. The number of public houses, theatres, and music halls must give a young enthusiast for Christ a sickening impression. The enormous number of hawkers must also have given a rather exaggerated idea of the poverty and cupidity which nevertheless prevailed. The Churches in those days gave the very uttermost idea of spiritual death and blindness to the existing condition of things; at that time very few of them were open more than one evening per week; . . . for miles there was not an announcement of anything special in the religious line to be seen.

To anyone who cared to enter the places of worship, their deathly contrast with the streets was even worse. The absence of weeknight services must have made any stranger despair of finding even society or diversion. A Methodist sufficiently in earnest to get inside to the "class" would find a handful of people reluctant to bear any witness to the power of God.[12]

This sincere Methodist found London not only a bit frightening, but unappealing. His world was one of Sunday worship, prayer meetings and class meetings throughout the week, and a strict, regimented Methodist approach to life. He despised many of the attractions of the "world" as contradictory to the gospel that constantly called the believer out of the world. London provided a glaring contrast to his own life and values.

But here was the question: What was he to do? As yet, young William had no idea of making a living by preaching the gospel, and he knew that his family responsibilities demanded that he find work. As much as he despised the pawnbroking business, that was the only trade he knew, and he found a job in a pawnbroker's shop in Walworth.[13] He lived in the attic above the shop, which was located at 1 Kennington Row, Kennington Common, and in the earliest extant letter from William Booth, he describes the shop as being "uncommonly pleasantly situated no shop in Nottingham anything equal to it. In front we look on to a beautiful Common on which there are constantly a number of people playing at cricket, flying kites or some other game and at the back we have a nice garden fountain."[14] However, he also speaks in that letter of an outbreak of cholera that was ravaging London at that time. So, there was good reason to fear for his health and well-being.

He worked for a nominally Anglican pawnbroker, William Fillmer, who lived next door to the shop. His early impressions of Fillmer were positive, but Booth's later reflections were that Fillmer's religion was a legal formality, and, according to Booth, he knew nothing of either personal godliness or compassion for others, both marks for a devout Methodist like Booth of the grace of God in the life of the believer. Both Fillmer and the foreman of the shop, John B. Neale, were hard taskmasters, insisting that William be home by ten o'clock each evening at which time the door would be locked against him. The daily routine—to which William had become accustomed during all those years in Nottingham—was numbing, and Sunday was not a day of rest for young William. He discovered churches that would allow this lay preacher to preach, and he generally preached twice on Sundays.

William was understandably despondent at this time. He was destitute and alone. He was, however, tenacious in his Christian faith, and apparently his preaching engagements were helpful for providing both a religious and a social outlet for this lonely soul in the big city. He wrote of this time:

> My way was complicated, but I stuck to my faith and the preaching of it as far as I had the opportunity. It is true that here and there I made friends in my preaching excursions with whom I fraternized, as far as my little leisure afforded, enjoying occasional seasons of useful communion. But my poor heart was desolate in the extreme. It seemed as though I had got launched out on a wide and dreary ocean without a companion vessel or a friendly port in view.[15]

On December 6, 1849, he wrote down six resolutions by which he was determined to conduct his life, reminiscent of the kinds of resolutions he would have seen or heard from other Methodists. These resolutions challenged Booth daily to the disciplined life of self-denial, and reminded him to read God's Word and, above all, to "strive to live closer to God, and to seek after holiness of heart, and leave providential events with God."[16]

While there is no evident call to preach the gospel as part of these resolutions, but rather more of an attitude of redeeming the time and seeking after the will of God, it is obvious that the author was striving for a better self, a more religious self, and a self given over completely to God and to holiness of heart. This prevailing attitude—these habits of the heart—would eventually allow William to consider the life of a preacher, but as yet the opportunity did not present itself in any clear and compelling way. He continued in the business that he despised during the week, and rejoiced in opportunities as a lay preacher to preach twice on Sundays and occasionally on a weeknight. He modeled his preaching after what he knew in his Methodist rearing, often preaching for an hour or more.

This turned out to be a time of testing. William would like to have contemplated a settled preaching ministry, but was often told that presently there was no need for preachers. On the other hand, he even contemplated in 1850 going to Australia on a convict ship as a chaplain, the need being great for such a ministry given the ongoing experiment at this time of ridding England of her "criminal class." Robert Hughes has written that

> in their most sanguine moments, the authorities hoped that it would eventually swallow a whole class—the "criminal class," whose existence was one of the prime sociological beliefs of late Georgian and early Victorian England. Australia was settled to defend English property not from the frog-eating invader across the Channel but from the marauder within. English lawmakers wished not only to get rid of the "criminal class" but if possible to forget about it.[17]

Booth's sympathies were with many of those innocent people who were being so mistreated by the authorities. After all, the circumstances being different, he could have been one of those persons on one of those convict ships, for truth to tell, those ships held thousands of people whose only crime was being out of work or being in debt when they were imprisoned. There was not only a restlessness in William at this time—a searching—but there was something of the adventurer lurking in William now that he had broken away from Nottingham and moved to London. He wanted to do something exciting and dramatic for the kingdom of God. But what?

It was at this propitious moment that William met Mr. Edward Harris Rabbits, a boot manufacturer by trade and a Wesleyan layperson.[18] Rabbits heard William Booth preach one morning at the Walworth Wesleyan Chapel and apparently was moved by the preaching of the young evangelist. Rabbits was sufficiently impressed by both the earnestness and the enthusiasm of the preacher, and he saw in William Booth the kind of evangelical preacher who provided a stark contrast both to the many monotonous preachers of the day and to the deadly formality of the worship service even within his beloved Methodism.

Rabbits heard William Booth frequently after that and eventually agreed to support him at twenty shillings per week for three months until Booth could find some sort of settled ministry among the Methodists. "Lucky Edward Rabbits to find a Founder of a great religious organization on such thrifty terms!"[19] By William's account, on April 9, 1852, which was Good Friday that year, he left his pawnbroker's trade forever. "I shook hands with my cold-hearted master and said goodbye," Booth later recalled.[20] The next day, April 10, 1852, was his birthday, and Booth remembered that day as his first day of freedom. He found modest quarters in Walworth, purchased some needed furniture, and celebrated his twenty-third birthday.

William Booth and the Evangelical Tradition

William Booth considered himself to be part of the broad evangelical tradition of his day. A religious spirit commonly referred to as "evangelical" pervaded Victorian England, such a spirit being traceable back to the preaching of John Wesley in the eighteenth century. "The direct descendants of Wesley formed the largest group outside the establishment."[21] William Booth was both influenced by that tradition and became a sustainer of it, especially the Wesleyan expression of evangelicalism.

However, that evangelical tradition, while predominately Wesleyan in its inception, was far-reaching; it influenced not only the Methodists, but also Congregationalists, Baptists, Quakers, and Anglicans. Owen Chadwick demonstrated the range of evangelical influence by writing, "In contemplating Victorian religion we need to remember The Salvation Army as well as Oxford University."[22] And G. Kitson Clark asserted that The Salvation Army "was in some way the climax" of the evangelical movement.[23]

Evangelicals became known for a desire to save the souls of themselves and others, a pious moral existence that sometimes included total abstinence from alcohol described gently by one author as "their want of appreciation of the spirit of cakes and ale,"[24] and a strong social conscience. It was often the latter that drew the working classes to these dissenters. Thus, there developed a distinct alliance between evangelicals and the working classes, evangelical chapels being filled with laborers.

Broader cultural influence for evangelicals outside of Anglicanism began politically with the repeal of the Test Act in 1828. This opened up the possibility of political office for these evangelicals, and such influence, combined with the rising humanitarian tide of Victorian England, brought many needed reforms to Victorian society. In that way evangelicals, though often uncomfortable with the culture in which they found themselves, profoundly influenced and shaped that culture.

Evangelicalism of the nineteenth century lost some support, especially among the intellectuals, over issues of biblical inspiration and science. Evangelicals generally believed in the verbal inspiration of the Bible, and held to a literalistic interpretation of its message. For them, the scientific affirmations of Darwin and others were incompatible with the biblical witness. As the Victorian world developed after the publication of Darwin's *Origin of Species* in 1859, the scientific community and the evangelical community grew farther and farther apart. Increasing numbers of intellectuals became antireligious. Many cultured despisers of religion wanted to relegate religion to the margins of life where only the ignorant would hold to cherished religious beliefs of the past. There was little attempt on the side of either community to strike a middle ground.

However, Booth was not only broadly evangelical, he was clearly Methodist as well. Although he was baptized in the Anglican Church, Booth's ministerial and theological sympathies were all with the Wesleyan Methodist movement in which he had been nurtured. He moved from Methodism in Nottingham to Methodism in London, and in Methodism he would formally remain until 1862. Even after his departure from the Methodist denomination that ordained him, he always thought of himself as Methodist and Wesleyan.

John Wesley, in the previous century, although living and dying as an Anglican priest, was one of the founders of Methodism, together with like-minded believers such as his brother Charles. The movement was founded initially by serious Oxford University students who had committed themselves to come together periodically throughout the week and on Sundays to study the classics and other writings, especially books on divinity. The activities of the group soon expanded to attending the University Church on Sundays, listening to the sermon, and participating in the Lord's Supper. Primarily through the instigation of one of its members, William Morgan, members of this Holy Club began visiting the local prison and their ministry expanded to visiting the poor in Oxford. These activities were enhanced as the members of the group increased their study to include the serious study of the Bible, and steadily grew in their determination to seek after holiness of heart and life, one of the manifestations of which was obedience to the command of the Lord to love God and love one's neighbor.

These Oxford Methodists were not spared the ridicule of fellow students, and although they suffered under various ludicrous labels—Holy Club, Godly Club, Bible-Moths, or Supererogation Men—the term *Methodist* was taken as a badge of honor. John Wesley was apparently the acknowledged leader, although the makeup of this religious society certainly included other men of similar gifts such as Charles Wesley and George Whitefield.

The early rise of Methodism can be seen in three stages—Oxford, Georgia, and London—and is inextricably connected with John's theological pilgrimage at all three of these stages.[25] Various Methodist societies arose throughout England, Scotland, Wales, and Ireland, and these societies promoted revivalistic preaching, holiness of heart and life, and clear evidence of the gospel through good works, especially directed to the poor and needy. The movement was consolidated in the 1750s, and as it reached maturity, its impact became evident during Wesley's lifetime throughout Great Britain and even in America where Wesley had been a missionary in Georgia in his earlier days.

Wesley embraced both the doctrine of justification by faith of Protestantism and the works of Roman Catholicism and developed a synthesis that would distinguish the Methodist movement theologically. Henry Rack has written:

> In the perspective of Protestant history, Wesley can be said to have been trying to find a solution to the old problem of how to reconcile the notion of a salvation that depends on a divine act of grace to save fallen men with the desire for a positive and progressive attitude towards a recreation of the personality by a progressive realization of the mind of Christ in which men can take an active part. If...Wesley brought together these two concerns, he did so in response to the practical needs thrown up by a revival situation as much as by way of a formal theological response to an old problem. In doing so, however, he mediated between the various strands of Anglican tradition with direct or indirect if highly selective and

reinterpreted elements from Catholicism as well as trying to make sense of the raw religious emotions of the converts.[26]

However, one would misinterpret Wesley in saying that there was some-thing besides grace at work in the believer in the scripture way of salva-tion. Wesley's notion of merit is not precisely that of Roman Catholicism, but of merit that is favored by God. Kenneth J. Collins is careful to note that,

> when Wesley described merit in a "loose sense" . . . he meant little more than that our works are in some sense "rewardable." This element of reward, however, does not mean that the redeemed have an independent claim on the grace of God; instead, it simply points to the already effec-tive grace of the Almighty, which results in works that will, again out of sheer grace, be favored and rewarded. In other words, God is so gracious that not only does divine empowering grace issue in the fruit of the Christian life, but God will also reward believers precisely for this fruit—fruit that they could never have brought about by themselves! Wesley's understanding of merit in the loose sense, then, does not underscore autonomous human achievement; on the contrary, it doubly highlights the graciousness of divine activity: once in the giving of grace; the other in the rewarding of its fruit. . . . Wesley's theology not only began in grace, but it culminated there as well. It highlighted not human prerogatives but the bountiful grace of God.[27]

As John Wesley developed his theology through his own constant quest for the assurance of salvation and in the context of the unfolding of the eighteenth-century religious revival in which he played so signifi-cant a role, the doctrine of holiness became central to his soteriological theology as well as to his pastoral ministry and his emphasis on "practi-cal divinity." For Wesley,

> justification is pardon and is received by a faith which is a divine, supernatural "evidence" or "conviction" of things not discernible by our bodily senses. Justification not only means that through Christ's death God reconciled the world to himself but is also a personal sense that this was done for *me*. Wesley carefully distinguishes this from sanctification: we are not actually *made* just and righteous, but simply pardoned from our sins. To be made just and righteous is a distinct work and gift of God, though in some degree it is an immediate fruit of justification. "The one (justification) implies what God *does for* us through His Son; the other, what he *works in* us by his Spirit." There

is no doubt that from 1738 to the end of his life Wesley adhered to this basic doctrine.[28]

Speaking of Wesley's quintessential sermon on the topics of justification and sanctification entitled "The Scripture Way of Salvation," Richard P. Heitzenrater states:

> One of the hallmark sermons in the Wesleyan repertoire was published in 1765. "The Scripture Way of Salvation" signals the maturation of his theology, hammered out during the years of contention and controversy. It stands as perhaps the single best homiletical summary of his soteriology, or doctrine of salvation (*Sermons*, 2:153-69). He had preached on this text, Ephesians 2:8, over forty times already, and had also published an early sermon on it, "Salvation by Faith." But the previous decade had witnessed the exceptionally unsettling controversies generated by Maxwell, Bell, and other Calvinists and antinomians who had challenged Wesley's view of the nature of justification and sanctification. Now, in this examination of faith and the "way of salvation," Wesley succinctly reiterates his emphasis on grace—prevenient, convincing, justifying, sanctifying—and strongly underscores his correlative stress on the necessity of good works.[29]

Part of John Wesley's enduring theological legacy to the church, therefore, was this distinction between justification and sanctification, or pardon and perfection.

> There was more to the Christian experience than faith and forgiveness. The new birth that resulted from God's forgiveness was only the threshold of holiness, which then entailed a process of continued openness to God's grace and the exercise of love within a fellowship of believers that would provide a nurturing environment for growth in grace and in service to the world.[30]

Ken Collins states in his significant work entitled *The Scripture Way of Salvation: The Heart of John Wesley's Theology* the following:

> Though regeneration is a significant work of grace, it marks only the beginning of the larger process of sanctification. As such, regeneration or initial sanctification is an important—though by no means final—approach to the ultimate goal of the Christian life, namely, the full restoration of the *imago Dei* in which we were created. This larger process of sanctification, of which regeneration is an ever important part, entails the implanting of the love of God, in all its richness and power, in the human

heart, and therefore involves the inculcation of holy tempers such as faithfulness, humility, meekness, and patience, which will displace such ungodly tempers as atheism, pride, self-will, and love of the world. This process of cleansing, of purifying human hearts so that the divine glory shines through, is nothing less than the very substance of salvation.[31]

William Booth clearly believed and taught the doctrines of salvation and sanctification, even during this early stage of his ministry, largely as he understood them from his Wesleyan heritage. When he spoke of seeking after holiness of heart, as he did, for example, in his fifth resolution written on December 6, 1849, he meant seeking after entire sanctification as he learned the doctrine from the Methodists, which was the natural pilgrimage for the believer after justification by faith. While Booth was not trained to explicate the nuances of the doctrines as Wesley had, he nevertheless understood the basic biblical aspects of these and other doctrines. The context of the revivalism in which he would be increasingly engaged compelled him to call people to repentance, embrace the salvation of God offered through his grace, and grow in grace. The believer should be open to all that God promises in this life, including full salvation. Booth preached redemption, and the biblical doctrine of holiness was part of God's redemptive purpose for every believer. That doctrine was not an amendment to his theology, but the core of his theology even from these early days of ministry.

Wesley's more practical legacy was in the Methodism that was his child, which became a powerful agency for revival in spite of the small membership during Wesley's life due largely to the discipline that Wesley enforced upon his people. However, while John Wesley was unquestionably the controlling and unifying agency for the people called Methodists during his lifetime, Methodism after Wesley's death was far from unified, and often found itself embroiled in conflict, especially conflict over church polity. On the one hand, Wesley feared that Methodism would leave the established church—a fear shared by his brother Charles—but on the other hand, Wesley created a religious society that increasingly identified itself apart from the church, especially as pressure from Methodists demanded that they worship at the same time as the local Anglican church, or as they demanded to receive the Lord's Supper from Methodist preachers. "Over a period of more than sixty years, Wesley had developed methods and procedures that, while intended to 'reform' the Church of England, in fact gave the Methodists a self-conscious identity distinct from the Church."[32]

Following Wesley's death in 1791, Methodism could not hold the center. While there remained a fairly consistent doctrinal focus within Methodism—stressing holiness of heart and life—tensions arose over polity. Some wanted the Conference to control Methodism, thus maintaining a strong central government. Others wanted more autonomy at the local level and formed a more democratic approach to church governance. Both sides of the argument appealed to Wesley's intentions, which were more ambiguous than either side would admit. Wesley often made accommodations to particular local needs as he established procedures. After all, he was not shaping a denomination but merely guiding a religious society whose controlling purpose was to spread scriptural holiness throughout the land.

By 1795 Methodism had effectively separated from the Church of England, and in 1796 a group of Methodists in favor of more democratic polity and local power followed Alexander Kilham, who had been expelled from the Conference, out of Methodism to form a separate denomination that took the name of New Connexion Methodism. In later years this denomination ordained William Booth to the ministry. In the nineteenth century, other groups continued to form, all generally claiming to be fulfilling Wesley's original intention for the movement called Methodism. The largest of these other groups was Primitive Methodism, formed in 1811. "By 1851 they were five times as large as any other seceded Methodist group, and were nearly a third as numerous as the Wesleyan Methodists."[33]

Methodism however, was Booth's religious home even though at this time there were family feuds going on. He claimed that by the age of twenty he had become an admirer of John Wesley. He said this of himself:

> I worshipped everything that bore the name of Methodist. To me there was one God, and John Wesley was his prophet. I had devoured the story of his life. No human compositions seemed to me to be comparable to his writings, and to the hymns of his brother Charles, and all that was wanted, in my estimation, for the salvation of the world was the faithful carrying into practice of the letter and the spirit of his instructions.[34]

In later life, as his ministry developed, Booth would be clearer about his own theological indebtedness to John Wesley. One biographer rightly refers to John Wesley as Booth's "hero and spiritual progenitor."[35] Booth also came to realize that he was the organizational heir to Wesley and he, like Wesley, would bequeath to the Church a dynamic religious society raised up to spread scriptural holiness throughout the land.

To understand William Booth's connection to Methodism and its founder is critical, even at this early and inconspicuous stage of Booth's ministry. William Booth's allegiance was not only to evangelicalism—although he considered himself a part of that tradition; he was consciously Wesleyan in doctrine, practice, and spirit. His understanding of Wesleyan doctrine, enhanced not only by reading Wesley but by listening to his own pastor as well as to itinerant American Methodist James Caughey, would be enlarged in him not only intellectually but spiritually as well. He sought after holiness of heart as well as the assurance that sanctification brings to the believer. Likewise, he, like the Methodism of which he was part of as a child, embraced the notion of an active holiness—loving God and loving one's neighbor. That Methodist impulse of reaching out to one's neighbor, and often and especially to the poorest and most destitute neighbor, was instilled in the young preacher, and had already manifested itself in his limited ministry in Nottingham. His own experience of poverty as well as his daily associations with those who came into his Nottingham and London pawnbroker shops further enhanced the compassionate side of his nature.

To miss this Methodist nurturing in the broader framework of the evangelicalism of nineteenth-century England, therefore, is to misinterpret William Booth from the beginning and to see him as a-theological. One of his biographers, Harold Begbie, while acknowledging Booth's Methodist rearing, misses the importance of Methodist doctrine to William Booth. Often Begbie treats Booth as though he was not really free to do what he had to do until he put that theology behind him. Speaking of Booth's early days in Nottingham, Begbie claims that "years were to pass before he broke free from sectarianism."[36] He reiterated such sentiment when he wrote that "for years he was plagued by theology," and commended William Booth for being such a spirit that "could revolt passionately from orthodoxy."[37]

William Booth never considered himself to be "plagued by theology," especially the living and dynamic biblical and Wesleyan theology that he embraced. He was rooted and grounded in Wesley's theology and tradition, and gladly so. It was from this theological platform that he began, rather tentatively, his preaching in London. He could not have envisioned in those early days what would come of his faithfulness to the gospel ministry as it unfolded within the Methodism that had been his home since his earlier years in Nottingham. Nor could he have imagined what would become of this Methodist preacher.

CHAPTER THREE

PROVIDENTIAL MEETING: WILLIAM BOOTH AND CATHERINE MUMFORD

Introduction

William Booth moved to London principally to find work, but he found much more. He found his destiny. His friend, Mr. Rabbits, had befriended a Methodist family named Mumford who, a few years earlier, had moved to Brixton, a suburb of London. The mother and daughter, Sarah and Catherine, were especially devoted in their Christian lives and in their relationship to Methodism, whereas Mr. Mumford was, by this time, religiously tone-deaf. Catherine Mumford and her mother attended a small Methodist chapel known as Binfield House in Binfield Road, Clapham, and were both impressed by the preaching of a lay preacher by the name of William Booth.

William Booth Meets Catherine Mumford

Mr. Rabbits, after speaking to William of the admiration that the Mumfords had expressed, arranged for William to meet Catherine. Both would later recount that it was love at first sight. However, who was this

Catherine Mumford who had so immediately captured the attention of the young preacher?

Catherine Mumford was born in the same year as William Booth—1829—and preceded him into this world by three months. She was born on January 17, 1829, at Ashbourne in Derbyshire, England.[1] Her mother, Sarah Milward, had married a lay preacher and avowed total abstainer from alcohol by the name of John Mumford, and bore five children, Catherine being the only girl. Of the four boys born to the Mumfords, only one, John, survived to his adult years. The father's trade took him and his young family from Ashbourne to Boston in Lincolnshire in 1834, and eventually to Brixton.

Catherine's father was an unstable and unreliable man, and would not play a formative role in her life. Very little is known of his background. He was a carriage maker by trade, committed to total abstinence from alcohol, and somewhat interested in politics. But there was a sort of sadness about him. He was forever disappointed with his lot in life, and this melancholy increasingly came to light during Catherine's lifetime. When Catherine was still a child her father gave up his lay preaching and became antagonistic toward religion. He was impetuous, perhaps moody, and definitely given to emotional peaks and valleys, as his joining of various causes demonstrates. He was sometimes religious, sometimes not; at one time all-consumed with the temperance movement, at another time an imbiber of alcohol; occasionally thoroughly immersed in his work, but many times likely to be out of work. He gave people around him reason not to trust him. And there were undoubtedly times when Catherine and her mother also doubted his stability, and justifiably so.

During Catherine's childhood, her father's troubles increased. Often penniless, he finally turned his back on the causes that were once meaningful to him—total abstinence from alcohol, politics, and religion.[2] Catherine did not speak much about her father, but the following entry appears in Catherine's diary, written when she was eighteen:

> I sometimes get into an agony of feeling while praying for my dear father. O my Lord, answer prayer and bring him back to Thyself! Never let that tongue, which once delighted in praising Thee and in showing others Thy willingness to save, be engaged in uttering the lamentations of the lost. O awful thought! Lord have mercy! Save, oh save him in any way Thou seest best, though it be ever so painful. If by removing me Thou canst do this, cut short Thy work and take me home.[3]

There were times in Catherine's adult life when she had to support her parents financially, and often things seemed desperate. Happily, in 1861 John Mumford was led back to the Lord and the church by his daughter and even attended some of her public meetings. Methodist theology allowed that genuine freedom of the will was lost at the fall but restored as a result of prevenient grace, the grace that comes before salvation. With this freedom, people can choose to accept or reject the offer of God's grace, and even once it is accepted, people can turn their backs on God and eventually lose their salvation. They would then have to come again to repentance and accept the offer of God's mercy. The likelihood of falling from grace, however, was slim in that once a person was walking in the light of God, he or she would not desire to leave that light for the darkness of their former life. However, it did occasionally happen, and Catherine certainly believed that her father had fallen from grace, lost his assurance that he was a child of God, lived a life of despair, and needed to repent again. In the previous century, John Wesley preached "A Call to Backsliders" and spoke of those Christians who are taken captive of Satan:

> This is frequently the case with those who began to run well, but soon tired in the heavenly road; with those in particular who once saw "the glory of God in the face of Jesus Christ," but afterward grieved his Holy Spirit, and made shipwreck of the faith. Indeed many of these rush into sin as an horse into battle. They sin with so high an hand as utterly to quench the Holy Spirit of God; so that he gives them up to their own heart's lusts, and lets them follow their own imaginations.[4]

Catherine's mother was a different sort altogether. She was an intensely religious woman and her convictions about such matters as religion and total abstinence from alcohol would remain steady throughout her lifetime, in contrast to her wayward husband. She educated her children at home, desiring, on the one hand, to instill godly principles in them, and fearing, on the other hand, the deleterious effects of education outside of the home. Except for a brief period in Boston of schooling outside of the home, Catherine's education was at home under the watchful eye and the disciplined regimen of her mother. Catherine's education not only involved the training of the mind in such matters as English, history, Bible, and theology, but also a shaping of the character. Education was focused not only on what Catherine would learn but also on the kind of person she would become. Her reading of the entire Bible eight times before the age of twelve bears witness to the educational center of the Mumford household.

Catherine was a sickly child, and her ill health forced her often to stay at home away from the company of children her own age. Her learning might have been broader had she been well and had mingled among other children. At times she felt isolated and alone due to her lack of fellowship with her peers. Catherine, however, did not complain.

Sarah Mumford reared Catherine in a strict environment, with strong views about matters pertaining to history, culture, the church, or Christian theology. However, it is not apparent that these views were forced on Catherine. Her natural tendency was to share her mother's views and opinions. A strong and lasting bond developed between mother and daughter. Kate—as she was affectionately called—both loved and respected her mother, and these feelings were mutual as Catherine matured. In general, Catherine viewed her childhood fondly, and her rearing was a rather striking contrast to the childhood experiences of the man she would eventually marry.

Two cultural matters shaped Catherine's formative years that would continue to be important to her throughout her lifetime. The first has already been alluded to several times: total abstinence from alcohol. She retained this position in spite of the fact (or perhaps because of it) that her father, from whom she had learned the importance of total abstinence, renounced this when Catherine was a young girl. Nevertheless, total abstinence meetings had been conducted in the Mumford home, and Catherine was exposed to the rhetoric of this position in her earliest years. This became a national movement by 1842, often championed by Methodists and considered a more morally respectable position than mere temperance.[5]

So critical was this matter that in her young adult life, while drawing up a list of qualifications that any future husband must possess, Catherine determined that he must be a total abstainer.[6] She spoke about this conviction with William Booth when she met him. At the time he drank moderately, and had been drinking beer since the age of thirteen for medicinal purposes.[7] Booth himself reflected that "from thirteen to twenty I was not a teetotaller. I drank a little for my health's sake, and as advised by the doctor. I was delicate, and medical men predicted that if I went in for preaching I should be guilty of suicide. When I saw the ravages of drink I gave it up for ever."[8]

Another social issue that was taking shape in the heart and mind of young Catherine was that of the treatment of animals. She suffered extremely, both physically and emotionally, when she saw animals mistreated, and she often interceded personally to prevent a horse from being beaten or a donkey from being harshly prodded. Catherine could not endure the suffering she witnessed of what one writer labeled "these little brothers and sisters of humanity."[9]

One poignant incident in her childhood was so dramatic and, as she believed, so utterly cruel that she recalled it years later with great sadness. The Mumford family owned a retriever named Waterford, and Catherine recounts a special bond between her and that dog, stating that they were "inseparable companions."[10] Catherine visited her father one day at his place of business, leaving the dog outside while she went in to speak with her father. She evidently stumbled after entering the building and cried out. Waterford, ever protective of his mistress, crashed through the large plate-glass window, causing, so Mr. Mumford thought, needless damage to his business establishment. Mr. Mumford was so incensed by this that he had the animal immediately destroyed. Catherine was inconsolable. Catherine's increasing sensitivity to all suffering creatures would continue throughout her lifetime.

These larger social and cultural matters were, however, secondary to Catherine's religious sensitivities. Catherine was reared in the Wesleyan Methodist tradition, and after the family moved to London, she began attending, with her mother, a Wesleyan Methodist church in Brixton. Being good Methodists, both Mrs. Mumford and her daughter attended the weekly Methodist class meetings. As mentioned, these meetings, formulated by John Wesley, were considered by Wesley himself to be the strength of Methodism and the source of its spiritual power and influence. The class meetings provided an opportunity for the members to study Scripture, confess sins, receive assurance of pardon, witness to lives of holiness, and otherwise support and strengthen the sisters and brothers of the movement. Membership in these classes would usually number about a dozen people, and the class meeting leaders were laypeople. Henry Rack wrote, "The class meeting became so vital and integral a part of the Methodist polity and seemed so clearly to express its values of a mixture of individual and collective piety and 'fellowship' that it achieved an almost mythical status as a picture of true Methodism. An early preacher found that the Methodists in class 'lived as the Christians of old, having all things in common.'"[11]

Neither Catherine nor her mother was completely pleased with life in that Methodist chapel and found the church rather lifeless contrasted with what they had known previously, especially in Boston. Nevertheless, Catherine decided to follow her mother's lead and join the church after she was "truly and savingly converted"[12] at the age of sixteen, which meant that she was assured both rationally and experientially that she was indeed a child of God. She speaks of this time in her life as passing through "a great controversy of soul."[13] On the one hand, she confessed that she had lived a blameless life as far as outward appearance was concerned, was undaunted in her zeal for the gospel, and had gladly used the means of grace of the church. On the other hand, she still knew herself as a sinner, filled with self-doubts and occasionally demonstrating an angry temper. She lacked all assurance that she was definitely a child of God by his grace mediated through the Holy Spirit. The experience at sixteen, encouraged no doubt by her mother, was one of searching for that assurance. Later reflecting on this time of her life, Catherine said, "It seemed to me unreasonable to suppose that I could be saved and yet not know it."[14]

She testified that one morning during that time of struggle, her eyes fell on these words from one of Charles Wesley's hymns with which she was quite familiar: "My God, I am Thine, What a comfort divine, What a blessing to know that my Jesus is mine!" She then related her experience in this way:

> Scores of times I had read and sung these words, but now they came home to my inmost soul with a force and illumination they had never before possessed. It was as impossible for me to doubt as it had been before for me to exercize faith. Previously not all the promises in the Bible could induce me to believe: now not all the devils in hell could persuade me to doubt. I no longer hoped that I was saved, I was certain of it. The assurances of my salvation seemed to flood and fill my soul. I jumped out of bed, and without waiting to dress, ran into my mother's room and told her what had happened.
>
> Till then I had been very backward in speaking even to her upon spiritual matters. I could pray before her, and yet could not open my heart to her about my salvation. It is a terrible disadvantage to people that they are ashamed to speak freely to one another upon so vital a subject. Owing to this, thousands are kept in bondage for years, when they might easily step into immediate liberty and joy. I have myself met hundreds of persons who have confessed to me that they had been church members for many years without knowing what a change of heart really was, and without having been able to escape from this miserable condition of doubt and

uncertainty to one of assurance and consequent satisfaction. For the next six months I was so happy that I felt as if I was walking on air. I used to tremble, and even long to die, lest I should backslide, or lose the consciousness of God's smile or favor.[15]

Her salvation assured, she decided to join the Wesleyan church near her home, and both Catherine and her mother participated actively in church life. Both of them became dissatisfied with their beloved Wesleyan Methodism and were sympathetic with the Reformers, a group of ministers and laypeople who were calling for the democratization of Methodism. "The *Wesleyan Times,* begun January 8, 1849, heralded the cause of the reformers, while the *Watchman* guarded business as usual. The battle for Methodism's soul in England, begun among the clergy, was taken to the local churches and to the laity. Everyone entered into the debate and wanted some voice in the future of the Methodism in which they had grown up and which they cherished."[16]

Because of this sympathy, Catherine's membership at the local Wesleyan church was not renewed after she had been warned not to show open support for the Reformers. Membership at that time was renewed quarterly and not to be renewed meant expulsion. Catherine Mumford, by this action, had been summarily dismissed from the Wesleyan Methodist Church in which she had been reared and which she loved. This caused Catherine great anguish.

It was a result of this action that Catherine and her mother began attending the Binfield House chapel at Clapham, a church of the Reformers. For three years, from 1852 to 1855, she taught a Sunday school class of fifteen girls whose ages ranged from twelve to nineteen. From all accounts this was a successful class. Catherine was personally concerned for each of her charges and conducted the class much after the model of the Methodist class meeting. She enjoyed a tranquil and settled life after the move to this church, living with her parents, teaching her class at the church, and participating in the shaping of Methodism through the Reform movement. However, her life was at a turning point that she could not possibly have imagined. It was during this time that she met another sympathizer with the Reformers: William Booth.

Mr. Rabbits arranged a dinner party at his home at 1 Crosby Row for some of his Reformer friends to which he invited William Booth and Catherine Mumford and her mother. This was a fortuitous meeting for Catherine Mumford and William Booth. Actually, Catherine's first close impressions of William were rather awkward because William had been pressed by Mr. Rabbits to recite a rather absurd American temperance poem entitled "The Grog-Sellers Dream." After the recitation there arose a bit of a dispute about the value of teetotalism, and only the call to dinner saved the argument from continuing. It can be supposed from what we know of her that Catherine Mumford willingly expressed her convictions on the subject, and perhaps her forthrightness is what first attracted William Booth to her.

They met frequently thereafter; the attraction quickened and the affection grew. After a meeting of Methodist Reformers—whom William had now joined—in a schoolroom in Cowper Street, City Road, in which both William and Catherine were present, William accompanied Catherine home to Brixton, and a genuine love affair commenced that would continue unabated through marriage until Catherine's death in 1890. Harold Begbie refers to the love of these two people as "a Methodist love story. Passion was there, deep and abiding, but passion restrained by duty and consecrated by devotion."[17]

William and Catherine had several common bonds that drew them together and made them inseparable through thirty-five years of married life. However, nothing was more important to them than religion, and particularly the Wesleyan Methodism in which they had been nurtured. They were Wesleyan in theology, in practice, and in spirit, and when Methodism found itself embroiled in the 1840s and 1850s, both William and Catherine took the side of a Reform party within Methodism.

Conflict within Methodism

It is critical to understand how Methodism came to this point of controversy. As has been mentioned, John Wesley was decidedly not in favor of Methodism breaking away from the established church. In spite of some of his own actions that seemed contrary to the establishment, he continued to see Methodism as a renewal movement within Anglicanism. He was upset upon learning that American Methodism, under the leadership of Francis Asbury and Thomas Coke, was leaning in the direction of a new and separate denomination. John Wesley kept autocratic control of the movement; but a democratic impulse began to shape the future of Methodism when, in 1784, a Deed Poll was established, an annual conference was commenced, and a group of one hundred ministers, appointed for life, was convened to assist Wesley in the administration of Methodism. Wesley died in 1791, and the democratic movement within Methodism gained ascendancy.

New denominations were formed in England, following the lead of American Methodists. Among the Wesleyan Methodists of England, however, it appeared that there was an entrenched bureaucracy, and a group of agitators or reformers—depending on one's point of view—were calling for a democratization of Methodism as well as for other reforms.

The conflict between the conservative and the reformed parties sharpened during a dispute over the American Methodist evangelist and holiness teacher, James Caughey, who, as mentioned earlier, was a person destined to have profound influence on William and Catherine Booth. In the spirit of trans-Atlantic revivalism, which was conducted in the nineteenth century and would be continued by such notable American preachers as Charles Grandison Finney and Dwight L. Moody, Caughey made four trips to England during his ministry to hold revivals, the first one being an extended visit, lasting from 1841 to 1847. As has already been mentioned, it was during this visit that William Booth was influenced by the preaching of Caughey in Nottingham.

Despite his effectiveness, there was considerable dissension in the Wesleyan ranks over Caughey. His detractors did not argue over his theology, because he essentially believed and taught the same things they did. What they could not condone were his revivalistic techniques. Owen Chadwick describes these disputes within Methodism:

> From 1843 onwards there were long arguments over an itinerant evangelist from the American Methodists, James Caughey. American methods were organized like a machine, and Caughey had enemies. English preachers of Leeds and Sheffield and Birmingham testified that he wrought wonders in their parishes and had rare gifts of bringing the indecisive to decision. They protested that interference with Caughey would obstruct the work of God. Others could not bear his devices and dodges. They accused him of using decoy penitents to lead others forward to the communion rail, and of pretending to miraculous knowledge about individuals in his congregations. He divided Methodists wherever he went. Conference of 1846 at last resolved to ask the Americans to recall him. It was not easy to persuade Methodists in York or Huddersfield to respect the ban.[18]

Caughey returned to America in 1847, not a moment too soon for some Methodists. Others, however, complained about the high-minded actions of the Conference.

The utmost stretch of charity could hardly invent any justifiable motive for their sudden banishment of the remarkable American evangelist Caughey, and this at a time when he was at the very zenith of his success. He was a Methodist minister, and his doctrines agreed in every particular with those of the Conference. Crowds flocked to his meetings from all the country-side, thousands of souls sought salvation, and the revival was at its floodtide, when the Conference compelled his withdrawal, causing widespread discontent among multitudes of the most loyal ministers and members of the Connexion, and exposing themselves to charges of envy and jealousy to which it was very difficult to reply.[19]

Richard Carwardine has expressed it this way:

Caughey's exclusion sent partisans rushing for their pens and produced waves of protest around the connection. Various circuits and special meetings issued testimonials to the revivalist's capabilities and good character; in pamphlets and journals, Conference came under fire. Caughey did not lack ministerial support, but most of his public defenders were incensed local preachers, leaders and trustees, and other prominent laymen ready to take matters into their own hands if their pastors would not act for them. The tone of their attack ranged from the mild to the vitriolic, but the argument in essence was always the same: Conference's inflexible standing by connectional discipline in a decade when denominational growth was low, relative to overall population and the increases of past decades, demonstrated that Conference's position was, "in effect, one of distinct opposition to revivals of religion and the salvation of souls." Church order was important, but was not an end in itself: "is there not reason to *fear* lest [Methodism] should become a mere compacted frame work of ecclesiastical guards and precautionary regulations . . . ?" Thrown on the defensive, Conference sympathizers tried to cast doubt on Caughey's revival figures and stooped on occasion to impugning the American's integrity on the slavery issue.[20]

Both William Booth and Catherine Mumford sided with the Reformers initially for two reasons. First, although they were both admirers of Wesley and recognized his autocratic control over Methodism during his lifetime, they supported at this time a more democratic approach to church government that was part of the Reformers' platform. Wesleyanism had to be rescued from what both of them perceived to be an autocratic group of ministers unsympathetic to the democratic impulses of the times and to the opinions of others in the denomination. For many Methodists, the actions taken against Caughey were arbitrary, and both William and Catherine would feel the backhand of such arbitrariness when they were expelled from the Wesleyan Church precisely because they demonstrated sympathy with the Reformers at this time.

However, for both William and Catherine, democratic sympathies could only go so far and eventually William would balk at what he perceived to be excessive congregational control. Catherine was not in the ministry and so had no concern about such control. However, later in life both William and Catherine would themselves revert to a more autocratic form of government that evolved after the founding of The Christian Mission in 1865 and was an essential aspect of founding an army for God in 1878.

It was more the second aspect of the Reformers' platform that attracted Catherine Mumford and William Booth to them. The Reformers supported Caughey because they saw in him the spirit of the Wesleys and primitive Methodism; they saw in him the spirit of revivalism. The Reformers were longing for revival to sweep through Methodism and thereby through the nation. The Reformers emphasized revival, the winning of souls for Christ; and holiness, purity of life and empowerment for ministry. These, along with his commitment to total abstinence from alcohol—especially appealing to Catherine—were the tenets of James Caughey, and his dismissal was generally lamented by the Reformers because his preaching continually brought these matters into focus for Methodism. William and Catherine were likewise committed to revivalism, and William began to see himself primarily as a revivalist rather than as a preacher settled to one local congregation. The spirit of revivalism, then, was the chief draw of the Reformers for the future founders of The Salvation Army.

Catherine was probably at this time more devoted to the Reformers than William was. He admired them, and especially their stance on revivalism and holiness, but he was not sure that he wanted to join them. Much of William's insecurity was also complicated at this moment because he was still a lay preacher with no denominational home, and, after all, Rabbits had agreed to support William for only three months at twenty shillings per week as a regular preacher at Binfield House.

Indeed, William's situation with the Reformers was not as steady as when he had been welcomed to that body by Rabbits; and as was often the case in William's life, he was prone to bursts of enthusiasm followed by times of despondency, despair, and doubt. The Reformers were learning that their rebellion against an autocratic Wesleyanism did not prevent similar autocratic tendencies within their movement, especially with those empowered to lead. They were also learning the hard lesson that congregational leadership had its problems as well, sometimes resulting in indecisiveness on the one hand, and downright combativeness against strong-willed preachers, on the other.

Added to that, the fervor of evangelism among the Reformers, while noble, did not deter jealousies from creeping into the movement among the pastors themselves, reminiscent of the jealousies that many felt against Caughey and his successes. Added to that, there was great divisiveness as early as 1852 among the Reformers—some wanting to return to the mother church, some wanting to align themselves with other Methodist denominations, while others stalwartly insisted on creating their own denomination. The uncertainty of the future of the movement caused William grave concern for his own ministry and future. Begbie summarized Booth's attitude toward the Reformers at this time by saying, "The more he saw of the Reformers the less he liked them."[21]

There is evidence that William was in great inner turmoil during this time, and was having considerable difficulty knowing God's will for his life and for the future. All the complicated matters of life burdened him, and he had to be careful lest he fall into depression and despondency. Added to this was his growing love and affection for Catherine. They were increasingly aware that they both wished to be engaged and married, in spite of their anxieties about a sufficient salary and a steady position in ministry, which were indispensable for a secure future together. Catherine Booth later recalled that "amongst the ways in which W. sought to obtain light was the old-fashioned one of opening the Bible and receiving the first passage on which the eye fell as the interpretation of God's pleasure, and this instance was rather curious, his eye falling upon, 'And the two sticks become one in my hand.' However, this controversy could not go on for ever with two such hearts as ours, and consequently we came to the conclusion and covenanted that come weal or woe we would sail life's stormy seas together, and on our knees we plighted our troth before the Lord."[22]

William and Catherine were often apart after their initial meetings, but a voluminous correspondence began during their separation that provides many insights into their lives from 1852 onward. In the letters of this period William raised the questions, concerns, and doubts, but Catherine is often seen consoling, counseling, encouraging, and comforting William. In the first extant letter from Catherine to William dated May 11, 1852, and addressed to "My Dear Friend," we see much sympathy from Catherine over William's present circumstances and his natural tendency to fret and worry. Her instruction, "Never mind who frowns, if God smiles," is followed after a couple of paragraphs by this friendly advice: "You have some true friends in the circuit and what is better than all you have a friend above whose love is as great as his power. He can easily open your way to another sphere of influence greater than you now conceive of."[23]

William and Catherine's Engagement

Resolution about William and Catherine's relationship came when they expressed their love for each other and were willing to trust the future to providence and commit themselves to a lifelong union in marriage. On Saturday evening, May 15, 1852, they were engaged.[24] Their future together was settled, but in the meantime there were several issues that had to be faced and William and Catherine would not be married for more than three years. The primary issue, however, revolved around William's feelings toward the Reformers and the as of yet open question about what denomination he would choose in order to prepare for the ministry. In this as in other matters he respected Catherine's opinions, and "Miss Mumford threw her whole heart into the question."[25] Also, to complicate matters, "They both agreed that the arrangement with Mr. Rabbits should come to an end when the three months were completed in July."[26]

The story of William Booth's entrance into a denominational home—New Connexion Methodism—will be dealt with in the next chapter. In the meantime it is important to note that the providential meeting of William Booth and Catherine Mumford, begun with the meeting in the home of Mr. Rabbits, led to the marriage of William and Catherine on June 16, 1855.[27] The wedding was a quiet affair held in the Congregational Stockwell New Chapel where Catherine had once worshipped. The officiating minister was Catherine's pastor, the Reverend Dr. David Thomas.[28] The only other people witnessing the wedding were William's sister Emma and Catherine's father.

The honeymoon was brief, only one week at Ryde on the Isle of Wight. However, it became immediately obvious that a partnership had begun in the lives of two become one. William and Catherine sustained both their love for and friendship with each other for the thirty-five years of their marriage, strengthening each other in the face of great obstacles and difficulties in what would eventually become a remarkable shared ministry. All of this was possible, they often reflected, by God's grace alone. And the grace that had led them to the altar on June 16, 1855, was the same grace that aided William in his struggle to find a denominational home.

CHAPTER FOUR

FINDING A DENOMINATIONAL HOME: WILLIAM BOOTH AND NEW CONNEXION METHODISM

Introduction

Both before and after his marriage to Catherine Mumford, William Booth was in search of a denominational safe harbor, preferably in the Methodism that he loved. He believed that he had been called by God for ministry, but his primary interest was in evangelism. He was looking for a denomination in which he could feel at home theologically and in which his gifts as an evangelist would be used.

William Booth and the Reformers

William's friend, Mr. Rabbits, agreed to support William for three months—from mid-April to mid-July 1852, and Booth's responsibilities were principally at Binfield House on Binfield Road, Clapham. This was a chapel controlled by the Reformers who were more democratically oriented than the rigid, autocratic Methodists with which the Reformers quarreled. Carolyn Ocheltree wrote that, the Reformers under the leadership of James Everett, Samuel Dunn, and William Griffith had agitated against undemocratic Methodist polity within Wesleyan Methodism. When these same leaders were expelled at the Wesleyan Conference of 1849, the Wesleyan Reformers became a popular movement. While this group never officially thought of themselves as a separate denomination, their ideas prompted 100,000 members to leave the Wesleyan Methodist Church over a period of a few years.[1]

It is interesting to note that Samuel Dunn, William's pastor back in Nottingham, was one of those expelled by Conference and became a leader of the Reformers. Dunn and others continued to press their claims upon Conference, but Owen Chadwick noted that "by July 1852 Dunn was convinced that they had no hope of forcing Conference to yield and became an Independent minister."[2] From 1865 to 1868 he ministered in America.

Among the Reformers the congregation pressed for lay input into matters of polity and finance. This may have been initially attractive to William because it was a step away from the sometimes-arbitrary rule of some local pastors whom he had known within Methodism. Also, William had worked for unreasonable bosses in the pawnbroking business and knew what it was like to be under the control of small-minded men.

However, it was never William Booth's nature, even at this young age and with limited experience, to submit totally to the will of the congregation. Booth was a leader, and he found it difficult to have to answer to committees. This conflict caused a strain at Binfield House even during Booth's brief tenure there, and Booth parted company with the Reformers and with the chapel on Binfield Road, a move supported by Catherine even though she wished the matter of a denominational home settled before she and William married. Catherine wrote:

> The discipline of the Reform Society was very unsatisfactory to us both, in denying the Minister what we considered to be his proper authority. The tendency of human nature to go to extremes found ample illustration in this particular. From making the Minister everything, treating him with the profoundest respect, receiving his word as law, putting him almost in the place of God Himself—they went over to regard him as nothing, denying him every shadow of authority, and only allowing him to preside at their meetings when elected for this purpose, and speaking of him in public and in private as their "hired" preacher. In W.'s case, it was worse than this. The leaders of the local movement with which he was connected not only denied him anything like the position of a leader, but refused to give

him reasonable opportunities for preaching. They simply dealt with him as a cypher, doubtless feeling that, did they give him any sort of position, he would earn for himself the leadership they were determined to keep for themselves. We both saw that these relations were too strained and unnatural to last very long; accordingly, at the end of the three months, for which Mr. Rabbits had engaged him in the first instance, and for which he remunerated him out of his own purse, the connection was dissolved.[3]

This naturally caused a strained relationship with Mr. Rabbits, who not only sided with the Reformers but probably also considered William as subject to his authority much as he would his employees in his factories. One biographer, usually fairly sanguine when referring to Rabbits, commented that "Booth, however, had a more aspiring spirit than Rabbits, who could scarcely see beyond the boundaries of a ledger and who attached more importance to an auditor's certificate than to uncertifiable salvation, and he knew his heart's business, which was his Master's, better than the boot manufacturer knew his, which was only his and of this world. Booth, too, remembering how preoccupied his father had been with business and practical affairs, may have been dubious of the worth of Rabbits' values."[4]

For the time being, William Booth parted company not only with the Reformers but also with Edward Rabbits—although his friendship with Rabbits was renewed in later years, probably because of an enduring respect that Rabbits had for the youthful evangelist. Booth later recollected that he would not have renewed his engagement with the church on any terms, and then recalled that "there was nothing for me to do but to sell my furniture and live on the proceeds, which did not supply me for a very long time. I declare to you that at that time I was so fixed as not to know which way to turn."[5]

William was understandably despondent, not knowing where he would go. Even though young and relatively inexperienced, he was captive to his own sense of right and wrong, and failed to see the value of other sides of an argument. His judgment was always the right one, and the only recourse for others was to see things his way. If this was a strength in William Booth, it was also a weakness, and would cause many personal troubles, especially in his later life.

Nevertheless, his impetuosity caused him some sleepless nights. He had no prospects. He had no money. And Catherine Mumford could well have decided to leave him to his own devices at this time. She had the security of living at home with her parents at Brixton. However, to her great credit, she viewed her engagement to William as divinely ordained and had agreed to marry him. The mutual love and respect of William and Catherine for each other at this time was genuine and growing. Catherine supported William's departure from the Reformers. She affirmed William's call to the ministry. She courageously looked to their future as one in which God was leading and she would enter that future with William, all other considerations aside.

William Booth and Congregationalism

Apparently Catherine suggested that William think about the Congregationalists. Catherine conceded that this would not be easy for William. She wrote:

It was at this time, when the way to the Ministry seemed totally closed in the Methodist direction, that W.'s attention was turned to the Congregational Church. I think this was my doing; indeed, I know it was; but, until he came to this dead stop, he would never hear of it, and even now his difficulties appeared almost insurmountable. To leave Methodism seemed an impossibility. His love for it at that time amounted almost to idolatry. . . .

Although I could sympathize with all this, and had a fair share of love for the Church to which I also owed much and in which I had experienced a great deal of blessing, still, I had nothing like his blind attachment. For one reason, I had not been actively engaged. Mine had been more the position of a spectator; and, moreover, I argued that, once settled in a Congregational pulpit, he could impart into his services and meetings all that was good and hearty and soul-saving in Methodism; at least, I thought he could, and consequently, I pressed him very strongly to seek an open door for the exercise of his Ministry among the Independents.

He was slow to accept my counsel. He had formed a very lofty notion of the intellectual and literary status of the Body, and was fearful that he was not equal in these respects to meet what would be required of him. But I was just as confident as he was fearful. I felt sure that all that was wanted by him was a sphere, and that once gained, I saw no difficulty in his being able to organize a church of workers, and make them into Methodists in spirit and practice, whether they were such in government or no.

Perhaps I was very simple in these notions; I had little or no experience at that time as to the difficulty of over-ruling the prejudices and changing the customs which had been handed down from generation to generation.

However, I was young and sanguine, and already had come to have con-siderable faith in the enthusiastic energy and devotion of my beloved, and I thought if he could once get into the leadership anywhere, he could carry the people whithersoever he would.

With such reasonings as these, and seeing that there was no other way by which he could reach the sphere to which his soul believed God had called him, he gave in, and resolved to seek an open door for the preach-ing of Jesus Christ, and to bringing lost sinners to God amongst the Congregationalists.[6]

Catherine began attending the Congregational Stockwell New Chapel near her home in Brixton, probably about mid-1852, the time when William was contemplating Congregationalism as a denomina-tional home. Evidently she retained her obligations of teaching a class of girls at the Binfield House and probably still attended some of the services there. However, because William was not yet settled about where his ministry would be, Catherine occasionally attended the local Congregational church as a means of helping William to make this deci-sion. The Reverend Dr. David Thomas was the minister.[7] It was he who, although once having incensed Catherine because of his doubts about the equality of women with men, nevertheless, would later preside over the marriage of William and Catherine.

Precisely why Catherine began attending this church is difficult to ascertain. It is possible that her growing uncertainties with the Reformers because of the way they were treating William at the Binfield church caused her to search for a church home elsewhere. And it is uncertain if, by attending this church and listening to the preaching of Dr. Thomas, she encouraged William to think about Congregationalism, or if she attended the church precisely because she had encouraged William in this direction and was seeking for confirmation of this new direction in their lives. The church was located near her parents' home, and so it was also convenient for Catherine to attend.

In any case, Congregationalism was seriously considered as an option for William's ministerial and vocational future from July to October 1852, particularly the Congregational Union, one of the branches of nineteenth-century Congregationalism. Is it possible that William was encouraged in this direction because of Samuel Dunn's move to an Independent ministry? In any case, upon the advice of Dr. Thomas, William made an appointment with the Reverend John Campbell, at that time a leading Congregationalist and minister of both the

Tottenham Court Chapel on Tottenham Court Road and Whitefield's Tabernacle, Moorfields, London. Catherine Booth later recalled that

> at that time the most influential man among the Nonconformists in London was a Dr. Campbell. He was the editor of a religious newspaper that was regarded as the principal organ of the Denomination, known as *The British Banner,* together with one or two other magazines. Dr. Campbell was mighty in controversy, and his paper had achieved no little notoriety in this line.[8]

William Booth was well received by Dr. Campbell and was assured that the doctrine of unlimited atonement that Booth supported, in contrast to the Calvinist doctrines of election and limited atonement, would not be a hindrance to his preaching in the Congregational Union. In that day Congregationalism taught Calvinist doctrines of election and limited atonement, which in the nineteenth century was to say that God had chosen those who were to be saved and the atonement applied to them alone. This, of course, had been the focus of the argument between John Wesley and his friend George Whitefield in the previous century, dividing Methodism. In his biography of John Wesley, Kenneth Collins wrote about the debate:

> Valuing their friendship, Wesley was undecided whether he should challenge the Calvinistic views of Whitefield so directly as to preach on the subject of free grace. To be sure, Whitefield would find the notion that salvation was available to all sinners very troubling. To break his indecision, Wesley cast lots on April 26 [1739], which indicated that he should "preach and print." Accordingly, a few days later, April 29, Wesley published the sermon "Free Grace" in Bristol. On the one hand, the sermon impugned Calvinist predestination and, on the other hand, affirmed that salvation is free for *all*, that all who are in *need* of Christ may come to the Savior. Naturally, George Whitefield was angered by this publication, and it caused a rift, not quickly healed, between the two principal leaders of the revival. No sooner had Wesley and Whitefield joined hands than they were already beginning to go their separate ways.[9]

The controversy continued into the nineteenth century, and although Booth may not have read Wesley's "Free Grace," he was theologically sympathetic to the doctrines explained in that sermon. In spite of a difference of opinion on this matter, the conversation between Booth and

Campbell went well, and Campbell gave William letters of introduction to other ministers in the denomination.

However, as supportive as Dr. Campbell was, another minister, the Reverend Dr. James William Massey, Secretary to the Home Missionary Society of the Congregational Union, was the opposite.[10] He discouraged Booth greatly, leading Booth to believe that he could not presently enter the Congregational college without extensive probationary experience in Congregationalism, and that it would be at least five years before Booth would be a Congregational minister, if at all! William wrote immediately to Campbell, and Campbell intervened on William's behalf. Had Campbell seen in William Booth a sincere determination to serve the Lord and his generation as a minister? Had he seen gifts in William Booth that he believed needed to be developed? Had he sensed a genuine religious fervor in William Booth? For whatever reasons, Campbell was able to override Massey. Booth appeared before an examination committee and was sent to the home of the Reverend John Frost at Cotton End for training in the Congregational ministry.

The question of the Calvinist doctrine of predestination was still a problem for Booth, however, and perhaps the members of the examination committee believed that, with proper training at Cotton End, William Booth would see his way clear to accept the tenets of Calvinism in good conscience. After all, Congregationalism of the nineteenth century was not as strident about Calvinist doctrines as were the followers of Calvin in the sixteenth century, and allowed for some latitude in interpreting doctrine. In addition, the Booths were aware that Charles Grandison Finney, whom they so admired, "had preached regularly from a London Congregational pulpit and with their admiration for Finney that may have been a factor in Booth taking this new direction."[11] Indeed, the Reverend Dr. George Smith, the Secretary of the Congregational Union and a member of the committee, stated that "the Committee has shown you great favour arranging for you to go into training, although not even a member of an Independent Church, and holding doctrinal views opposed to those of the Committee; but on examination at the close of the first term, the Committee will certainly expect that you will be more nearly in harmony with their opinions."[12]

Two books were recommended to Booth to help him achieve such desired harmony—Abraham Booth's *Reign of Grace*, and George Payne's *Divine Sovereignty*—both spelling out a thoroughly Calvinist theology. William was conscientious in reading the books, but found in them a theological rigidity that he could not accept and that the good Dr. Campbell had led him to believe was not universal within the Congregational Union. He had lingering doubts about how free he would be to teach and preach the views he believed to be soundly biblical, even if they departed from standard Congregational thinking.

Booth's Wesleyan theological background—which taught that God's prevenient grace was granted to every person, thereby providing the opportunity for all to respond to the atonement offered by Christ on the cross—prevented him from considering any doctrine of election that excluded free grace to everyone to be biblically unsound as well as a road-block to evangelism. Booth believed that Christ died on the cross for "the whosoever" and likewise believed in the possibility of all people who trusted in Christ by faith being saved. In that regard the atonement was universal rather than limited. He was unable and unwilling to change his theology to conform to the Congregational Calvinism of his day, and so he decided that the Congregational ministry was not for him. He later reminisced that

> in my emergency a remarkable way opened for me to enter college and become a Congregational minister. But after long waiting, several exami- nations, trial sermons and the like, I was informed that on the completion of my training I should be expected to believe and preach what is known as Calvinism. After reading a book which fully explained the doctrine, I threw it at the wall opposite me, and said I would sooner starve than preach such doctrine, one special feature of which was that only a select few could be saved.[13]

In his opinion of Calvinism he had a theological companion in Catherine Mumford. Her own antipathy to Calvinism had begun to take shape at age fourteen and she was well aware of the theological and evan- gelistic issues involved. However, like William at this time, she was per- haps most concerned about the pastoral implications for a Calvinist theology. She, like William, wanted to make the gospel available to all and wanted to invite all to accept by faith God's grace, manifested most surely by a universal atonement. Any doctrine of election and limited atonement suffocated the fullness of the biblical message as both William and Catherine understood it. These had been Wesley's concerns also. "Wesley would have liked predestination to be an 'opinion,' not break- ing communion, but could not gain agreement on this and indeed often treated it as a deadly poison not be tolerated."[14]

In the end there were enough misgivings about Congregationalism that William finally declined Campbell's gracious offer of admittance into Cotton End and thereby, after six months' training, into the Independent ministry. He wrote to Dr. Smith, the Secretary of the Congregational Union, "thanking him for all his kindness, but intimating that he had not the slightest intention of altering his doctrinal views, or of even deliberately setting to work to prepare for doing so."[15] The Home Missionary Society minutes of the Congregational Union for October 5, 1852, recorded the following: "W. Booth, candidate. The secretary reported that Mr. Booth had withdrawn from being a candidate for admission to Cotton End, disapproving of the manner in which the committee had conducted his examination and the disputed doctrine."[16] And even after considering Congregationalism briefly again in March 1853, William finally decided for Methodism. He wrote to Catherine, "I am for *Methodism* most *unquestionably*. I am determined to stand by it."[17]

Other Prospects

In the meantime, although not formally matriculated at a college, William was reading, probably on the advice of Catherine, who was more naturally disposed than William toward the training of the mind, and whose "undoubted intellectual superiority"[18] was evident even to William. On July 28, 1852, William wrote to Catherine, "I am reading Finney and Watson on election and final perseverance, and I see more than ever reason to cling to my own views of truth and righteousness."[19] Catherine was constantly advising William to study more.

In leaving the prospects for a Congregational ministry, all appeared lost to William. However, help and hope came from some of his friends who were still in the Reform movement. William was asked by a group of Reformers from Spalding in the Midlands to take charge of their Methodist circuit in Lincolnshire. The Reformers were predominant among the Wesleyans in that country town, and the laity there were mostly Reformers. Word had come to them that William Booth was still searching for a pastorate and, although greatly disillusioned with the Reform movement generally, might be more receptive to an invitation to a country circuit far removed from the movement's political realities. Again, it is necessary to rely on Catherine Booth's recollections. She said, "Here the great majority of lay preachers and people sided with the expelled Ministers, and were, in course of time, by expulsion or from choice, separated from the original fold, whereupon they formed themselves into a Community consisting of Societies and lay Preachers."[20]

The churches of the circuit covered twenty-seven miles, and William had to preach in the churches and oversee their business affairs. One of Booth's biographers, often unduly critical of many things, remarked that Lincolnshire was a county "which . . . remains depressing because of its flatness, which seems to afflict the spirits of its inhabitants and to make them symbolic of the illimitable dullness of the villages. When one wishes to find the Methodist chapel in a South Lincoln village, one looks for the ugliest and meanest building in the ugly and mean place."[21]

William did not find Lincolnshire so. By all accounts he was delighted to go to the Midlands and minister among his Methodist friends and found the people anything but dull. Indeed, William was warmly and gladly welcomed at Spalding. He recounted that "the Spalding people welcomed me as though I had been an angel from Heaven, providing me with every earthly blessing within their ability, and proposing that I should stay with them for ever. They wanted me to marry right away, offered to furnish me a house, provide me with a horse to enable me more readily to get about the country, and proposed other things that they thought would please me."[22] This, of course, is a much later recollection by Booth of his time in Spalding, but such optimistic and glowing accounts of his ministry would become normative for William Booth throughout his lifetime. There was either a fear or an inability in William Booth to admit to any failures or defeats, especially with regard to the ministry of the gospel. His "lists of triumphs seems endless."[23] Therefore, his recollections always have to be read with caution.

Booth remained in Spalding from November 1852 through February 1854.[24] Many people experienced conversions under Booth's ministry and often knelt at the Communion rails at the various churches in his circuit, such as at Donnington or Swineshead Bridge or Holbeach, in repentance for their sins.

The move to Spalding did have one negative side effect. It meant that William and Catherine were separated for the first time since their engagement, though such sacrifices had to be made if William were going to find a settled ministry and eventually a denominational home. They had enjoyed, since their first meeting, their nearness to each other, which nurtured their love. A separation of this sort would be a trial for both of them. Added to that were Catherine's misgivings still about the

Reformers and what future William could possibly have with this disjunctive movement. Catherine thought that this move to Spalding might delay William's training and eventual ordination, but she was ready to submit to what she perceived to be the working of God in their lives, and knew from previous experience that God's ways were often mysterious.

The parting of William and Catherine was made easier to bear by a lengthy correspondence between them that would continue throughout their lifetime of partnership whenever they were apart. Catherine counseled William on many matters—both doctrinal and practical—and strengthened his despairing heart whenever he felt fatigued by his work. She wrote to him about such weighty matters as the spirit of prayer, life in Christ, and how profitable it is to read good biographies. She warned him about the danger of ambition, especially in light of the fact that William was becoming a favorite son of the people in Spalding, and even had to caution him about an infatuation from an admirer about whom William wrote. Catherine likewise shared with him her views about how to preach, how to conduct revivalistic meetings, and the importance of study to his ministry, she being the more intellectually inclined of the two. Also, it was critical that William get settled views on various social issues, especially that of total abstinence from alcohol. Make no mistake, when Catherine spoke of settled views she was referring to *her* views. In fact, "it was Catherine's habit—infuriating to everyone except William—to begin her frequent dissertations on faith and morals with the assertion that she had thought very carefully on the subject. Her tone implied that, since her protagonists had not done the same, she could only hope that they would gradually come to see the truth."[25]

William was also faithful in his correspondence to Catherine, although "his letters were rarely so didactic and never so patronizing."[26] He reported on the many successes of his work, but was free to admit to times of despondency and illness. Depression plagued William Booth during his entire adult life, and even during a relatively peaceful ministry in Spalding the signs of depression were already apparent. And so the correspondence between William and Catherine flows with rhythms of anguish and comfort; advice and counsel to each other; to professing love for each other and looking forward to being together in marriage; and occasionally to disagreements with each other over such things as the measures used in revivalism. William was probably more disposed than Catherine to allow for emotionalism in the revivalistic meetings. In one letter she wrote:

Watch against *mere animal excitement* in your revival service. I don't use the term in the sense in which . . . revivalists would use it, but only in the sense in which Finney himself would use it; remember Caughey's silent, soft heavenly carriage; *he* did not shout; there was no necessity; he had a more potent weapon at command than *noise; I* never liked noise and confusion, *only so far* as I believed it to be the *natural* expression of deep anxiety—wrought by the Holy Ghost.[27]

Added to all of this was William's concern that some Reformers in Spalding were considering reunion with the Methodist bodies, which would mean that William would have to be more subservient to the growing democratic impulses within Methodism and answer to laypeople and committees. Both William and Catherine, who knew that the New Testament laid down no single pattern of church government for all times and ages, appreciated the variety of denominational organizations, and would not have liked to have seen the ascendancy of one type of organization above another.

However, William's experience in his ministry in Spalding had caused him to consider more seriously matters of polity and ministerial authority. There was a kind of vocational self-awareness dawning in William, shaped, to some extent, by Catherine. William Booth was never one by temperament to bow to the control of people in the church, and that on two counts. First, he believed that the minister should be the authoritarian figure in the church by virtue of his office as pastor (the issue of women in ministry had not yet arisen between William and Catherine). As the pastor, he was not going to be treated as an employee of the church. The nature of authority was at stake. The power of his word would, he believed, lose all meaning were he subservient to church governance. He was sure that his preaching would be hindered and his vision for the salvation of the lost dampened by endless questions and bickering about polity and policy. Although he did not have the social standing of his mentor, John Wesley, who, by virtue of that standing, as well as his office as Anglican priest, refused to be subservient to some kind of lay control, William Booth nevertheless believed that the office of preacher gave him a biblical authority that demanded recognition.

Second, even at this time in his life it is evident that William Booth possessed leadership qualities, and as a leader could not see himself constantly answering to committees and yet more committees. He demonstrated already an autocratic personality that began to take shape as the leader of the other young evangelists back in Nottingham. Again, it is important to note that such authoritarianism was not the result of place or position in society, as it had been with the Oxford-educated Wesley. It was simply the disposition of the man. Such authoritarianism would become evident in later years as the leader of The Christian Mission, and especially as the first General of The Salvation Army. By temperament, then, it was impossible for William to consider coming again under the control of a local church. That is why he left the chapel in London, and he did not want to go through that experience a second time. And on this point Catherine was in full agreement, perhaps because she began to recognize a similar authoritarian personality in herself, and she surely supported William in his dilemma.

It was at this crucial moment that William began to contemplate other options. Was this a sign that the Lord was leading him out of the ministry and into something else? He considered entering the business world. After all, he had acquired some business skills and acumen in several years of the pawnbroking business. Should he move to America and minister where he believed more liberty was given to the pastor? Undoubtedly the accounts of Finney's and Caughey's ministries and the influence of the Methodist itinerant preacher, Richard Poole, who came to Spalding in November 1853, stirred him. Bennett is of the opinion that "Pool's influence over Booth seems to have been considerable."[28] Poole's preaching moved Booth. Poole was direct in his preaching and simple in his method, and Booth determined that he would copy Poole's preaching style. In addition, Poole, dissatisfied with Methodism in England, considered going to America to join the Methodist Episcopal Church there.

Catherine assured William that she would support him in this venture, writing on December 1, 1853, that

> if our prospects fail here; our path being blocked up, and the interests of our family demand it, I will brave all the trials of the voyage and the climate and cheerfully accompany you across the Atlantic, because then I should feel "well we tried the only path conscientiously open to us in our native land and it failed, therefore if evil befall us we shall be sustained by the belief that it was in the path of duty and in the order of providence."[29]

One can hardly blame Catherine for her natural fear of traveling across the Atlantic in the middle of the nineteenth century. Such travel was most uncomfortable in the best of circumstances and often treacherous and dangerous in difficult ones.

However, in the meantime, the Reformers of his circuit continued to consider joining an association of Methodist churches and leaving behind them their rather tenuous connection with Methodism and their sense of disunity. Deciding precisely what Methodist association to join was causing some bickering among the Reformers and wearing poor William out! Should there be some kind of official connection with the Methodists? A denomination called New Connexion Methodism seemed to appeal to Booth, and it is referred to in correspondence between William and Catherine at this time.

William Booth and New Connexion Methodism

The Methodist New Connexion arose after the death of John Wesley in 1791. Methodism after Wesley's death began breaking away from Anglicanism and even began separating internally. Initial Methodist separations from Anglicanism came in spite of Wesley's continual protestations during his lifetime that Methodism was not a separatist movement. However, as has already been witnessed with the Reform movement, the Methodists endlessly discussed matters of organization, polity, and the extent of the use of revivalism. William Booth sometimes felt that all such discussions hindered the work of the kingdom of Christ.

One young minister who wanted reform within Methodism at the end of the eighteenth century was Alexander Kilham, born into Methodism at Epworth in Lincolnshire, the birthplace of the Wesleys.[30] He published pamphlets pushing reform, especially the use of the laity in the management of the church. The issues Kilham raised were not unknown to Wesley himself, and Wesley's own resolutions on these matters never pleased everyone; in fact, they often caused dissension among his own Methodists. The force of Wesley's personality, his autocratic leadership, and his ability to argue his positions with an acute, Oxford-trained mind kept Methodism basically connected. Nevertheless, even during Wesley's lifetime some wished to press the reform issues that Kilham and others later espoused, while others, desiring to remain clearly under the authority of Anglicanism, knew that such measures would eventually lead to expulsion from the Anglican community. Kilham was, nevertheless, much more influenced by the democratic impulses unleashed in the broader culture at the end of the eighteenth century. The growing democracy within Methodism reflected a political and social ethos that Wesley disliked and eventually weaned much of Methodism away from autocratic control.

Kilham's reform measures were too radical for some of Methodism's leaders and he was expelled from Conference in 1796. The proposals that he had made for a more democratic Methodism in a treatise entitled *The Progress of Liberty Among the People Called Methodists* "became the basis for the formation of the Methodist New Connexion, a new denomination into which two other Methodist preachers and five thousand members followed him."[31] It must be noted, however, that Kilham was no renegade. "It cannot be denied that Kilham was an intrepid reformer, whose sole concern was for the welfare of the Church, which he deeply loved, and for the progress of the gospel."[32] He published a magazine espousing his views, which eventually evolved into the *Methodist New Connexion Magazine*. He also purchased the Ebenezer Chapel in Leeds as a place to preach, all along hoping for reconciliation with Wesleyan Methodism.

By July 1797 it became apparent that no such reconciliation was forthcoming, and so the new Methodist denomination came into being, first called The New Itinerancy but later called the Methodist New Connexion. Wesleyan theology was maintained, but a constitution was established based on the reform measures for which Kilham and others had been fighting. Chief among those measures was lay representation in the governing of the denomination. When William Booth was considering New Connexion Methodism as his denominational home, he was not opposed to this as far as broad denominational governance was concerned, but he still wanted a balance between denominational lay representation and the authority of the local preacher.

When Kilham died at age thirty-six, on December 20, 1798, he was honored by some and vilified by others. Nevertheless, by then the denomination was established. Some Reform societies, convinced that reconciliation with the Wesleyan Methodists was impossible, joined with the Methodist New Connexion, and William considered doing likewise with his independent circuit at Spalding. He took such a proposition to the quarterly meeting of the circuit, but the motion failed. However, he resolved to join the Methodist New Connexion denomination himself, regardless of the Spalding circuit's direction. New Connexion Methodism appeared to offer William what he had been looking for in a

denomination: a thoroughly Wesleyan theological base, a strong emphasis on revivalism, and a governance that included representation from
the members of the congregation and from both the local lay preachers
and the ordained ministers alike, without, however, undermining the
local preacher's authority or the ordained minister's authority. One of
Booth's biographers noted that the Methodist New Connexion "was a
society after Booth's own heart, able to be influential in various directions, and he began overtures for an amalgamation of the Reformers with
the New Connexion for that reason, and because he was sick of the inter-
minable petty arguments with which the Reformers imagined they were
establishing the Kingdom of God on earth."[33]

There was, however, an odd turn of events in 1854. The Reformers did
resolve to join New Connexion Methodism, but by that time were
declined. The Reformers were on their own. Some were able eventually
to join New Connexion Methodism and some joined other denominations. And, as has already been mentioned, Booth's proposal for the
Spalding circuit Reformers to join New Connexion Methodism was
declined.

However, by this time William himself was determined to join New
Connexion Methodism, and to that end wrote to the Reverend Dr.
William Cooke for information regarding formal training in Dr. Cooke's
home at 3 The Crescent, Albany Road, in Camberwell, South London,
in preparation for ministry in the New Connexion movement.[34] He was
accepted by Cooke, and entered the seminary in London, much to the
dismay of many in his congregation in Spalding. They tried to entice him
to stay with them with the promise of providing a home, a horse, and the
prospect of immediate marriage to Catherine rather than having to wait
the four years' probationary period before being married, which was New
Connexion policy. Also, some London Reformers tried to lure him to the
Hinde Street Circuit at an annual salary of one hundred pounds, a fine
salary for that time. Other friends were pressing to persuade William that
his gifts were as a revivalist and that he should launch out in an independent ministry unfettered by any denominational structure or
bureaucracy.

Truth to tell, William was in a dilemma over leaving the Reformers,
who offered so much financial promise and security, and stepping out in
faith with New Connexion Methodism. William wavered in his decision.
Voluminous correspondence flowed between William and Catherine
regarding the decision. Catherine completely favored the move to New

Connexion Methodism and stated so many times. In a letter from Holbeach dated January, 1854, William wrote to Catherine:

My Dearest Kate:—The plot thickens, and I hesitate not to tell you that I fear, and fear much, that I am going wrong.

Yesterday I received a letter asking me if I would consent to come to the Hinde Street Circuit (London Reformers), salary £100 per year. I have also heard that the committee in London are about to make me an offer. I would give a great deal to be satisfied as to the right path, and gladly would I walk it whether here or there.

You see, my dearest, it is certainly enough to make a fellow think and tremble. Here I am at present at a circuit numbering 780 members, with an increase for the year of nearly two hundred. Am invited to another with nearly a thousand. And yet I am going to join a church with but 150 members in London, and a majority of circuits with but a similar number.

I fear that with all my cautiousness on this subject I shall regret it. Send me a kind letter to reach me on Friday. Bless you, a thousand times! My present intention is to tear myself away from all and everything and persevere in the path I have chosen. They reckon it down here the maddest, wildest, most premature and hasty step that ever they knew a saved man to take.

I remain, my dearest love, Your own William.[35]

Catherine's response was immediate. In part, she wrote:

My Dearest William:—I have with a burdened soul committed the contents of your letter to God, and I feel persuaded He will guide you. I will just put down one or two considerations which may comfort you.

First, then, you are not leaving the Reformers because you fear you would not get another circuit or as good a salary as the Connexion can offer. You are leaving because you are out of patience and sympathy with its *principles* and *aims*, and because you believe they will bring it to ultimate destruction.

Second, you are not leaving to secure present advantages, but sacrificing present advantages for what you believe to be *on the whole* (looking to the end) most for God's glory and the good of souls. And the fact of Hinde Street offering £200 would not alter those *reasons*. If it is right in *principle* for you to leave the movement and join the Connexion, no advantages in the former or disadvantages in the latter can possibly alter the thing.

But mind, I do not urge you to do it, and I do not see even now that it is too late to retreat, if your conscience is not satisfied as to the quality of your motives. But I believe it *ought to be*. I wish you prayed more and

talked less about the matter. Try it, and be determined to get clear and settled views as to your course.[36]

William finally settled the dispute. He resolved to leave the Reformers
and join New Connexion Methodism. In later years he recounted the
move in this way:

> The people with whom I had come into union were sorely unorganized,
> and I could not approve of the ultra-radicalism that prevailed.
> Consequently, I looked about for a Church nearer my notions of system
> and order, and in the one I chose, the Methodist New Connexion, I found
> a people who were, in those days, all I could desire, and who received me
> with as much heartiness as my Lincolnshire friends had done.[37]

The decision made, William left for London in February 1854, delighted
again to be with Catherine, but probably still sorrowful that "his friends
in Lincoln were rueful because of his impending departure and disposed
to blame her for it."[38]

William entered Dr. William Cooke's training college for prospective
New Connexion Methodist ministers on February 14, 1854. Cooke was
a leader in New Connexion Methodism, and his book entitled *Christian
Theology* was a basic text for New Connexion Methodist ministers. It was
customary in the nineteenth century for clergy outside of the established
church to receive ministerial training by studying with an experienced
minister, learning the trade, as it were, under the watchful eye of a senior pastor. The training given was varied, and was considered necessary
for the minister of the gospel. Sermon preparation was critically important to this training, and was complemented with lessons on writing,
grammar, rhetoric, and logic. Elementary Greek and Latin were taught,
as well as some basic work in moral philosophy. The daily schedule was
rigorous and always under the control of Dr. Cooke. Personal and academic disciplines were emphasized. The more practical and evangelistic
work was conducted in the neighborhood of the training college and was
intended to complement the academic training of each student.

A friendship developed between Booth and Cooke, whom William
later recalled as "a man of beautiful disposition . . . and an imposing presence."[39] One unconfirmed story has it that one of Cooke's daughters was
converted under Booth's ministry. In any case, it is evident that Dr. Cooke
allowed his student sufficient time for preaching and evangelization, for
Booth was at heart an evangelist. Cooke saw that and respected it.

William soon discovered that he had neither the patience nor the temperament of a student. Much of the academic side of the training at Camberwell was tortuous for him and much too confining. He describes his approach to study in this way: "However, I set to work, and, with all the powers I had, commenced to wrestle with my studies."[40] William was still trying to develop the study habits recommended by Catherine, but he confessed that he found the academic side of his training difficult and, for him at least, perhaps actually uninspiring. "That William did not make a good theological student goes without saying. Into the speculations of philosophy he never entered, and for the laborious study of theology it is quite certain that he could never have had a fruitful inclination.... Yet he was conscious in himself of the need for knowledge, and agonized more than was good for his health over intellectual deficiencies."[41]

Cooke was wise enough to see the conflict in young William between the active evangelistic side that enlivened him, and the passive student side that was crippling. Cooke resolved the conflict by suggesting that Booth had had enough training and it was time for him to engage in ministry full time. He suggested that young William become the superintendent of the London Circuit of the denomination, and in that capacity he would be the first minister on probation of the Packington Street Chapel in Islington, recently opened on July 19, 1854.[42]

As flattering as such an offer was, William did not have confidence in himself for such a task even though the circuit was small and the membership numbered only about 150. He especially doubted his administrative skills because evangelism was his first love. Therefore, a compromise was made, and it involved his old friend, Mr. Rabbits, who, although estranged from William in 1852 over William's leaving the Binfield House, remained an admirer of Booth's and was following him into New Connexion Methodism. There is very little information regarding this friendship during the previous two years, but it is obvious that by now they had settled their differences, and Rabbits would once again come to the aid of Booth. The deal was made: another man, the Reverend P. T. Gilton, was to be made superintendent of the circuit, and Rabbits would financially support William Booth to be Gilton's assistant, thereby allowing William time and energy for his evangelistic work. Also, it was conceded that Booth could marry within a year, although most probationary ministers had to wait four years to marry. Catherine was delighted with the turn of events and saw all of this as providential.

If officially he was the assistant to the Superintendent of the London Circuit of the Methodist New Connexion, in reality he had quickly become that denomination's itinerant evangelist. Mr. Gilton, it would seem, for much of this time was left to serve alone. No doubt, like his Queen, he was not amused.[43]

However, Josiah Bates, "a leading layman and keen supporter of Booth, had written to the *New Connexion Magazine* [suggesting] that Booth be appointed as the denomination's full-time evangelist."[44]

William launched out from London. He renewed his revival work back in Lincoln where he was known. He went from there to Bristol and then to Guernsey, where his meetings were very successful by revivalistic standards, many sinners being converted and many saints finding holiness. In January 1855, he was off to Longton in Staffordshire for revival meetings, invited there by the president of the denomination himself. There he stayed for a month, and up to twenty-five hundred people heard him preach each evening. His reputation as an evangelist was growing in the Potteries, and from there he continued successful preaching tours in the Midlands and in the north of England—Shelton, Hanley, Nottingham, Burslem, Newcastle, and Mossley.

There were times, as had been the case in the Wesleyan revivals in the previous century, that the public meetings became rather emotionally charged. In writing to Catherine, William said,

> Last night twice or thrice I became alarmed, the excitement was almost overwhelming, I feared for the people. I feared lest we should not be able to keep the reins of the meeting. The cries of distress were thrilling, piercing, running, as one gentleman expressed it, through to your finger ends. Some were violent, commenced shrieking, clapping the forms, etc., these I stopped directly; in fact all the more violent I stopped as soon as I could. If I doubted, as in two instances, sincerity, I stopped them authoritatively; if I had confidence in them I poured on the balm of Jesus' salvation and the sweet promises of His Word, and they soon turned their tears and wailings into joy.
>
> Amid all this I could not help but reason, Is it right? Is this the best way? Perhaps I was severely tempted to believe it all a delusion? Perhaps it was my own unbelief, but it was strange that these thoughts should be passing in my breast while I stood upon the form, the calmest and at times the most unmoved in all that dense assembly, directing and controlling every movement of the meeting so far as such a number of beings could be controlled and guided.

The people are more *ignorant* here than in other places I have visited, many who come are backsliders, and they wring their hands, and strike their breasts, and beat the communion-rail enough to melt and break hearts of stone.[45]

William most certainly recalled Catherine's earlier warning against excessive emotionalism when she wrote that he was to be careful of mere animal excitement in his revival meetings. However, William was able to bring order to the meetings both by his preaching and by his authoritarian word, and he never lost control of the meetings. Nevertheless, newspaper reports of the meetings, as well as accounts from people attending the meetings, caused concern for many of Booth's contemporaries in the denomination, and, in spite of continued invitations coming to Booth to preach, many felt that he should return home to resume his responsibilities in the London Circuit.

Nevertheless, William was pleased with how things were going. He had developed a good daily working routine, and continued to report great crowds at his meetings. His apparently disciplined schedule allowed him to get his needed work done, and in a letter to Catherine from Birmingham he wrote that "I have announced to the lady where I am now staying that I do not go out at all to visit, and I intend sticking to it."[46] Booth is referring here to social visits and to taking tea with members of the church. He abhorred such visits as a complete waste of time and a detraction from his work. This would remain true throughout his ministry.

His health, ever a concern of his, was steady at the moment. Both William and Catherine were often ill, even at this young age, and felt comfortable telling each other about such illnesses and sharing thoughts on remedies. Catherine, especially, believed in the value of such alternative medical treatments as hydropathy and homeopathy, and even at times believed in galvanism. Hydropathy is treatment by water—drinking it or bathing in it. Homeopathy "is a method of treatment that used a range of drugs, usually administered in very small doses, which would, if given to a healthy person, cause similar symptoms to the ones being treated."[47] And galvanism was the use of electricity to stimulate muscle activity. Both William and Catherine were also vegetarians, although there are a few references to their eating fish or fowl. "Catherine, it is not unfair to say, had an obsession with sickness, particularly her own, and its cure, so much so that it is possible that her general health at this stage in her life was not as bad as she imagined."[48]

Both were convinced, for example, of the value of cold-water baths and William refers often to the value of such baths, combined at times with large doses of horehound tea, used as a cough remedy. In one letter to Catherine he wrote,

> My health is better, my chest stronger. . . . I adhere to the cold water bathing of my chest and shoulders and back. I do not return much before 12 on an average—sleep well, rise about 1/2 past 8, breakfast and walk till dinner—afterwards do my correspondence, read a little and prepare for night, leaving the prayer meeting about 10—last night they did not leave the chapel until 1/4 to 12.[49]

Personal family matters intruded upon William and Catherine, and the illness of Catherine's mother was a cause for some concern during this time, as was the continuing near-poverty existence of William's mother and two sisters still living in Nottingham. William sent them money when possible, although his income from the revival meetings was often meager.

In spite of various distractions, William and Catherine made plans for their future life together and often discussed what arrangements would be made to accommodate his traveling, especially if they had children. William's concern for the future welfare of his wife and possible family was lessened a bit when he finally took out a life insurance policy. William and Catherine spoke often of their love for each other, and continued to correspond about such matters as the importance of study, the need occasionally for rest and recreation, and the ever-present concern about money to support them in their married life.

There was only one issue that seriously threatened this otherwise loving and tranquil relationship, and that was a disagreement about the equality of men and women. Catherine was convinced of their equality in every way, although sadly recognizing that women had not been given the same intellectual training as men, and therefore were not the equal to men in that respect, through no fault of their own. However, by nature, women were equal to men, and all that was wanted now was for women to be given equal privileges and opportunities. William "quoted the old aphorism that woman has a fibre more in her heart and a cell less in her brain."[50] As has been mentioned, Catherine had already confronted her pastor, the Reverend Dr. David Thomas, on the issue of the equality of women and men, and now she knew that it was necessary to write to her love about this matter, even supporting the equality of women and men in ministry, although this matter was not of immediate concern for her because she had not yet entered into a public ministry and was at this point in her life not even entertaining such a notion.

The most crucial and direct letter from Catherine to William on the subject of the equality of the sexes even in ministry is dated April 9, 1855, just before their marriage in June. This was a lengthy epistle of sixteen pages dealing with many matters, but the heart of it exemplified Catherine's most precise thinking to date related to these matters, and in the letter she advised William to get settled views on these subjects.[51] William's reply on April 12, 1855, was not exactly what Catherine was hoping to hear from her betrothed. He responded:

> The remarks on *Woman's* position I will read again before I answer. From the first reading I cannot see anything in them to lead me for one *moment* to think of altering my opinion. You *combat* a great deal that I hold as firmly as *you* do—viz. her *equality*, her *perfect equality*, as a whole—as *a being*. But as to concede that she is man's *equal*, or *capable* of becoming man's equal, in intellectual attainments or prowess—I must say *that* is contradicted by experience in the world and my honest conviction. You know, my dear, I acknowledge the superiority of your sex in very many things—in others I believe her inferior. *Vice versa* with man.
>
> I would not stop a woman preaching on any account. I would not encourage one to begin. You should preach if you felt moved thereto: felt equal to the task. I would not stay you if I had the power to do so. Altho', *I should not like it*. It is easy for you to say my views are the result of prejudice; perhaps they are. I am for the world's *salvation*; I will quarrel with no means that promises help.[52]

If there was any issue that nearly broke off the engagement of this couple, this was it. There was a strain in the relationship over this matter, but William and Catherine were reconciled and married two months later. To William's credit, his views both on the equality of women and men and on the ministry of women would evolve into what Catherine believed to be biblical views. Both their marriage and the ministry of the organizations that they founded would demonstrate such biblical equality.

In any case, William was now settled into a ministry with a denomination in which he felt at home. Here was a group of people who espoused the kind of biblical and Wesleyan theology that were important to Booth, who believed in evangelism as he did, and who were seeking to balance the ministry of the laity with the ministry of the pastors in the denomination. At this point, William probably believed that he was with New Connexion Methodism for better or for worse until the Lord called him home. However, such was not to be the case. There were yet to be many difficult turning points in William Booth's life until he found his destiny.

CHAPTER FIVE

DIFFICULT DECISION: LEAVING NEW CONNEXION METHODISM

Introduction

Following his marriage to Catherine, William Booth was initially appointed as an evangelist with the denomination. Their married life began with constant itinerancy as they moved from town to town and city to city to fulfill William's evangelistic calling and responsibilities. There were times when ill health prevented Catherine from traveling with him, but she was able to stay with her parents in Brixton and, when possible, meet William during one of his engagements. As mentioned in the previous chapter, both the Booths were absolutely consumed by matters of health, and often thought of themselves as more sick than they actually were.[1] However, in spite of these concerns, Catherine was strong enough to bear eight children, all of whom lived into adulthood, no small task in the nineteenth century. And as far as we know, Catherine had only one miscarriage.[2] The first child, William Bramwell, named after an English holiness teacher and "a legendary figure in Methodism of all shades,"[3] was born on March 8, 1856.[4]

William Booth's Ministry with New Connexion Methodism

William generally experienced success in his ministry, preferring ministry in the Midlands and the north rather than in London. He did face some opposition, coincidentally enough, in his own home city of Nottingham. There the superintending minister was the Reverend P. J. Wright, who may have been guided both by genuine concerns about revivalistic methods and by personal jealousy, given the success of William's meetings in Nottingham. The first concern had been leveled against both James Caughey and Charles Grandison Finney, but both of these men eventually returned to England in spite of some opposition.

> The emotional religious meetings certainly were disconcerting to those who wished for quieter and more orderly ones. Religious respectability was indeed at risk.... There were serious questions about revival measures used to control people's emotions, which placed doubt on the authenticity of some conversions. There were also reasonable reservations about the lasting results of thousands of conversions both for the local churches and for impact on society.[5]

However, there is no doubt that some of the opposition was motivated by jealousy, as Wesley had experienced in the previous century, and both Caughey and Finney had experienced both in America and England at various junctures of their ministries. Some local ministers, whose ministry was lackluster, could not abide the work of itinerant ministers, who were free from Conference control. What one author has well stated concerning Caughey might also be said of Booth at this time:

> Threat to authority caused "settled ministers" to point with envy at their itinerant brother's freedom. Caughey had come to England without an invitation and had remained for five years without any official connection to a Methodist conference. His popularity had kept him in demand even when circuit superintendents preferred that he stay away. More ominous, he had encouraged "irregular ministers," uneducated men like Booth, who might overrun the denomination.[6]

The Annual Conference in 1857 met in Nottingham, and by a vote of forty-four to forty it determined that William Booth should be relieved of his evangelistic status and placed in a circuit in spite of the fact that

Booth was supported in his desire for evangelistic work by people of the Hull Circuit where he had labored.[7] There is every evidence that P. J. Wright convinced delegates that this was the wisest move. There were petty concerns that Booth's itinerancy was costing the denomination too much money, and that Booth was too young to have the kind of influence on the denomination that was his by virtue of his travels. These were patently absurd reasons for any change. However, the Conference was convinced that William had to be tried in a circuit before ordination was granted, and this was a legitimate concern. Booth resigned himself to the will of the Conference, and at the 1857 Conference he was appointed to the Halifax Circuit, with primary responsibility for Brighouse. Catherine acquiesced only for the sake of her husband and family, but was convinced that the denomination was led by jealous and resentful men, and would like to have seen William leave New Connexion Methodism immediately. She was indignant with this decision by the Conference, and moving to Brighouse did not help her disposition.

William expressed his sentiments in a letter to Catherine's parents:

> You will have been expecting a line from us containing Conference information, and now that our suspense is ended in certainty, or nearly so, I take the first opportunity of sending you a line. For some time I have been aware that a party has been forming against me. Now it has developed itself and its purpose. It has attacked and defeated my friends, and my evangelistic mission is to come to an immediate conclusion. On Saturday, after a debate of five hours, in which I am informed the bitterest spirit was manifested against me, it was decided by 44 to 40 that I be appointed to a circuit. The chief opponents to my continuance in my present course are *ministers*, the opposition being led on by the Rev. P. J. Wright and Dr. Crofts. I care not much for myself. A year's rest will be very acceptable. By that time, God will, I trust, make plain my way before me, either to abide as a circuit preacher, or by opening me a door which no man or number of men shall be able to shut. My concern is for the Connexion—my deep regret is for the spirit this makes manifest, and the base ingratitude it displays.[8]

Going to Brighouse was a move contrary to their every instinct. Booth-Tucker in his biography of Catherine Booth claimed that the superintendent of the Halifax Circuit "was a sombre, funereal kind of being, very well-meaning no doubt, but utterly incapable of co-operating with Mr. Booth in his ardent views and plans for the salvation of the people."[9] Brighouse was known as "one of the most obscure and least successful circuits,"[10] and Catherine was not in good health. She was pregnant with their second child, and soon after arriving in Brighouse, on July 28, 1857, Ballington Booth was born, named after an uncle of Catherine's. In February 1858, their second son was baptized by James Caughey.[11]

Added to that, the accommodations were not to the Booths' liking, and Catherine wrote to her mother soon after their arrival in the early summer of 1857 that "it is a low, smoky town, and we are situated in the worst part of it."[12]

The next Annual Conference, held in Hull in 1858, was important for two reasons. First, it provided yet another opportunity for William to plead his cause and once again be appointed as an evangelist by the denomination. Second, it was the Conference in which William was ordained to the Christian ministry, his four years of probation having been completed. James Caughey had advised William to wait until his ordination before pressing again the issue of an itinerant revivalistic ministry. William was ordained and was now in full connexion with the denomination. However, following his ordination he was reassigned to a circuit rather than to the evangelistic ministry for which he had hoped. William Booth had apparently agreed to this decision.[13] Nevertheless, he was not to go back to Brighouse—good news for the Booths—but to Gateshead, a town of about fifty thousand across the Tyne from Newcastle.

Now that William was ordained, he most likely wanted to stay with the denomination at least until his position became intolerable. Catherine, however, was less sanguine. Writing to her parents regarding the forthcoming appointment of William, she said,

> The resolution of Conference we have not yet seen. I do not feel as anxious about it because I feel confident God will open our way either in, or *out* of the Connexion and I don't care much which. I have no fears about the future if we are only ready to do his will at all risks and I think we have both come to that decision.[14]

She was equally forthcoming in another letter to her parents about her feelings for Brighouse: "I feel just like anyone liberated from prison getting from that hated Brighouse."[15]

If Brighouse was darkness, Gateshead was light. It was a place where Methodism was well established by John Wesley, and Methodist chapels of various denominations, including New Connexion Methodism, were erected. Gateshead provided opportunities for William's evangelistic new measures to be tried at the local level. Catherine had agreed to be a class leader. House-to-house visitation was established, special prayer meetings for revival were inaugurated, and street meetings, which William had already tried both in his early days in Nottingham and in his recent itinerant ministry, were begun. He even followed the lead of the Primitive Methodists and held camp meetings. These measures, many of which were introduced by Whitefield and Wesley in the eighteenth century and reinforced in the ministry of Charles Grandison Finney, helped to reinvigorate the Gateshead church. A report on the history of the Bethesda Chapel on Melbourne Street in Gateshead, which had been built as recently as 1836, recounted the following:

> Probably the heyday of Bethesda Glory was when the Rev. Wm. Booth came as its Minister in 1858. His earnest evangelical work and preaching soon gathered crowds. Young and old to the number of 4/500 met every Friday night at a religious meeting for Prayer, Praise and Testimony, called a Band Meeting. The congregations packed Bethesda every time he preached—and it held 15/1,600 people, being then the biggest building in the town.[16]

William was reappointed to Gateshead at the Annual Conference in 1859 in Manchester. Catherine was especially pleased with the more settled life that the family was experiencing, which was important as the family increased. The eldest Booth daughter and Catherine's namesake was born on September 18, 1858,[17] and a second daughter, Emma Moss, was born on January 8, 1860.[18]

The Booths were pleased to go to Gateshead in spite of the poverty and misery that they encountered there. They both saw opportunities for ministries that they had not seen at Brighouse. The following has been written about Gateshead:

> Providence could not have provided William and Catherine Booth with a more spectacular example of Victorian poverty and the personal degradation which it creates. All over Britain children were growing up in festering slums without the benefit of either education or medical care. One child in three died at, or soon after, birth, and a third of those who survived did not live beyond their tenth birthday. But in Gateshead—which had felt but not absorbed the shock of the Industrial Revolution—men and women lived in continual destitution.

A huge influence of Irish—driven out of their homeland by the potato famine and attracted to England by hope of work in the new factories— had helped to double the population in less than fifty years. More than half of the adult men had no regular work. The twin pressures of population and poverty crowded families together like animals. The mid-century census reported that seventy-one persons (members of sixteen separate families) lived in one small house. The result of the overcrowding was three outbreaks of cholera in five years. The Rawlinson Commission into the causes of the second epidemic described living conditions in the poorer parts of the town.

Houses built back to back, usually in squares, drew drinking water from rusty communal stand-pipes at the centre of the yards or at street corners. A whole row of houses—perhaps eight families in all—shared a single earthly privy. When they were cleared, the ordure was stored in the yards and then sold as manure. A single sewer, which flowed down the main street, had been badly designed and regularly flooded. So the steep roads which sloped down to the river carried away the refuse of daily living and human effluent. Sheep and cows which grazed on nearby wasteland were slaughtered in the yards, and their hides were tanned on the spot—adding another smell to the stench that always hung in the air. Three years before the Booths arrived a fire helped to cleanse the city by destroying some of the more fetid premises. But the destruction added to the desperation of the poor.[19]

The tenure at Gateshead provided two new opportunities for Catherine that would prove to be exceptionally beneficial a couple of years later when the Booths launched out into an independent ministry, both such opportunities being noted in a report on the first hundred years of the church. "His wife, Catherine Booth, ably assisted him, and often preached in various places in the Circuit—in fact Gateshead is the first place in which she did preach."[20] First, she gained some experience in administration. She was forced to take responsibility for much of the business of the circuit when William was ill in the summer of 1860. Booth-Tucker described the illness as "nervous prostration and complete breakdown."[21] Ervine's assessment of William at this time is more pointed. He wrote, "William, so resentful about the refusal of the Manchester Conference to appoint him to evangelistic work that he did not attend the next Conference, had a complete breakdown."[22] This would not be the last time that Catherine would have to substitute for an ailing William. "Whatever the cause of William's incapacity, a period of rest and recuperation away from Gateshead was required as well as hydropathic treatment under the direction of a Mr. John Smedley at his clinic in Matlock. William's absence forced Catherine to assume the many responsibilities for the business of the circuit."[23]

Second, Catherine began preaching at Gateshead. Her mother had instilled in her a commitment to the equality of women and men, and even as early as 1853 she wrote a letter to her pastor at the time, the Reverend David Thomas, defending such equality in the face of remarks by Thomas to the contrary.[24] She did likewise in her correspondence with William after their engagement, the most important letter on this subject being two months before their marriage, when she encouraged William to get "settled views" on this matter.

Catherine's most systematic defense of equality, including the equality of women and men in preaching, came in 1859[25] with her published pamphlet originally entitled *Female Teaching: or the Rev. A. A. Rees versus Mrs. Palmer, Being a Reply to a Pamphlet by the Above Named Gentleman on the Sunderland Revival.*[26] The title of the pamphlet partially explains the reason for its being written. Mrs. Phoebe Palmer, a Methodist layperson, had conducted revivals in Sunderland, near Gateshead, and although she did not formally preach, but considered her ministry one of teaching the biblical doctrine of holiness, a local pastor wrote a pamphlet challenging women in public ministry.[27] Catherine, incensed by what she read and being a supporter of Mrs. Palmer, wrote the pamphlet. She had, however, not yet begun preaching herself. She had taught both a class of girls and Sunday school at Brighouse, lectured on temperance at Brighouse, and was the leader of a class in Gateshead.

Her preaching began on Pentecost Sunday of 1860. She had been struggling internally with whether or not she should preach for some time. Catherine's holiness theology converged with her commitment to revivalism. She was now thoroughly convinced that the ministry of the Holy Spirit in the lives of women and men had liberated them, for the sake of the kingdom, to use all their gifts and abilities to the glory of God. The cause of revivalism was empowered and sustained by a theology of holiness. Also, her personal commitment to female ministry was undoubtedly strengthened at this time because she had accepted some leadership responsibilities at Gateshead. Pamela J. Walker has noted the following in her *Pulling the Devil's Kingdom Down: The Salvation Army in Victorian Britain:*

But in the late 1850s, the reappraisal of the role of women created by holiness theology was critical to Catherine Booth's understanding of female ministry. Revivalists like Finney and Caughey encouraged women to speak at meetings and to pray before mixed audiences. Women in the United States took up these opportunities in a number of ways. Mrs. Palmer's ministry remained within a tradition that the revivalists deemed highly acceptable for a woman. Others, including Amanda Berry Smith and Antoinette Brown, established independent preaching careers and created a new model for female ministry. These innovative women were important to Catherine's growing conviction that the restrictions placed on women were unscriptural and damaged women as well as the church.[28]

At the conclusion of William's sermon on that Sunday morning, Catherine rose from her seat and walked to the front of the chapel. "My dear husband thought something had happened, and so did the people."[29] She then went on to recount the incident:

> He stepped down to ask me, "What is the matter, my dear?" I said, "I want to say a word." He was so taken by surprise, he could only say, "My dear wife wants to say a word," and sat down. He had been trying to persuade me to do it for ten years. I felt as if I were clinging to some human arm—and yet it was a Divine arm—to hold me. I just got up and told the people how it came about. I confessed, as I think everybody should, when they have been in the wrong and misrepresented the religion of Jesus Christ. I said, "I dare say many of you have been looking upon me as a very devoted woman, and one who has been living faithfully to God, but I have come to know that I have been living in disobedience, and to that extent I have brought darkness and leanness into my soul, but I promised the Lord three or four months ago, and I dare not disobey. I have come to tell you this, and to promise the Lord that I will be obedient to the heavenly vision.[30]

Catherine returned to Bethesda Chapel that evening and preached her first sermon, "Be Filled With the Spirit."

And so when William was absent from the Gateshead Circuit because of his illness, Catherine was pressed into the preaching ministry in the circuit, something that she could not have imagined even a few months before. When William returned at Christmas, he and Catherine shared the preaching on Christmas Day, and Catherine continued to preach on Sunday evenings at the request of the lay leaders of the chapel. Her preaching ministry was well established by the time it was necessary for William to leave the denomination, and from that time on she shared the preaching ministry with her husband.

William's ministry was a disappointment at Brighouse, but successful at Gateshead, and he was certainly theologically grounded in New Connexion Methodism. However, all was not well. William's proclivities for evangelism beyond the borders of the local church were still strong. He felt stifled by the local pastorate, and wanted an appointment that would allow him to be an itinerant evangelist for the denomination. Indeed, his son, Bramwell, claimed that "when he joined the Methodist New Connexion there was a distinct understanding with the authorities of that time that he became one of their ministers for *evangelistic* work, in which he had already gained a great measure of success in various parts of the country. It was their subsequent refusal of that work which brought about the rupture."[31] Some of the denominational authorities, whom even the most objective observer would have to admit were narrow-minded bureaucrats, thought otherwise, and William, with the full support of Catherine, left the denomination in 1861. His resignation officially took effect the following year.

Leaving New Connexion Methodism

The Gordian knot in this controversy was over the issue of whether or not William Booth should be set free for an itinerant evangelistic ministry supported by the denomination, or confined to a circuit with perhaps the promise of some time off during the year for evangelistic work as allowed by his superiors. William Booth felt called by God for evangelism, and the urgency of winning souls was the driving force of his ministry. His gifts and abilities for evangelistic preaching had already been used and improved, and it is beyond doubt that local churches benefited from William's efforts by adding converts who thereby strengthened the life of local churches.

However, certain methods used by William still caused concern for the more decorous pastors, as had been the case with the Wesleys and Whitefield in the previous century. Also, jealousies arose over the young evangelist's popularity among the people (although the Booths often attributed opposition to jealousy). One biographer has summed up these two concerns well by stating:

We do not wish to imply that this opposition to William Booth was entirely without reason. His methods were ardent and unusual; he must have shocked or offended a great many pious people; his appearance in a town did, no doubt, lead to certain manifestations of violent emotion. But he was opposed on other grounds as well as these. Certain ministers in the New Connexion were his enemies; many felt that he was too young for such perpetual prominence; others were unquestionably jealous of his powers.[32]

When this issue had first arisen, there is no question that some thought that because William had not yet been ordained by the denomination, he should demonstrate his abilities in the local pastorate; not an unreasonable request from denominational leaders whose primary responsibility was for the work of the local church. And now that he had been ordained only for three years, some in the denomination thought that his administrative and pastoral abilities had not yet been tried sufficiently. More time was needed.

However, William Booth was not willing at this time to attribute any pure motives to fellow ministers who might have been genuinely offended by his methods. He was not willing to consider even well-intended criticisms. "Nothing could have been more offensive to other New Connexion ministers than a constant demonstration by one of their number that he regarded himself as their moral superior."[33] Nor did Booth sympathize with the argument that more time was needed to enhance and direct other skills wanted in a New Connexion Methodist minister. "Booth, for the greater part of his life, believed himself to be divinely inspired, and his belief caused him to regard all who tried to thwart him as the enemies of God."[34] Booth viewed the opposition as motivated solely by petty jealousies. As one biographer noted, both William and Catherine were "incapable of considering the possibility that they were wrong."[35] Both sides became more resolute in their convictions.

Even after the move from Brighouse to Gatheshead, both William and Catherine still held out hope that provision would be made by the Conference for William's talents as an evangelist. Before going to the 1861 Conference, William wrote a letter to the Reverend James Stacey, the retiring president, outlining his reasons for wanting evangelistic work.[36] At the beginning of the letter Booth stressed that

> for the last seven years I have felt that God has specially called me to this work. The impression has been clear and decided. I am as satisfied of it as I am of my call to the ministry. It is now four years since I was put down

from it, and the impression, instead of dying away, is as strong and vivid as ever.[37]

While Stacey was unable to meet personally with William, it was agreed at the Annual Committee that William's request would be brought to the attention of the Conference when it met in Liverpool in May.[38]

William sought counsel on this matter, especially from his spiritual mentor, James Caughey. However, in a letter to her parents, Catherine

> shows some disappointment with James Caughey, the man whom she so admired. "William has written to Mr. Caughey and another friend, and neither of them seems disposed to risk any advice. Mr. C. is evidently afraid but our trust is not in man and if we take the step it will be solely trusting in the Lord" [Booth Papers, Mss. 64805, The British Library]. . . . There is no indication as to why Caughey acted as he did.[39]

Very successful evangelistic campaigns at both Gateshead and Hartlepool preceded the Conference. Booth was supported in his desire for evangelistic work by his circuit as well as the annual district meeting, and Mr. Joseph Love, "a wealthy lay member of the Conference and Treasurer of the Chapel Fund, allowed it to be known that if the cost of making an evangelist of Booth were a consideration, he would bear the whole of the expense in excess of the ordinary allowances and salary of a minister."[40]

Catherine accompanied William to the Conference of 1861, which commenced on Monday, May 20th. Even with the financial support of Mr. Love, as well as William's long-suffering friend, Mr. Rabbits, the matter of being allowed to pursue his evangelistic work did not appear hopeful. Dr. Crofts, generally supportive of William, was the president of the Conference. The Booths hoped that he would see things their way. This was not to be the case, and Crofts, as well as several other influential ministers such as the Reverend Philip James Wright, believed that it was in the best interests of the denomination, the circuit, and Booth himself to remain confined to a local church.

There were some attempts at compromise at the Conference, Mr. Crofts being evidently unfit to thoroughly defend his colleague. This was the question: Would William be willing to continue in a circuit for one more year while also accepting some invitations to conduct revival campaigns, with the permission of the leadership of the circuit? The denomination might appoint William as the superintendent of the Newcastle Circuit.[41] A resolution was put before the Annual Conference by William's former teacher, Dr. Cooke, who himself received a setback from Conference, being asked to resign as the editor of the *New Connexion Magazine*. Nevertheless, Ervine's evaluation of this resolution follows:

> The appointment, combined with Dr. Cooke's Resolution, was tanta- mount to a reversal of the ban on Booth's evangelical activities, for it allowed him to engage in a considerable amount of revival work and really left the decision as to the extent of that work to his judgment; for he was the Superintendent Minister whose opinion was to be consulted! His withdrawal from the Methodists was, indeed, due to a disagreement between him and the Annual Committee on the proper interpretation of that Resolution. It is possible that had he been permitted to act on his understanding of its terms, he might never have left the Connexion, and The Salvation Army might never have been founded. That is vain specu- lation, vainer, perhaps, than speculations usually are, for if Booth had not withdrawn from the Connexion after that Conference in 1861, he proba- bly would have withdrawn a little later.[42]

William may have been still hopeful for some kind of settlement. Catherine was perhaps more convinced at this time that William should leave the denomination and launch out on his own, and, as Hattersley rather wryly remarked, "She often discovered that God supported her judgment."[43] She saw Crofts's indecision on this matter as weakness of leadership and a failure on Crofts's part to govern by principle rather than by compromise. There was a dramatic account, begun by Booth-Tucker in his biography of Catherine Booth and often repeated in Salvation Army literature, that Catherine was in the balcony when the compromise was being discussed, but was unable to remain silent. The Coates biography, embellishing even what is recorded in Booth-Tucker's account, rehearses the incident, stating,

> Rising from her seat and bending over the gallery, Mrs. Booth's clear voice rang through the Conference as she said to her husband, "Never!" . . . There was a pause of bewilderment and dismay. Every eye was turned towards the speaker in the gallery. The idea of a woman daring to utter her protest, or to make her voice heard in the Conference, produced little short of consternation.[44]

The operative word here is *never*. Crofts cleared the balcony before a vote was taken on the resolution, and Catherine left the balcony with the other guests. Eyewitnesses to this event evidently challenged Booth-Tucker's dramatic revision of the events at this Conference, and Booth-Tucker did not repeat the story in a later abridged version of Catherine Booth's life. The final decision to leave New Connexion Methodism is more finely nuanced than this story allows.[45]

Following the Conference, Catherine Booth wrote to her parents, and revealed in that correspondence the personal struggles that the inevitable decision of the denomination would force upon the Booths. In June 1861 Catherine wrote:

> Our position altogether is about as trying as well it could be. We have reason to fear that the Annual Committee will not allow even this arrangement with the circuit to be carried out, and if not, I don't see any honourable course open but to resign at once and risk all; if trusting in the Lord for our bread, in order to do what we believe to be His will, ought to be called a risk. . . . I am sick of the New Connexion from top to bottom. I have lost all faith in its ministry and I see nothing for it but a slow consumption. . . .
>
> The President has written to know the nature of the arrangements . . . with the Newcastle circuit. William will send them, and if they object I shall urge him with all my might to resign.[46]

She also wrote, "If my dear husband can find a *sphere* where he can preach the Gospel to the masses, I shall want no further evidence of the will of God concerning him."[47]

Dr. Crofts visited with the Booths, explaining the compromise to them. While one biographer described the Newcastle Circuit as "one of the most important in the Connexion,"[48] and another writer referred to "the prestigious Newcastle-upon-Tyne circuit,"[49] it is entirely possible that the opposite was the case, and that the circuit was in near ruin and would require all the attention Booth could give to it. There would not be time for evangelistic work.

The home of the circuit superintendent at Newcastle was made available to the Booths, and the experiment initiated at the Annual Conference had begun. Regardless of the state of the Newcastle Circuit, the question needs to be raised as to whether or not William himself was faithful to the compromise put forth by the Conference. The fact of the matter is that William continued to pursue his evangelistic interests even outside of New Connexion Methodism. He first preached outside the circuit at Alnwick, but many New Connexion Methodist preachers were reluctant to invite him to their churches because they did not want to get involved in the controversy between Booth and the denomination.

> William also made a trip to London to speak with some gentlemen about various independent ministries of revivalism in Britain, and with one independent group he preached in the open air twice near the Garrick Theatre. He was testing the possibilities of an independent revivalism apart from his denomination, but none of the ministries about which he inquired appealed to him.[50]

While in London he met on separate occasions with evangelists Reginald Radcliffe, Edward Hammond, and William Carter, and was often given the advice to leave any denominational moorings and launch out in an independent ministry, as they had done. And his preaching in the Garrick Theatre was under the auspices of the East London Special Services Committee, recently established by George Pearse. In any case, the trip to London "had been profitable. He said at the end of it, 'I am very much easier in my mind. In fact, I have a measure of trust and confidence that all things are working for the desired end, to a degree that I have never had before.' It had also been very helpful with regard to laying foundations for his later work."[51]

The denomination, understandably, interpreted William's searching as a neglect of his duties as superintendent in Newcastle and therefore as a deliberate ignoring of the compromise hammered out in Liverpool. William was culpable. All attempts to exonerate him cannot escape the fact that he was knowingly disobedient to the denomination to which he had sworn allegiance. So sure was William of his high calling that he could not see God's will working through the denomination or its leadership.

It was impossible for either William or Catherine at this time to see God's will as anything other than a private calling to an individual. The will of God was measured solely by their own experiences and they did not seek the confirmation of their calling from the broader Christian community outside of that experience, except occasionally from someone like James Caughey. They were unable to perceive the call and will of God in a corporate sense in the context of the broader body of Christ—in this case, New Connexion Methodism. That denominational structure required autocratic control over the ministers as well as lay input into evaluation of its ministers. When all is said and done, William Booth disdained both, and saw these matters of church polity as a hindrance to his evangelistic gifts and abilities and to the wider evangelistic mission of the denomination, and thereby the Church universal.

> Booth's resignation came two months later, after he had tested the waters to see if he could succeed as an itinerant. Only then did he reject appointment to the prestigious Newcastle-upon-Tyne circuit. His departure was due less to the conference's push than to the pull of the Booths' desire for independent evangelism. It was not an impulsive act, but a calculated decision. Anti-revivalist Methodists did not reject him as much as he later wanted to believe. He was no martyr to the cause of revivalism among the poor.[52]

Any discussion of the complicated motives for the Booths leaving New Connexion Methodism must also include the fact that William's own autocratic personality was beginning to show through, and he was not going to submit to either ministerial control or lay evaluation. This autocratic penchant is true notwithstanding Bramwell Booth's disclaimer when speaking about the founding of the Army that "it was not that he wanted to be an autocrat. All his predispositions were the other way."[53]

Truth to tell, both the Booths were rather high-handed in their dealing with the denomination, and certainly in later years as the heads of The Christian Mission and The Salvation Army, they tended to see those ministers who appealed to the same personal calling by God, and thereby left the Army, as nothing less than traitors to the cause. The privilege of a personal calling that they allowed for themselves, and that thereby superseded denominational requirements, would not be tolerated in others who came under their command in later years.

However, there was certainly also blame on the denominational side. The fault for their departure from New Connexion Methodism was not all on the side of the Booths. In July, after William had been in Newcastle only about a month, Dr. Crofts wrote to him, and reprimanded William for not giving enough attention to the circuit, a charge that was inexplicable given William's brief tenure in Newcastle. There was a bureaucratic mind-set among the leaders of the denomination that prevented them from seeing that William Booth did indeed have gifts that ultimately would prove beneficial to the denomination, and thereby to the kingdom of God. "Denominational authorities were glad to see him go. The ferment his ministry fostered inconvenienced bureaucrats."[54] However, as has been noted elsewhere,

Even the most impartial observer of the unfolding events and the struggles between the Booths and the denomination would have to conclude that the denomination was being controlled by small-minded bureaucrats, unable, even for the sake of the gospel and the Kingdom, to rise to the occasion of supporting one of their own during a time of personal introspection and obvious good will. The July 16 letter from Crofts displays a deplorable lack of leadership resulting in his inability to guide the deliberations of the denomination toward a solution beneficial for all concerned.[55]

The two sides were intractable, and there was enough blame to go around. However, William now felt that he had no recourse but to resign from New Connexion Methodism. He wrote his official letter of resignation on July 18, 1861, in which he stated his understanding that the arrangements made for his appointment to Newcastle were to be observed for the year. Booth wrote the following at the beginning of the letter:

> My Dear Sir:—Yours of the 16th is to hand. Its contents certainly much surprised me. You say, "I am sorry to learn that you are not taking your circuit according to the rules and usages of the body, nor according to the resolution of Mr. Cooke." But, sir, I informed you of every particular respecting the arrangement, immediately after it was made; since then I have received two letters from you on circuit business, in which you do not refer to it; if, then, as you say, this arrangement was calculated to grieve my best friends of the Connexion, and of sufficient importance to bring before the Annual Committee, how is it that you have waited five weeks before writing me on the subject?[56]

William's resignation was formally accepted at the Annual Conference the following year at Dudley, and after the letter of resignation was sent to Crofts, Catherine wrote to her parents that "we both intend to brace ourselves for all its consequences and manfully face all difficulties. The Lord help us and show us His salvation! Continue to pray for us."[57] Carolyn Ocheltree has observed that

> two factors characterize Booth's development from a Wesleyan preacher to free-lance evangelistic preacher. First, the influence of James Caughey's and David Greenbury's modelling as *irregular* evangelists; secondly, the inability of the Methodist Churches (Wesleyan, Reformed and New Connexion) to conceive of Booth's work outside the traditional definitions of circuit ministry.[58]

The Booths were able to stay in Newcastle for a few weeks, and then for a brief time the Booths moved to London and lived with Catherine's parents in Brixton. This was to be their base of operations as they moved into an independent revivalistic ministry.

In his biography, Begbie reported that "after seven years of devoted service, he was penniless; and this time he had a wife and children whose care he and no other could provide."[59] Ervine corrects this mistaken notion of the state of affairs in the Booth family at this time.

> It is important here to correct a misbelief, unfortunately given currency in the official Life by Begbie, that the Methodist New Connexion allowed Booth to leave Newcastle in a penniless condition. "After seven years of devoted service, he was penniless," Begbie asserts . . . and on the next page refers to "the stranded and penniless family." The Booths undoubtedly were poor, as were all the ministers of the Methodist New Connexion, but to be poor is one thing and to be penniless and stranded is another. Booth was actually better paid than the majority of his brethren in the Methodist ministry. In the second year of his probation, his salary was £100 per annum, which was more, by £30 or £40, than was paid to his fellow-probationers, and in addition to this salary, he received a quarter's salary and allowances and was repaid all the contributions he had made to the Superannuation Fund during his seven years' service. He was also allowed the free use of the minister's house for several weeks after his resignation was accepted. He did not leave the Methodists in affluence, but neither did he leave them in penury. They rewarded him as well as they could.[60]

And so the Booths moved out into somewhat of a wilderness experience. It is beyond doubt that William especially felt called to evangelism, and this step of faith would provide him with opportunities of fulfilling that calling. However, he was not alone either in the decision or in the ministry of preaching. William would have left New Connexion Methodism earlier if Catherine had had her way. In any case, as has been mentioned, Catherine also had begun preaching, and so the ministry from now on would be a shared ministry. Catherine wrote to her parents in July 1861 that "I have no fear of being able to speak in public for some months to come, and we must make the most of our opportunities at first."[61] Together the Booths were facing the future.

CHAPTER SIX

THE ROAD TO FREEDOM

Introduction

Andso the Booths began their new life living with their four children at the home of Catherine's parents, waiting for some sign from the Lord about their future. Two of the Methodist denominations had forbidden their churches from inviting the Booths into their pulpits. William was too evangelistic, and Catherine was a woman, thereby challenging their understanding of a New Testament prohibition against women preaching. However, friends within these denominations, as well as others, invited the Booths to conduct evangelistic meetings in various places in England.

The Booths felt that they were in good company. They took special notice of the fact that the Conference had also closed its church doors to James Caughey and the Palmers, whom the British considered as outsiders.

> The same resolution which closed their doors against William Booth closed them also to James Caughey, and to Dr. and Mrs. Palmer, who had been instrumental at that time in strengthening many of the Non-Conformist Churches in the United Kingdom. No doubt, some of the

opposition that developed in the long run against the Booths was originally due to a prejudice against "foreigners,"—the evangelists just mentioned having come from the United States. The very strong, not to say bitter, feeling then prevailing against the ministry of women, had also to be reckoned with, for Catherine Booth had shared in the Founder's work.[1]

The Beginning of a Ministry of Revivalism

The first invitation to the Booths came from Hayle in Cornwall, issued by a New Connexion preacher by the name of Mr. Shone, who had been a convert of William's. Although there was no promise of remuneration for their efforts, both William and Catherine viewed this as a vindication of their decision to leave New Connexion Methodism, and paid their own expenses to go to Cornwall. William found Cornish revivalism to be rather emotional, especially as people knelt at the penitent-form or mercy seat, in response to William's preaching. The Wesleys had experienced great revivals in Cornwall, often marked by crying and fainting and people in emotional and spiritual distress. As well, the Wesleys witnessed great numbers of conversions, as the Booths would in this first campaign. Henry Rack has noted that:

> Cornwall . . . was to become remarkable for cycles of revival of this kind, which gathered in fringe and loosely attached adherents.
>
> The characteristic features of these revivals seem to be the prominence of children, the role of house and prayer meetings, and the fact that the work seemed to come mainly from local lay people and not the itinerants who, if anything, failed to consolidate it. There are also strong indications that a good many of those influenced were already well in touch with Methodism, if not actually members: there were evidently good crops of perfection experiences as well as recoveries of "backsliders."[2]

The work of the Booths did not end at Hayle. It continued as the Booths moved from Hayle to St. Ives and St. Just, where conversions were registered in the hundreds and several people signed the pledge not to drink alcohol.[3] In a letter William wrote during this time, he is positively jubilant about the ministry in Cornwall, and also makes reference to a request from the Palmers that the Booths take their place in Liverpool because they had to return home rather hastily due to Dr. Palmer's failing health. It was Mrs. Palmer's ministry, as well as the broader issue of the ministry of women, that Catherine had defended two years previous in her pamphlet. William wrote the following to his friend, Mr. John Atkinson, on November 18, 1861, from St. Ives:

> I know you will be glad to hear a few particulars respecting the Lord's deal-ing with me and with His church in this part of the vineyard, in addition to those you may already be possessed of. The good work is still sweeping gloriously along. Yesterday was my eighth Sabbath in this town and a high day it was. Chapel crowded morning, afternoon and night, and in the prayer meeting very many were saved....We have had a very pressing invi-tation to take the place of Dr. and Mrs. Palmer at Liverpool. Mrs. Palmer wrote herself but we have not decided. I feel much impressed with the importance of the work in this county. About 700 have professed to obtain mercy. I have laboured in New Connexion, Wesleyan and Primitive chapels, chiefly the former. We have a most blessed union of all denomi-nations. Will you unite in prayer that the good work may spread on every hand? I expect to be here three weeks longer and supposing that we do not go to Liverpool I expect to go either to St. Just or Camborne. Yours affec-tionately, William Booth.[4]

An eyewitness to Booth's revival in St. Ives wrote that "I have heard Mr. Booth preach a great many times, and can therefore say something about him. He is the best I ever met with for rivetting the attention of the ungodly part of the people. There has not been a minister in St. Ives for the last thirty years who could attract such congregations night after night for such a length of time."[5] There is also some indication of the preaching style of the Booths at this time. Of William it was written that "the preacher's loving earnestness—not his logic—conquered us and we felt in very deed that it was good to be there."[6] Of Catherine it was said that "the sermon was one of the most closely reasoned and logical dis-courses we have heard for a long time, and accustomed as we have been for many years to hard and close thinking, it was to us a refreshing and sanctifying discourse."[7]

The four Booth children, who had stayed with Catherine's parents dur-ing the first eight months of the Cornish campaign, joined their parents. And it was during this time that Catherine learned that she was pregnant again. Such good news was counterbalanced by personally disappointing news, at least to William, that in its 1862 Annual Conference, New Connexion Methodism had formally accepted William's resignation.[8] This marked a finality that was inevitable. But William nevertheless felt it as a personal defeat and a source of frustration.

It was during this time in Cornwall, while the Booths were ministering in Penzance, that Herbert Henry (whose name was altered to Herbert Howard six months later),[9] their third son and fifth child, was born on August 26, 1862.[10] Other revivals followed, and the Booths completed their ministry of eighteen months in Cornwall with a revival in the Free Methodist Chapel in Redruth and then in Camborne.

They then moved from Cornwall to Cardiff, Wales. In Cardiff there were two events that proved to be providential for the Booths. First, although some churches had opened their doors to the Booths, the revivalistic impulse in William prompted him to use other venues for his meetings. William had long ago found preaching in the open air to be quite effective, as did Whitefield and the Wesleys in the previous century. William had preached in the open air in both Nottingham and Gateshead, and so this ministry was not new to him. At Cardiff, the meetings were held in the local circus. In a letter to a friend in February 1863, William wrote, "On Sunday we commenced in the *circus*, a large building capable of holding a great number of people. The services were much blessed. In the afternoon and evening it was very full."[11] Such use of secular buildings, the Booths discovered, sometimes attracted larger crowds and thereby provided more opportunities for evangelism. People who had no interest in entering a church were quite willing to go to a local circus or theater to hear speakers, especially those who were evidently as engaging as the Booth duo.

Second, the Booths established friendships in Cardiff that would prove to be beneficial both emotionally and financially for years to come. Two brothers, John and Richard Cory, began to lighten the Booths' financial lot during their time in Cardiff, and continued to do so in the future. The Cory family had earned their wealth as ship owners and coal merchants, even naming one of their ships after William Booth and "announced their intention of devoting part of its profits to any evangelistic cause in which he might be engaged."[12] Also, a generous couple, Mr. and Mrs. J. E. Billups, supported the Booths at this time, and their support would likewise continue in the future. Mr. Billups had made his money as a contractor. Mrs. Billups became a friend to whom Catherine often corresponded.

However, in spite of successes in places like Cornwall and Cardiff—the Booths had registered seven thousand converts in their Cornwall campaign—there were also some disappointing failures. The ever-anxious William was often dejected because of the burden of trying to support a growing family and the weariness of an itinerant life where the billets were often less than one would wish. After all, William had "a tendency to develop sudden and mysterious illnesses at moments of great pressure."[13] Through the support of his friends, William was off again to Matlock for hydropathic treatment while Catherine was left tending the family. One of the Booths' daughters rather humorously remembers the confidence placed in hydropathy in the Booth family in this way: "My mother was a great believer in hydropathy. At the first unfavourable symptom we were either stewed in soap-baths or sweated in tepid damp sheets, or roasted in tropical Turkish heated rooms or gargled with liquids that would do to choke on or fed with benefits derived from plain water in gruel and meal."[14] As helpful as these treatments were for William, he was still despondent over financial anxieties and remained worried desperately about the future.

At times, the ministry could not support both William and Catherine, and that often meant weeks of separation, which furthered William's despondency. Catherine would stay with the children either in a home in one of the cities nearby William or take the children to her parents' home in Brixton. After Matlock, William continued conducting revival meetings without Catherine, but he seemed unable to shake his depression. In one letter to Catherine during this time he wrote that "I don't feel disposed to persevere much longer in a life the results of which are really so trifling."[15] Imagine Catherine with her growing family of five receiving this kind of news! Should she prepare for William's leaving the ministry and perhaps entering into some kind of business venture? And if that were to happen where would the family settle?

But Catherine was stronger than she knew. The responsibility for rearing the children during this time fell on Catherine, and she did so in the strictest Victorian way. Her primary goal was to bend the will of the child to the will of the parents. However, this was done not only for the sake of rearing obedient children but also for an ultimate religious reason. This conforming of the will in human relationships would prepare the children to bend their will to the will of God when they reached an age of religious accountability. Catherine followed the pattern of Susanna Wesley before her, and so she was strict with the children, but not unreasonably so.

While both William and Catherine appeared at times to be rather distant from their children, and relied on servants and governesses to assist in the rearing of the children, there is no indication that they did not love their children or treat them in ways different from the Victorian world in which they lived. Certainly the reflections of the children in later life upon their home life and upbringing were very positive in spite of both the discipline exercised upon them and the expectations placed on them. It would be difficult indeed to substantiate Hattersley's assessment that "even judged against the behaviour of the most pious Victorian Nonconformists, the Booths' treatment of their children was bizarre."[16] As Bennett has pointed out, "Roy Hattersley paints an unfairly negative picture of the Booth household. To him the intensely religious atmosphere caused as many problems with the children as it solved, and while it is true that too much was often expected of them, they none-the-less, for the most part, seemed to revel in it."[17]

As had been their custom during their engagement, William and Catherine carried out a long correspondence during their frequent absences from each other, and that correspondence reflects matters both great and trivial at this time in their lives. They wrote about the Lord's work, but also about the need to fire the governess and hire a new one. They reflected on what their future might be like, but also commiserated when one of them had a toothache. This correspondence reflected nearly daily communion with each other, and in spite of William's depression, the love between this husband and wife was evident in the correspondence.

Evidently, by the middle of 1864 the financial support that the Booths needed during this time of independent ministry was finally coming in at more regular intervals. William's anxieties over financial matters were temporarily lifted, as were also his bouts with depression. Optimism filled their letters to each other because of the favor that they had received, and William constantly expressed his genuine gratitude for a loving wife and healthy children. Healthy, that is, but for one. It was during this time that Marian Billups Booth was born on May 4, 1864, while the Booths were at Leeds.[18] Marian, or Marie as she was known to the family, was not a well child, but the nature of her illness is shrouded in mystery. One biographer noted that she, "following an accident, developed serious physical weakness, and was only reared to an invalid life with considerable difficulty."[19] Ervine, on the other hand, wrote that "this child, soon after her birth, became subject to convulsive fits and is still delicate."[20] Evangeline Booth, Marian's younger sister, recorded, "At a very early age smallpox weakened her health and she could not profit by study as did the rest of us, nor in later years take part in public life. Being nearest to her age, my mother asked me to make it my duty to help her with her lessons and see that she had a place in the games."[21] In any case, suffice it to say that Marian was incapacitated all of her life, and her care was shared by members of the family.[22]

After only five weeks after delivering Marian, Catherine commenced preaching again. This time she conducted a revival campaign apart from her husband, the first time she would do so. However, the toil of caring for the children, preaching, being separated from her husband, ill health, and constant worry about personal debt was beginning to break Catherine. And William's advice to take some time for reading (it was usually Catherine who had to encourage William to study more!) did not work. St. John Ervine is rather hard on William at this juncture. He wrote:

> It seems not to have occurred to him that a delicate woman, delivered of six children in nine years; constantly embarrassed by insufficiency of money; left for long spells to manage her difficult brood, one of which, a baby, suffered from convulsions; and continually agitated by his health and the emotional excitements of revival meetings, had little time in which to divert her mind with reading, that her mind, indeed, was already over-diverted, and that what she needed was rest, some security of means, and a settled life.[23]

William himself was also again feeling the strain, and he briefly considered joining the Independents in Nottingham, "demonstrating that he realistically did not see a future in a ministry apart from denominational support."[24] Depression came and went for William. Catherine was working as hard as William, but also suffered times of despondency. However, as difficult as this period was for the Booths, in the final analysis they found the ability to rise above their circumstances and see their lives as being directed, sometimes mysteriously, by the providence of God. In spite of their extreme anxiety about the future, they were able to place themselves in the hand of God and follow wherever he chose to lead them—even to London.

The Move to London

The Booths' move to London in 1865 had nothing to do with William. In fact, he would have preferred staying away from London. That move—which was to prove to be so providential—had everything to do with Catherine, and that for three reasons. First, Catherine was tired of an itinerant life. She wrote to her mother, "I should like to live in London, better than any place I was ever in."[25] In the words of one biographer, "She had had enough of being God's gypsy."[26] Second, ever the faithful daughter, she was concerned about her aging parents, and she wanted to be nearer to them permanently. However, the third reason was the most important one. Catherine had been invited by the Southwark Circuit Free Church Methodists to conduct an evangelistic campaign at Rotherhithe, in southeast London, "very much an isolated community, separated from the rest of London."[27] The advertisement bills, capitalizing on the novelty of Catherine preaching, read, "Come and Hear a Woman Preach." Those meetings commenced on February 26, 1865, and concluded on March 19, 1865. Catherine was well received, her meetings were successful, and she was also introduced to the Midnight Movement for Fallen Women, a ministry among the prostitutes of London.

It was at this time that Catherine began to gain prominence as a preacher and orator. Many people who heard her testified to the power of her spoken word. Also, "what she saw in London greatly influenced Mrs. Booth to make the metropolis her centre, although her idea was still to work through existing religious agencies."[28] After Rotherhithe, she was invited to preach at the Free Methodist Chapel in Grange Road, Bermondsey, "a squalid part of South London, densely inhabited by very poor people, many of whom lived on casual labour at the docks."[29]

To accommodate Catherine's ministry, the family moved to a home in Hammersmith, 31 Shaftesbury Road. Soon after settling in London, William left to continue his ministry in the provinces, his first engagement being in Louth, Lincolnshire. Their income at this time was supplemented by sales of a songbook that William had compiled and by Catherine's *Female Teaching* pamphlet that she wrote in 1859, which was renamed *Female Ministry; or Women's Right to Preach the Gospel* in 1870. In good times the family income exceeded the income of most ministers of the day, but the income was not steady, and there were some lean times. "It was the uncertainty of their income and not necessarily the amount, that kept them in turmoil."[30]

Frugality of lifestyle, which the Booths had learned in their Methodist rearing, now helped them get through difficult times, and Mrs. Booth often took in up to two lodgers to make ends meet. The best known of the lodgers were Jane Short, who first met Catherine Booth while Catherine was preaching in Margate, and Miss Billups, the daughter of the Booths' friends in Cardiff. The itinerant life now over for Catherine, she could well supervise the home during this time.

The two conditions that always seemed to be present in the Booth home were orderliness and tidiness. Life was lived in that household according to a strict schedule, and the home was always neat and clean. All of the children's pets—and there were many of them—were kept in the backyard. Catherine loved animals and nothing disturbed her more than seeing an animal mistreated.

> To her children Catherine handed on that love of animals, which had been second nature to her when a girl. Keeping of pets was encouraged, for were they not to be accepted as a part of the divine and wondrous universe that included flowers and trees and mountains? Caring for animals, moreover, was training in that thoughtfulness for others which is the very essence of Salvationist principles.[31]

It must have indeed been difficult for the Booths to live by such strict standards given the size of the family, enlarged by lodgers and servants, and also given the hectic pace of life, especially after the founding of The Christian Mission. However, both William and Catherine were involved in home life and their sitting side by side at meals rather than William sitting at the head of the table signaled to all in the home a partnership in marriage that complemented the Booths' partnership in mission.

The children undoubtedly felt the strictness of their parents' authority, but also knew that they were loved. All appearances to the contrary, William often played with his children at home and on family outings. However, one biographer notes rather tragically that while Catherine was very attentive to the children's physical and spiritual needs, "neither her health nor her engagements, nor perhaps her disposition, allowed her to play with them."[32]

In November 1865, the family moved from Hammersmith to Hackney to be nearer the work that William had commenced in the East End of London. Their home in 1 Cambridge Lodge Villas, Mare Street, Hackney, was not the best location because a church was being built next door to the home. However, it did accommodate a growing family, and soon after the family moved into this residence, the seventh Booth child, Evelyne Cory Booth, was born on Christmas Day, 1865, the middle name—Cory—signifying the namesake of the Booths' Welsh supporters.[33] Interestingly, she later changed her name to Evangeline.[34] And while the family was still living in that residence, the last Booth child, Lucy Milward Booth, was born on April 28, 1868, her middle name signifying that she was named after her maternal grandmother.[35]

The joy of bringing children into the world was counterbalanced by the sadness of the death of a loved one. Catherine Booth's mother died of cancer on December 16, 1869, while staying with William and Catherine. This loss was difficult for everyone in the family, but especially for Catherine because there had been a close bond between mother and daughter.

The Booth home was a sanctuary from the cares of the world, much as the Mumford home had been for Catherine as she grew up under the watchful eye of her mother. Catherine determined that her home would be the same for her children. And so their basic education was given in the home, under Catherine's supervision. She was constantly suspicious about the influence of other children or teachers outside of the home. Evangeline Booth's principal biographer records that

> over the five-foot bookcase in this home . . . was exercized a vigilant—it should be added a broad-minded—maternal censorship, calculated to reserve the children's attention for what in literature was really worth their time. Nor did they worry very much over what in the second-best they were missing. For they had quite enough to satisfy their absorbent minds, and to neo-pagans it will be a surprise to learn that their bill of fare consisted mainly of the Bible.[36]

The education of the children was guarded, but Catherine also loved taking the children outdoors and thought that many useful lessons could be learned by playing sports, and so tennis, football, and cricket were common outdoor activities for the children. Such activities had been denied Catherine in her rearing because of constant sickness, and so she was especially diligent in seeing that her own children enjoyed playing games.

But life in the home was also preparation for mission. Evangelical religion was the religion of the household, and the urge to reach beyond the home in ministry and mission was strong in both William and Catherine. A passion for mission was shared by the children, all eight of them eventually becoming Salvation Army officers, with only Marian, because of her limitations, unable to participate in Christian Mission and Salvation Army leadership.

William Booth can be understood only by seeing him as someone driven by a religious impulse to save the world from itself—from its own sin and well-deserved misery. That religious drive was evident both within the home and outside of the home, and all who came in contact with William Booth immediately recognized that drive in him. His compulsion to save eventually found institutional expression in the founding of a mission in the East End of London.

THE BEGINNING OF A MISSION

Introduction

Upon William Booth's return to London from the north, two gentlemen were waiting to speak with him. One, R. C. Morgan, was a member of the Plymouth Brethren. Truth to tell, he was rather scandalized to hear a woman preach—Catherine Booth by name. He was further upset with her occasional remarks against what she perceived to be the entrenched Calvinism of the Plymouth Brethren. He also found it difficult to accept her defense of certain doctrines that she claimed were biblical, such as holiness of heart and life. He and Samuel Chase, his partner in the publication of a weekly paper entitled *The Revival*, the name of which was changed to *The Christian* in 1870, tried to convince both William and Catherine that Catherine should stop preaching and pay more attention to domestic matters. Based upon their reading of certain Pauline texts, they were convinced that their argument would win the day. They were, to say the least, naive in their evaluation of the Booths, especially Catherine, on the matter of women in ministry.

William Booth Finds His Destiny in London's East End

It is surprising, therefore, that these two gentlemen, as well as John Stabb, who, along with Morgan and Chase, was a member of the East London Special Services Committee, nevertheless wanted William to lead a mission in the East End of London, the name for that part of London that became popular in the 1880s. Many descriptions of this area of London give the impression of it as a place of horror, a community of poverty, disease, and crime unmatched in the nineteenth century. Anyone walking through the East End at that time would witness the bleakest of living conditions and the utter disregard for human life and human values. Here is one description of conditions with which the Booths would eventually become very familiar:

> Trade disruption during America's Civil War increased East End unemployment. Famine stalked back streets. While twenty-five thousand obtained handouts, the unemployed lived in East End warehouses. In 1867, as shipyards closed, unemployment in Poplar and Bromley was up nine thousand over the previous year.... As many as one hundred thousand unemployed, uneducated children became petty thieves. Girls and some boys became prostitutes. Lack of sanitation bred cholera; London's sewerage emptied into the Thames, from which inhabitants drew drinking water. In the summer epidemic of 1866, eight thousand died, four thousand of them in the East End districts of Bethnal Green, Poplar, Stepney, and Whitechapel, where Booth's mission was located. Smallpox was common, and Bethnal Green matchbox makers suffered from the industrial illness of phossy jaw. Nor did the habits of the poor improve their health. Cheap licenses permitted the sale of untaxed beer, cider, and perry. There were 49,130 licensed beer-shops by 1869.[1]

There were countless Methodist chapels and small missions in the East End, ministering in the midst of devastation. The City Mission Movement and the Home Mission Movement had been inaugurated many years earlier, and many evangelicals working in the cities were looking for cooperation with one another as a means of ministering to the masses.[2] Glenn Horridge writes that

> the various agencies of the Home Mission Movement frequently had a temperance facet to their operations. Alongside and sometimes

intertwined with the missions and temperance lay a host of other charities. In London alone 144 charities had been founded in the 1850s. These
ranged from religious missions to housing charities, money for distressed
gentlefolk, and the R.S.P.C.A.[3]

Motives for these many agencies varied, some wanting to bring a prevailing civilizing influence into the culture, while others desired to
express a deep and abiding humanitarian concern. However, as Bennett
has noted, "It was not uncommon for the Booths, particularly William,
to ignore or at least underestimate the work of other people, and at times
they spoke almost as if they were the only ones working in the East
End."[4]

In spite of the seemingly impossible circumstances of life in the East
End, Booth accepted the invitation and the challenge to preach there,
and the beginning of his mission is officially dated as Sunday, July 2,
1865. On that day, William preached in a tent erected in a Quaker burial ground until the old tent was blown to the ground sometime after
August 27 and other venues for meetings had to be found. William was
no stranger to the East End, and had preached with a group of missioners outside of the Blind Beggar public house. Those missioners invited
him to preach in their tent because they were taken by the power of this
evangelist, and some thought that in William Booth they had found the
leader for whom they had been praying.

The phenomenon of preaching in the open air was common in East
London at that time.

> By 1866 the number of persons preaching in the open air in London every
> Sunday *during the season*—some in groups, but many singly—amounted to
> hundreds. Yet over and over again it was stated that the need remained
> greater than the attempt to meet it. And there was always an underlying
> lament of a lack of permanency in the results, seen especially in oft-
> repeated public discussion of the question, "What can we do to keep our
> converts?" To which none among the preachers was able to give a satis-
> factory answer.[5]

The Christians who heard Booth preach in the open air and pressed
him into further service came from various missions such as The
Christian Community, originally a Huguenot community but by
William's day undenominational, or the East London Special Services
Committee, a group with which Booth had had previous contact in

London. In fact, as has been mentioned, as early as the summer of 1861, while exploring the possibility of a home mission work in London, Booth had preached for this group at the Garrick Theatre in Whitechapel. The missioners from these and other groups were all committed to ministry in East London—in Whitechapel and Bethnal Green.

The loss of the tent meant that this mission was on the move and looking for other places to preach. On the first Sunday in September, services were held in Professor Orson's dancing academy, the Assembly Rooms, on New Road in Whitechapel. One woman who joined the mission, Mrs. Eliza Collingridge, as well as two converts, John Gore and Honor Fells, played an important role in Booth's mission. As these rooms were available only on Sundays, however, various other places had to be rented for weeknight meetings. Venues varied and included an old chapel, a carpenter's shop, a wool warehouse in Bethnal Green, a stable, a penny gaff, a pigeon shop, a skittle-alley, and a shed in Poplar "polluted by smells from adjacent pig-sties."[6] Finally, by 1867 there were more permanent quarters for meetings on Sunday evenings at the Effingham Theatre on Whitechapel Road. Here was a site more suitable for preaching, and East Enders felt comfortable here because they were used to visiting it during the week for other than religious purposes.

This was, nevertheless, a nomadic life and difficult existence, especially in the face of angry mobs and ridiculing East Enders. William Booth, however, was nothing if not persistent, and he continued ministering in various venues and conducting open-air services in front of public houses such as the Vine or the Blind Beggar. At the same time, Catherine was preaching to the wealthy in the West End of London. On one occasion, although seven months pregnant at the time, in October 1865, she held services in the Horns Assembly Rooms at Kennington, near the site of the pawnbrokers shop where William had worked upon his arrival in London at the age of twenty. The Booths depended primarily on Catherine's income during this time, since there was not enough money coming in from the East Enders to whom William was ministering for him to receive a steady income.

As mentioned in the previous chapter, to be nearer the work in East London and Mile End Waste (so named because snow was dumped there in a patch of land off Mile End Road in the winter), the Booths moved from Hammersmith to Hackney in November 1865. William had been walking from Hammersmith to East London, and that would not be possible for long. The Booth home on Mare Street was closer to the place of William's ministry.

It is beyond question that William Booth felt called by God to this ministry. He was haunted by the desperation of the inhabitants of East London, and although at this time he had no social plan for the alleviation of their physical poverty, he did believe with perfect faith that he had the answer to their spiritual poverty. That simple answer was the message of salvation—faith in Christ who had paid the price for their sins. The motivation for helping the poor was primarily biblical and theological—he believed in the redemptive power of the gospel in the lives of people, and that obedience to the injunction of his Lord to love God and love one's neighbor was the essential mark of the Christian.

Secondarily, he knew intuitively that alleviating the suffering of the poor would prevent society from falling into chaos. This was not his primary motivation for preaching the gospel, but an outcome of that preaching. But one must be careful not to imply that the most compelling reason why Booth ministered to the poor was to create a more stable society. Booth was primarily an evangelist and a revivalist, pressing the hope that spiritual regeneration would manifest itself in social stability. To state that the Booths "also brandished the threat that, if religion failed to ameliorate poverty and crime, all society would suffer"[7] is to place too much emphasis here. The salvation of society and of British homogeneous culture from an increasingly diverse heathenism in England was not Booth's first concern. He was driven primarily by a vision for the salvation of the lost of East London.

The work of William Booth came to the attention of Mr. Samuel Morley, whose father was from Sneinton, Booth's birthplace in Nottingham. St. John Ervine describes Samuel Morley as "a wealthy and philanthropic Liberal Member of Parliament."[8] He represented Nottingham and later Bristol and had acquired an immense fortune from a textile business founded by his father. After hearing of William Booth's work in East London and after a long personal interview with Booth— probably in October 1865—he decided to support Booth financially. This was the first visible support for the East London Christian Revival Society.[9] Until his death in 1886, Morley continued to support Booth.

Such generous support, however, was not enough to keep the Mission and family going, and the Booths still depended on income from Catherine's preaching even though the year 1866 was a particularly difficult one for Catherine. Severe diarrhea and nausea caused weight loss, and Catherine seemed more frail than ever. Her constant worry about health was justified now. This was not enough, however, to curtail her preaching, and not only because the family depended on Catherine's income to put bread on the table but because Catherine was compelled to preach the gospel regardless of consequences to her health. Her venues varied. She ministered in Tunbridge Wells, where she went to recuperate but was asked to preach at the home of Mr. Henry Reed, whom Ervine described as "Rabbits over again, but richer."[10] He had made a fortune in sheep farming in Tasmania, and decided to help William Booth in his struggling work. But Booth could not always rely on the finances of wealthy supports, Reed being a case in point. He was particularly difficult at times and withheld funds from the Mission when it was not run to his liking. Reed really wanted to control the Mission, which was unthinkable to Booth.

Catherine's preaching also took her back to London and then to Ramsgate and Margate. The latter two engagements at seaside resorts to the east of London were taken because these places would be better for her health. Her converts at Margate included the previously mentioned daughter of the Billupses, whom the Booths had met in Wales, as well as Miss Jane Short, who moved back to London with Catherine, boarded in the Booth home, and helped with the care of the children.

Upon her return to London, her mission to the West End continued, as did support for the Mission. One person who heard her preach and subsequently heard William preach convinced the Committee of the Evangelization Society, another group supporting ministries in East London, to help support the work of the Mission. Since February 1867, the primary venue for preaching on Sunday evening had been the Effingham Theatre, renamed the New East London Theatre. But William Booth finally formally acquired a place of his own—a beer shop named the Eastern Star at 188 Whitechapel Road.

> The Mission's first official report, in 1867, bore a picture of the Eastern Star on its cover. The once notorious tavern had become a bookshop, reading room, mission hall, penny bank, and later added service as a soup kitchen. In addition, administration was moved from Cambridge Lodge Villas and the Eastern Star became William Booth's first headquarters, which it remained for nearly three years.[11]

By the beginning of 1868, the Mission was finally enjoying some success. The Mission had thirteen preaching stations—apparently named after the term *preaching-houses* that had been used in Methodism—seating a total of eight thousand persons. Although there was as yet no organized and centrally controlled social ministry for which Booth would later be so well known, there were a variety of local ministries as the local needs warranted—reading rooms, penny banks, soup kitchens, mothers' meetings, and a system for distributing food, clothes, boots, and blankets to the poor. The lodger, Jane Short, became a visitor for the Mission, and thereby followed up on people who had been served by the Mission. Jenty Fairbank writes of Jane Short:

> Jane Short's priorities were uncompromising. She it is who gives us one of the first clear statements of intent as far as the relationship between evangelism and good works is concerned. Writing in *The Christian Mission Magazine* of April 1870 she explains: "While the chief object and aim of The Christian Mission is to bring sinners to Jesus, we feel it a duty and a privilege to minister to the bodily wants of the necessitous. . . . Parcels of old clothing and old boots and shoes will be most gratefully received."[12]

The inclination to care for the poor in any way possible had been inherited from Booth's Wesleyan rearing, which placed constant emphasis upon loving God and loving one's neighbor, after the injunction of Jesus.

At that time, William Booth relied on "a Council of ten well-known philanthropists and religious workers, and a Committee of nine other persons, one of whom acted as Honorary Secretary, while another was Treasurer."[13] Among the members of the council were Morgan and Chase, the editors and publishers of *The Revival*, and Morley who had decided to support the work of the Mission financially. In October 1868, Booth began producing *The East London Evangelist* to give an account of the work of the Mission, which was published by Morgan and Chase.[14]

Another move for the Booth family was necessary by late-1868. The home in Cambridge Lodge Villas was troublesome to the ailing Catherine because of the incessant traffic and construction noise outside her window. In December 1868, the family moved a few streets away to Belgrave House, 3 Gore Road, Hackney, overlooking Victoria Park.[15] It was in this house that a second boarder, Miss Mary Coutts Billups, was taken in to help with the expenses of the house.

Although located in a beautiful setting, the house did not prove to be a place of refuge for the family, as Catherine had wished. It served as overflow offices for the growing Mission. And just over one year after moving into the house Catherine's mother died. The Mission was expanding beyond the East End to Croydon and Edinburgh. In October 1869, the Mission purchased a people's market—a failed venture of Mr. John McAll, a member of Booth's Mission committee—which was converted into a fine Mission station and proved to be a good central meeting place for the Mission. "It was large enough to seat 1,500 people and the adjoining 10 small rooms, shop and soup kitchen could meet a multitude of needs."[16] The premises, renamed the People's Mission Hall, was opened on Sunday, April 10, 1870, appropriately William Booth's forty-first birthday.

William was very ill, however, and Catherine preached in both the morning and evening services. William's illness took him away from East London, except for his presence at a couple of committee meetings, from that time until September. Catherine ran the Mission. And again in 1872, William's health prevented him from participating in Mission business for six months. "His doctors pronounced his trouble to be a nervous breakdown, resulting from overwork, and expressed fear that it would be impossible for him to return to duty."[17] Again, Catherine, in spite of her own illnesses and anxiety over William, was strong enough to continue the work of the Mission, and she proved to be more than able for the task. She administered the business affairs of the Mission and frequently preached. Writing to a friend from Smedley's Hydropathic Establishment in Matlock on April 17, 1872, William Booth stated that

> I am still alive, although not worth much. Have been here 5 weeks and am likely to be away from London a month longer. My wife and friends are determined that I shall have a fair chance of getting strong before my return. I have been in a very poor way a long time. I have had much trial, business and otherwise the last 15 months, and it has told on me. However, I am rallying now and hope to be myself again 'ere very long. The Mission goes forwards. I don't know that we were ever doing much better on the whole. You know a little of the faculty of my wife for superintending, and she has had a merciful increase of health and strength of late as though on purpose to take my place. Bless her, she has been most useful.[18]

It was apparent, however, that all was not well. In 1870, two financial matters caused Booth great concern. Both personal finances as well as finances for the Mission—and later for The Salvation Army—constantly perplexed Booth, and were frequently a cause of his depression. First, the renovations of the people's market were going far over budget and demands were made upon Booth that he was not prepared to meet. Second, with Catherine's declining income due to her frequent illnesses, Booth was rightly concerned with the financial security of his family. He had never taken his salary from Mission funds, and funds from the sale of books were not enough to keep bread on the table. He briefly considered turning over the Mission to others while he went back to business ventures to support his family.

His despair was so great that he even humbled himself and pleaded with the ever-recalcitrant Henry Reed for help. He received no money from Reed, but only what may be described as a vicious and self-righteous letter condemning Booth for getting into debt. The insult was, of course, made worse as Reed signed off at the conclusion of the letter with "Yours in Christ, Henry Reed." Even though it may be said that this same Henry Reed later provided more funds to support the Booths in the autumn of 1880, at this time of need his lack of support was insufferable and beyond comprehension. Reed never proved to be the trusted friend that others had become to the Booths. So for now the Booths would have to continue without Mr. Reed and find funds elsewhere, thank you very much.

Booth once described his father as "a Grab, a Get. He had been born in poverty. He determined to grow rich; and he did. He grew very rich, because he lived without God and simply worked for money; and when he lost it all, his heart broke with it, and he died miserably."[19] His happiness had been tied completely and only to personal wealth. William was determined not to follow that path. He abhorred his father's attitude, and tried to instill in his children the virtue of living for others rather than for oneself.

Booth had established a Food-for-the-Millions program, which was his only attempt at an organized social ministry throughout the entire Mission. This program provided nourishing meals for the poor at reasonable prices, and helped support the Booths until Catherine was able to resume her preaching and speaking engagements and once again bring funds into the home. The program was placed under the leadership of Bramwell Booth, the eldest of the Booth children, and James Flawn, who, before his conversion, had been in the food catering business, and who provided various food services for the Army as a Salvationist until his death in 1917. Different cultural crises had caused the Mission to give away soup and bread in the past as need arose among the poor, such as during a cholera epidemic in 1866. The Food-for-the-Millions program, however, was a much more concentrated feeding program, and Flawn was adept in this business. This program ran for four years, from 1870 to 1874, when it was sold to a man named Cooper, the brother-in-law of Mr. Billups. Booth was convinced that the program, although helpful, was too much of a financial and personnel strain upon the growing Mission.[20] Sandall wrote:

> General relief work seems later to have been abandoned by The Christian Mission, for writing to the Rev. Arthur Wedgwood (hon. Secretary of the Whitechapel Union Division of the Charity Organization Society) in June 1877 William Booth stated that the Mission had ceased almost entirely to administer relief to strangers, but instead referred them to the Charity Organization Society.[21]

The first Annual Conference of the Mission was held in November 1870.[22] This was a turning point in the history of the Mission. In the previous year, the name of the Mission was changed to The Christian Mission "because its activities were no longer only metropolitan."[23] A constitution for The Christian Mission was written in 1870, and after that time the control of the Mission was placed solely in the hands of William Booth, hereafter called the General Superintendent according to the Rules of the Mission. Technically, the Conference (a term Booth borrowed from the Methodists) was in charge of the administration of the Mission, but Booth was, for all intents and purposes, in control of the Mission. In 1875, it was determined that he could even override decisions of the Conference. An autocracy was fully established at that time. Booth despised the control imposed upon him by committees, and several of his Missioners, led by George Scott Railton, trusted Booth's autocratic control implicitly.

The Enduring Work of The Christian Mission

Some have suggested that The Christian Mission had failed in East London, and that "Booth could only hope that his East End failure was only temporary and would go unnoticed."[24] However, both Booth and his supporters measured the work of The Christian Mission not only by what was being done in East London but by the increasing ministry of the Mission. Christian Mission stations numbered eighteen in 1870. By 1878, when the Mission evolved into The Salvation Army, the fledging Mission could boast of fifty-seven stations. There can be no doubt that the durability of The Christian Mission and its eventual evolution into a worldwide religious movement cast a different light on the Mission. Booth certainly saw his work as that of kingdom work, and any measure of failure or success was inconsequential as long as he and his Missioners were faithful to the work that God had given them to do.

But the question is not really one of success or failure. The critical question is: In the great metropolis of London, in general, and in East London, in particular, how did this mission survive when countless others failed? What were the enduring qualities that sustained Booth's work when other equally sincere religious societies and evangelists are unknown today?

There are three compelling characteristics of The Christian Mission that account for its eventual durability and allowed it eventually to evolve into The Salvation Army.[25] The first is that Booth rooted the constitution of The Christian Mission in 1870 within the Methodism in which he had been nurtured. "The Christian Mission's polity from 1870 to 1878 was Methodism's conference plan from its founding by John Wesley. In structure and discipline, Booth's Christian Mission was Wesleyan."[26] One author is convinced that "the Mission and the Salvation Army which followed, were the high water mark of Methodist enterprise in Britain. The Mission was and the Salvation Army remains part of the Wesleyan heritage."[27] Even though the Mission might appear independent, it lodged its conference system, rules, regulations, and doctrines within the Methodist tradition, and so was not inventing something new as many missions then did and as many independent churches today are prone to do. While Booth was not trained, as Wesley was, to understand the richness of the tradition of the Church going back to its earliest history, and the implications of that tradition for Methodism, he did, nevertheless, have a certain innate attachment to the tradition of his own Methodism. With the formal establishment of The Christian Mission at the 1870 Conference, he was not about to start something completely new.

Second, the Mission clarified its doctrine. Here again the Methodist influence upon the Booths is evident, as there is an emphasis in their doctrines at this time upon the doctrine of sanctification.[28] The East London Christian Revival Society had established seven doctrines by about 1866. But by 1870, the doctrines evolved to ten with the addition of a doctrine of sanctification that stated: "We believe that it is the privilege of all believers to be 'wholly sanctified,' and that 'their whole spirit and soul and body' may 'be preserved blameless unto the coming of our Lord Jesus Christ.' (1 Thess. V.23)."[29] The Christian Mission Conference of 1876 further clarified the meaning of sanctification.[30]

In an address on holiness to the 1877 Conference of The Christian Mission, William Booth claimed that the power of evil still existed in the soul of the believer after justification by faith, even though that power was diminished. But, said Booth, God has taken evil from the throne of the soul in the act of sanctification and given the believer power over evil. "He is no longer under sin but under grace."[31] Deliverance is partial at justification, but complete at sanctification. "Not only can Agag be taken captive, but hewn in pieces. Sin can not only be held in bondage, but destroyed."[32] In that same address, William Booth pronounced the centrality of the doctrine of holiness in The Christian Mission in this way:

> Holiness to the Lord is to us a fundamental truth; it stands to the fore-
> front of our doctrines. We write it on our banners. It is in no shape or
> form an open debatable question as to whether God can sanctify wholly,
> whether Jesus does save his people from their sins. In the estimation of
> The Christian Mission that is settled forever, and any evangelist who
> did not hold and proclaim the ability of Jesus Christ to save his people
> to the uttermost from sin and sinning I should consider out of place
> amongst us.[33]

Later, in "The General's Address at the Wesleyan Conference" in which William Booth was asked to elaborate upon the principles accounting for the success of The Salvation Army, Booth stated, "We go on the three broad lines of Repentance, Faith, and Holiness of Heart."[34] The centrality of the doctrine of holiness to the Booths and The Christian Mission and The Salvation Army is beyond dispute, even including an understanding of entire sanctification. Hattersley asserted that "in fact, 1876 was the one 'Holiness moment' in the life of both the Mission and the Army which it became. From then on the idea was in steady decline—denied a central place in doctrine because its metaphys-ical complications were not to William Booth's taste and only what he regarded as important survived."[35] This statement can be made not only by ignoring both the social and theological foundations of the Booths and their movements, but also, incidentally, by ignoring the central place of the doctrine in the continuing life of the Army today. While Murdoch questions the timing of the holiness doctrine in the life of the Booths, even he acknowledged that "the Booths particularly embraced the Wesleyan doctrine of holiness, salvation from all sin, a point at which traditional English Wesleyanism and mid-nineteenth century revivalism merged."[36]

In any case, the present handbook of doctrine published by The Salvation Army, entitled *Salvation Story*, has well articulated the connection between the doctrines formulated by The Christian Mission and later by The Salvation Army and Methodist doctrine. That work states the following:

> While their [Salvation Army Articles of Faith] origin is nowhere stated, their roots are clearly in the Wesleyan tradition. The articles bear a striking similarity in words and content to Methodist New Connexion doctrines, which can be traced back to at least 1838. William Booth was an ordained minister of the New Connexion, whose founders claimed their doctrine to be "those of Methodism, as taught by Mr. Wesley."...Our doctrinal statement, then, derives from the teaching of John Wesley and the evangelical awakening of the eighteenth and nineteenth centuries. While there was significant correspondence between evangelicals in the mid-nineteenth century, indicated especially in the [eight]-point statement of the Evangelical Alliance of 1846, the distinctives of Salvation Army doctrine came from Methodism. Our strong emphasis on regeneration and sanctification, our conviction that the gospel is for the whosoever and our concern for humanity's free will all find their roots there.[37]

There has been speculation that some of the doctrines such as the ninth doctrine—which was added under the Rules of The Christian Mission in about 1873 or 1874 and which read, "We believe that continuance in a state of salvation depends upon continuous obedient faith in Christ"—were formulated because of a strong Calvinist influence in the ranks of The Christian Mission, but this cannot be substantiated.[38] In fact, Horridge's study has shown that "once the Movement became identifiable, the numbers of officers and members increased, thus enabling the Army to expand further. Of those officers with previous religious experience, two-thirds were Methodists of Wesleyan or Primitive ideology. A small but growing number of Anglican women were joining and in late 1878/1879 there was a marked influx of women."[39]

To reiterate, the doctrines of The Christian Mission evolved from seven to ten to eleven by 1874. There were minor changes in wording and explanations after 1874, but the substance of the doctrines did not change. The Deed Poll of 1878 that legally affirmed The Salvation Army contained those eleven doctrines.[40]

The third characteristic of The Christian Mission that accounted for its permanence while countless other similar missions faltered was its leadership. Many early leaders of the Mission—especially George Scott Railton, who was appointed General Secretary of the Mission in 1873— saw the rule of the Mission by one leader, Booth, rather than by committee, as a strength and a signal of future usefulness and growth. George Scott Railton himself had been attracted to the Mission after having read Booth's *How to Reach the Masses with the Gospel,* a description of Booth's work in East London, and after having traveled to London to meet the Booths. Railton soon joined the Mission and quickly became an invaluable leader of the Mission and leader in the evolution from Mission to Army.[41]

Others with leadership ability also assisted the Booths. For example, Eliza Collingridge, who has already been mentioned, became the first paid worker of the Mission in 1867 and was given the title of Biblewoman. She had responsibilities for visiting, distributing tracts and Scriptures, counseling, and conducting Bible studies for women. In 1870, she was appointed Superintendent of the Shoreditch Circuit. Others, such as James Dowdle, the saved railway guard; Elijah Cadman, the converted chimney sweep and a Methodist lay preacher; and John Lawley, formerly a Primitive Methodist, joined the Mission, providing invaluable leadership and remaining faithful to William Booth after the Mission evolved into The Salvation Army.[42] In the late 1870s, the son of a gypsy family in East London, Rodney "Gypsy" Smith, joined the Mission and eventually became a Salvation Army Captain. He left the Army, however, and gained a reputation as an international evangelist.[43]

There is no doubt that people were attracted to the Booths, perhaps inspired by their preaching, secure in the organizational abilities of both Booths, and somewhat driven by the theological vision of the Booths that, at this point, highlighted the grand themes of holiness of heart and life as well as the conversion of the world. It became evident, especially as the ministry of William Booth evolved, that Booth was finally and fully convinced that the whole world could be brought into submission to Christ, and that driving theological conviction began to take shape in the theology of The Christian Mission.

However, as long as the Methodist Booth was in charge, discipline was part of the life of the Missioners and rules and regulations were established—to which those in the Mission were to conform. The rules, modeled largely after the rules and regulations of Methodist life in which the Booths were reared, at Catherine's insistence included total abstinence from alcohol for officeholders in the mission, which was a departure even from the rules of New Connexion Methodism. Catherine wanted to expand total abstinence from alcohol to all members of the Mission and pressed that issue again in 1876, but she was surprisingly unsuccessful. "The conditions of membership in the Mission were exceedingly complicated and detailed in their requirements, but while it was insisted that members should not in any way traffic in intoxicating drink, personal abstinence therefore was not more than strongly urged."[44]

As Hattersley has rightly noted, "William Booth's attempt to turn the Mission into a temperance organization failed. He had hoped that total abstinence would be made a condition of membership. . . . The failure of the Conference to follow his lead on the subject confirmed that, although he had gone a long way toward establishing his autocratic authority, he had not gone far enough. More constitutional reforms were essential."[45] And so it was not until 1878 that Catherine entirely won the battle with this rule, and at that time total abstinence from alcohol for all officeholders and members of the Mission was required. This rule continued in force with the evolution of the Mission into The Salvation Army.

The Booths' family life revolved around the work of the Mission, a pattern that continued until well after the Mission became The Salvation Army. Extremely helpful to the Booths as the Mission took shape were their children, especially the eldest son, Bramwell. He inherited from his father certain organizational abilities, which is why he was able to administer the Food-for-the-Millions program beginning in 1870, although he was merely fourteen years of age at the time. On August 27, 1876, William Booth, in writing to Bramwell, stated that

my own and a growing conviction is that God wants you to assist me in directing and governing this Mission, and at my death, if it should anticipate yours, to take my place. With my present feelings *I should certainly name you to take my place in the event of my decease.* True, at present, your youth would be very much against you with some of the men, but you would have Mamma to counsel you and she would have much weight. But my feeling is that God will spare me for some time to come—and every year now will tell in your favour.[46]

Other Booth children helped as well, as they were able. It was during the Mission days that the children took part in open-air services, gave testimonies, led meetings, and even preached. Their skills were being tested and refined, and when the Mission evolved into the Army, they played leading roles in the developing of that movement.

The work of the Mission continued unabated by using various means of ministry that Booth felt had been essential to the success of the Methodists and to the American revivalists whom the Booths admired. Therefore, preaching, open-air meetings, class meetings, prayer meetings, and visitation were particularly stressed in the work of the Mission. William wrote to Bramwell:

> I have been reading Tyerman's *Wesley* in my illness and have, by comparing his experience with my own, I think, derived some *important lessons*. One is that, under God, Wesley made Methodism not [only] by converting sinners, but by making well instructed *saints*. We must follow in his track, or we are a rope of sand. He laid as much stress on visiting the members privately, and in classes, as on preaching.[47]

As one biographer has noted, the spirit of The Christian Mission was a reflection of the character of William Booth himself. That spirit

> called for a real self-denial, but counseled reasonable care of oneself. It preached the most arresting form of the Christian Gospel, but prescribed an extreme tenderness with the broken-hearted. It denounced sin with an energy that was almost violent, but sought the sinner with a loving-kindness that was entirely beautiful.[48]

Statistics demonstrate that in 1868 through 1869 there were a total of sixteen Christian Mission stations and that by 1877 that number had risen to thirty-one, the highest number of Christian Mission stations up to that time being in 1875 with a total of thirty-nine. The changing numbers demonstrate two things. First, some stations, most notably those in Brighton, Edinburgh, and Norwood seceded from The Christian Mission and became independent missions. The motivations of the preachers and the missioners are difficult to discern, but both William and Catherine viewed these people as traitors to the cause, thus once again confirming a major weakness in both of them. What they allowed for themselves in terms of the leading of God, they did not allow in others. God had led them into New Connexion Methodism and surely God had led them out. They were being faithful to the call of God in their lives. This was, however, a privilege that they refused to acknowledge for other people, especially anyone who left the Mission and later The Salvation Army. What the Booths valued in themselves they often questioned in others.

> While they were certain of the righteousness of their own motives, they sometimes impugned the motives of those who disagreed with them. And while they saw their break from New Connexion Methodism as an act of great courage motivated by God Himself, similar actions by Christian Missioners or later by Salvation Army officers would be viewed with suspicion. This attitude would be reflected in Catherine and William's tightening control, such control proving in later years to be both a great strength to the Mission's ongoing work and later of The Salvation Army but also a weakness, especially as it sometimes revealed the all too human sides of the founders of the Mission and the Army.[49]

St. John Ervine wrote that "it was characteristic of the Booths that they rejected authority over themselves, and at the same time sincerely and vehemently resented any question of their own authority over others, and they were remarkably successful in persuading other people to share their resentment."[50]

Second, all was not left to chance. There was the flexibility and practicality of opening and closing Christian Mission Stations as need arose. George Scott Railton, in a letter dated August 3, 1876, wrote that "we have abandoned several small station[s] in order to use up all our strength on those we can make something of.... It is of no use keeping up appearances. We must lay the axe to the tree roots and make a real living Mission all round."[51] And in a letter dated June 15, 1877, that William Booth wrote to his friend, William Stephenson Crow, he remarked that "we have given up 9 Stations during the year voluntarily with 616 members."[52]

Such disciplined administration apparently had some success, for by 1878, *The Christian Mission Magazine* reported fifty-seven stations. In a letter written on May 23, 1877, to William Stephenson Crow—Booth's printer in the Christian Mission days whom he had first met at Gateshead and who was a sort of confidant for Booth—William Booth wrote that "we are I think in a stronger [underlined twice] position than ever since the commencement of the work."[53] This is a witness not to a failing Mission, as some have suggested, but to a thriving but struggling

Mission. There was no need to confine the Mission to East London, and if some stations failed there this was a sign to Booth that he should move on to establish other Mission stations elsewhere. It is always critical to note, for better or for worse, that Booth saw himself led providentially in the matters of the Mission, as was the case with the move beyond East London. The year 1877 to 1878 proved to be a turning point, for it was during that year that the Mission that began so inconspicuously in the East End of London twelve years previous and evolved beyond East London, emerged into an Army, a Salvation Army.

CHAPTER EIGHT

THE EVOLUTION OF A MISSION AND THE CREATION OF AN ARMY

Introduction

There were several turning points in the history of The Salvation Army, and one of the first and most crucial ones occurred in the years 1877 and 1878. There was a gradual understanding during this time among the Booths and the leaders of the Mission that the Mission was evolving into something different from what it had been. The original intention, of course, was no longer in effect: to be a mission to the unconverted, and upon their conversion to send these people back to local churches. Both the critical attitude of some church people toward converts from East London, as well as the attraction of new converts to the preaching and ministry of the Booths kept people attached to the local Christian Mission stations, appropriately called Preaching Stations. These factors, accompanied by the fact that the Booths needed some of their converts and others who had joined the Mission to assist them in their work, kept people tied to the Mission and loyal to the Booths.

A Period of Transition

So something resembling a new denomination was taking shape, although William Booth at this time refused to admit that he had a church on his hands. Rather, he continued to refer to the Mission as a mission for salvation purposes, and thereby a mission in service to the wider Church. He had not, at this point, established a clear ecclesiology by which he could identify his Mission as a church. Nevertheless, all the accoutrements of a church existed in each Christian Mission Station; there were congregations who assembled on a regular basis, preaching of the gospel was done at those meetings, the sacraments were practiced, and there is some evidence that class meetings were conducted after the pattern established by Methodism to help nurture the converts in the life of holiness.

The 1877 Conference of The Christian Mission, held fom June 11 through 14, formally instigated that evolution, the Conference henceforth continuing not as a committee conference, but as a council of war that Booth had already declared as early as January of that year. Governance of the Mission by committee was officially discontinued and autocratic control of the Mission by William Booth replaced representative control.

> The result of the June Conference of 1877 was therefore that the Conference Committee was to be abolished, but an annual gathering for meetings was to continue; that Booth would make all the decisions and appoint the evangelists personally to stations; that instead of allowing complicated organization, legislation would be simplified; that teetotalism would be universal for all members of the Mission; and Sunday Schools would be temporarily abandoned, as would soup kitchens and food shops.[1]

William Booth wanted to return to his original and rather simple concept of the Mission—to save sinners and raise up saints.

There can be no doubt that John Wesley was the model for this renewed direction in the leadership of the Mission. William Booth attributed the success of Methodism partly to the example of John Wesley. "He [Booth] felt himself as time went on to be placed in circumstances in many important respects similar to those in which Wesley had ultimately been placed, and his position was very like Wesley's in one respect at least, that people would come to him and say, 'Take us under your care. We have loosed our anchors.' "[2] What Booth failed to possess was the natural social recognition of Wesley's authority in eighteenth-century society where the Oxford-trained rector was in a social position in which people depended on him and looked to him for leadership. While English society was somewhat flexible in the eighteenth century, and people could rise to higher stations by virtue of their occupations or acquired wealth, nevertheless "one explanation for Wesley's attitude to his authority and one source of the broad acceptance of it was the hierarchical 'dependency' nature of eighteenth-century society.... As a clerical gentleman he was, for most of the time, dealing with social inferiors as accustomed to obey as he was to command."[3]

Booth had no such social standing that would help to establish his authority over others. Rather, as was also true with Wesley, he did have an authoritarian nature, and consequently was bored with committees and others' rules and regulations. And apparently he enjoyed his position of authority, contrary to the protestations of his son, Bramwell, who wrote, "It was not that he wanted to be an autocrat. All his predispositions were the other way."[4] Catherine Booth also exhibited autocratic inclinations, and so the Mission was going to be in the hands of not one Booth, but two. And along with the Booths came their children, many exhibiting the leadership qualities of their parents. Catherine had already demonstrated both her ability and her desire to lead when William had to be absent from the Mission for health reasons for long periods of time and Catherine effectively ran the Mission. The authority of the Booths over the Mission would have been impossible had not a number of people willingly submitted themselves to that authority. The Booths nurtured such obedience for the remainder of their lifelong ministry, and, generally, people complied with the wishes of the Booths, with a few notable exceptions that will be evident in later chapters.

> None of the Missioners dissented. Just as John Wesley, William's mentor in this move, was accused of "surrounding himself with flatterers: the standing temptation, indeed, of autocrats,"[5] it is possible that some of the thirty-six evangelists or some of the conference delegates could be called flatterers. Indeed neither William nor Catherine were free from attracting those kinds of people. Nevertheless, most of the Missioners genuinely shared Catherine and William's vision for the Mission and were excited about their ministry in this Army of God.[6]

Along with this new style of leadership came a military discipline upon the members of the Mission, by which William Booth and his Mission became better known by the general public. Up to this time, Catherine Booth's name was known to more people because of her preaching to a wider London audience than was William Booth's name through his work in the various Christian Mission Stations. "It is possible to say that nine people out of ten who knew the name of Catherine Booth had never heard of William Booth's work in Whitechapel."[7]

Because the Mission had established itself outside of London, it was now known as The Christian Mission, while *The Christian Mission Magazine* recorded the work of the Mission at its various Stations, as well as the pronouncements of William Booth, who provided a single vision for the work of the Mission. Although the idea of a Salvation Army was not yet in the picture, Booth's language at the June 1877 Conference was filled with military imagery.

> What is the good of a council of war? The commander in chief calls the principal officers around him to receive information and counsel from all. Each brings his facts and expresses his judgment as to what is necessary and important to do, and then in view of all this he resolves upon a programme of operation. This is our Council of War. We are here to consider practical questions and how we can best deal with them: to receive reinforcements and re-station our army; and, above all, we are here to help each other's souls, to cry together to the Living God for the rebaptism of the Holy Ghost.[8]

This military language was not new, especially to the converted chimney sweep, Elijah Cadman, now one of the most important Mission leaders. As early as 1873, he referred to himself as a lieutenant and to William Booth as his general, an abbreviated title of general superintendent. On another occasion, Cadman, in advertising meetings in the town of Whitby, identified himself as a captain. During the time of evolution from Mission to Army the military language became commonplace. In a letter dated August 14, 1878, Booth addressed Cadman as "Captain." Again, in a letter addressed to Cadman on September 24, 1878, Booth signed the letter, "Yours in the Army."[9] And then there was George Scott Railton. He

> had long been referring to William Booth as General and thought of himself as Mr. Booth's lieutenant before there ever was a Salvation Army. In fact, while laid aside with a serious illness in 1876, Railton wrote *Heathen England* as a kind of apologetic for the work of The Christian Mission. "Before the name of the movement existed the idea of The Salvation

Army leaps at one from every page.... All through *Heathen England* we
see that General Superintendent, William Booth, and General Secretary,
George Scott Railton, had an army on their hands."[10] Subsequent editions of *Heathen England* were well suited for explaining the work of the
Army.[11]

This military language was not completely strange to the broader culture. As one historian has noted, "The possibility that Great Britain was
about to enter a war against Russia meant that militarism was the theme
of topical conversation."[12] Likewise, military language was common
among other churches, and Joel A. Carpenter, speaking of the use of such
language and imagery in fundamentalism and evangelicalism of the
twentieth century, wrote that "the imperial language of conquest had
pervaded the British missionary rhetoric during the prior century and
reached its apex, perhaps, at the great Edinburgh World Missionary
Conference of 1910."[13] And David Malcolm Bennett wrote that "a military mood was fast developing in the Christian Mission, and it reflected
the wider mood of the Victorian Church and Britain generally."[14] So,
while military language and imagery was "in the air" so to speak, Booth
was the religious leader who developed the metaphor most comprehen-
sively as his Mission moved into becoming an Army.

This was the time of the solidification of the Mission's doctrines, purposes, and controlling ideology. It is true that some Missioners had left
the Mission since 1875 over such issues as women in ministry, Booth's
insistence on open-air work, his exacting demands upon the Mission
workers, his Wesleyan teaching of holiness, and even the emotional
nature of some of the public meetings. These meetings sometimes witnessed people jumping and dancing, crying and shouting, or falling to the
ground as if—by their own admission—smitten by God and convicted of
sin. One report from Hayle after The Christian Mission had become The
Salvation Army read, "Glory, glory, glory, glory to Jesus, to JESUS. We
must conquer and win Hayle for Jesus. Good times all day on Sunday.
Saints jumping, dancing, crying, shouting, and rolling on the ground. We
disgusted some people. Hallelujah. Blood-washed Johnny."[15] Bramwell
Booth reported instances of levitation at the public meetings as well as
instances of divine healing.[16]

But, just as Wesley before him had encountered similar emotionalism
in some of his meetings, Booth and his officers controlled the more deliberate zeal of people who came to the meetings. Catherine was often suspicious of such overt emotionalism. The proof of genuine religion, the

Booths believed, was not only in what a person felt, but also in what a person did. William Booth always admonished his listeners to "go and do something."

So, in spite of controversy in the Mission over such matters, and in spite of some rather devoted Missioners leaving the Mission, 1877 was the time to articulate the purpose of the Mission, consolidate the work of the Mission, and encourage the workers of the Mission. This was the time for Booth consistently and clearly to remind his people that the primary purpose of the Mission was to concentrate on preaching—not the merely intellectual kind that Booth abhorred, but preaching that led people to conviction of heart and life. Charles Grandison Finney, the American evangelist, represented Booth's favorite example of the kind of preacher he wished his preachers to be. Finney's preaching style grew in refinement as his opportunities to preach developed, and by the time he took his two tours of England, he was an accomplished public orator, pressing home the claims of the gospel like the lawyer he was, and calling for people to respond to the call of God, repent, believe the gospel, and live out the gospel for the redemption of society.[17]

Booth was convinced that such preaching by the Missioners would accomplish the same purposes—convert the sinner, raise up the saint, and put the saint to work. Booth wrote, reflecting the language of Finney, that "true godliness is practical benevolence."[18] Missioners were to demonstrate measured success in their preaching ministry. He wrote, "If you bring statements of large numbers of converts, and small or no increases in membership, you will leave it open for people to infer either that the conversions are not real, or that, being real, they are not properly looked after."[19]

Largely through the influence of Catherine Booth, women were participating in the life of The Christian Mission and in the preaching at the Mission's preaching stations. At the 1870 Conference, the following stipulation was enunciated in Section XII, Female Preachers:

> As it is manifest from the Scripture of the Old and especially the New Testament that God has sanctioned the labours of Godly women in His Church; Godly women possessing the necessary gifts and qualifications, shall be employed as preachers itinerant or otherwise and class leaders and as such shall have appointments given to them on the preacher's plan; they shall be eligible for any office, and to speak and vote at all official meetings.[20]

Even before this official statement, women had served prominently in the Mission. Eliza Collingridge was the first woman to hold office in The Christian Mission. She was at one time the superintendent of the Shoreditch Circuit and presided at the meetings. The minutes of the Shoreditch Circuit Elders' Meeting for February 6, 1870, list Sister Collingridge as the superintendent,[21] which demonstrates a recognized sanction of women in ministry, but predates the official written rules of The Christian Mission at its Conference that year. After the 1870 Conference, the number of women actively involved in The Christian Mission increased, as did their influence and responsibility. In 1870, of the thirty-four delegates, six were women, including Catherine. "The idea of a mixed Conference was very unusual for the 1860s or 1870s or before, but one where women were held to be on an equal footing with men was unheard of and, in religious circles, generally considered heretical."[22]

And the leadership of the Army recognized the impact of Salvation Army women preaching. In a letter from Bramwell Booth to Elijah Cadman on December 10, 1879, lamenting that some congregations were falling off, he wrote, "If there is no other plan of working the place we had better send lasses."[23] Such "Hallelujah Lasses" as Louisa Lock, Louisa Agar, Lizzie Jackson, and others—many still in their teens— brought the Army to public attention and helped to forward the cause of the Army. There were times when thousands of people turned out to hear these young women preach.

Also, Catherine's 1870 edition of *Female Ministry* proved useful as an apologetic for the somewhat radical position of women in ministry taken by The Christian Mission. It is beyond doubt, however, that as the work of the Mission increased, and as the Mission evolved into The Salvation Army, the place of women in ministry became prominent. The public awareness of the Army and the growth of the Army may be attributed to many things, but having women in ministry was critical. Pamela J. Walker wrote:

> The Mission's 1870 policy on women was enacted immediately; it may have simply codified existing practice as many women were already listed on the circuit plans. Women were present at the annual conferences from 1870, and in 1875 Annie Davis was the first woman to take charge of a mission station. These were not measures born of crisis, nor did the work require an extraordinary call. The Mission believed women had gifts and talents that they should exercise freely. Women's authority was thus sanctioned and institutionalized.[24]

Booth's theology was taking shape along with his growing ministry as the leader of The Christian Mission. The Wesleyan doctrine of holiness had always been important to William Booth, and undoubtedly would have been stressed in his training for New Connexion Methodism under his theological tutor, the Reverend Dr. William Cooke. Cooke wrote voluminously on theological matters, and in his book entitled *Christian Theology: Its Doctrines and Ordinances Explained and Defended,* he devoted a chapter to entire sanctification in which he wrote: "As to the manner in which the blessing of perfect love may be obtained, we believe with the venerable Wesley, that 'it is wrought in the soul by a simple act of faith; consequently, in an instant.' But we believe, also, in a 'gradual work both preceding and following that instant.' "[25] Although the book was written after Booth studied with Cooke, this undoubtedly would have been the kind of teaching passed on to Booth.

There obviously remained discussions about the ramifications of the doctrine of holiness, especially on matters of "residual sin" and "perfectionism" as John Pentecost has pointed out. Nevertheless, "the Booths' doctrinal orientation was essentially Wesleyan—as demonstrated by the early publication of their doctrinal statements/articles of faith."[26] As I mentioned in the previous chapter, Booth made clear the importance of the doctrine of holiness at the 1877 Conference of The Christian Mission. He stated:

Holiness to the Lord is to us a fundamental truth; it stands to the forefront of our doctrines. We write it on our banners. It is in no shape or form an open debatable question as to whether God can sanctify wholly, whether Jesus does save his people from their sins. In the estimation of The Christian Mission that is settled forever, and any evangelist who did not hold and proclaim the ability of Jesus Christ to save His people to the uttermost from sin and sinning I should consider out of place amongst us.[27]

The Birth of The Salvation Army

The Christian Mission Magazine in August 1878 announced a "War Congress" in which the Mission was formally announced as a Salvation Army, although the transition was gradual. The possibility of changing the name of The Christian Mission to a Volunteer Army had been briefly considered.[28] Such a title was in keeping with the cultural sensitivities of

Great Britain at the time because of the formation of a Volunteer Army, or Home Guard, in 1870.[29] In fact, "the new volunteer movement was just then the subject of some ridicule."[30] Bennett reiterates this fact, "In the mid- and late 1870s this force did not have a good reputation and received some uncharitable treatment in the press."[31] And so Booth, not wanting to be identified with such a Volunteer Army, chose the name Salvation Army for his Mission. Stationery from these early months of the history of the Army read "The Salvation Army, called The Christian Mission." But by October 1878, in most of the stationery, references to The Christian Mission were dropped and the stationery simply read "Headquarters of The Salvation Army."

William Booth became the first General, a suitable shortening of the title of General Superintendent that he held as the head of The Christian Mission, and the *Deed of Constitution* outlined and clarified the duties and responsibilities of General Booth, which included the power to appoint his successor. Mission station preachers were given the rank of captain, and many of the songs of the early Salvation Army utilized the military metaphor by which the Missioners were expected to live and to die.

Uniforms suitable to the ranks followed, and a military discipline governed the lives of the officers (ministers) and soldiers (laity) of the newly founded Army. The use of the uniforms was optional at first, different styles suiting the tastes of the various officers. Women's uniforms were finally fashioned in June 1880 under the direction of Catherine Booth. Uniforms included a bonnet, made attractive but durable since women officers in the early Salvation Army frequently came under attack by mobs in the open-air services. Uniforms served the purposes of the Army well, but the idea of plainness of dress had always been important to the Booths, perhaps as part of their Wesleyan heritage. Indeed, Wesley, upset with more fancy dress among his Methodists as they became wealthy and more respectable, "wished that he had imposed a Quaker uniform."[32]

The public of Great Britain might very well have been surprised to find that they had another Army on their hands, a religious Army at that. However, this was not as strange as it first appears.

There is a striking link between Victorian England's use of military metaphors and the naming of the Salvation Army. By 1879, the mission informally had adopted "salvation army" as its title; but the military's new popularity after the Crimean War and Indian Mutiny of the 1850s stimulated formal acceptance. Excitement had surrounded the formation of a

Volunteer Army of home guards in 1870. So Booth was not affronting popular norms in adopting a military title; rather he was catching the public eye by co-opting jargon that was then popular. Also, a military motif suited a mission that was evolving an imperial command structure, a London bureaucracy, and, within a year, an international scope.[33]

Appropriately, the name of *The Christian Mission Magazine* was changed to *The Salvationist* in 1879. Within the article entitled "Our New Name," the mission statement of the Army was articulated: "We are a salvation people—this is our specialty—getting saved and keeping saved, and then getting somebody else saved, and then getting saved ourselves more and more until full salvation on earth makes the heaven within, which is finally perfected by the full salvation without, on the other side of the river."[34]

After the founding of the Army, William Booth consistently used military language in his public pronouncements and writings. This was, after all, an Army of salvation and as such it was intent on overcoming, conquering and subduing the world. In *The Salvationist* Booth hints at the ultimate goal of this new Army: "To subdue a rebellious world to God."[35] This goal represents William Booth's growing postmillennial theology that eventually became one of the controlling visions for the Army, reflecting the growth of the Army and, in turn, partly accounting for that advance.[36]

The evolution from Mission to Army was led by Booth himself, but also aggressively championed by George Scott Railton, the first to hold the title and rank of commissioner in The Salvation Army, Bramwell Booth, Catherine Booth, and others such as Elijah Cadman, John Lawley, William Ridsdel, James Dowdle, and Annie Davis, all Christian Missioners who had helped to establish the work in various Preaching Stations. It is beyond doubt, however, that William Booth was at times reticent not about the evolution that was happening, but about some of the advances taking place. "Bramwell Booth describes his father at this period as *watching* the movement."[37] William Booth was both adventurous and cautious at the same time. "To challenge the world was right and necessary, but to annoy the world was foolish and hazardous."[38] Writing to Bramwell on March 16, 1877, William said, "I wish we did not do so many *silly* things. I think I see a great difference between *manly, natural, bold, daring action* and weak, *frivolous*, childish comicaliy."[39] Indeed some of the tactics used by Christian Missioners and even by early Army officers in both outdoor and indoor meetings to win the world for Jesus were scandalous.

> The sight of perhaps dozens of people in trance-like state leaping or dancing around in the open-air or in their halls cannot have enhanced the Army's reputation. Added to this were ribald and militaristic-sounding brightly-colored posters; strange outbursts of behaviour such as a woman officer riding a carriage through a town and playing the fiddle while a soldier banged a drum from the top; periodic allegations of immorality; and extensive reporting of faith-healing.[40]

Bramwell Booth even records instances of levitation in Christian Mission meetings.[41] William Booth basically would have none of that, in spite of occasional caricatures of him in local publications. He wanted to attract the attention of the world, and the brass bands marching to the street meetings, the all-night prayer meetings, and the occasional use of religious lyrics set to popular tunes were as far as he would go, and at times were a stretch even for Booth, not to mention some of his followers.

The Army Encounters Opposition

In any case, the tactics of the Mission and the early Army were enough to incur opposition from two ends of the social spectrum: from the mobs on the one end and churches on the other. Attacks on religious groups were not new in religious history. In the previous century the Wesleys and Whitefield suffered attacks from mobs of ruffians who often poured out of the pubs upon the unsuspecting evangelists. Richard P. Heitzenrater described religious opposition to the Wesleyan revival, "Some people took stronger steps to oppose the Methodists. In a land where 'risings' were not uncommon, it was not hard to raise a mob to protest any number of disruptions to the public peace."[42] Others such as the Quakers, the Congregationalists, the Primitive Methodists, and the Baptists also experienced mob attacks in their early histories.

Glenn K. Horridge devotes an entire chapter to the opposition to The Christian Mission and the early Salvation Army in his book *The Salvation Army Origins and Early Days: 1865–1900*. He wrote:

> Large-scale riots as a means of social expression were on the decline by the 1850s as trade unions, social and friendly societies, political associations

and effective policing increased. However the violence against the Salvation Army was one response in the centuries-old tradition of opposition to anything considered to deviate from the norm. Such reaction normally related to sexual deviance but also encompassed others such as swindlers, gypsies or those introducing and supporting new religious ideas. For many years missionaries of any denomination might be "attacked." If the group survived, they were generally accepted or at least tolerated. If they failed, the social control exercized was vindicated. Methodism is an example of the former and the Coaklers of the latter. The generic name for opposition such as this is "rough-music" but local names varied.[43]

Horridge goes on to mention that "such mobs often adopted names . . . the name commonly associated with such anti-Army violence was 'Skeleton Army' but it could vary; it was the 'Unconverted Salvation Army' in Whitechapel, the 'Red(-Nose) Army' in Guildford, the 'The Society for the Suppression of Street Parading' in Salisbury."[44]

The first organized opposition against the Army occurred in Whitechapel in August 1880 by a group of local thugs who labeled themselves "The Unconverted Salvation Army." These mobs were often fueled by the local brewers, ignored by the local magistrates, and sometimes implicitly encouraged by the Establishment. Salvationists did not retaliate, but William Booth eventually applied pressure on the head of the Metropolitan police authority, the Home Secretary, and Prime Minister Gladstone, defending the right of Salvationists to assemble publicly without fear of brutal attack, and asking for a privilege that all of Her Majesty's subjects should enjoy. The mobs' opposition often encouraged Booth's followers because they were convinced that they had been found worthy to suffer the same persecution as the early Christians. So they were able to take heart from this side of the persecution.

These attacks came to public attention through the newspapers, and the Home Secretary, Parliament, and the Queen's Bench became involved in questions concerning the legality of Salvationists marching on the streets. Catherine Booth personally wrote to the Home Secretary, and in May 1882 received the following reply from John Bright, indicating some sympathy from legislators in England:

> DEAR MADAM—I gave your letter to Sir W. Harcourt. He had already given his opinion in the House of Commons, which will be to some extent satisfactory to you. I hope the language of Lord Coleridge and

the Home Secretary will have some effect on the foolish and unjust magistrates to whom, in some districts, the administration of the law is, unfortunately, committed.

I suspect that your good work will not suffer materially from the ill-treatment you are meeting with. The people who mob you would doubtless have mobbed the Apostles. Your faith and patience will prevail,—I am, with great respect and sympathy, yours sincerely,

JOHN BRIGHT[45]

Local magistrates, however, often turned their backs on rulings that favored The Salvation Army. The opposition of the gangs, as well as the more sophisticated opposition of the churches, continued until the early 1890s. Finally "on 1 July 1890, Lord Chief Justice Coleridge again found for the Army, and categorically stated that the Army had a right to parade the Queen's highways providing they were not intentionally causing an obstruction."[46] By that time, the Army won the fight to march on the streets, and likewise became part of the religious landscape of England whether people liked it or not. So, as social acceptance increased, and as the Army settled into a denominational life, violent opposition finally died a natural death.

However, the religious opposition was troublesome. In a letter to William Crow dated November 8, 1878, William Booth wrote, "I shall have to appeal to each station to do something for the parent fund and that right off. The rich are giving us up on account of our vulgarities so we must help ourselves. I hear we were denounced very thoroughly in the recent Missionary Convention and that Spurgeon is going to denounce us."[47]

"Public antagonism troubled Mrs. Booth deeply, but chiefly because it came from religious people."[48] One of the first and strongest oppositions from the established church came from Dr. Goodwin, the Bishop of Carlisle, in October 1880. It was not William but Catherine who answered the bishop, first in a public address in Carlisle and then in the pages of *The War Cry*:[49] "All I shall say in respect to the Bishop is that I feel quite certain that if his lordship is a spiritually enlightened man—if he had himself attended those meetings on which he founded his remarks, he would have come to very different conclusions."[50]

[Catherine Booth] was constantly convinced that if the Army were objectively examined, and if the results of its work were carefully scrutinized, then people—even the Bishop of Carlisle—would rejoice in what they saw. This would be especially true if it could be emphasized, as Catherine did in her speaking and writing, that the working classes were disenfranchised from the established churches of nineteenth century England and that the Army had the means and methods, as Wesley did a century earlier, of bringing religion back to the working classes and the working classes back to religion. Of that she had no doubt, and she was astonished that the Church of England could not see this as an ultimate benefit to the life of the Church and the health of the social fabric of England.[51]

The Creation of an Intentional Community

With doctrines, discipline, leadership, and polity now in place, the evolution from Mission to Army was critical for setting the future course of the growing movement. The contention that the Mission was extended beyond London to the provinces as a ploy because it was stagnating in the East End of London fails to recognize the theological and missional drive of Booth and his fellow Missioners. Booth was for the conversion of the world, which is clear from his earliest writings.[52] In spite of having to close some stations in the East End, there was still overall growth in The Christian Mission and that continued in The Salvation Army as the Army advanced to countries beyond England's borders. However, in 1868 there were only sixteen Christian Mission stations and ten years later, in 1878, and at the time of becoming The Salvation Army, there were fifty-seven Christian Mission stations. And on August 3, 1876, George Scott Railton admitted the strategy of the Mission when he wrote that "we have abandoned several small station[s] in order to use up all our strength on those we can make something of."[53] And even during the time of evolution into an Army, as early in the history of the Army as December 19, 1878, in a letter to William Crow, Booth wrote, "And as I have fully decided that until we can get District Generals I will not extend further."[54]

The expansion of the Mission, and later of the Army, resulted largely from a theological base as well as a strategy for mission rather than a plot to cover failure in the East End. The evolution into an Army was seen not only by Booth but also by those around him as a novel and exciting way to give voice to such a theological vision. Far from seeking absolute control in order to establish his own empire, Booth had to be convinced to use the title of "General" for himself, but was finally sure that the ecclesiastical model of an Army of God made use of a legitimate military metaphor and would work in such a way that would enhance the kingdom of God.

It cannot be denied that Booth was an autocrat, like Wesley before him. However, any objective observer of both William and Catherine Booth would have to admit that these people were not schemers, self-promoters, and religious charlatans looking out for their own interests. For all their faults, they believed in the biblical doctrines of The Christian Mission and The Salvation Army, were primarily intent on advancing the kingdom of God, served their generation to the best of their ability, and earnestly sought what was best for the world.

An intentional community had been created. The Army could now be included as one of evangelicalism's "alternative communities."[55] As Joel A. Carpenter has observed,

> Grassroots religious movements are sectarian virtually by definition; they tend to establish clear boundaries of belief and behavior that will mark their followers as distinct and special, as a chosen and set-apart people. But in a situation where such movements can hope to grow and flourish if they are broadly attractive, their leaders find it tempting to smooth out some of their rough edges.[56]

In 1878, then, Booth had an Army on his hands. What happened in that year was similar to what occurred in 1744 when John Wesley called a conference that was "to become an important benchmark of Wesleyan doctrine and discipline."[57] And what was written about Wesley's conference could also describe the year 1878 in Army history. "This conference was an organizational watershed for Wesley and the Methodists—a gathering of their forces, a recapitulation of their ideas, a sorting out of their structure and methods, and a plan for their growth. The Methodist movement had come of age, and the Wesleys had taken a firm hold on their future."[58]

So now the same could be said of William Booth and his new Army. The Salvation Army had come of age and the Booths had taken a firm hold on their future. Precisely where this would lead was, of course, unknown during this time of transition. However, sometimes to his own amazement, Booth witnessed the advance of his Army and would himself be indispensable both to that advance and to the ongoing character and shape of this Army.

THE ARMY IN THE PUBLIC SQUARE

Introduction

I n spite of difficulties, trials, and problems, the Army was finding a place in history that would have been impossible to imagine in July 1865 when William Booth began preaching in that Quaker burial ground in East London. Even those who still opposed the Army were rather astonished by the support that the Army was continuing to enjoy from Samuel Morley and T. A. Denny. It was Denny who paid the first year's rent on a new headquarters for The Salvation Army located at 101 Queen Victoria Street, and ten years later Booth was able to purchase the freehold on the property. Previous to that the Booths moved their residence to 114 Clapton Common. The census records for that time reveal something of life in the Booth home. In the household there were "two adopted sons—Hythe-born George, who was given the Booth surname, and Henry Andrews, who in 1893 was to become the pioneer of Army medical work. In addition, Heléne Bunot, a French governess, attended to the education of the children, and a cook and her son, a housemaid and a dressmaker assisted with the smooth running of the home."[1]

Also, new friends—such as Archbishop Tait, Lord Coleridge, W. T. Stead, and Dr. Lightfoot, the bishop of Durham—had joined in the defense of the Army when it encountered opposition. These and other friends were doubtless a bit astonished at the tactics that the Army was continuing to use to attract the masses, but they were nevertheless interested in the broader principle of the Army's right to conduct its religious life as it saw fit. Also, the number of those attracted to the Army was growing significantly, and so English clergy, as was true of Wesley's day, looked wistfully and perhaps a bit jealously at the Army's evangelistic drive, its strong sense of mission, its appeal to the masses, and its growth.

The Salvation Army and the Church of England

The year 1882 was critical in the history of the Army and in the shaping of William Booth's thinking about several theological matters. Up to this time the Army's relationship with the churches, and especially with the Church of England, had been tenuous. The Army was beginning to evolve into a denomination, with all the structures and appearances of what would be called a church. Unfortunately, neither William nor Catherine had developed any particular ecclesiology to match their other theological loyalties, and at this point William Booth's view of what constituted the church was rather weak. He had not had to consider what happens to a sectarian movement when it moves into a second generation.

Various denominations had opinions about The Salvation Army, but Catherine was always ready to affirm that "neither are we diverse from the Churches in the great fundamental doctrines of Christianity."[2] Generally, the Methodists were open to what the Booths were doing, and some Methodist groups were even enthusiastic about their work.[3] Indeed, in 1880 William was asked to address the Wesleyan Conference, an invitation that must have pleased Booth who was reared in Wesleyan Methodism. Likewise, during his earlier independent ministry the Wesleyan Methodists had banned William from their pulpits. Booth spoke about the reasons for the success of The Salvation Army. As David Malcolm Bennett writes, "Booth had never been one to bear grudges, unlike his wife, so it is unlikely that at any time in his address he gloated to the assembled Methodists. But there can be little doubt that he spoke with great satisfaction, and saw the invitation as justification of all he had stood for over the years."[4] Bennett goes on to note the most important reason for this address:

> In some ways this was an important step in The Salvation Army becoming accepted by respectable Christians. Before this Booth and his followers had been accepted and supported by individuals from various classes and religious denominations, while others had looked on in puzzlement, disapproval, or horror. But for the first time here was a large and influential denomination giving its seal of approval to his work.[5]

And even Cardinal Manning of the Roman Catholic Church commented at length on The Salvation Army in his article in *The Contemporary Review*.[6] In a sense, however, giving some kind of definition to a growing Army was forced upon William Booth by the Anglican Church. Anglican clergy at this time had mixed views about The Salvation Army. Some, like the bishop of Carlisle, were positively antagonistic, but others, like Archbishop Tait, were supportive and even eventually subscribed to the Army's appeal to purchase the Eagle Tavern and Grecian Theatre in London, two rather notorious properties in London off of City Road, and to turn them into a place for religious meetings.[7] The bishop of Chichester perhaps summarized much Anglican opinion when in November 1882, in speaking of the Army, he warned his audience, "Let us beware of looking at them with indifference or contempt or dislike, lest haply we be found to fight against God."[8] Likewise, J. A. Atkinson, in a paper entitled "The Salvation Army and the Church," stated the following:

> What should be the attitude of the Church towards The Salvation Army? In my opinion, neither that of opposition nor condemnation. The Army is employed in a good work, to which the Church herself ought to have been equal, but which she has neglected to perform. God's blessing has manifestly been on the movement. How far the Army should be encouraged and supported by Churchmen is a question which will be differently answered by different minds. My own feelings are in sympathy with it, and I think it ought to be welcomed wherever it will undertake its distinctive mission of winning to Christ those whom no religious bodies have hitherto been able to reach.[9]

Differences of opinion notwithstanding, the leadership of the Anglican Church could not ignore the popular attraction of Booth and his Army at home, as well as the expansion of the Army into other countries including the United States, Canada, Australia, France, Switzerland, Sweden, and India. "William Booth was now not merely the head of an unsectarian mission society in England, but the General of an Army which [was] spreading its influence to all parts of the world."[10] Anglican leaders also undoubtedly looked back at the relationship of the Church with the Wesleys and probably pondered whether or not Anglicanism could have kept Methodism within the fold with some creative conversation and negotiations from both sides. However, "though Wesley repeatedly affirmed that he had no desire for Methodism to leave the Church of England, he was realistic enough to prepare for just such a possibility."[11]

Also with a loss of clergy, an entrenched bureaucratic and organizational system that could not meet the needs of growing urbanization, and the loss of many Anglicans to Roman Catholicism due to the impact of the Oxford Movement, the Anglican Church was losing ground quickly, especially in ministry among the working classes. Norman Murdoch wrote,

> As a direct result of its establishment, the Church of England suffered enormous losses in the late-nineteenth century. According to Peter d'A. Jones the church was losing strength relative to the Nonconformists at the same time its identification with the ruling classes injured its image with the urban masses it hoped to reach. Its organization was "top-heavy, inflexible, and unwieldy." It was no match for either the "direct tactics of The Salvation Army" or the "self-governing congregations of the urban sects."[12]

Archbishop Tait "spoke favourably of the Army in the House of Lords, and he explored the possibility of bringing the Army under the aegis of the established Church."[13] In 1882 the Upper House of Convocation appointed a committee first "to issue general instructions to the Church on its attitude toward the Army"[14] and second to investigate the possibility of a union of The Salvation Army with the Anglican Church. One who was present on the committee recorded that the negotiations lasted for several months. The committee was impressive, consisting of the following members: Dr. Edward White Benson, the chair of the committee, then bishop of Truro who was appointed archbishop of Canterbury in January 1883; Dr. J. B. Lightfoot, then bishop of Durham; Canon B. F. Westcott, who followed Lightfoot as the bishop of Durham; Canon Wilkinson, later bishop of Truro and St. Andrews; and Dr. Randall J. Davidson, then dean of Windsor and chaplain to his father-in-law the archbishop of Canterbury, Dr. Archibald Tait, who in 1903 became the archbishop of Canterbury.[15]

The negotiations—that were, incidentally, on all accounts quite respectful from both sides—continued until early 1883.[16] The negotiations eventually centered on three questions. First, should a union be accomplished what would be the place of William Booth? Would he be accorded some kind of ecclesiastical office given the fact that he had raised an Army within the space of a few years that rivaled in some places the strength of the Anglican Church? Second, what would be the place for Army officers in the Anglican Church, and especially the female officers? It became particularly evident that the best that could be hoped for the female officers was that they would be appointed as deaconesses. Ordination for women officers was at that time out of the question. Finally, and inextricably connected with the issue of the possible ordination of officers (and the exclusion of female officers from ordination and therefore from administering the sacraments as they had done in the Army), what would be the Army's position on the sacraments, a question already being raised by Catherine Booth and George Scott Railton?

These negotiations continued for about a year, but by 1883 it was clear that there would be no official connections between the Church of England and the Army, and the proposal that the Army be linked to Anglicanism as a Church Salvation Army came to nothing. There were many reasons for this, and it is clear from correspondence that the Army was not as forthcoming in the negotiations as it should have been, especially in answering in writing specific questions placed before the Army by the Anglican Church.[17] William Booth was hesitant. First, there were still Anglican leaders, such as the bishops of Oxford and Hereford, parading scandalous accusations against the Army, and especially the worship services of the Army. While one has to admit that there were certainly excesses in some indoor and outdoor worship services, and while some Salvationists were not discreet when speaking about organized religion, nevertheless, the bishops' accusations that the Army was conducting "Creeping for Jesus" meetings at midnight in their barracks (Preaching Stations) at which time all the lights were turned out and the worshipers crept around on the floor, were patently absurd. The fact that the Booths had to entertain such accusations was ridiculous. Needless to say, the bishops later recanted their statements for lack of evidence. In spite of exaggerated stories about early Army meetings, both William and Catherine Booth were concerned during the early Army days about displays that appeared to be comical or vulgar. Their public meetings stressed singing especially of the hymns of the Wesleys, sermons, and opportunities for people to kneel at the mercy seat to ask forgiveness of sins or seek holiness of heart.

Second, it became increasingly clear that Booth, although constantly protesting that he did not want to create a new sect, was doing just that, and he refused to give up his autocratic control of the Army to the leadership of the Anglican Church. Randall Davidson's "objection to the General's autocratic rule was the insuperable barrier to any union between the Army and the Church."[18] St. John Ervine described this final decision:

> Why Dr. Davidson, now that Booth had brought his forces to a high state of efficiency and popularity, should have expected him to yield them to other people, some of whom had striven, and were still striving, to destroy them, is hard to understand. Booth, though he might appear unimpressive to Dr. Davidson, had done what Dr. Davidson had not: made an Army where none had been, and had sent it fighting across the world. As the General sat and listened to the young Dean of Windsor and gazed round the room at the distinguished ecclesiastics who had come to solicit his co-operation, he must have felt a glow of pride in his heart as he reflected that he had achieved what none of them had achieved, and that the once absurd evangelist who banged a Bible and waved an umbrella to attract attention on Mile End Waste, was now being entreated to help the Established Church to relate itself to the poor! . . . Booth had not raised his Army to be spoil for the Church of England: he had raised it to make war on hell. And he, better than any of these bishops and canons and deans, knew how to lead it into battle. God helping him, he would die at its head.[19]

But for all of Booth's theological sensitivities, his lack of an ecclesiology at this point proved to be problematic. These negotiations forced the issue upon Booth: Was the Army to continue as a sectarian movement, or was it to become another denomination? Was the Army merely a sect or was it a church? While other aspects of Booth's theology were strong and well founded by this time, he had no sustaining doctrine of the church that provided a theological framework as his movement evolved into a denomination in succeeding generations. Now that he had distinguished himself from the Anglican Church, Booth should have confronted the question about the identification of his movement. But he failed to do so. When it served his purpose he referred to the Army as a

Mary Booth, William Booth's mother.

Catherine Booth in Army uniform.

The Booth family: Catherine, William, and children.

William Booth in later ministry.

Catherine Booth on her deathbed in 1890.

William Booth Motor Car Campaign.

William Booth meeting Swazi chiefs in his Hadley Wood home in 1907.

Funeral cortege of William Booth on August 28, 1912.

movement for salvation purposes, but at other times he used churchly language when speaking of the Army. The weakness of Booth's understanding of the church was exacerbated by the fact that Booth's evangelistic nature did not allow for the nurture of the saints. In spite of Booth's Wesleyan heritage, he failed to appreciate the place of the class meetings for Salvationists. Although many were won to Christ through the revivalistic impulse of the Booths and their Army, the Army was not sustained in future generations by the nurturing inclinations of Methodism. At this time, Booth was unclear about what his newly founded movement would become, and nowhere was this matter more obvious than in his deciding whether or not the Army would retain its observance of the sacraments.

The Salvation Army and the Sacraments

In an article in *The Contemporary Review* Randall Davidson stated that regarding the sacraments "there seems still to be much uncertainty in the Army's Councils."[20] It is clear that at this point William Booth and the other leadership—principally Catherine Booth, Bramwell Booth, and George Scott Railton—had not made a firm decision about the sacraments. Should they be administered more regularly by the Army? Should the Army negotiate with the Anglican Church about sacramental observance at the local level by Salvationists at the Anglican Church? Should the Army drop observance of the sacraments altogether?

In this light, and heavily influenced by Catherine's growing suspicions of rites and rituals and liturgies, which she was convinced were often covers for sham religion, Booth had to deal with the sacramental question. Both baptism and the Lord's Supper had been administered in The Christian Mission and in the early days of The Salvation Army.[21] The record is unclear as to the prominence of either ordinance during this time.[22] However, it was evident that especially the sacrament of the Lord's Supper was causing some grief in the hearts of William Booth's closest advisors such as Catherine or George Scott Railton, and this was so even though both Catherine and Railton, like William, were reared in Wesleyan Methodism and found comfort in the sacraments. As late as 1853, after receiving the Lord's Supper in Dr. Thomas's church, Catherine "told William, 'It has been a very long time since I felt so deeply in this calling to remembrance my Saviour's sufferings.' This suggests that though on this occasion observing the Lord's Supper had left a definite mark upon her, this was not usually the case."[23] It is possible that this was such a wonderful occasion for Catherine because the taking of the sacrament was so well connected to the biblical preaching of Dr. Thomas, whom Catherine so admired. Nevertheless, both Railton and Catherine were convinced that some people were relying on the ordinances for their eternal salvation, thus denying the biblical doctrine of salvation by grace. They were likewise concerned about the disunity of the church caused by differences of opinion about the nature and administration of the sacraments. These differences threatened the unity of the church and jeopardized the church's mission to a fallen world.

In spite of such misgivings, William Booth was reluctant to dismiss the sacraments, especially the Lord's Supper. Indeed, as late as July 1881 *The War Cry* reported that "on Sunday morning we administered the Sacrament of the Lord's Supper to about 120 soldiers; it was a glorious time and the power of God was evident."[24] There are likewise *War Cry* reports that on two successive Good Friday services at the Army's headquarters there was the partaking of the Lord's Supper.[25] Likewise, upon occasion, the visitation of entire corps to local Anglican churches for the Sacrament of the Lord's Supper had been arranged.[26] Indeed, Susie Swift, a Vassar graduate and an Episcopalian who met the Army in Scotland in 1884, worked for the Army on its International Headquarters, and eventually became an officer in The Salvation Army before leaving the Army and entering a Roman Catholic order, wrote about the days when she worked on headquarters: "To those who find it hard to understand how an Episcopalian of 'High' tastes could work with the Army, I answer that the Army taught in those days that it was 'not a church but a mission' and placed no obstacle in the way of my receiving the 'sacraments' of my own or any other denomination."[27]

However, it is evident that Booth was being pressed to decide on the sacramental question, the major issue being not baptism but the Lord's Supper.[28] St. John Ervine noted "that abortive conference confirmed Booth in his determination, first made on Mile End Waste, to keep separate from churches. It confirmed him, too, in his opposition to the use of sacraments."[29] However, Ervine's observation is not accurate. Booth was less decisive on this matter than was usual for an admitted autocrat, probably because he had not yet been settled in his own mind about the future of the Army as either a church or a permanent mission to the poor. His tentativeness about this is best seen in his *War Cry* article of January 17, 1883, entitled "The General's New Year Address to Officers":

Now if the Sacraments are not conditions of Salvation; if there is a general division of opinion as to the proper mode of administering them, and if the introduction of them would create division of opinion and heartburning, and if we are not professing to be a church, nor aiming at being one, but simply a force for aggressive Salvation purposes, is it not wise for us to postpone any settlement of the question, to leave it over to some future day, when we shall have more light, and see more clearly our way before us?

Meanwhile, we do not prohibit our own people in any shape or form from taking the Sacraments. We say, "If this is a matter of your conscience, by all means break bread."[30]

This statement is remarkable for three reasons, the first being that it is highly unusual for Booth not to give a final and definitive answer on any topic and every decision affecting the Army. Booth was used to stating decisions that he expected to be obeyed without question.[31] Second, Booth did not bring closure to the matter, but postponed the settlement of the question to some future day. It is impossible to know precisely what he meant by this. Booth's reticence to close the door on this discussion gives credence to Begbie's observation that "to his life's end, certainly for many long years after his decision, he was occasionally disturbed as to its [giving up the sacraments] wisdom."[32] Finally, Booth did not prohibit Salvationists from taking the sacraments, but went on in that article to describe his own theological understanding of the Lord's Supper and baptism.

Meanwhile, Cardinal Manning, while appreciating the work of the Army, was perplexed by Booth's protestations that the Army would not become a sect, but nevertheless wished to maintain absolute autocratic control over this newly energized movement. Precisely why the Army would retain absolute autocratic control if not to establish itself as a sect was unclear to Manning, whose own perception was that eventually Booth would establish another denomination. Manning wrote:

Mr. Booth declares his firm resolve the Salvation Army shall never become a sect. He cites the failure of John Wesley in his attempt to maintain an unsectarian position. The meaning of this would seem to be that the aim of the Salvation Army is to promote general and personal religion apart from all bodies and, apart from all controversies. . . . The head of the Salvation Army is resolved that it shall never become a sect. . . . He seems to wish that it may not be a sect but a spirit which, like the four winds, may blow upon all the valley of dry bones—men, women, children, sects, communions, and, as he perhaps would say, Churches, quickening and raising them to a higher life. . . . Nevertheless we have a conviction that the Salvation Army will either become a sect, or it will melt away. This world is not the abode of disembodied spirits.[33]

As late as 1895, in an interview with Sir Henry Lunn, William Booth expressed again his various opinions about the sacraments, stressing yet once more his emphasis on conversion and the subsequent holy life and holy living as the essence of the Christian gospel. Booth feared anything that would detract from that, and in that interview readily admitted that "we have found the existing notions with reference to these ordinances seriously interfering with the inculcation of right views of penitence and holy living. Men and women are constantly in danger of putting their trust in ordinances, and thinking that baptized communicants must be in a secure position, no matter how inconsistently they are living."[34]

While that statement underscores Booth's theology of redemption as the central doctrine by which he measured the doctrine and practice of the church, that interview is interesting for two other reasons. First, Booth reiterated many years later what he had said in his *War Cry* article in January 1883: "Moreover, I should like to emphasize the fact that this with us is not a settled question. We never disclaim against the Sacraments; we never even state our own position. We are anxious not to destroy the confidence of Christian people in institutions which are helpful to them."[35]

Second, Lunn's questioning of Booth also caused Booth to reiterate something else that he had stated earlier in the January 1883 *War Cry* article. Lunn completed the interview by asking the General this question: "Would you be willing to sanction your soldiers being baptized and partaking of the Lord's Supper if they desired? To this the General gave an unqualified answer in the affirmative."[36] In fact, this had already been officially sanctioned in *The Doctrines and Disciplines of The Salvation Army, 1885*. In Section 26—Baptism, Question #6 asks, "What is the teaching of the Army on the subject of the Lord's Supper?" The answer given is, "When such an ordinance is helpful to the faith of our Soldiers, we recommend its adoption."[37]

For better of for worse Booth finally made the decision of the non-observance of the sacraments for his own Army, with no indication of precisely when the matter would be open for future discussion. Here is one significant place where he made a departure from his Wesleyan and Methodist heritage, and this is the one doctrinal area where the

Methodists were uncomfortable with the Army. Methodists were concerned that "the sacraments were almost wholly ignored,"[38] and any claim by Booth to be a devout follower of John Wesley—whose decided opinion of the sacraments as means of grace was strong and who admonished the frequent partaking of the Lord's Supper—was somewhat mitigated by his nonobservance of the sacraments.

What many Methodists undoubtedly did not understand is that the nonobservance came largely through taking the doctrine of holiness to its logical conclusion. Catherine Booth argued that if all of life is holy, if all of life is a visible sign of God's invisible grace, then any particular observance was unnecessary. She had also correctly concluded even in her earlier years that salvation comes by God's grace alone. These theological convictions, along with Catherine Booth's suspicion of formality, liturgy, and ceremonies, provided a convincing argument that the observance of baptism and the Lord's Supper should be dropped by the Army. David Rightmire has noted:

> The emphasis on sacramental living by the early Army leaders was the result of a dialectic between their pragmatic theology and explicit pneumatological presuppositions. The abandonment of sacramental practice by no means implied a denial of the sacramental aspect of life. For the Army, the emphasis was upon the reality of new life in Christ, experienced spiritually. The sacraments, as memorial ritual, were not essential to spiritual religion. What was essential was the necessity of spiritual communion with Christ. This was possible only in the experience of entire sanctification.[39]

Nevertheless, some Methodists perceived dropping sacramental observance as a problem, and were convinced that the problem could be solved by creating a Methodist Army, one of the tasks being to assist the Army in the administration of the sacraments, and also "watch over the care of the young and the pastoral oversight of the converts. . . . They, on the other hand, would furnish suitable spheres of open-air and aggressive work for tens of thousands of our people who . . . are hungering and pining for it, but who do not care to engage in it in any way that separates them from the Methodist Church."[40] Nothing came of any union with the Methodists, and in spite of Booth's move to the nonobservance of the sacraments, Methodists still considered the Booths and the Army to be part of the Methodist family.

A third reason why the negotiations with the established church broke off revolved around the matter of women in ministry, and Pamela Walker well connects the dropping of the sacraments with this critically important issue. Walker noted that the decision to drop the sacraments "reinforced a refusal to countenance distinctions between men's and women's relationship to the sacred. . . . By rejecting material forms of receiving grace, the Army underscored the meaninglessness of outward, human physicality and the significance of the transforming grace of the Holy Spirit."[41] It was indeed such transforming grace that empowered women as well as men for ministry. One does not have to be very creative to hear Catherine Booth speaking up at this point. It became clear that the women of the Army, who had become accustomed to freely preaching, teaching, and perhaps, at times, administering the sacraments, were not going to be allowed those same privileges in the Army's union with Anglicanism. Freedom for female preachers was a distinct Army characteristic, and the Army was proud of its accomplishments in the area of women in ministry.

> For Catherine the relegation of her women officers to deaconesses and the subsequent limitation of their powers was out of the question. Any curtailing of the rights and privileges of women to preach the gospel would be debilitating to the privilege for which Catherine, and by now countless followers, had fought and suffered. Women were equal to men in ministry. That, to Catherine, was clear and nonnegotiable since, in her mind, the justification for it arose from the pages of the Bible itself.[42]

As a result of the discussion with the Anglican Church, the place of women in ministry, firmly established since Christian Mission days, was further enhanced with the decision not to join the Anglican Church. That Church's reluctance—not to say overt opposition—to giving Army women any ecclesiastical place in the Church only strengthened the Army's resolve to affirm its allegiance to an equality of ministry between women and men. Catherine Booth's tract defending the right of women in ministry, originally entitled *Female Teaching* and by now renamed *Female Ministry*, still continued to be read among Salvationists and others. And William, who took some convincing on this subject, was not only theologically convinced of the position taken by the Army, but pragmatically knew that one of the most important reasons for the growth of the Army in the early 1880s was due to the public attention coming the Army's way due to the phenomenon of women in their unique Army dress preaching in streets and in halls all over England. W. T. Stead himself befriended the Army because of his first encounter of hearing women preachers in his hometown of Darlington.

The Anglican Church and the Army went their separate ways, but not before the Church flattered the Army by copying it. As many as four imitations of the Army were formed within Anglicanism in the early 1880s, but the one that endured and was sanctioned by the Anglican Church was the Church Army, founded by Wilson Carlile.[43] In the meantime The Salvation Army moved on at a rather frantic pace—opening up work in other countries, beginning various social ministries as need presented itself, answering its critics, and becoming part of the British public life. The early 1880s witnessed the beginning of the Army in Australia, Canada, France, Germany, India, Italy, New Zealand, South Africa, Sweden, Switzerland, and the United States. And in many of these places, as there was opportunity to demonstrate the gospel of love to God and neighbor, needed social ministries sprang up.

The Salvation Army and the Purity Crusade of 1885

However, no event would better demonstrate the Army's political and social will and impact upon British life than its involvement, primarily through Catherine Booth, in the Purity Crusade of 1885. The Army had already come to public attention—how could it be otherwise with literally thousands of Salvationists marching on the streets of towns and cities of Great Britain every Sunday and often on weeknights to conduct their open-air services, to take their message of redemption to the whosoever? By this time "The Salvation Army was not marching. It was charging."[44] However, if by chance someone had not yet heard of Booth's Army of Salvation, that was about to change. The British public was going to be reading in their newspapers about a national scandal, and the Army would be part of that story.

One of the dirty secrets of Victorian England was that underneath the veneer of respectability was, among other evils, a white-slave trade where girls were sold into prostitution, often by their own families, at the age of twelve or even younger,[45] thus violating the age of consent. The age of consent was "the age up to which it shall be an offense to have or attempt to have carnal knowledge of, or to indecently assault a girl."[46] The age of consent "was set at the age of thirteen in 1875, and three times between 1875 and 1885 the House of Lords passed a bill recommending the raising of the age of consent, all three recommendations failing in the House of Commons."[47] It comes as no surprise that that Army encountered many of these girls in its ministry in East London. The Army's international ministry to women, who were then known as fallen women, begins with a soldier of the Whitechapel Corps by the name of Mrs. Elizabeth Cottrill. She was the converts' sergeant of the corps, the person who ministered to people who went forward to pray at the conclusion of the sermon. In dealing with the young girls who came to the mercy seat after the sermon to pray and to find Jesus, Mrs. Cottrill could hardly send these new converts back to the brothels from whence they came. So beginning in 1881, although she had a large family of her own, she took them into her home on nearby Christian Street.

From this inauspicious ministry, and through the convincing witness of a young girl named Annie Swan who had escaped from a brothel and was found by Bramwell Booth sleeping on the steps of the Army's new international headquarters at 101 Queen Victoria Street, the Army began to investigate and, indeed, expose the vicious white-slave trade in England. The first order of business was to establish homes for these girls, and Bramwell's wife of two years, Florence Soper, was placed in charge of the Army's first rescue home located at 212 Hanbury Street in May 1884. Florence Soper was a woman of privilege, her father being a physician practicing in Wales. However, in spite of her comfortable rearing, she had already been through difficult times with the Army when she assisted the Booths' eldest daughter, Catherine, in beginning the work of the Army in France. This was no easy task as she and her fellow Salvationists withstood the mockery and cruelty of their listeners as they preached the gospel on the streets of Paris and attracted the whosoever to the evening meetings. So Florence Soper Booth was well prepared for battle. Although only in her early twenties, she happily accepted this assignment because she, like her husband, had become morally enraged at what they were beginning to learn about the plight of thousands of young girls in England. Ann R. Higginbotham has written this about Florence Soper Booth:

> Despite her youth and retiring nature . . . Florence Booth succeeded in establishing and expanding Salvationist rescue work. During the nearly thirty years that she headed the Women's Social Services, its operations grew from one rescue home in Whitechapel to 117 homes for women in Britain and around the world. Under the direction of Florence Booth and her assistant Adelaide Cox, a vicar's daughter who joined The Salvation

Army in 1881, the Women's Social Services earned the reputation as one of the largest, most effective, and, to some extent, most innovative rescue organizations in Britain.[48]

In the meantime, Catherine Booth (the elder) entered into the fray and became a leader in the attack upon this social evil. She had been preaching at Midnight Movement meetings for fallen women, and her friendship with Josephine Butler, one of the leaders of that movement, developed.[49] An alliance of religious and social leaders was formed to deal with this matter, but it would have been impossible to bring this social scourge to public attention without the help of the journalist William Thomas Stead, the son of a Congregational minister, "one who exemplified the nonconformist conscience of the nineteenth century,"[50] and a fast friend and supporter of the Booths, especially Catherine and Bramwell. William, however, always had lingering doubts about Stead.[51]

Bramwell Booth convinced Stead of the possible magnitude of the evil of trafficking young women in England and solicited his help. Bramwell Booth used evidence gleaned from several prostitutes of various ages now under the Army's care and from lengthy discussions with the city chamberlain, Benjamin Scott, who had firsthand knowledge of the Continental traffic in young girls and of the magnitude of prostitution in England, particularly London.[52] Others had urged Stead "to probe this traffic in teenagers to the regulated brothels of the Continent—among them Benjamin Scott, 75-year-old Chamberlain of the City of London, head of a committee to expose white-slavers and Benjamin Waugh, founder of the Society for the Prevention of Cruelty to Children. After talks with Scott, Bramwell had felt Stead was the one man in England to help him."[53]

It was Stead who devised a plan to expose this evil and publish in his newspaper, *The Pall Mall Gazette*,[54] stories that would become the forerunners of the sensational journalism of the following century. The plan was complicated and risky—involving the purchasing of a young girl named Eliza Armstrong from her mother. Rebecca Jarrett, formerly a prostitute and procuress but now under the care of the Army, would make the purchase.[55] Eliza would then be certified as a virgin by a midwife, Stead would spend time alone with the girl through the mediation of a Madame who was part of the plot, and Eliza would then be certified again as a virgin. The whole point, of course, was to demonstrate that it was indeed possible to procure a twelve-year-old girl from her parents for the purpose of prostitution in England. Stead then exposed the whole plot, bringing the evil of child prostitution to light in a series of articles in *The Pall Mall Gazette* entitled "The Maiden Tribute of Modern Babylon,"[56] but did not print the articles until Eliza Armstrong and Rebecca Jarrett had been taken to Paris by an Army friend and supporter, Madame Combe. The Queen was not amused and neither were people of polite society. These things, after all, were not discussed in public, and surely not printed in the newspapers for all to read! Stead had his detractors, but also had supporters. One biographer wrote,

> But additional support for Stead quickly came from a wide range of people. Amongst them were: Lord Shaftesbury, Lord Dalhousie, Canon Wilberforce, Charles Haddon Spurgeon (Baptist preacher), Hugh Price Hughes (Methodist leader), Millicent Fawcett (feminist), Percy Bunting (editor of the *Contemporary Review*), Ernest Hart (editor of the *British Medical Journal*), and Auberon Herbert (younger brother of Lord Carnarvon and a keen supporter of the under dog), who offered his country home as a refuge for Stead and his colleagues during the crisis. The first Friday after the exposures had begun the *Pall Mall Gazette* received about a thousand letters. Only one opposed the stand Stead had taken. The tide was turning. The ordinary men and women of Britain had been deeply moved by the revelations, and they were expecting action.[57]

William Booth remained unconvinced of this method of attack, partly because he had suspicions about Stead's motivations, and, of course, partly because he intensely disliked Stead's religious inclinations toward spiritualism. Booth perceived that to be Stead's equivocation of genuine Christianity. As one biographer observed, Booth "never greatly warmed to him."[58] Booth feared that Stead's sensationalism would bring discredit to the Army, and Booth was ever ready to protect the honor of his beloved Army. However, in fewer than five years Stead would use his journalistic skills to help Booth write *In Darkest England and the Way Out*, and in 1891 would write a biography of William Booth, which he concluded by stating that General Booth was "one of the greatest men of our time."[59] In 1912 Booth would speak sympathetically of Stead when he learned that he had gone down on the *Titanic*.

Nevertheless, some lingering feelings of animosity were evidently mutual because in his articles in *The Pall Mall Gazette* Stead made frequent references to the help of Bramwell Booth and others in the Army, but made no mention of the Army itself. Also, in the American edition of his biography of Catherine Booth the book was subtitled *The Founder of The Salvation Army*. In any case, *War Cry* articles clearly demonstrate that William Booth was involved in the Purity Crusade at the level of supporting the crusade with articles and public speeches, although he was not nearly as involved as his wife and his son.

The elaborate plan to expose the evil of white-slavery backfired. Stead's articles both stirred people's consciences and created enemies. Technically, Stead had broken the law in procuring Eliza Armstrong without the father's consent, and the government prosecuted Stead, Bramwell Booth, Rebecca Jarrett, as well as others involved in the plot in two separate trials with two juries. The first trial dealt with a charge of abduction and the second with a charge of indecent assault. Both William and Catherine were indignant that the light of the law should be shed on them rather than upon the predators of young girls. The British public, too, was divided; some, like Josephine Butler, came to the defense of those charged, while others, including those from competitive newspapers, decried Stead's inflammatory method of lifting the veil.

While Bramwell Booth was acquitted, Stead was committed to prison for three months and Rebecca Jarrett for six months. The midwife, Madame Mourez, was committed to six months' hard labor and she died in prison. Stead took his imprisonment for a just cause as a badge of honor, and following his release from prison he wore his prison uniform to work every year on the anniversary date of his imprisonment.[60] Stead was pleased with the support that he received from the Army, but felt that William Booth himself had been noticeably silent during this time. "There is no doubt that Stead felt bitter about the way that William Booth had abandoned him—indeed refused to play any part in the campaign for his remission and release."[61] Following Stead's release from prison there was a rally at Exeter Hall, but as Roy Hattersley writes, "No senior member of the Salvation Army was present at the meeting to hear the hero of the hour express his gratitude for the support which the Army had given him, 'from the Chief of Staff down to the humblest private'— thanks which clearly excluded the commanding General."[62]

There was, however, vindication, in spite of the trials that followed the Purity Crusade. Something permanent arose out of the crusade. Catherine Booth appealed both to Her Majesty and to Prime Minister Gladstone to forward the cause of a bill that was being introduced in the House of Commons. Largely through the efforts of the Army nearly four hundred thousand signatures were gathered and that petition was sent to the House of Commons on July 30, 1885, asking that the age of consent be raised to eighteen.[63] The Criminal Law Amendment Act was passed on August 14, 1885, in conformity with the request of that petition, with the exception that the age of consent was raised to only sixteen. Three previous attempts to raise the age of consent in the House of Commons had failed, and so the passing of this law was especially pleasing to Catherine Booth, Josephine Butler, W. T. Stead, Bramwell Booth, and others who had engaged in this battle.[64]

In the midst of the trial, however, William Booth began questioning the wisdom of organized social ministry that this work was beginning to necessitate. In a letter to Catherine dated November 10, 1885, he wrote:

> I am sure our work has materially suffered by our attention being taken from it to give the other [Purity Crusade]; we may have been paid back to a certain extent, and in the long run much good may be done, but I thoroughly believe in "Salvation" being a panacea for the world's sin and sorrows, and that while there are other medicines that look in the same direction, the largest amount of good can be accomplished, with the least expenditure of time and money, by simply getting the people's souls saved and keeping them saved.[65]

Booth was obviously conflicted at this time about the primary work of the Army. "It is characteristic of him that he hung back from a crusade for sexual purity while his son Bramwell persuaded W. T. Stead to undertake it in the *Pall Mall Gazette*."[66] The day after the sentences were handed down, William Booth was concerned that the Army's time would need to be taken up in protesting the sentences. He wanted the Army to get back to salvation business. "From the outset of this campaign the General had been uneasy about his Army's involvement in it. Apart from any other factor, such issues, he felt, tended to detract from the essential task of preaching the gospel of Jesus Christ."[67] St. John Ervine's assessment that until the time of the Purity Crusade "Booth had devoted his energies exclusively to the spiritual regeneration of the world"[68] is not accurate. There had been attempts to meet the physical needs of people in The Christian Mission with one organized program entitled Food-for-the-Millions, as I pointed out earlier.

But it is fair to say that some years passed before William Booth saw the necessity for giving theological justification to social ministry, and organizing that social ministry in such a way that it moved the Army in new directions of ministry. He simply did not yet understand Stead's grand vision of what Stead referred to as the salvation of the state.

However, Booth's theology would eventually evolve in such a way that he could embrace a broadened vision of redemption, and Stead was one of those pushing and urging him in that direction.

In the meantime, however, there is still much of Booth's story to be told. The 1880s were not only about the advancement and consolidation of the Army but about personal battles and victories as well. And herein the story continues, leading up to 1890, the year of the great turning in the personal lives of the Booths and in the history of The Salvation Army.

TURNING POINTS

Introduction

T he Booths' family life in the 1880s reflected the hectic pace of Army life. William and Catherine were in the center of the storm and much was happening around them. In 1885 the family moved from Clapton Common to 1 Rookwood Road, only one hundred yards north of their Clapton Common home. The work of the Army had become all consuming to the Booths and their family, especially with the Purity Crusade of 1885. The Booth house continued to serve as part home, part office, and part headquarters for the planning of the Army's battles. Catherine maintained the order and discipline of the household with great difficulty, and often wished for a more tranquil life, although she herself was frequently out preaching or opening new corps.

The Booth Family

Bramwell Booth was now the Chief of the Staff and constantly at his father's side. As I mentioned in the previous chapter, he married Florence Soper, a physician's daughter, on October 12, 1882. He knew every aspect of the work of the Army, and was chosen as the natural successor to his father as the next General of the Army when William died. The second child, Ballington, married Maud Charlesworth, a vicar's daughter, on September 17, 1886, she having to wait until after her twenty-first birthday to marry because her father refused his consent to the marriage.[1] Ballington was likewise being groomed for leadership in the Army and was eventually sent to America as his first overseas appointment. The third child and eldest daughter, Catherine, had already suffered persecution and slander when she opened the work of the Army in France and Switzerland. She showed the Booth mettle, however, and, ably assisted by Bramwell's future wife and by her mother's visit to France, she overcame the obstacles of beginning the Army work on what to British eyes was foreign soil. She married Colonel Arthur S. Clibborn, formerly a Quaker and one of the officers who worked with Catherine in France and Switzerland, on February 18, 1887. All the sons-in-law took the Booth name, and so the married name of this couple was Booth-Clibborn.

Emma was especially close to her father. He saw in Emma the same spirit as her mother and in many respects Emma manifested the Christian graces and virtues better than any of the Booth children. She was also bred as a leader in the Army, but was capable of leading with natural Christian humility and with a servant's heart that was difficult, if not impossible, for some of the other Booth children. Emma's untimely death in 1903 is a story yet to be told, but was absolutely devastating to William Booth. He not only lost a daughter, he lost a friend and a confidant.

Emma married Commissioner Frederick Tucker on April 10, 1888, William Booth's fifty-ninth birthday.[2] Even before her marriage, she was already in charge of training female Salvation Army officers. Frederick Tucker had served in the Indian civil service and had joined The Salvation Army in England years earlier. He was reared an Anglican, but was converted in a meeting held by Moody and Sankey in London in 1875. For the wedding he wore the Indian dress and turban of a beggar. He was barefooted and his begging bowl was on the platform during the ceremony. He had gone back to India to commence the work of the Army there in 1882, and now he and Emma, the Booth-Tuckers, would return to India to continue the work together.

Herbert, the third son, was also destined to participate in Salvation Army leadership, serving first in Canada and then in Australia. He married a Dutch Salvationist, Cornelie Ida Ernestine Schoch, on September 18, 1890. Herbert was reluctant to go ahead with the wedding because his mother was so ill at the time and near death. Catherine, however, insisted that the wedding go forward, and her presence at the wedding was symbolized by her picture being placed on a chair on the platform. The three remaining children were daughters. Marian Billups Booth was, as I have mentioned, an invalid all her life and, although given the rank of Staff Captain, never participated in the public life of the Army.[3] Eva Booth never married, was actively engaged in Salvation Army ministry, and became the fourth General of The Salvation Army in 1934. The eighth child, Lucy, married a Swedish Salvation Army officer by the name of Emanuel Daniel Hellberg on October 18, 1894. Apparently one of the Booths' adopted sons, Georgie, eventually moved to America, but there are no further references to him in any written records, diaries, or correspondence after his going to America.

It is beyond question that the children and the sons-in-law and daughters-in-law were in a privileged position in the Army and enjoyed benefits far beyond what other officers received. As if to establish their authority, some of the children had titles as well as rank, and so, for example, Ballington was known as the Marshal, Catherine was known as La Maréchale, Emma was the Consul, Eva (Evangeline) the Commander, and Herbert the Commandant. When rank-and-file officers were ill they often had to keep working. When one of the Booths was ill, arrangements were often made for months of recuperation. William and Catherine Booth had established a visible family dynasty, and this came to the notice of other officers in the Army and caused some hard feelings. Probably both William and Catherine passed this sense of privilege on to their children, and as one biographer has commented, William "genuinely believed that to be a Booth was to be one of the Lord's anointed. *The War Cry* exalted them each week."[4]

The problem of according such a privileged place for the Booth children and spouses was especially exacerbated because not everyone in the Army viewed all of the Booth children or their spouses as possessed of the extraordinary gifts and abilities needed for the work and responsibilities that were given to them. Some of them achieved rank and privilege only by virtue of being children of William and Catherine or being married to one of the Booth children. And, especially in later life, the potential for leadership that some of the children had was mitigated by petty jealousies and a love for bureaucratic control over other people. On the other hand, some of the Booth children earned their rank because of their natural gifts of leadership. And some, such as Emma, were able to exercise their leadership within the Army with great humility, while others often failed to demonstrate the Christian graces necessary for leadership within a Christian context. The complicated relationship of William to his grown children as well as the relationships among the children themselves will be dealt with in another chapter.

William Booth's International Travels

It was during this time that William Booth began to travel far and wide to visit his growing Army. One of the first expressions of the Army beyond the borders of Great Britain was to America. The first excursion to America was actually during The Christian Mission days. James Jermy had taken the Mission to Cleveland, Ohio, as early as 1872, but the work lasted only until 1876 when Jermy returned to England. In 1879 a young Salvation Army officer, Eliza Shirley, sailed to America with her mother, Annie, to join the father of the family, Amos, in Philadelphia where he had gone to find work. The Shirleys unofficially began the work of the Army in America, rather inauspiciously in an abandoned chair factory. The numbers of those attending the meetings were disappointing, but the Shirleys persevered in the work, with Eliza being promoted to Captain.

There was apparently enough promise in the reports that were being sent to William Booth that he decided to send George Scott Railton to open the work officially. Edward McKinley, in his incomparable history of The Salvation Army in America, begins his book with an apt description of the landing of Railton on American shores:

> They came to launch a great crusade. By all odds, they should have failed on the spot, outright and finally. Led by an amiable eccentric as single-minded as an arrow in flight (who nonetheless proved in the end to be as ill-fitted to this grand endeavor as he was to many smaller ones) were seven women so graceless that their leader referred to them affectionately as "half-a-dozen ignoramuses." This was the pioneer party of The Salvation Army. They struggled with a flag, luggage, and the other passengers down the gangplank of the steamer *Australia* at Castle Garden, New York City, on March 10, 1880, to claim America for God.[5]

But from that inauspicious beginning the Army began to grow in America, and Booth saw potential there for the development of his Army. No wonder, then, that Booth chose North America as his first overseas visit. Only six years after the landing of Railton and his party, the Army in the United States reported 238 corps and 569 officers, and Booth saw great promise in the continued advancement of the Army in the United States. He was also delighted with his visit to Canada on that trip. Both James Jermy and George Scott Railton, on two separate occasions, had had a brief ministry in Canada, and Army work had been opened there informally by two young men, Jack Addie and Joe Ludgate, both converts of the Army in England. They met each other at a revival meeting in London, Ontario, and decided, with no official backing from England, that they would begin the work of the Army in Canada. Attired in their makeshift uniforms they held their first open-air service on May 21, 1882, and "by the end of 1883 more than 200 corps and outposts were being worked by over 400 officers. During that year alone 20,000 persons had been recorded as having knelt at the penitent-forms of the Army. The first building to be erected by The Salvation Army in Canada was opened in Toronto in May 1883."[6] And by the time Booth visited Canada, Thomas B. Coombs, the youthful Commissioner, only in his twenties, was in charge of the work in Canada.

As one would expect, Booth's personal reflections of his travels through his correspondence with Catherine and Bramwell are filled with glowing reports. There is no reason to doubt that the work of the Army in North America was prospering at this time in spite of a near disastrous secession of the National Commander of The Salvation Army in America, Thomas E. Moore, who, upon leaving formed The Salvation Army of America, took many officers and soldiers with him, and confused the general public about which was the real Salvation Army. Frank Smith was sent from England in 1884 to replace Moore, and Booth's first visit to the United States was critical toward consolidating the work of the Army there. Edward McKinley wrote:

> A major factor in the Booth triumph was Booth himself. Effective in the print—his *War Cry* letters were widely read—the General was overpowering in person. His first trip outside the British Isles came in the fall of 1886, when he arrived in America, via Canada, to survey the distant front and to encourage the loyalists. The Army was not only encouraged; it was delirious.... The decline of Moore's troops became precipitate.[7]

And Booth, of course, was flattered when the most popular Methodist minister in St. Johns, New Brunswick "greeted me on Friday night on leaving for Halifax in the most respectful and affectionate manner, saying that next to John Wesley he hailed me benefactor to the world."[8]

Catherine Booth's Illness and Death

William Booth returned home from a personally uplifting visit to a time of extreme personal sorrow. Catherine was ill, and in the summer of 1888 the family moved from their Rookwood Road home to Hadley Wood "thinking that even purer air might help improve Catherine's health."[9] In Catherine's consultation with an eminent physician, Sir James Paget, she learned that she had cancer and that she would live only another couple of years at the most.[10] She was alone when she heard the news, and her ride home in the cab must have been sad indeed. William was waiting for her at home, preparing for a trip to Holland. He ran out to greet her and helped her up the front stairs of their home and into the parlor. She broke the news to William, and years later he reflected on that moment:

> I was stunned. I felt as if the whole world was coming to a standstill. She talked like a heroine, like an angel, to me. She talked as she had never talked before. I could say nothing. I could only kneel with her and try to pray.
>
> I was due in Holland for some large meetings. I had arranged to travel there that very night. She would not hear of my remaining home for her sake. Never shall I forget starting out that evening, with the mournful tidings weighing like lead upon my heart. Oh, the conflict of that night journey! I faced two large congregations, and did my best, although it seemed to me that I spoke as one in a dream. Leaving the meetings to be continued by others, I returned to London the following evening. And then followed, for me, the most painful experience of my life. To go home was anguish. To be away was worse. Life became a burden, almost too heavy to be borne, until God in a very definite manner comforted my heart.[11]

Catherine preached her last sermon on June 21, 1888, at the City Temple, the church of the well-known preacher, Dr. Joseph Parker.[12] She was feeling the effects of her illness and at the conclusion of her sermon had to sit quietly on the platform to regain her strength. Some officers then helped her into a cab for the journey home. Other private appearances followed, but there was never a public occasion such as this again for a woman who had become such a well-known preacher in Britain. She was able to attend some subsequent Salvation Army events, and as late as April 10, 1889, she managed to attend the sixtieth birthday celebrations for William held in Clapton Congress Hall.[13] However, her appearance at the City Temple gave her opportunity to deliver her last sermon, and for that reason this appearance is of historical importance.[14]

In 1889 Catherine was taken to Clacton-on-Sea, Essex, so that she could die near the sea as she had wished. The home there was made into a kind of headquarters away from London so that William could spend as much time with Catherine as possible. The Booths continued their family life and William continued his work as normally as possible under such sad and, at times, excruciating circumstances. Catherine lingered, ever welcoming visitors and dictating correspondence whenever possible. Staff-Captain Carr was a faithful nurse to Catherine. There were times when Catherine was sure that the end was near and the family gathered around the bed.[15] These deathbed scenes continued for some time. But Catherine was stronger than she knew. Henry Rack reminds his readers that these deathbed scenes were not uncommon to the life and culture of the Methodism that Catherine knew so well. He wrote:

> Almost as important for the early Methodists as a life well lived was a death well died, and indeed a number of short accounts of Methodist worthies in the *Magazine* were simply extended deathbed scenes with little else; blow by blow accounts of the last scenes were a prominent feature of all biographies. This kind of account has a long pedigree in Christian hagiography, and once again the old Puritans provide the closest parallel to the Methodist variety.... The histories of holy dyings were valued, as a later Nonconformist said, "to perfume the name of the deceased; to console surviving mourners; to gratify descendants; and to instruct and edify the church." They were also a proof of the truths taught by the dying saint: an important part of Methodist apologetic.[16]

Mercifully on October 4, 1890, Catherine was promoted to glory. William was inconsolable. Catherine Booth lay in state in the Army's Clapton Congress Hall, and an estimated fifty thousand people filed past her coffin. There was a long procession to Abney Park Cemetery where she was buried. William delivered an address at the cemetery and spoke of his love for Catherine. With the death of Catherine Booth ended one of the great love stories of the Victorian world.[17]

William left the funeral determined to continue the work to which God had called him and Catherine alike, although to continue it in loneliness. Truth to tell, after Catherine's death "nothing was the same again in either the Salvation Army or the family which founded it."[18] William wrote in his diary on October 14, 1890: "And now I am restarted on the same path, the same work. A large part of my company has gone before, and I must travel the journey, in a sense that only those can understand who have been through it, alone."[19]

William Booth's Social Ministry

William had no idea when he penned those words of the tumultuous times facing him, for it was at the time of Catherine Booth's death that William published *In Darkest England and the Way Out* to outline the social problems that the Army was encountering as well as the solutions to those problems. However, the book was also written to raise money for the ever-developing social ministries in The Salvation Army. The inauguration of that ministry signaled another turning point in the life of William Booth and his Salvation Army in 1890.

As I previously mentioned, The Christian Mission had no organized social ministry, save the Food-for-the-Millions program, administered by Bramwell Booth and James Flawn, which ran from 1870 to 1874. Each Mission Preaching Station tried to meet human need as much as possible, but no organized, centrally controlled ministry to the poor was undertaken in those days except for that Food-for-the-Millions program. What moved William and Catherine Booth as they surveyed Whitechapel Road in East London was that men and women were living in rebellion against God. They were sinners who needed to be saved, and the preaching of both Booths called sinners to repentance and raised up saints in the life intended by God. Once The Christian Mission was established, the purpose of the Mission was to save sinners and raise up saints after the model provided by William and Catherine Booth, George Scott Railton, and others. This emphasis was continued after the founding of The Salvation Army in 1878. The Booths were not unsympathetic to the physical plight of people, but that aspect of ministry was relatively unimportant to them initially.

In explaining the change from The Christian Mission to The Salvation Army, Booth affirmed this single mission.

> We are a Salvation people—this is our specialty—getting saved and keeping saved, and then getting somebody else saved, and then getting saved ourselves more and more, until full salvation on earth makes the heaven within, which is finally perfected by the full salvation without, on the

other side of the river. . . . My brethren, my comrades, soul saving is our avocation, the great purpose and business of our lives. Let us seek first the kingdom of God, let us be SALVATIONISTS indeed.[20]

In defining the work of The Salvation Army to the Wesleyan Conference in August 1880, Booth stated that "we go on the three broad lines of Repentance, Faith, and Holiness of Heart."[21] One would search in vain in this entire address in which he set forth the principles of The Salvation Army, and in many similar addresses during this period, to find any references to soup kitchens or lodging houses, let alone any biblical or theological justification for the extended ministry of social salvation. William Booth and his Salvation Army were still involved in the single mission of converting sinners. That, it was thought, was the highest service that could be rendered to the poor. "This impulse was purely evangelical; it did not become what is called humanitarian or economic till ten years later. At its beginning, The Salvation Army was a society of men and women which existed only to preach the repentance of sins."[22]

However, others in the movement began to recognize the complexity of their ministry, and there dawned an awareness in some of Booth's officers and soldiers that it was not enough to preach the gospel to the poor, but that preaching had to be complemented by taking care of the physical needs of the poor. And so it is a fact of history that the organized social ministry of The Salvation Army did not begin at the initiation of William Booth in East London, but with Salvationists in Melbourne, Australia, with the establishment of a halfway house for released prisoners.[23] The center was opened on December 8, 1883, as a kind of loving Christian reversal to the brutal transportation of the "criminal class" from England to Australia to empty English prisons of all those unwanted citizens.

> In their most sanguine moments, the authorities hoped that it would eventually swallow up a whole class—the "criminal class," whose existence was one of the prime sociological beliefs of late Georgian and early Victorian England. Australia was settled to defend English property not from the frog-eating invader across the Channel but from the marauder within. English lawmakers wished not only to get rid of the "criminal class" but if possible to forget about it.[24]

Little wonder that the compassion of these English Salvationists toward their countrymen was manifested in this practical way. "Within four years five such centres had been set up in the state capital, and Booth dis-patched an officer from England to Australia to study how this develop-ment could be applied to the home base."[25]

It was not until 1884 that social work began in an organized fashion in Booth's backyard, as it were. The rescue home for prostitutes, the Purity Crusade, and the Criminal Law Amendment Act, which came as a result of that ministry were prime examples of this social work. In the mean-time, various officers and soldiers continued to involve themselves in diverse aspects of social ministry. In Toronto, Canada, in 1886 the Army opened the first institution to give attention to alcoholic women, and in 1887 there was the opening of a daycare center in one of the "slum posts" of London so that working mothers could be relieved of the responsibil-ity of their children.

The crippling dock strike in 1889 "tested the faith of settlers and Salvationists who responded with sympathy, enthusiasm and practical aid."[26] A food and shelter center for the homeless was established in the West India Dock Road. In 1889 a women's shelter was opened on Hanbury Street, and on June 29, 1890, The Salvation Army opened the first "Elevator," a "sheltered workshop" for men.

However, until 1889 Booth was still making few public pronounce-ments about these social operations. He was apparently pleased with the initiative that his people were showing in taking care of the needs of the people. But his theology still reflected only a single purpose for his Army—that of winning souls. A typical article of Booth's is found in *The War Cry* from January 1887. After a thirteen-week journey of sixteen thousand miles, he wrote, "I have come back with the impression that the need of the world is bigger than ever I thought it was, and I have also come back with the impression that The Salvation Army is equal to it, if The Salvation Army will only do its duty."[27] In the entire article Booth made no reference to a second mission, to social salvation, or to social work. His references were only to the soul-saving mission of The Salvation Army and to spiritual redemption.

The magnitude of the social problems that The Salvation Army was addressing in Great Britain came into sharp focus during the mid-1880s. Booth's sensitivity to the poor, to whom he had been preaching for many years, was heightened through the experiences of his Army. A severe economic depression had taken its toll in England, and the effects of that depression manifested themselves in the places where Booth's Army was at work, "1873 being the date normally given for the beginning of the 'great depression' and 1874 as the beginning of the nineteenth century disaster to British agriculture."[28]

An analysis of poverty, homelessness, unemployment, and religion in East London originally entitled *Life and Labour of the People* was written by Charles Booth in 1889, and was eventually expanded into the seventeen-volume work entitled *Life and Labour of the People in London*.[29] But the first volume was published before William Booth published his *In Darkest England and the Way Out*, and so William Booth made use of Charles Booth's work, and was disturbed by the plight of the people with whom the Army and he had been working and to whom the gospel had been preached. There is no question that "[William] Booth wrote *In Darkest England* against a background of both social unrest and growing political concern."[30] Hattersley has written:

> In the previous year, the London dockers had struck for a standard wage of sixpence an hour and, after a month of picketing and protest, won. Public opinion—at least the increasingly educated and articulate working classes—was on their side. The dockers—casual labourers who reported for work each day, but worked at best for three, had once been the powerless poor. But, although they remained amongst the worst paid of British workers, by 1889 they were powerful enough to defeat the increasingly prosperous dock owners. Part of their success was due to the energy and ability of their leader, Ben Tillet. But Tom Mann and John Burns guaranteed the dockers' success by bringing out the engineers "in sympathy." Victory for organized labour was, in itself, frightening enough for the political establishment. But building on the experience of the dock strike Tillet, Burns and Mann began to organize unskilled workers. The result was the powerful force of New Unionism. And it was created by men who might—had their inclination not been for politics—have marched with the Salvation Army. Tillet was brought up a Methodist. Mann and Burns were campaigners for total abstinence from drink. Their great victory was won on the battlefield of London's East End where William Booth had first taken up arms against the devil. New Unionism and the Salvation Army were for the poor and of the poor.[31]

Finally it was decided that an office be created to coordinate the social reform operations of The Salvation Army. Therefore, by 1890 the tentative efforts of The Salvation Army at social reform were placed under the office of what became known as the Social Reform Wing of The Salvation Army, commanded by Commissioner Frank Smith.[32] Smith played a significant part in moving General Booth's sympathies in the direction of social ministry. And a "Darkest England" Trust Deed was executed on January 30, 1891, in a public meeting in St. James's Hall, London.[33] To answer critics of the Darkest England Scheme that the money was misused, a Committee of Inquiry was established and a report was issued on December 19, 1892, completely exonerating the Army and its General. Booth had always been very careful to give an accurate account of funds given to The Christian Mission and The Salvation Army.

With the establishment of that Social Reform Wing, The Salvation Army entered into a new stage of its ministry under the direction of its General, which one biographer has characterized as "an immense change in the direction of the Army."[34] Booth and his Army finally recognized institutionally the importance of the second mission that had gradually gained acceptance. In 1889 and 1890 the commitment to social salvation became fixed. The timing was significant in the history of The Salvation Army. Hitherto its chief concern had been for personal salvation from sin, and social concerns were secondary, but increasing in importance. Now, however, the movement was engaged in two works—personal salvation and social salvation. It now had, as I have mentioned, a dual mission. There is little evidence to substantiate John Kent's statement that "*Darkest England* appeared when the original religious basis of the Army was proving too weak to sustain the initial success."[35] In fact, it is altogether possible that the opposite is true—that *Darkest England* was written precisely because of the success and strength of The Salvation Army in many places in the world and because Booth had developed a biblical and theological justification for his growing work. This will be noted again below.

The surest public expression of this mission came from Booth himself. In October 1890 he published *In Darkest England and the Way Out* in which he gave theological expression to the necessity of social salvation in which The Salvation Army had already been engaged. However, the question needs to be asked: Why did the transition take place, and why was Booth ready to focus his enlarged vision of salvation as a double mission? Indeed, W. T. Stead himself, who used his journalistic skills to assist Booth in the writing of *In Darkest England and the Way Out*, stated the following in *The Star* on January 2, 1891: "Everyone knows perfectly well that two years ago, nay, even one year ago, General Booth did not see his way to the utilization of The Salvation Army as an instrument of social reform."[36] W. T. Stead had intimate knowledge of *In Darkest England and the Way Out* because Booth asked Stead "if I could get him a literary hack who could lick his material into shape, and get the book out in time. I said, 'I will do your hack-work myself,' and I did. I was very proud to do it."[37]

There are many possible answers to this question, and many factors—both personal and institutional—coalesced at this time and gave rise to an expanded ministry. The first has already been noted, but bears repeating. William Booth, reared in poverty himself, demonstrated social sensitivity toward the poor and needy in Nottingham, in Whitechapel Road, and in the ministry of The Salvation Army. However, at one time these social concerns were fleeting compared with the concern for the personal conversion of men and women. Experience—both personal and institutional—had heightened his sensitivities about people's physical impoverishment. He wanted to help the poor.

This heightened sensitivity was shared by many who had joined Booth's Army, and culminated in the 1880s through their continual exposure to the stark realities of depressed urban life in London and in other parts of the world. The experience gained by Booth and his Social Reform Wing, especially in the context of a great depression in England in the 1880s, caused them to come to grips with the fact that people were not interested in an escapist gospel, but welcomed a gospel that sustained them physically as well as spiritually. W. T. Stead himself noted that the experience gained by the Social Wing of The Salvation Army "encouraged the General to take a decided step in advance."[38] This was especially true in 1889 during the London dock strike, a devastating strike to the dockers and their families. Thousands of people were out of work and seeking food and shelter for their families.[39]

Second, William Booth certainly recognized that virtually hundreds of other people and organizations were engaged in social work. Much of the work in England was under the auspices of an agency known as the Charity Organization Society, founded in 1867. The Charity Organization Society consequently saw no need for the Army's social ministry, and often opposed it, probably because, in Bennett's words, "Booth had valued his independence too much to become part of it, so there existed a degree of tension between the two organizations."[40] The work, so claimed the Charity Organization Society, was already being done. However, if the reports of Charles Booth were accurate, the work was inadequate and certainly was leaving no lasting results, especially in the area of serious unemployment and its attendant problems. "The General was never good in acknowledging the work of others."[41] The basic problem was not that there was no charity toward the poor taking place at that time, but that there was too much of sentimental charity with no lasting results. In speaking specifically about Catherine Booth in this regard, Barbara Robinson wrote:

> In 1884, Catherine Booth delivered the sermon, "Sham Compassion and the Dying Love of Christ," a succinct critique of trends in late nineteenth-century social policy and philanthropy. It must be acknowledged that the social context she addressed was very different from the one faced by John Wesley. While Wesley sought to overcome widespread indifference to the plight of the poor, Catherine believed that Victorian charitable intervention had run wild. She was reacting to the late-nineteenth century proliferation of charities—a flood of what she termed "schemes without a Savior" or "religions of bodily compassion" which ignored serious soul-need. She ardently believed that much of the Christian activism of the period would only result in "a more eternal weight of misery at the cost of little present relief."[42]

William Booth echoed Catherine's critique and, convinced that he was now ready to improve on the work being done, offered the following criticism:

> And yet all the way through my career I have keenly felt the remedial measures usually enunciated in Christian programmes and ordinarily employed by Christian philanthropy, to be lamentably inadequate for any effectual dealing with the despairing miseries of these outcast classes. The rescued are appallingly few—a ghastly minority compared with the multitudes who struggle and sink in the open-mouthed abyss. Alike, therefore, my humanity and my Christianity, if I may speak of them in any way as separate from one another, have cried out for some more comprehensive method of reaching and saving the perishing crowds.[43]

Third, Booth perceived that much of the Church was unwilling to enter into a second mission in spite of the glaring needs of the people before the eyes of the Church. Booth was convinced, "and with good reason, that the respectable churches—both Anglican and Nonconformist—would not reach out to offer either spiritual or material comfort to the undeserving poor."[44] Andrew Mearns, a Congregational minister, had published his book entitled *The Bitter Cry of Outcast London* in 1883. As Tim Macquiban has noted, that book "stirred up the public conscience as no other work had. It was a devastating indictment of the failure of churches to respond to the needs of the poor in any way other than to build churches and chapels and offer limited aid."[45]

And so by 1890, Booth, convinced that it was theologically correct to address social redemption systematically, was willing to commit himself and his Army in a way that he wished for the church. He was at times critical of the church for not understanding either the necessity of or the nature of social redemption. "Why all this apparatus of temples and meeting-houses to save men from perdition in a world which is to come, while never a helping hand is stretched out to save them from the inferno of their present life?"[46]

This theological foundation was based on the great commandment of Jesus to love one's neighbor, a theological text that Booth referred to often in his later ministry.[47] However, this foundation was not only biblical but also Wesleyan.[48] The Wesleyan theological option for the poor found expression in Booth's social ministry.

> There exist many parallels in the Army to the radical side of Methodist preaching. Booth remarks in his book *In Darkest England and the Way Out* that "The Scheme of Social Salvation is not worth discussing which is not as wide as the Scheme of Eternal Salvation set forth in the Gospel. The Glad Tidings must be to every creature, not merely to an elect few who are to be saved. . . . It is now time to fling down the false idol, and proclaim a Temporal Salvation as full, free and universal, and with no other limitations that the 'Whosoever will' of the Gospel." Here one finds many of the Wesleyan themes of a personal "gospel egalitarianism" overflowing into a social vision for the poor, though perhaps not with the same theological sophistication but with the same anti-Calvinistic polemic.[49]

William Booth refused to make a distinction, as others had done, between the deserving poor and the undeserving poor. All must be offered the redemptive gospel message and the means to overcome their poverty.

Fourth, the authoritarian structure of the Army was important to Booth in spite of the growing democratic impulses of the nineteenth century, and was well in place and functioning by 1889 and 1890. Booth related that structure to this second mission—he believed that because of his organization's structure, it was best suited for redemption in two worlds. The dual redemptive mission of The Salvation Army would succeed through proper leadership and management where other less authoritarian enterprises had failed. He wrote that "so far from resenting the exercise of authority, The Salvation Army rejoices to recognize it as one great secret of its success, a pillar of strength upon which all its soldiers can rely, a principle which stamps it as being different from all other religious organizations founded in our day."[50]

A final reason—and perhaps the most important—why Booth was now ready to enter into this second mission revolved around the changing influential persons in his life and ministry. Two of the most significant persons in Booth's life up to this point were Catherine Booth and George Scott Railton. Both were adamant that the primary work of the ministry of The Christian Mission and The Salvation Army was the conversion of sinners and the raising up of saints. However, Catherine's and Railton's influence upon Booth diminished with Catherine's death in 1890 and with Railton's continuing lack of sympathy with the growing social emphasis of The Salvation Army, climaxing with his protestations in 1894 of the launching of a Salvation Army Assurance Society.[51] There is no doubt that Railton "feared that the new departure would detract from the Army's work in winning people to Christ. It proved to be another step in his increasing isolation from the rest of the Army hierarchy."[52]

As noted, Catherine Booth had been ill for quite some time prior to her death in 1890. Her influence in the Army was chiefly in the realm of encouraging the officers and soldiers, and preaching and teaching such doctrines of holiness and the role of women in ministry. This is not to say that she did not have some sympathy with the second mission, as her involvement in the Purity Crusade amply testifies. William Booth consulted her on the writing of *In Darkest England and the Way Out*, and dedicated the book to her. However, it remains a moot question of precisely how critical Catherine Booth would have been of the new direction of redemption once she saw it fully inaugurated. In his biography of Catherine Booth, W. T. Stead, himself one who influenced Booth in this new direction, quoted from a letter that Catherine Booth had written to him: "Praise up humanitarianism as much as you like, but don't confound it with Christianity, nor suppose that it will ultimately lead its followers to Christ."[53] One author has rightly noted that Catherine's "Wesleyan creed rested on the doctrine of human depravity. Soup and soap were, at best, ancillary to soul saving. Had she lived longer, she might have shared others' concerns about the gap between the army's spiritual and its social work."[54]

On the other hand, Railton at this time was a tireless evangelist, traveling the world for the Army. In that capacity, he was, however, far removed from Booth and the organizational and administrative development of the Army in London. Those closest to Booth in the development of the Darkest England Scheme were Bramwell Booth, W. T. Stead, and Frank Smith. Bramwell Booth, the eldest son and Chief of the Staff, had long been convinced of the necessity of social ministries, but was cautious about the relationship of that ministry to the more overtly religious work of the Army.[55] W. T. Stead was the journalist whose sympathies were for the betterment of society by any possible means, not the least of which was the work of the Army, and he assisted Booth with writing *In Darkest England and the Way Out*. He protested, however, that the book was primarily Booth's own work, but Booth needed an editor. And W. T. Stead, who left *The Pall Mall Gazette* to begin the *Review of Reviews* was a natural choice, even though Booth did not always agree with Stead. "He tolerated the editor and used him, but he did not like him, and certainly would not have trusted him to have a free hand at writing a book that was always going to result in significant changes to The Salvation Army."[56] Finally, there was Frank Smith. "More than anyone, Frank Smith got Booth to champion the lot of the poor after 1887. Under Smith's tutelage, Booth adopted ideas from Henry George, Arnold White, H. Rider Haggard, Sidney and Beatrice Webb and others. . . . Smith filled Booth's ears with social reform and used *War Cry* reports to represent his own social views as Booth's."[57]

However, Smith had other loyalties, and his political involvement and socialistic sympathies eventually caused him to leave the Army, but not before his significant influence in the Darkest England Scheme. Apart from Bramwell Booth, W. T. Stead, and Frank Smith, there were others who may have influenced Booth with the writing of *In Darkest England and the Way Out*, but these three were the most important shapers of this new direction in ministry.[58]

By 1890 The Salvation Army was well launched on a second mission. It was now a movement that was committed to both spiritual and social redemption, and Booth's theology from this time forward reflected this dual mission. His public pronouncements attempted to maintain the tension of the dual mission. This developed theology of redemption still included personal salvation from sin for the individual who believes by faith. However, now Booth embraced a theology of redemption that included social salvation from the evils that beset people in this life. And just as there was the possibility of universal spiritual redemption in Booth's theology, reflecting his Wesleyan theology, so there was the possibility of universal social redemption, reflecting his postmillennial vision for the salvation of the world before the return of Christ.

William Booth was nothing if not a military strategist for God. He knew that before launching this new ministry publicly, he had to bring his own people into line with his enlarged theological vision, and knew that it would not be possible to win the hearts and minds of all his soldiers and officers on this issue. Many, like Railton, and perhaps even Catherine, would still hold that the salvation of the soul is the surest way to bring about social redemption. However, as part of his strategic plan Booth wrote one of his most important articles in 1889 appropriately entitled "Salvation for Both Worlds" published in *All the World* in January 1889. In that article he explained that he had always been aware of the physical impoverishment of the people to whom he had preached, having experienced poverty himself. He nevertheless saw no remedy for such poverty and so was determined to save people's souls even if he could not help them in this world.

However, he noted that his own and his people's experience had taught him "that the miseries from which I sought to save man in the next world were substantially the same as those from which I everywhere found him suffering in this."[59] And Booth concluded that he now had two gospels to preach—a gospel of redemption from personal sin and a gospel of redemption from social evil. He broadened his theological language to take into account his changed theology. He added new meaning and a new dimension to the redemptive theological language that he had been expressing for years. Salvation now had social obligations and dimensions as well as spiritual ones.

Ten months after writing "Salvation for Both Worlds," designed obviously to prepare his own people for a personal and institutional allegiance and commitment to a double mission, Booth began writing *In Darkest England and the Way Out*. Booth's Army had already demonstrated in many parts of the world both a willingness and a capacity to enter into social ministries. William Booth was convinced of the theological justification of both personal and social salvation, and with the writing of this book he was now ready to commit his Salvation Army to war on two fronts. He wrote *In Darkest England and the Way Out* to explain his developed theology and thereby explain the evolution that had taken place in his own thinking and in the mission of the Army, which was increasingly placing itself in the public eye. And the date of the publication, October 1890, was a critical date in the theology of William Booth because it most clearly represents not only his broadened theological vision of redemption but also his desire and his willingness to act in a way that was consistent with his own theology.

In Darkest England was Booth's most extensive work and proved to be his most widely read work, read not only by Salvationists but by the general public for whom it was intended. Booth and Stead were wise in capturing the public imagination that was already enthralled with Stanley's bestseller, *In Darkest Africa.* "Booth always had a good eye and ear for a catchy title or tune, particularly if it was popular, and he borrowed and adapted this one for his own purposes."[60] Once Booth's book was published it did not escape notice and certainly did not escape criticism. Booth had his critics, many of them caustic and some vitriolic. He also had his share of defenders.

> As Canon Dwyer pointed out, all of England became divided into Boothites and Anti-Boothites. Among Booth's sympathizers were Cardinal Manning, Archdeacon Farrer, Sir E. Clark (the Solicitor-General), and the Marquis of Queensbury; among his critics, Thomas Huxley,[61] C. S. Loch (Secretary of the Charity Organization Society), Bernard Bosanquet, and Canon Dwyer. But even a critic like Dwyer had to admit Booth had the right objectives in mind, although he was going about the matter quite wrongly.[62]

The Darkest England Scheme incorporated many ideas envisioned primarily by Frank Smith, but were also embraced by W. T. Stead, especially championing the poor and putting programs in place that would aid and assist the poor with money from the wealthy. Booth would only go so far, however, because "he did not share Smith's socialism. He did want to repair capitalism's flaws, however. Booth's aim was to change the man when character was the reason for failure. For him, man's nature was grounded in the heart, not the environment. He was not a classic Christian Socialist; he believed that only conversion could rid the heart of sin and change outer maladies, although at times the cause of ruin was beyond one's control."[63]

The Scheme was intended as a crusade to assist the "submerged tenth" of Britain's population, those whose lives were enslaved by poverty, vice, prostitution, and any number of circumstances that kept these people from the security of work, income, home, family, or safety. Booth expected the Scheme to help not only England but also the world by providing a model of social salvation. The first part of the book dealt with an analysis of the problems, and this part was labeled "Darkness." The second part of the book, "Deliverance," proposed solutions to the problems, those solutions being divided among the city colony, the farm colony, and the colony overseas, each colony designed to bring light to specific aspects of England's darkness through various programs established for each colony. The city colony provided food and shelter for the poor as well as employment for the unemployed. The farm colony took people from the city and established them on farms to learn agricultural trades that would benefit them for the remainder of their lives. The best known of the farm colonies is still operated by The Salvation Army today, the colony at Hadleigh in Essex, originally established with 215 men.[64] Both Cecil Rhodes and Lord Loch (the High Commissioner for South Africa) visited the Hadleigh Farm in 1898. One of the most important Governors of that colony was David C. Lamb, who entered the Army under the Booths and helped with the shaping of the social ministry of the Army. The overseas colony helped the poor of the cities through the Army's emigration bureau to find work overseas, primarily in Canada, Australia, and New Zealand. Booth had hoped to establish such work also in Rhodesia, but that project failed. Farm colonies were also established in the United States for those needing employment from the cities of America.[65]

However, those who read and interpret Booth's book only in the light of its social analysis and constructive programs will seriously miss an important intention of the book, and in doing so will misunderstand William Booth at this important time in his life and ministry. The book is also an expression of Booth's expanded view of redemption to include social redemption. He wanted to maintain the delicate balance between personal and social salvation. Doing so was important to Booth for at least two reasons. First, he feared that social salvation would break loose from its ties to spiritual salvation, thus rendering The Salvation Army merely an ineffectual social agency. Second, he wanted to respond to his critics on the one hand who denied the validity of his social work, and his critics on the other hand who denied the validity of his religious work.[66]

Booth was not equally clear, however, in spelling out those intentions. Nevertheless, it was important for Booth to explain that the social ministry of the Army was not an end in itself. The work of social redemption was preparatory, necessarily, to the work of spiritual or personal redemption. Experience had taught him that some people were so disastrously oppressed by their present physical circumstances that "these multitudes will not be saved in their present circumstances."[67] A similar theme is reiterated throughout his book. Booth was convinced that "if these people are to believe in Jesus Christ, become the servants of God, and escape the miseries of the wrath to come, they must be helped out of their present social miseries."[68] The clearest statement of Booth's intentions is found in his assertion that "at the risk of being misunderstood and misrepresented, I must assert in the most unqualified way that it is primarily and mainly for the sake of saving the soul that I seek the salvation of the body."[69] Years later that theological position is reiterated in a letter to his officers on the occasion of his eightieth birthday:

> But while you strive to deliver them from their temporal distresses, and endeavour to rescue them from the causes that have led to their unfortunate condition, you must seek, above all, to turn their miseries to good account by making them help the Salvation of their souls and their deliverance from the wrath to come. It will be a very small reward for all your toils if, after bringing them into condition of well-being here, they perish hereafter.[70]

Only when Booth's social mission is placed within the framework of his entire theological vision will it be completely understood. His newly formulated theology of redemption was sustained and supported by other aspects of his theology that he had articulated prior to 1889 and 1890. He had already conceived of his Army as a part of the universal church that was blessed by God and sanctified by the Holy Spirit. He had developed his imagery of Christ to include the conquering Christ who was the model for deliverance from the evils of this world as well as from the wrath of the next world. He believed that evil was not finally triumphant, but that universal redemption, both personal and social, was possible. All people needed to be given the opportunity to respond to the gospel message by faith. He believed in an ultimate eschatological goal— a goal that would embrace both spiritual and social redemption, and he held out that goal as hope for ultimate redemptive victory for his Army of salvation. It is interesting and not inconsequential that his most important article dealing with this eschatological goal was written in August 1890, the same time that he was completing the writing of *In Darkest England and the Way Out*.[71]

Finally, however, the question needs to be raised: Was Booth completely settled with the direction that The Salvation Army took, especially after 1890? At the very least, there appeared to be some lingering questions in Booth's mind as to whether the decision to enter into social ministries was a wise one. In his book entitled *The Salvationists*, John Coutts refers to the issue of the Army's opening up a full-fledged medical work in India in 1893. Bramwell Booth tried to persuade William Booth of this necessity, and Coutts wrote, "The old man took some persuading. Might not the care of sick bodies divert attention from the salvation of perishing souls? But at last he agreed."[72] Owen Chadwick raised the same question in *The Victorian Church*. He wrote, "The most revivalist of sects was now willing to allow that a Christian had other duties to his neighbor apart from his duty to convert him. Yet in Booth's lonely old age...he sometimes wondered whether he had been right to allow the Army to divert its energies from conversion."[73] Tim Macquiban wrote that there is evidence that Booth "drew back in trepidation from the diversion from what he still saw as the primary tasks and preoccupations of his ministry—sin and salvation, hell and heaven, the devil and the Lord, features of the older-style evangelism."[74]

Booth's official biographer, Harold Begbie, raised this question of differing duties when he wrote that "after many years of incredible labour in the social work of the Army he came to wonder...whether he ought ever to have diverted any of the energies of the Army from the strictly evangelical responsibilities of the preacher's vocation."[75] And St. John Ervine, when writing about William Booth getting back to preaching after so much of his energy had been given to the Darkest England Scheme, wrote that "schemes of social reform had no interest for him any more, and he sometimes doubted his wisdom in adopting any."[76] This question obviously lingered even after William Booth's death, and upon his becoming the second General of The Salvation Army, Bramwell Booth had to face the question again. A newspaper reporter asked him about the Darkest England Scheme. Bramwell Booth's reply is important not only because he was one of the shapers of that Scheme but because now as General he would be leading the Army to move the Scheme into the twentieth century. Therefore, his vision of the Scheme is critical in providing some comprehensive view of what evolved in the ministry of the Army several years earlier. Bramwell Booth said:

> My answer...is that I have always looked on the Darkest England scheme and what came out of it as a comparatively small, though essential, part of the work of The Salvation Army—as a link rather than the main body of the thing. I say essential because it was, and is, an expression of the pas-

sion at the heart of the organism itself, but as such it takes a subordinate place in my own conception of the history—and, shall I say the hopes?—of the Army.

At the same time, there is no doubt that the scheme has done two good things for the Army, as well as a good thing for the world. It helped the Army into the eye of those who were compassionate for the poor, but under the influence of a generous humanitarianism which hitherto looked upon the Army as little more than a small religious sect struggling for its own existence. Secondly, it opened the way for the Army to use a vast weight of previously unemployed power in its own ranks, because it provided a platform for action other than the platform of talking and solo singing, of great religious functions, and the publication of religious literature. It provided work for another type of soldier—the man or woman who could act but not talk. So far as its reflex effect upon the Army is concerned the Darkest England scheme has fully justified itself.[77]

William Booth moved forward with his beloved Army into an unknown future, but without Catherine by his side. He had undertaken immense responsibilities with the development of the Darkest England Scheme, and as the General of a growing Army he would have to maintain a delicate balance of all ministries of the Army. His love for the Army and commitment to its cause became the dominant force in his life. For this love and commitment he paid a price since, at times, the interests of the Army came above the interests of the family. His subsequently losing three of his children from the ranks of the Army as well as another daughter to a premature death was almost more than he could bear. William Booth would learn the lessons of the pain as well as the glory of leadership as he moved beyond the events of 1890.

CHAPTER ELEVEN

THREE WHO LEFT

Introduction

After the death of Catherine and the launching of the Darkest England Scheme, Booth gave much attention initially to defending the Scheme and answering its critics. However, he longed for the pulpit, and the preacher, pastor, and evangelist that New Connexion Methodism and The Christian Mission had shaped once again set out to conquer the world by proclaiming the gospel of the kingdom of Christ. From the early 1890s Booth immersed himself again in his first love: preaching and evangelism. This meant that control of the daily operations of the Army passed from William to Bramwell. This did not indicate that William was unaware of the smallest details of the Army's operations; his correspondence and diaries readily demonstrate such attentiveness. It did mean that Bramwell often made the daily decisions, both great and small, from the Army's International Headquarters at 101 Queen Victoria Street, with the advice and consent of William.

Conflict in the Booth Family

And herein was cause for trouble, especially among the other members of the Booth family who could endure the autocratic nature of William Booth as the founder of the movement and the head of the family, but who could not abide Bramwell's high-handed control of other family members. There were bound to be difficulties ahead; confrontation was inevitable. All of the Booths, including the spouses of the Booths, thought of themselves as extraordinary people, and enjoyed the many privileges of being a Booth—privileges denied to ordinary officers. As I mentioned previously, only the Booths were given titles as well as ranks, and often the titles were conferred in public meetings, which set the Booths apart from the rank and file. Only the Booths were allowed to take months to recuperate from any number of illnesses in very comfortable circumstances when other officers had to keep in the fight. The Booths' illnesses, as well as prayers solicited for their recovery, were reported in *The War Cry*. Frequently, the Booths' public meetings were reported in *The War Cry* and always in glowing terms with astonishing results. And the marriages of the Booth children were always festive public occasions, again reported at great length in *The War Cry*. The family was constantly before the public eye. Little wonder, then, that their own sense of self-importance was exaggerated.

The choice of marriage partners for the children was controlled by Catherine and William, and after the death of Catherine by William alone. In one of the most unfortunate incidents played out before the Army public, Lucy Booth was engaged to Colonel John Lampard. He, evidently for quite noble reasons, called off the engagement. Lucy Booth, ever the Victorian lady now embarrassed by this inexplicable situation, did what many Victorian ladies did. She collapsed! And she remained in a state of ill health for quite some time.[1] In the meantime, William Booth considered disciplining Lampard for such a despicable action, and the rumor was circulated that Lampard was mentally deranged.[2] After all, "anyone who declined the opportunity to marry a Booth must have seemed to the General to be out of his mind."[3] "A deputation of officers has been here," Bramwell Booth wrote, "to see the General today to express their sympathy and to request that there should be either a court martial on Lampard or that he should be expelled."[4]

Lucy Booth gradually recovered her strength, being allowed over three months to do so, and "continued to appear in the official organ [*The War*

Cry] in the role of an ill-used lady."[5] Lampard disappeared from Salvation Army history, "branded as a lunatic, and his subsequent career is not known to the authorities, although there is a belief that he went to the United States, where his eccentricities, if he had any, would not be noticed, and there became an evangelist."[6] Lucy went back to India where she had served with the Booth-Tuckers and there she met one Emanuel Daniel Hellberg, a Swedish Salvation Army officer.[7] They were married on October 18, 1894, and Hellberg took the Booth name, as did the other sons-in-law. The Booth-Hellbergs initially retained their separate ranks—she a commissioner and he a colonel—and were sent back to India. Lucy Booth was the Territorial Commander and her husband was the Chief Secretary.

This incident gives some indication of the self-absorption of the Booths. They had been protected from the wider society and from evil influences, whether real or imagined, by their ever-watchful mother. And they had been so convinced of their exceptional gifts and abilities that they expected officers and soldiers of the Army to recognize them immediately and constantly. After all, most of the Booths entered public life in their teens, and were in their early- to mid-twenties when they were appointed to positions of leadership and authority within the Army. And with the absence of Catherine and her mediatory influence among the members of the family, William now found difficulties in managing the family.

In many instances that sense of self-importance created in the Booth children and inherited by the Booth daughters-in-law and sons-in-law caused great conflict within the family and was destructive both to the life of the family and to the mission of the Army. William Booth's allegiance was now solely to his beloved Army and the principles and discipline of the Army had to be upheld even at the expense of some of his children. He had become a General first and a father second. To complicate matters, "Bramwell seemed not to share the belief of his brothers and sisters that they were fully as inspired as he was, and he endeavored to dominate them. In this endeavor he had the support of his father."[8] And, as David Malcolm Bennett has stated, "Towards the end of 1895 the Salvation Army hierarchy was given a drastic overhaul. No less than 20 territorial commanders were given new postings. Amongst them were several members of the Booth family. . . . There had been little consultation with those involved in these transfers."[9] As a result of these new postings, one of William's sons and his wife left the work. Other children and their spouses would leave a few years later.[10]

Those Who Left the Army

The first to leave the Army was Ballington Booth along with his wife Maud.[11] They had been sent to America as joint National Commanders to replace Commissioner Frank Smith, "worn to the thread by his labors"[12] while trying to heal a breach in the Army in America caused by his predecessor, Thomas E. Moore. The Ballington Booths arrived in New York on April 21, 1887, and continued to bring healing to an Army that was still in disarray from the Moore split. They were, by all accounts, indefatigable leaders of the Army in America and enjoyed remarkable success in preaching, writing, and administering a growing Army. Edward McKinley speaks of them both as

> officers of exceptional ability whose administration was marked by advances that the rank and file were eager to attribute to their leadership: the reconciliation of Colonel Holz and most of the remnant of the Moore rebels; the construction of the new national headquarters on Fourteenth Street; and the origin, by Maud, of a range of activities designed to convert convicts and to help them into honest and useful lives on their release from prison. One of the Ballington Booths' most important contributions to the future of the Army was the rejuvenation of the Auxiliaries, who formed the first stage of the massive public support upon which the Army's social programs would come to depend.[13]

In *The History of The Salvation Army* Arch Wiggins noted that "during Ballington and Maud Booth's leadership the number of corps more than doubled and the officer-force was increased two and a half times."[14]

Imagine, then, the surprise of many Salvationists on both sides of the Atlantic when they read in *The War Cry* from February 29, 1896, that Commissioners Ballington and Maud Booth had resigned from The Salvation Army. In January Bramwell Booth had ordered several command changes, and he ordered the Ballington Booths to come home to England. They refused. Bramwell Booth insisted that they follow his orders. They resigned on January 31, 1896.

In their letter of resignation they made it clear that they were not unwilling to leave America. They were, however, convinced that the American expression of the Army was unique and that a change in command might mean leaders who did not understand either the Americans or the way the Army worked in the American culture. Likewise, they were not disposed to follow the orders of a Chief who treated them and others not as servants together in the great salvation war, but as subservient officers who should obey his every command.

It is evident from their letter of resignation to Bramwell Booth that their primary grievance was with General Booth, and they feared that in any appointment they would be treated by William Booth the same way that he had treated them during a visit to America. They had no hope that a change in appointment would heal irreparable wounds. Indeed their words, while some might consider them rather self-serving and holding out no promise of compromise, do give a glimpse of William Booth in his later ministry. He was becoming more autocratic, more out of touch with the feelings of his officers and soldiers, and losing the common touch that was so evident at the beginning of his ministry. Ballington and Maud wrote that

while in the States, the General showed himself, not only unkind and unappreciative to us personally, but he was hard, ill tempered and impossible to please. (a) From the hour of his arrival he treated us without fatherly regard or affection, and often with contempt, and that in the presence of our own people, who had confidence in us and who were watching every action. He alienated our affection from him. (b) He appeared to us so utterly inconsistent with regard to the swells. According to implicit instructions we had notable persons on the platform (though understand, we had never had them on an Army platform, or given them precedence over our own people before). In many places he hardly took any notice of the loyal troops who had come miles at personal sacrifice and expense to see him, but he went out of his way to show consideration and affection even to some of these outsiders. Then in council, and in particular to us privately, he would make out that he despised these outsiders, and that he had no hope for them. (c) He belittled the Army work, even saying to us "he could have drawn just as large crowds and had just as much success without any Salvation Army at all," and remarked in anger, that he "would have done much better in money if he had hired himself out, like the lecturers do with an agent to get up his meetings," thus showing that he was utterly unmindful of the toil and effort of our dear officers and soldiers, who had sacrificed, lost rest and worked themselves sick to please him and to show him something worthy of the Army and the nation. (d) It became to us quite evident, before he had been long in the country, that he did not come to inspect the troops, or enter into our battle here, but to express his preconceived and prejudiced ideas, and to ride roughshod over us all. This was painfully patent at the first staff council, where he said, "I'm not going to let you suck all the juice out of this plum," and many other things which caused surprised comment among the officers. (e) He never talked to us, or invited us to talk to him concerning our difficulties, trials and plans in the work, or its needs, etc. If he asked our opinion, it was invariably merely that he might contradict it and prove us wrong. He would accept the notions and opinions of any minister or outsider before ours, and this, mind you, concerning capacity of halls, suitability of cities, to visit people he ought to meet, etc., and many other matters which these very persons would themselves in many instances refer to us from our wider knowledge of the country. He utterly refused to receive our opinions upon anything, until to save constant friction and unpleasantness we had to close our mouths. It was, indeed, the saddest chapter of disappointment in our lives.[15]

It is interesting in light of the American experience of The Salvation Army that not only had they lost their confidence in the General and the Chief, and therefore the movement, but also they were at odds with the Army's growing emphasis on social work. They wrote:

We could not take a command in a country where the Social Work is being pushed while the Spiritual Work is at a low ebb, or is suffering therefrom. The work of the Army, which really ought to commend itself to the world, and hold its respect and make us the greatest power, is the Army's Spiritual Work; but we feel that the Social Work has, and is, being pushed, exploited and boomed, so that the people's eyes are now drawn from that side of the Army upon which the world will be only too glad to turn their backs, viz.: The Spiritual side. Your officers are afraid to speak, and yet there are a great many who say and feel that the Social Work is undermining the Spiritual and diverting the public funds and attention from the Army's first blessed aim and work.[16]

While the social ministry of the Army had by now been well launched, it became evident from these and other protests from high-ranking officers that a clear theological foundation and justification for that social ministry had not been made. The very fact that the Ballington Booths could still speak of the social work and the spiritual work as though they were two competing operations rather than two aspects of the same holistic ministry of salvation is telling. Important leaders within the Army still did not comprehend clear biblical and theological justification for the Army's social ministry.

The Ballington Booths had a loyal following. They were supported both within and without the Army. Pressure was put on the Army from outsiders such as Josiah Strong of The Evangelical Alliance for The United States of America. He first wrote directly to William Booth himself about this matter. And then he wrote a letter to W. T. Stead, asking him to intervene with General Booth on behalf of the Ballington Booths.

> There is but one opinion on the subject among the Americans, and unfortunate as this incident would be at any time it is peculiarly so just now in view of the present relations of Great Britain and the United States. The order to "Farewell" has already been used to my certain knowledge in various parts of the United States very much to the detriment of the Army. The circulation of "The War Cry" has already fallen off, the income of the Army already been curtailed. Not only for our own sake but for the sake of the world-wide work of the Army, which must in the future so largely draw its resources from the United States, we profoundly deprecate this recall.[17]

Both William and Bramwell wrote lengthy replies to the Ballington Booths, but to no avail. The decision had been made. And in spite of William Booth's protestations that he did not want to accept their resignation, a couple of years later, on January 25, 1898, he wrote to Bramwell hinting that Ballington really engineered a schism in the Army, although for what possible reason remains unclear. William wrote,

> I notice all you say with respect to the controversy with Ballington. I am quite satisfied now in my own conscience that not only is he wrong today, but that he was meditating the possibility of this schism for some time before I came to the States, and that he seized upon my criticisms, and the little mortifications that I made manifest as the ground for the step he took.[18]

Truth to tell, there was fault on both sides of this argument, but that the Ballington Booths had been most wronged in this dispute is beyond question. Perhaps they did not give enough consideration to William Booth's desire to maintain unity in the Army by way of the London hierarchy. In that system of government, orders must be obeyed or the entire structure is at risk. However, the Ballington Booths expected a father's love, understanding, and sympathy to prevail in this dispute, but instead, the General's will won the day but not the family. And when all is said and done, both William and Catherine believed that officers who left the Army, even their own children, for whatever noble reasons, were traitors to the cause. They were bound to find hidden and dark motivations behind the actions of their officers who left, and this was no less true as

William looked back on the resignation of his son and daughter-in-law. The privilege William and Catherine allowed for themselves in leaving New Connexion Methodism—that it was the leading of God and they were his obedient servants—they did not allow for others. "It is a very narrow view, dear Catherine," Ballington wrote to his sister eight months after his resignation, "for you or anyone else to take that God cannot bless anyone who happens to be separated from the Army. Why, we are being blessed daily, and have hourly evidence of God's presence and favor."[19]

William Booth was intractable over this affair. On March 13, 1896, he wrote to his daughter, Catherine,

> I go forwards. I feel that I stand for the Truth, and stand for the Principles of the Army—*immovable* [which he underlined three times]. I am sure God is with me, and I feel confident of greater victories in the coming years than anything we have ever dreamed of; but even were it otherwise, God has called me to rear this Banner. If I hang on to it alone, I will die with it in my grasp.[20]

Ballington and Maud Booth left the Army, stayed in America, and on March 9, 1896, founded the Volunteers of America, copying the military model of the Army. Ballington became the first General of that movement, and was succeeded by Maud as General upon his death in 1940. She remained in that position until her death in 1948.[21] Ballington Booth was ordained a presbyter of the "Church in General" at St. James's Episcopal Church in New York City. After the resignation of the Ballington Booths, Evangeline was appointed as the temporary National Commander before the appointment of the Booth-Tuckers, who were sent to America to take over the leadership of the Army there.[22]

The next to leave the Army were the Booth-Clibborns, but for purposes far less noble than those that caused Ballington and Maud Booth to leave. Arthur Booth-Clibborn lacked the gifts and abilities of many in the Booth family that he had joined by marriage to the eldest daughter, Catherine—known by the family as Katie or Kate. He had been a member of the Society of Friends, and in many ways was still a seeker. He was captivated by the ministry of a sect leader named John A. Dowie, whose cult of the Zionites was headquartered in "Zion City," Illinois.[23] Dowie was the self-proclaimed reincarnation of Elijah and therefore the precursor of the Second Advent of Christ. Catherine Booth-Clibborn was wisely not convinced, but remained with her husband, although their marriage was not a particularly happy one.[24] But despite her disagreement with Arthur's captivation with Dowie, Catherine was faithful to Arthur and went with him. During this time of trouble William Booth, in a letter to Bramwell, let his opinions be made known regarding Arthur: "If I didn't think the fellow was out of his mind I should then think him a fool to entertain any hope that such a letter as that he has written would do anything effectual toward healing the big breach that he has made by his folly and conceit and selfishness."[25]

The Booth-Clibborns resigned on January 10, 1902, their letter of resignation being written only three days after Percy Clibborn, Arthur's brother, resigned from the Army because of his own attachments to the teachings of Dowie.[26] In the letter they claimed that in the Army they lacked the liberty to preach divine healing, pacifism, and the premillennial return of Christ—three positions of Dowie and his Zionites that the Booth-Clibborns constantly referred to as part of the "full gospel."[27]

Catherine did not think much of Dowie. She saw him for the fraud that he was, and challenged Dowie's vilifying both the work of the Army and William Booth himself. Years later she wrote, "I was to blame in going to Zion City (Chicago) when from the very first Dowie *violated every God given instinct in me*, and *all* I had learned of *Christ!* Dowie always struck me as a '*monomaniac*' so full of himself was he! The torture of my mind and conscience neither *you* nor Percy (my Brother in Law) will ever *know or understand*."[28] Evangeline had similar reservations and in a letter to her father written only three years after the Booth-Clibborns resigned, she wrote, "There has been quite a sensation just now over a report that is widely spread through the press that Dowie is dying of cancer. The consternation in Zion City is of a perplexing and unique nature. What a fraud the man has been. I wonder what his end will be like."[29]

The Booth-Clibborns entered into independent ministries, Catherine becoming rather well known in evangelistic circles. At the time of their departure, "submissive to the point of apathy, Kate put her name with Arthur's to the founding of what was called a Christian Mission of the Friends of Zion."[30] Their connection with the Army, however, was severed, and their relationship with William Booth remained strained. Catherine Booth-Clibborn once wrote to her brother, Ballington, that "again and again did I make journeys to I.H.Q. [International Headquarters] to see Father, to try to get reconciliation apart from the Organization, but all in vain. Bramwell would not have it."[31] Tragically,

William Booth saw Katie only twice more in his lifetime, their first visit being in 1905 in Paris. However, it is William's final meeting with his eldest daughter that demonstrates the tragedy of human relationships. Carolyn Scott wrote about Katie going to see her father on his deathbed.

> When Kate arrived and asked to see him, the request was refused. It was thought that the shock would be too much for him. "I must go to him," she insisted, and eventually she was allowed into his room on condition that she would not say who she was. . . . As she bent over him, he stirred and asked, "Who is it?" but she looked at him for a long time and then, keeping her promise, came away without answering.[32]

The next family member to leave the Army was Herbert Booth, along with his wife, Cornelie. Herbert had been recognized by his father for his leadership ability, and William once suggested to Bramwell that Herbert should be the natural selection for General following Bramwell.[33] However, Herbert had long been discontented with the Army's international control and wished for a decentralized system of authority. As was the case with others in the family, Herbert's argument was not only with his father but also with his brother, Bramwell, and with the increasingly ironclad authority that he exercised. Herbert's immediate concern was his ill health and his need for a change of appointment. But the far deeper matter was that of not having the freedom to determine his and his wife's own future. They were both less and less inclined to place their destinies in the hands of an autocratic father and an implacable brother. "The uncompromising attitude of his father and brother had forced Catherine and Ballington, not to mention the many others, to renounce their allegiance, not to the principles of the Army, but to the iron-handed rule over them, and by repeating that folly they were driving Herbert to a like renunciation."[34]

The Herbert Booths were in command of the Army in Australia. The Army had established a Limelight Department before Herbert's arrival. That department, existing from 1892 to 1909, "filmed several important public events associated with the Commonwealth Parliament in 1901."[35] The Army, who had been early to accept this new technology, soon was not the only group using it, and when movie houses opened up in major cities, the Army no longer had a corner on the cinema market. However, while in Australia, Herbert Booth immediately realized the evangelistic value of such technology, and while there produced "Soldiers of the Cross," one of the world's first lectures illustrated with short films and slides. Herbert Booth's biographer wrote the following about this gospel adventure:

In 1896, when he arrived in Australia, the Army had a limelight department that consisted of one lantern and three hundred ordinary slides. Under his personal supervision the plant was expanded until he had perfected an organization that enabled him to realize his dreams and create a dramatic representation of the heroism and sufferings of the early Christians.

In the production of this extraordinary picture a company of six hundred men, women and children, costumed as were the early Christians, were staged in scenery true to history and there patiently trained to enact their part to express the tragic drama. The pictures were then taken and reeled to follow the lecture at the rate of one to every forty words spoken. Both the still and motion pictures were executed in color by the best artists in Paris, London and New York. There were two hundred and twenty pictures and three thousand feet of film. Twelve months were consumed in preparing the drama for public presentation.

The Commandant delivered the Lecture in all parts of Australia and, after his retirement from the Army, in Europe, South Africa, Canada and the United States.[36]

However, in spite of rather creative and energetic leadership of the Army in Australia, there were tensions arising between Herbert and his father and Bramwell. Finally the relationship was irreconcilable. The Herbert Booths wrote their letter of resignation, dated February 3, 1902, less than a month after the resignation of the Booth-Clibborns.[37] The lengthy letter, written to "Our Dear Father and General," gives many reasons for resigning from the Army, but the heart of the matter can be read beginning on page two. They wrote:

> We must sorrowfully admit that after the greatest thought and sincerest prayers we have come to the conclusion that the present method of Army administration will no longer commend itself to our judgments nor is it in harmony with the dictates of our consciences.
>
> Recent constitutional changes in our government have compelled us to come to the conclusion that *you yourself* have lost faith in the one man control as it relates to all but the General for the time being and the Chief of Staff.
>
> The system which subjugates all the chief officers of the Army to the vote of their subordinates and yet leaves the supreme heads in *absolute control* seems to us *unjust, unreasonable and oppressive.*[38]

Herbert Booth continued his ministry for the remainder of his life primarily in Australia, Canada, and the United States. However, Bramwell and Eva were ever suspicious that Herbert's ministries were intended to interfere with Salvation Army ministries and thus confuse the people about the reasons for his leaving the Army, and would be an intrusion upon Army work. This family strife continued for years to come.[39]

The most immediate effect upon William Booth, now with the loss of his third child from the Army, is best summarized by St. John Ervine: "The pain which had been suffered by his wife baffled him, and now, as he grew old and his loneliness pressed more closely upon him, this bewilderment increased. He wanted affection and he wanted power, and the two desires continually fought in his heart."[40] Booth's eldest daughter once wrote, "My own father told me twice that he 'had no children or grandchildren outside the S.A.'! This was said to hold me; it had the opposite effect."[41]

Ultimately, William Booth's tragic flaw—and the same might be said of Bramwell as well—was that he resented "any attempt to dispute his leadership or to reduce his authority. Those who left the Army were deserters!"[42] As far as he was concerned, Ballington, Catherine, and Herbert left the Army "for trivial, selfish, or at the best, most heartless reasons," and they "handed in their solemn pledges and left me to struggle forward as best I could."[43] As for Bramwell, "Booth's mutinous children were complaining, not because they were forbidden to do the work of their Creator, but because they were expected to render obedience to their brother who would eventually become their General. They were puffed up with pride. They said to themselves, We are as good as Bramwell. We also are William Booth's children. We also are eloquent and capable of handling crowds. Why, therefore, should we serve our brother any more than he should serve us?"[44]

Emma Booth's Death

However, whatever grief William Booth felt over the departure of his children from the Army, it could not match his sorrow when he learned of Emma's tragic and premature death. She had been on a western tour, beginning in Buffalo, New York, which included an inspection tour at Fort Amity, Colorado, one of America's farm colonies. She was the only passenger killed in a train wreck at Dean Lake, Missouri, on October 28, 1903.[45] Frederick Booth-Tucker "was inconsolable, barely able to struggle through the several mass memorial meetings and the three enormous public funerals—one in Chicago, where Booth-Tucker had been waiting for her when he received the news of her death, and two in New York—that Army tradition demanded."[46] Unfortunately, family disputes continued, even at Emma's funeral in Carnegie Hall.[47] Booth-Tucker did not allow Ballington or Herbert, Emma's two brothers, to participate in the funeral. Ballington and Maud Booth remained in an adjoining room during the funeral. Herbert and his wife were allowed on the platform, but Eva and Booth-Tucker refused Herbert's request, even as the funeral service progressed, to speak. This bitterness toward Ballington and Herbert would have been unconscionable to the very gracious Emma. Booth-Tucker returned to England in August 1904, and his sister-in-law, Eva, succeeded him as the National Commander. She "reigned—no other word will do—over the American Army for the next thirty years."[48]

Emma's death was felt intensely not only by her husband; the loss was equally grievous to William. Of all his children he was closest to Emma, and for good reason. William referred to her as his "left" hand. He wrote in his diary for October 29, 1903, that

> while the Chief was my "right hand" in this great enterprise, she was my "left," and I had fondly reckoned on her being his right hand when I had passed away. While all these years he has helped me so manfully and skillfully in brain, she has cheered and sustained me in heart, and yet both have excelled in the possession of each other's qualities, for she has had skill of the highest character and he has had the tenderest qualities of the soul.[49]

"Bramwell said that she might have been 'the most gifted member' of the Booth family, and described her as having 'a remarkable capacity for bringing the best out in people.'"[50] Emma certainly displayed the ego of the other Booth children, but possessed a lovely grace—which many of her siblings lacked—that balanced that strong ego. Emma possessed the balanced nature that her mother possessed, and of all the women in the family, Emma was most like her mother. Therefore, her loss reminded William once again of the loss of Catherine those many years earlier, and served to increase his loneliness and isolation.[51]

William Booth was determined to continue his work and the work of his beloved Army. As at no other time in his life, the world would know of William Booth—preacher, evangelist, social reformer, and tireless leader of a growing Salvation Army. But his family and other officers of the Army who were close to him, like George Scott Railton, would see a darker and more complex side to William—that of an egotistical autocrat who had lost perspective of the ministry of servanthood to which he genuinely believed God had called him. To be fair, Booth was not altogether unaware of this, and, at times, his better sense of humility and his finer nature of grace came through.

But William was now served primarily by his two children who were most like him and therefore least likely to confront him with his weaknesses—Bramwell and Eva. They too often lacked the grace of the biblical servant-leader. Had their counsel and advice to William been more honest and less flattering, they would have done him an immense favor. Had they reached out to their siblings rather than treating them so contemptuously, they could have brought some measure of peace to the family and to William's heart. They had forgotten that the Army was founded as much by the battles fought by Ballington, Catherine, and Herbert as by their own hard work. But "Bramwell, whose deafness helped to make him inaccessible to argument, became increasingly absorbed in ruling the Army."[52] And the same may be said of Eva, who eventually became the fourth General of The Salvation Army in 1934.

There is no doubt that if, by providence, Catherine Booth had lived, these breaches would not have taken place. She was the mediator. She was the one who knew when to exercise strict discipline and when to temper that discipline with grace. She was the strict but loving mother, and once recognizing the strong-headedness in her children, would have exercised a judicious and fair mediatory role in these family disputes. Little wonder, then, that William constantly longed for her and lamented her premature departure.

However, Catherine was gone and the family had been broken. But William Booth's ministry continued into an unknown future. He was, nevertheless, convinced, in spite of all personal tragedies and triumphs, that God was with him. That was all the assurance he needed.

CHAPTER TWELVE

INTERNATIONAL EVANGELIST

Introduction

Afterthe Darkest England Scheme was fully launched, both William Booth and his Salvation Army received international attention primarily from the press, but also from the comments of influential politicians and social critics. The British public had known of William Booth and his Army for many years, but now as they talked about his Social Scheme, his popularity broadened. However, there was conflict in Booth's mind, heightened by the comments of many senior and respected officers in the Army, about precisely how far the Army ought to go with its social ministries. Earlier biographers were aware of such conflict, and the official biographer of William Booth, Harold Begbie, wrote that "after 1898 . . . he began, if not to lose faith in the efficacy of social reforms, at least to question whether he had done wisely in throwing so much of his energy into this tremendous struggle."[1]

William Booth's Return to Preaching

In any case, once the Darkest England Scheme was on firm footing, Booth left the administration of the Scheme primarily in the hands of

Bramwell Booth, and to others as well such as Elijah Cadman, Randolph Sturgess, and David Lamb.[2] But, of course, he could not let go completely, and kept an eye on all of the details of the Scheme. In the meantime, with the administration of the Scheme well attended, William Booth returned to his first love—his role of preacher and evangelist— and he concentrated his energies in these areas for the remainder of his life.[3] His Army was growing not only in Britain but also in other parts of the world, and he longed to give attention to his officers and soldiers abroad and to win the lost and raise up the saints in other countries. And in return he liked the international attention now given to him.

From 1893 onward, "he himself turned more and more to the centre of his Army, and with as much ardour as in the earliest years, but with more breadth and profounder sympathy, preached the great gospel of the changed heart."[4] It is clear from his writings during this time that his energies were turned away from the Scheme and channeled once again to the conversion of the world. During this time he wrote to Bramwell that

> I cannot go in for any more "campaigns" against evils. My hands and heart are full enough. And, moreover, these…reformers of Society have no sympathy with the S. A. nor with Salvation from *worldliness and sin*. Our campaign is against *Sin*! And our great difficulties lie in the direction of a lot of professed followers of Jesus Christ who are full of humanitarian pleasant Sunday afternoon Moodyism or the like. The Christ people who are not for a religion of deliverance from sinning are God's great enemies.[5]

In order to fulfill his mission, his world travels greatly increased since the time he had first set off for America in 1886. His travels were all-encompassing wherever the Army was at work—as far away as India and Australia and as near as Denmark, Sweden, or Norway. While it is evident that some of Booth's accounts of the numbers attending his meetings as well as the tremendous success of all his endeavors were exaggerated, Booth and his Salvation Army did, nevertheless, catch the public's attention. He was a striking, propheticlike figure who commanded attention from a public platform in a General's uniform. The General and The Salvation Army were inextricably connected in the public imagination.[6]

There are many indications that Booth's Army was growing and developing, especially on the Continent. Arch Wiggins noted:

> An outstanding event was the holding of a North-European Congress in Copenhagen in the April and May of 1893. Such a get-together was ren-

dered necessary by the remarkable growth of Salvation Army operations on the Continent. In the three years which were completed by the date of the Congress, in the nine commands concerned—France, Switzerland, Belgium, Holland, Germany, Denmark, Sweden, Norway and Finland— the number of corps had been increased from 287 to 896; officers from 500 to 1800; social institutions from 1 rescue home to 3, and 19 other centres, including food depots, shelters, factories and labour yards had been established. Copenhagen was chosen as the place of meeting because of its geographical position. The Congress lasted five days. The General was assisted by the Chief of the Staff (Bramwell Booth), a staff council being the central engagement.[7]

Reasons for the Growth of The Salvation Army

There were many reasons for the growth of Booth's Army at this time, which provided him with a worldwide platform for his brand of religion. Those reasons for the Army's growth likewise explain the popularity of Booth himself. However, five reasons stand out. First, the nineteenth century in which Booth preached and established his Army was a religious environment, dominated by a Protestant theology and a Protestant ethos. Of that, a strong segment of Protestantism considered itself evangelical, with its tenets tracing back to the preaching of John Wesley in the eighteenth century. "The direct descendants of Wesley formed the largest group outside the establishment."[8] And, as I mentioned in chapter 2, William Booth was both influenced by that evangelical tradition and became a sustainer of it as one committed to the Wesleyan expression of evangelicalism. In spite of the fact that Christianity came under criticism from the intellectual community in Great Britain, it was still central to the religious and cultural life. William Booth was not one to be silenced or placed on the margins. He was an avowed evangelical, nurtured in the Wesleyan tradition, with a biblical and Wesleyan vision of what was best for the world.

Second, while there had been women in various ministries of the Church since the time of the New Testament, no denomination had ever before had the concentration of women in ministry that The Salvation Army had. This was a new cultural and religious phenomenon, and women preachers—some as young as their mid-teens—were attracting great crowds of people in Britain. Andrew Eason, in his book entitled *Women in God's Army: Gender and Equality in the Early Salvation Army*, rightly sees some ambiguity in the commitment to women in ministry in the early Army, especially in the minds of some of the leaders such as William Booth, George Scott Railton, and even, to some extent, Catherine Booth herself. And Diane Winston, in her *Red-Hot and Righteous: The Urban Religion of The Salvation Army*, wrote that "as the first Christian group in modern times to treat women as men's equals, the Army offered a compelling, if sometimes contradictory, vision of gender."[9] While Winston readily admits the ambiguous record that Eason explores, she nevertheless criticizes Eason for not pressing hard enough the positive role of women in the Army and the contribution of the Army in this area to both the culture and the Church of the twentieth and twenty-first centuries.[10]

Therefore, a case can be made that a commitment to women in ministry was more deliberate, and the results of women in ministry more influential than Eason admits. In her work entitled *Pulling the Devil's Kingdom Down: The Salvation Army in Victorian Britain*, Pamela J. Walker concludes that

> The Salvation Army was among the first denominations to proclaim "women's right" to preach the gospel, and under its aegis thousands of working-class women assumed a spiritual authority that defied injunctions requiring female silence and submission. The Hallelujah Lasses stood in the streets, claiming spiritual authority for themselves while calling on others to repent. They drew on the urban working-class culture that surrounded them to create an evangelizing style that expressed their religious convictions. These convictions were not limited by institutional boundaries nor were they focused on the interpretation or creation of texts. Rather, they were expressed in words and through the body in dramatic conversions, sensational and physical preaching, and a willingness to withstand the opposition of street gangs and the indignity of jail. Salvationist women contributed to the Victorian social-purity movement and the expansion of women's employment, and they offered one model of reformed gender relations that addressed many of the conflicts that plagued working-class urban households. The Salvation Army integration of aspects of Victorian feminism and evangelical Christianity introduced these ideas into new circles, bringing working-class women in particular into a wider women's movement. After the vote was won in 1918, many leading suffragists "went on to champion women's leadership in religious contexts," supporting women's ordination and preaching themselves. The

Hallelujah Lasses were pioneers in establishing an authoritative, public, religious voice for women.[11]

William Booth, however, may well be criticized that he did not place women in leadership positions proportionate to their numbers in ministry, beyond his own family members. This was in spite of the fact that he recognized the importance of women in ministry to the advancement of The Salvation Army. In 1880, while speaking at the Wesleyan Conference in London of the reasons for the growth of The Salvation Army, he stated as one of the principles that "we employ women. And for this we have the authority of Mr. Wesley."[12]

At the same time, perhaps Booth was aware of the dangers of putting women on the margins of ministry in order to conform to Victorian culture and mores. His intent was to be faithful to the biblical principle of the equality of women and men in ministry. In a speech recorded in *The War Cry* on May 12, 1888, William Booth acknowledged that

> in the way of our salaried officers we have a great difficulty to meet, because nearly every week there are two officers turned into one. That is, the male officers are joined with the female officers, and then, by some strange mistake in our organization, the woman doesn't count. That is altogether contrary to the principle of The Salvation Army. . . . I propose from this night that we count the woman as one; and if you don't count the woman the same as the man, count the woman two and the man one![13]

In spite of some ambiguity in putting biblical principles into practice, the place of women was critical to the advancement of the Army in many areas—preaching, social ministry, literary work, and administrative ministry. In the words of Diane Winston, "One could make the case that the Army mounted a significant challenge to nineteenth-century notions of women's roles, even when it failed to live up to its own promise."[14]

A third reason for both the growth of the Army and the international recognition of William Booth was that the Army's message was obviously clear and compelling, and it was centered on the biblical doctrine of holiness. As his ministry progressed, Booth continued to embrace the biblical and Wesleyan doctrine of sanctification by faith for the individual believer. In fact, his best work on this subject, *Purity of Heart*, was published in 1902. Sanctification for the believer was Booth's ultimate answer to the problem of personal sin and guilt. The Army continued to teach and preach the basic tenets of the doctrine of sanctification: it was a second definite work of God's grace in the heart of the believer; it was appropriated by faith; it was available to all believers; and believers could rest assured that they were sanctified.[15]

However, as Booth's ministry broadened, he began to understand the doctrine in corporate categories as well as personal ones. It becomes clear in his later theology precisely why he interpreted sanctification in this wider dimension. First, sanctification was the final answer to the problem of evil. By connecting sanctification with the ultimate conquest of the world and of evil—only a holy people could do a holy work—Booth destroyed any concept of the finality of evil.

Second, his doctrine of sanctification gave legitimacy to the Army. He became convinced that God sanctified not only individuals but groups as well. The doctrine of sanctification took on a new dimension for Booth as his Army grew and developed. Corporate sanctification, or institutional sanctification, became an important sign that The Salvation Army was of divine, and not merely human, origin. In a *War Cry* article in 1892, the Founder exhorted his readers in this way: "Cast yourselves upon God. Keep on watching and praying and believing and expecting for me, for yourselves, for the whole Army at home and abroad, for the mighty baptism of burning fire!"[16] He reiterated this in one of his most important letters to his officers in 1909:

> The Salvation Army has known a great deal of this Divine inspiration. It is itself the creation of the Holy Spirit. All it knows of life and vitality, and all the power it possesses to bless the world, come from the Holy Spirit; and to this day waves of Divine influence, in a lesser or greater measure, are sweeping over it which proceed from Him alone.[17]

Third, Booth's wider understanding of sanctification became fundamental because this work of God in believers and in the church was preparation for the final redemptive purpose of God—the establishment of the kingdom of God. This aspect of sanctification prevented Booth's concept of holiness from being monastic; it was not a doctrine that called for separation from the evil world until the work of redemption was completed by God alone. As with the Wesleyan revivals in the previous century, people learned their theology not only by hearing the preacher but also by singing the songs. One of Booth's songs clearly reflected his enlarged vision of sanctification for his Army:

Thou Christ of burning, cleansing flame, Send the fire!
Thy blood-bought gift today we claim, Send the fire!
Look down and see this waiting host,
Give us the promised Holy Ghost,
We want another Pentecost, Send the fire!

God of Elijah, hear our cry: Send the fire!
To make us fit to live or die, Send the fire!
To burn up every trace of sin,
To bring the light and glory in,
The revolution now begin,
Send the fire!

'Tis fire we want, for fire we plead, Send the fire!
The fire will meet our every need, Send the fire!
For strength to ever do the right,
For grace to conquer in the fight,
For power to walk the world in white, Send the fire!

To make our weak hearts strong and brave, Send the fire!
To live a dying world to save, Send the fire!
O see us on thy altar lay
Our lives, our all, this very day,
To crown the offering now we pray, Send the fire![18]

A fourth reason for the growth of the Army was that Booth further developed his postmillennial vision for winning the world for God, and at this juncture in his ministry and theology there was a natural transition from the doctrine of sanctification as a means of preparation for redemption, and the doctrine of the kingdom of God as a result of the work of redemption by God's holy people here on earth. In brief, the doctrines of sanctification and the kingdom of God became so inextricably linked to one another at this time that it would be impossible to consider one doctrine without considering the other. They cannot be treated separately. "If you are a holy man or woman," Booth wrote, "you will help forward the War, and spread the glory of Christ's name far more effectively than you will if you are not fully saved. Holy people are the great need of the world. I am sure they are one of the great wants of the Army."[19] Those who shared the organizational and institutional power with Booth espoused the same theology that they believed was both biblically based and socially functional in giving legitimacy to the organization. They, too, were convinced of these doctrinal principles: the nature of institutional holiness, and the ultimate redemptive purposes of that holiness—the conquest of the world."[20]

William Booth's vision of the kingdom of God was shaped by his post-millennialism. Postmillennialism "holds that the millennium will come first, usually 'as the fruit of the present Christian agencies now at work in the world,' and that the Second Coming or the delivering agency will occur at the end of the process."[21] A clearer and more succinct definition of postmillennialism, and one that relates postmillennialism to the social reform work of the Army and other movements, is found in Donald Dayton's *Discovering an Evangelical Heritage*. Postmillennialism is the expectation of "Christ to return in judgment *after* a millennial reign of one thousand years."[22] Dayton goes on to affirm that "reform activity was in part to prepare the way for the millennium, which was in turn a reflection of the vision of the 'state of the perfect society' that drew Evangelicals into reform."[23]

Millennial themes of various stripes had been the subject of countless books, articles, discussions, and movements from the period of the New Testament to the nineteenth century. Neither Booth's concepts nor his practical application of those concepts were new. However, his distinctive contribution and focus was in the relationship of the Army and his theology to the establishment of the kingdom. His postmillennialism provided a grand triumphant vision for an Army on the march, and the constant growth of the Army, likewise, sustained that postmillennial vision.

Booth's millennial thinking, therefore, became part of the fabric of the working theology of The Salvation Army in his day, although no millennial statement or position was ever included in the official doctrinal statements of the Army. However, Booth's millennialism, taken in the context of his total theological system; in the context of The Salvation Army and its ministry and social concern; and in the context of other millennial visions was neither strange nor insignificant.

William Booth was convinced—and in his international travels he was constantly persuading his people—that this work of redemption was the will of God. He reasoned that just as God willed that an individual be saved, so God extended that will to the whole world, and God wanted the entire world to be saved. "We must increase the speed if we are to keep pace with the yearnings of the Almighty Heart of Love that would have all men to be saved."[24] Given that fact, Booth was equally convinced that God's people on earth were the agencies of that redemption, and none were better suited or qualified for that than Salvationists.[25]

Here William Booth's single-mindedness and his inextricable relationship with The Salvation Army came to his service as an international evangelist and religious figure. He became increasingly convinced that he and his people were to have a significant part to play in the establishment of such a kingdom. Booth had no interest in setting some sort of time frame for the establishment of the kingdom of God by reading the nineteenth and twentieth centuries back into the books of Daniel and Revelation. He was concerned, however, that his people understand their place in God's redemptive activity, and that they be well motivated, realizing all along that there was a divine organizational goal to which they were marching: the kingdom of God. It was that goal that Booth was constantly preaching and that, in turn, gave such significance in the lives of his followers. "When God's people wake up to the importance of this great War, and go forth to engage in it after this fashion, the millennium will not be very far away."[26] On that practical, pastoral level rested the chief concern of William Booth for his Salvationists. On May 30, 1885, he wrote:

> I want to see a new translation of the Bible into the hearts and conduct of living men and women. I want an improved translation—or transference it might be called—of the commandments and promises and teachings and influences of this Book to the minds and feelings and words and activities of the men and women who hold on to it and swear by it and declare it to be an inspired Book and the only authorized rule of life.... It is of no use making correct translations of words if we cannot get the *words translated into life*.... Wayfaring men, though fools, can make this translation, and fifteen years' perseverance in it will, I have not the shadow of a doubt, go a long way towards bringing in the millennium.[27]

Such hopeful relationship between The Salvation Army and the establishment of the kingdom of God prevailed in Booth's thinking throughout the remainder of his life. His single-mindedness continued unabated, and Booth—and thousands of his followers—believed The Salvation Army was the agency best suited for the work of universal redemption.

As Booth's ministry expanded, so did this vision of the kingdom of God. And this was happening at the same time that Booth developed his view of salvation to include social as well as personal salvation. In fact, his clearest expression of the millennium was written in 1890 in an article entitled "The Millennium; or the Ultimate Triumph of Salvation

Army Principles."[28] And only two months after the publication of that article, Booth published his *In Darkest England and the Way Out*. And so, with the publication of "The Millennium," followed almost immediately by the publication of *In Darkest England and the Way Out*, 1890 proved to be a critical juncture in both theology and ministry for the founder of The Salvation Army. His Salvationists would understand that the dual mission of the Army, undergirded by a theology of redemption that was both personal and social, was preparatory to the establishment of the millennial kingdom on earth, and thereby a harbinger of the Second Advent of Christ. Likewise, Booth's increased emphasis on the possibility of a millennium provided a final eschatological vision of the conquest of God over the forces of evil as well as of the work of universal redemption. And in Booth's mind, he and his Army were the center of that salvation story. His article on the millennium, therefore, is important because Booth spells out the various characteristics of the millennium, and thereby provides goals to be obtained by his Salvationists. This motivation for the mission of the Army was not taken particularly from a Wesleyan theology, but more from the cultural and social context of Booth's day. Booth's postmillennial expression was not derived specifically from a doctrine of creation that would lead toward the redemption of creation. Rather, it was more of an expression of the perceived natural result of the methods of revival coupled with an English version of ruling the world.

Here Booth reached beyond his spiritual mentor, John Wesley. The Wesleyan revivals, as well as the revolutionary activities of Europe in Wesley's days, "induced in him a touch of 'post-millennialism'—an expectation of a notable out pouring of gospel grace and progress on earth. Rank-and-file Methodist attitudes varied."[29] But basically, millennial speculation did not concern either Wesley or his Methodists. Such matters "were not of central concern to him. What did matter was doctrine concerned with personal salvation as the achievement of holiness to the point of perfection."[30] And the same could be said of Charles Grandison Finney. While Finney was a postmillennialist early in his ministry, the Civil War inevitably dampened his proclivities toward postmillennialism.[31]

Finally, William Booth was a military strategist for the gospel, and that practical strategy strengthened the corps life of the Army wherever Booth went preaching. There were many aspects of that strategy that were critical. For instance, Booth often opened up a "circle of corps" rather than corps in isolation from one another. It was intended that the corps would help and strengthen one another, and that the stronger corps could assist the weaker corps. Several examples of this could be given, but the work of the Army in Manchester, England, is undoubtedly a prime example. "Between 1878 and 1883 inclusive, the Army opened twelve corps within Manchester Parish, five of these in 1883 itself. This growth corresponds with the fastest period of Army growth nationally. Manchester had the largest concentration of corps in any city throughout the Army's history."[32] The total seating capacity of these corps was 10,100, the largest corps with a capacity of two thousand and the smallest three hundred. Glenn Horridge summarized the success of these corps:

> Once a number of corps were established within an immediate area, mutual aid played a very important part in maintaining momentum. Great encouragement must have been derived by soldiers and bands from one corps visiting another, visits from staff-officers, officers on their way to India, and the numerous activities taking place within the corps. All such factors contributed to keep the Army to the forefront of local life. In addition the discipline of the officers and soldiers insured persistence. This persistence came in not stopping open-air meetings because of the weather and, once out, marching and spreading the Gospel with well-drilled efficiency. Such drill included stopping every few minutes when on the march to allow soldiers to enter side streets to sing a song (hymn) of "fire a volley" (shout Gospel verses).[33]

Another military tactic used by Booth was to close the small corps or the corps that were not succeeding, a tactic taken from Christian Mission days. As I mentioned previously, George Scott Railton wrote to James Dowdle, an important Christian Mission preacher: "We have abandoned several small station[s] in order to use up all our strength on those we can make something of."[34] That adaptability continued in the Army.

A World University of Humanity

Even though William Booth was a conservative autocrat, there was a creative and imaginative side to him, already evidenced by his bringing the Army to birth. But even at this period of his life, he continued to show his creativity by outlining strategies for the future work of the Army. During this later ministry as an international evangelist, Booth had a dream of a World University of Humanity, and drew up a lengthy proposal for such a university in 1903.[35] While The Christian Mission had not established any training centers for its preachers, the Army early on recognized the need to do so. The first attempt at any kind of systematic officer training was in Manchester, England, in 1879, but that did not last. Training centers were permanently established in London, first for women in 1880 at the Booths' Gore Road house. Emma Booth, then barely twenty years of age, was placed in charge of that training center. And at the end of that year, a house was adapted in Hackney for the training of men. Ballington Booth, in his early twenties, was put in charge of the training of the men. And, of course, the ever-reliable "James Flawn was caterer for both homes."[36]

The training given was simple: Bible history and doctrine, as well as basic educational and pastoral skills. The training lasted for only a few months. In 1882 both the women and the men moved into the new Training Barracks, as they were called. "By the time the International Congress met in June, 1886, 2,600 men and women had passed through the training homes to serve as Salvation Army officers among nineteen nations."[37]

Booth was concerned that there were ineffectual officers and soldiers in his Army. As early as February 10, 1893, he wrote the following to Bramwell:

> I have got a feeling floating in my mind that we shall have to shake ourselves loose from a lot of trammels and get away from some of our old fashioned notions, which make us responsible for keeping Officers, whether they succeed or whether they don't. I don't see why we should not strike out and have something like a "Free Trade"; let them marry, and go if they don't succeed, only keeping the men that do well. As it is, one good fellow has to carry three or four lame and helpless fellows round his neck, and if we don't mind we shall be landed with a lot of incapables, and also further difficulties.[38]

On December 1, 1901, Evangeline Booth wrote to Bramwell Booth regarding the training of officers:

> The Training question has been on my mind for a long time, though only now am I in a position to consider the proposed alterations. I am fully persuaded that if we can improve this branch of our work, one of the finest strokes for the bettering of the whole Territory will be accomplished. I feel sure that the leakage in our younger ranks is almost entirely to be attributed to an insufficiency in their training, and believe that the plan I have proposed will meet the difficulty and supply the lack.[39]

But the concern for education and proper training was not limited to officers. William Booth wrote in 1905, "A great many of the Soldiers, and this applies especially to the Locals [lay leaders], are able to do important work in the Corps and yet get very little work given to them; their idleness leads to their decline and decay. Now this I am convinced arises not only from weakness in carrying out our system on the part of the F.O. [Field Officer], but from the fact that we have no method of Training our Locals or our Soldiers."[40]

Booth also spoke about the need for training in piety, after the model of the Methodist class meeting. This had been used effectively in The Christian Mission but became neglected, probably because of the heavy emphasis on revivals and mass meetings, in the Army. It is true that thousands of people were converted in those meetings, but the Army was weak in nurturing those people in the Christian faith. William Booth admitted as much when he wrote:

> It is also another reason for losing a great many Soldiers—especially does this apply to people with families. They say they want to take the young people where they can get some proper instruction in piety and for the battles of life. . . . I am very much exercized about the piety of many of the Soldiers also. They get very little to help them in the direction of deep spiritual things.[41]

Booth simply did not find the training of officers or soldiers sufficient to meet the needs of the world and his expanding Army. Therefore, he envisioned the establishment of a university "having its main Wings in England and the United States, with affiliated Colleges throughout the world, and to provide it with Officers of every rank capable of supplying the training needed for the discharge of every variety of work at present engaged in by The Army, or in which it may feel called upon to engage in the future."[42] He envisioned that training would be given in four areas: evangelistic work, missionary and medical work, social work, and departmental work including instruction in medicine, engineering, architecture, accounting and auditing, finance, and editorial and literary work. To Booth, this would include a broad educational training in what he called "the science of humanity."

Booth's proposal included the finances needed for beginning this university, and Booth's correspondence during this time gives evidence that he certainly talked about this idea frequently, especially to potential donors. However, the university was not formed, surely to Booth's disappointment. Nevertheless, he was not one to dwell on the past. He had other worlds to conquer.[43]

William Booth's Motor Car Campaigns

Booth was excited about the invention of the motor car because he saw the potential for its use in spreading the gospel. Booth became the Methodist circuit rider brought up to date. He began his first motor campaign in August 1904 from Land's End and went as far as Aberdeen.

> The physical endurance of this old man of seventy-five is revealed by the itinerary of the tour which lasted for twenty-nine days and covered 1,224 miles. He spoke at seventy-five indoor, thirty-six outdoor, and fifty-three overflow, meetings; one hundred and sixty-four in all. He received, and replied to, thirty-six addresses of welcome. The average length of his indoor addresses was seventy minutes, and of his outdoor addresses, fifteen minutes.[44]

The remaining campaigns throughout England, Scotland, and Wales—six in number—covered similar mileage and followed the same routine. Booth's car, a white, open car with red wheels and with a large sign at the back of the car that read "Get Saved," led the way. His was followed by other cars in the caravan with other officers such as Commissioner Lawley and Major Fred Cox, Booth's faithful aide-de-camp.

Here was a peculiar sight by contemporary standards, all the riders in goggles, protective hats, and waterproof overcoats as they rode along—a company of traveling evangelists enduring the exigencies of such travel. William once wrote to Bramwell that

> I don't know what other people have discovered but I certainly have not yet found out where the pleasure of Motoring comes in, you are either blown through and through by Gales, or wetted through and through by Rain, or choked through and through by Dust, and what the roasting through and through by the Sun is like I do not yet know.[45]

But Booth was undaunted by this task, and his reports of these campaigns are often glowing. "The Campaign grows in volume as we roll along," he wrote of his 1906 adventure. "Yesterday at the five places where I spoke we had enormous crowds, the Open-airs were so vast as to be all but unmanageable. Still I got some truth out. A rough fellow at Eadie's elbow kept on punctuating almost every sentence to which I gave expression with the words 'That's a damn good speech.' "[46] So, he could also find humor in the journey, and he journeyed on with single-minded devotion to the work at hand.[47]

Whether on a motor car campaign or traveling abroad, one of Booth's most dedicated officers, Fred Cox, was at his side for many years as his faithful and loyal aide-de-camp, meeting Booth's every need. Cox even had a special uniform made, with forty-three pockets, so that he could carry everything needed by the General. Cox's responsibilities were many, from preparing the platform before the meetings to ensuring that the billets were well prepared before the General arrived. A typical letter from Cox not only demonstrates Cox's attention to detail but gives evidence of Booth's careful vegetarian diet, as well as the conditions that were expected when Booth was in someone's home. William Booth especially despised small talk with people, feeling it a complete waste of time and energy. And so Fred Cox wrote the following to Alderman John Mawle, J. P. of Banbury:

Dear Sir,

Understanding that you are entertaining General Booth on the occasion of his visit to Banbury on Monday next the 11th inst., I thought that perhaps you would like to know that the General's requirements are most simple.

He takes neither Fish, Flesh, nor Fowl, but lives chiefly on Bread and Butter, Mild Cheese, and uncooked Fruit such as Apples, Bananas, etc., etc.

Dinner he likes about 12:30 and will take a little Vegetable such as boiled Potatoes, Spinach or French Beans, and sometimes a little plain Milk Pudding (prepared without sugar).

These with warmth and quiet, enable the General to meet the heavy demands that are so constantly made upon him.

I would like to add that if you would Kindly refrain from inviting anyone to meet the General I should be greatly obliged, as the consequent necessity to talk in addition to his Public speaking is too taxing on his strength.

Yours very sincerely,

Fred R. Cox

MAJOR[48]

As Cox prepared the homes for the General's stay in these travels, one of his responsibilities was to string a wire from the General's bedroom to his own bedroom. A buzzer of sorts would be placed next to the General's bed and the bell would be at Fred Cox's side. Therefore, whenever the General—who often had sleepless nights—needed Cox, all he had to do was to ring the buzzer. "It was no uncommon thing—indeed it occurred with increasing frequency as the years went by—for Cox to be called several times during the night."[49] The tasks were many, and while occasionally Cox complained in his letters to his wife of the way he was being treated not only by the General but also occasionally by members of the Booth family, he nevertheless remained faithful to the General for the last years of Booth's life, first as a secretary, and toward the end as a friend and comrade.

General Booth kept marching on with his loyal contingent of officers, like Fred Cox, at his side. But there was trouble ahead for Booth. His sixth motor campaign, begun on July 24, 1909, had to be interrupted because Booth was having serious trouble with his right eye. So the remaining years of Booth's life were filled with triumphs and agonies, but perhaps the story of his triumphs is best told first.

CHAPTER THIRTEEN

ENGLAND RECOGNIZES HER SON: HONORS BESTOWED UPON WILLIAM BOOTH

Introduction

It is fair to say that William Booth did not seek all the recognition that came his way in his later years; although he enjoyed it, as would anyone, when he was so honored. Part of the burden of leadership was that he continued to be vilified by the likes of Thomas Huxley after the launching of the Darkest England Scheme, and there were enough disgruntled former officers who wrote about their bad experiences with the Army to make life difficult for Booth.[1] However, like Wesley and Whitefield before him, Booth had the fortitude to move forward with the cause and did not allow the disgruntled, either within or without the Army, to set the pace of his ministry or the ministry of his beloved Army.

To be sure Booth's detractors were probably rankled by the increasing attention he received through his international travels as well as his travels in his own homeland. He was coming to a place where he would be honored by kings and princes, United States presidents and city council members, and emperors and statesmen. In addition, some people within the church had already begun to recognize and appreciate Booth's work before the public honors were bestowed upon him. After all, the archbishop of Canterbury was the person who initiated the discussions with the Army in 1882, and Cardinal Manning of the Roman Catholic Church long recognized the importance of Booth and his Army and admired Booth's attention to people's spiritual lives.

Recognitions Come to William Booth

But recognition by other Christians was eventually matched by similar recognition—and sometimes even admiration—by the larger culture. Booth had always had influential friends around him such as E. H. Rabbits, the Corys, T. A. Denny, or W. T. Stead who supported his work. But these people were principally from the world of business and industry. But now recognition came from another level. One of the first times for such recognition occurred when Booth was received by Mr. William Ewart Gladstone, four times prime minister of England, on Monday, December 21, 1896, at Hawarden Castle. In a pamphlet that William Booth published after this interview, he mentioned that the conversation ranged from the work of the Army around the world, to the ranking system of the Army, to religion in general, including the matter of disestablishment.[2]

How Roy Hattersley, in his biography of William and Catherine Booth, could have determined from the written record that after introductions "there followed a dialogue which showed every sign of Mr. Gladstone fulfilling an unwelcome commitment with patience and courtesy"[3] is impossible to say. Were this remotely the case, perhaps two American presidents were better disposed to receive Booth. President William McKinley welcomed Booth on February 10, 1898, while Booth was touring America yet again. During this visit Booth was asked to open the Senate in prayer. And in his travels to America in both 1903 and 1907 Booth met President Theodore Roosevelt. In 1903 Roosevelt again asked him to open the Senate in prayer. In writing to Bramwell about his opening the Senate in prayer in 1898, William wrote:

> You will see from Nicol's report that by invitation I opened the Senate by prayer this morning. It was only a kind of slight formality, three minutes the limit given me for the prayer. Still I made the acquaintance of the Vice-President, who was exceedingly cordial, and Mr. Millburn, the Chaplain, and of several prominent people, besides being seen and heard by a number of Senators and others. This afternoon I have had my interview with the President. No stranger ever received me in a more friendly and hearty manner.[4]

These occasions pleased Booth for the attention they brought to him as well as to the Army. However, for Booth personally, a high point of his life was his reception by King Edward VII. The Booths had sought the approval of royalty for their work, beginning especially with Catherine's correspondence with Queen Victoria during the Purity Crusade. But the Booths had not personally met royalty, although, as faithful subjects of the Crown, they showed a sincere interest in the well-being of the royal family. The King asked, through his private secretary, Lord Knollys, to see William Booth—an invitation that delighted Booth. The only other time an Army officer had met with the King was in 1902 when Bramwell Booth had represented the Army, wearing his Salvation Army uniform—a privilege granted by the King himself—at the coronation of Edward VII.

And so, all other considerations aside, Booth prepared to meet the King. On the morning of the interview, June 22, 1904,[5] Booth stopped to inspect a temporary building on the Strand that the Army had erected for its forthcoming International Congress. He then washed his hands in a workman's pail and left for Buckingham Palace for the interview. His Majesty, who evidently knew of the work of the Army in several parts of his empire, by all accounts, cordially received Booth. Soon after, there followed a message from the King and Queen Alexandra to the International Congress assuring Salvationists of their interests in the good work of the Army. Following the Congress, on July 23, 1904, Queen Alexandra received Booth at Buckingham Palace.

Perhaps because of this personal contact and perhaps also because Booth was becoming more aware of his own mortality, the death of Edward VII affected Booth greatly. William Booth was on a campaign in Switzerland when news reached him of the King's death. Bramwell Booth first sent a telegram to William informing him of the King's illness, and then wrote to him a letter dated May 7, 1910, describing how the Army's leadership heard the news of the King's death and what plans were in progress for a memorial for the King and for condolences to the widowed Queen. William responded:

> We were appalled at the receipt of your telegram, which arrived here at 6.O'clock last night. We heard nothing about the matter; nobody here seems to know anything about it either, until we got at the German newspapers. However, I sent off immediately two telegrams of which the following are copies:
>
> > Her Majesty the Queen—London.
> > Distressed tidings King's illness—
> > Praying God's intervention healing him
> > And supporting Your Majesty. William Booth.

His Royal Highness Prince of Wales—London.
Just received tidings King's illness—
Praying for recovery and Divine support
Yourself, Princess and Royal family. William Booth.

I was much agitated all the evening and through the night, waking frequently with the words "God help the King" involuntarily on my lips. I felt the matter was serious; in fact I seemed to all but give up hope right away. This morning we hear, in an irregular fashion, that His Majesty died at 11.40 last night. What a mysterious, sudden, painful, nay, tragic affair it is. We understand that his malady has been Bronchitis. I wonder what the five Doctors who signed the bulletin did for him. However, I suppose we shall have some sort of details in the newspapers during the day, this morning's papers having gone to press before the news of the fateful termination of the malady was received in Zurich. I don't know what to say more; it seems little use me saying anything at all. When I left him that morning it was with the feeling that I had prepared the way for another interview, in which I might speak more freely to him about spiritual matters. Alas, alas, the second interview never came off, and never will do in this world, and in the next it will be too late for it to be of any advantage to either of us. Oh how true it is, "in the midst of life we are in death."[6]

And in a letter to Bramwell the following day, he again wrote the following:

This terrible and almost tragic death of the King has harassed me no little for many reasons, one of which has been the seemingly utter unbelief in the religious bearings of the event. There is nothing about Eternity, about the relations between the conditions in which men die and the conditions in which they live again. If there were no God, no Jesus Christ and no Cross, no Judgment Day and no Heaven and no Hell, the feeling could not have been much worse. I can understand the conduct of the worldly crowds, but when it comes to people professing to believe the Bible, it goes to my very soul. . . . Since dictating the above I have received your wire of this morning, and have telegraphed Princess Victoria as follows:

Her Royal Highness Princess Victoria. London.
Your Highness will certainly be amongst those who
will feel most deeply the loss of His Majesty.
May I not hope that the God, whom I have known
perform such miracles in the way of consolation,
will support and comfort you and make your sorrow
work out for the joy of others. I am praying for this.
William Booth.[7]

Following the death of Edward VII, Booth sent a telegram to Edward's son, the new king, George V.

While meeting with King Edward VII was a high point in William Booth's life, other honors bestowed on him as the Founder and General of The Salvation Army brought pleasure to him also, not only for the personal recognition but for the advancement of the cause of the Army in the mind of the public. He received the Freedom of the City award or its equivalent four times from four different cities or boroughs. In fact, when the first such honor was given to him—the Freedom of the City of London on October 26, 1905[8]—one thousand officers escorted Booth from the Army's International Headquarters on Queen Victoria Street to the Guildhall. This grand march caused one newspaper to report that "it is unusual, if not unprecedented, for a candidate for the City Freedom to be escorted to the Guildhall by a procession of his admirers, and it may be hoped that the example set yesterday by The Salvation Army will not be followed."[9]

William Booth was well received by Sir John Pound, the Lord Mayor of London, and the City Chamberlain, The Right Honourable Sir Joseph Cockfield Dimsdale. It was Dimsdale who read the citation for that occasion, the last few lines of which read as follows:

> This imperial City, through its Corporation is pleased to recognize publicly its indebtedness, and mark its gratitude, by placing the name of William Booth on the Register of her Honorary Citizens, which already bears the names of Britain's best and most valued sons.
>
> The Citizens of London are proud, General Booth, to offer you, through me, the right hand of fellowship, and to receive into their body one whose aim has been the rescue of the hopeless and the elevation of human nature.
>
> On behalf of the Lord Mayor, the Court of Aldermen, and the Court of Common Council, I beg to ask your acceptance of this Casket containing the copy of your Freedom, and also a warrant for £100 towards the funds of your noble work.[10]

Booth responded with a rather lengthy address about the Army, probably longer than was anticipated. Nevertheless, Booth did have a flare for such public occasions, and never missed an occasion to talk in colorful ways about himself as well as the work of his Army around the world. The beginning of the speech began with some high drama about his work for the kingdom of God:

My Lord Mayor, Aldermen, and Gentlemen of the Common Council—I must confess to feeling at a loss, when I look the task in the face, of making any fitting response to the generous and gracious sentiments that have just been spoken by the Chamberlain, or to adequately testify to the gratitude I feel for the gift of the Freedom of this great City. I have all my lifetime, my Lord Mayor, faced audiences of various descriptions. I have faced the howling mobs of Whitechapel and other places in the Empire; I have talked with boulders flying through the windows of buildings on the Continent; I have spoken to thousands and tens of thousands gathered in mighty conclaves in our Indian Empire; I have talked to the scattered populations of our Colonies up and down the world; but I have never faced an audience in which I found so great a difficulty to construct my ideas or give expression to them.[11]

But, of course, Booth did find the words necessary for this occasion. Following the ceremony at the Guildhall was a luncheon at the Mansion House and then a tour of various Army facilities in the City of London. Booth had to have had a rather strange feeling about the events of the day. Here he was being honored, but the first time he set foot on London soil he was virtually penniless and had no hope for the future. He took work in that pawnbroker's shop and hated every moment of it. And he began to preach. Even his Christian Mission began rather inauspiciously, and, but for what Booth perceived as the grace of God, his Christian Mission could have gone into obscurity as had many similar missions of that sort. But here he was on this day being honored in this very public and distinguished way. Over fifty years had passed and he never could even have imagined such an event those many years earlier.

Not long after this, on November 6, 1905, William Booth received the Freedom of the City in the place of his birth. The ceremony began in the Exchange Hall and then there was a procession to Mechanics' Hall. Following the ceremonies, Booth enjoyed tea with the Lord Mayor of Nottingham. After all, Nottingham was "not to be outdone by London,"[12] and honored William Booth as "the greatest man that Nottingham has ever bred or seen."[13] Again, as Booth experienced that day, he must have felt strange indeed. Here was the place of his birth that he knew only in poverty, and where—since the age of thirteen, after the death of his father—he experienced all but destitution as he tried to keep food on the table for himself and his mother and three sisters. And now he is told that he is Nottingham's greatest man.

The next year, on April 16, 1906, the ceremony was repeated. This time, Booth "received the Freedom of the royal and ancient borough of Kirkcaldy, Scotland, from the hands of Provost H. M. Barnet, in the King's Theater."[14] Finally, Booth became a Freeman of Boston, Massachusetts, thus completing four such recognitions.

One of the honors bestowed upon William Booth in his later years that seemed to please him most—because he felt it would help the cause of the Army—was the honorary Doctor of Civil Law degree he received from Oxford University. That honor was bestowed on Booth on Wednesday, June 26, 1907. Booth had evidently heard that he was going to receive this degree while he was on a campaign in Japan. On May 6, 1907, he wrote to Bramwell about the degree from Osaka, Japan:

> I am not surprised at it, but still it is not what I should ever have coveted. My people here are much set up and think that it will help my influence greatly with students here and with similar classes elsewhere, and therefore I assent in the spirit of submission. You will send me the details as to the character of the ceremony, and the part I shall be expected to play in it. It has no charm for me apart from utility.[15]

It must have been an interesting day for William Booth. He was certainly in fine company. Among those who received honorary degrees that day were the American ambassador, the prime minister, the speaker of the House of Commons, Auguste Rodin, Rudyard Kipling, Charles Camille Saint-Saëns, and Samuel Langhorne Clemens, otherwise known as Mark Twain. How interesting it must have been to have heard a conversation between William Booth and Mark Twain! The stately procession of all of those receiving honorary degrees and other degrees, as well as many other officials of the university, proceeded from the Hall of Magdalen College to the Sheldonian Theater. And there, in that historic setting, William Booth received his honorary degree. The recently elected chancellor of the university and the late Viceroy of India, The Right Honorable George Nathaniel Lord Curzon of Kedleston, presided and read the citation in Latin, which translates:

> O Man, Most Venerable, Compassionate Patron of the lowest of the people, and Commander of the Army for the winning of souls, I admit you as a Doctor of Civil Law to this ancient University.[16]

It would, of course, be no small matter to Booth that he was recognized by so prestigious a university on such an important occasion for being a winner of souls. Booth began his ministry with evangelism as its focus, and many years earlier once again made evangelism his own personal priority while leaving the details of the Darkest England Scheme to Bramwell and others.

As I have mentioned, all of these honors undoubtedly were somewhat strange occurrences for Booth, this son of poverty from the streets of Nottingham whose entrance into London in 1849 was inauspicious to say the least. His Christian Mission was not immediately identifiable apart from several other missions of the same sort, and he and Catherine Booth struggled to support a growing family. After the founding of the Army he was ridiculed, probably by some of the same people who attended the occasions at Buckingham Palace, the Guildhall, or Oxford University. Nevertheless, in these final years the honors came and a now-grateful nation paid its respects in several ways not only to William Booth but also to his Salvation Army. There was even talk about making Booth a Peer of the Realm, to which Booth wrote that he "would certainly be willing to go to the House of Lords, or any other lawful place, if only I could thereby assist the Suffering Classes for whose betterment I have devoted my life."[17]

International Honors

International honors paralleled what was happening in England. In 1907 he had an interview with the king and queen of Denmark, the king of Norway, the queen of Sweden, and was admitted to the presence of the emperor of Japan. And while home he would meet occasionally with the current prime minister, chiefly to talk about the colonization project of the Darkest England Scheme. Harold Begbie has noted that "there is no doubt that next to his spiritual work, the idea of emigration occupied the chief place in his mind at this time. It was part of his dream of converting the world."[18] In 1908, we find further signs of his royal acceptance. Before going again to the Continent and on to Russia, he was received by the Prince and Princess of Wales at Marlborough House, and King Edward VII personally gave a contribution to Army funds. And while on the Continent, the king of Norway attended one of Booth's meetings, and Booth was again received by the king of Sweden. "These signs of royal favour steeled his soldiers' hearts. They were proud of their old commander who had risen from the Mile End Waste to be received in royal palaces and parliaments. On his return to England, he was commanded again to Buckingham Palace, where he was received on April 6 by Queen Alexandra and her sister, the Dowager-Empress of Russia."[19]

During the time when these honors were being bestowed, William Booth continued his motor campaigns in his homeland. The second campaign in 1905 covered 2,250 miles, and the third, beginning on July 28, 1906, covered 1,700 miles and lasted for thirty days. The fourth campaign, beginning on July 16, 1907, lasted for thirty-three days and covered 1,678 miles. And on June 20, 1908, even though he was now nearly eighty years of age, he began his fifth motor campaign, which covered 1,000 miles. But after the campaign the wear and tear began to tell on Booth, and he was having eye trouble.

And so, in spite of all the honors and in spite of his now-international reputation as a preacher and evangelist, and compassionate patron of the poor, he would enter into a difficult period. Even though Booth was uncertain what the future would hold, he was a man of faith and he trusted himself into the hands of his God. The remaining few years of his life included times of suffering, but at the end of the road there was light. And so Booth now entered into a time of darkness and light, and his response to what providence gave to him in his declining years is perhaps the best measure of the man.

CHAPTER FOURTEEN

DARKNESS AND LIGHT

Introduction

The motorcar campaigns continued. Booth the evangelist was still driven by his postmillennial vision of saving the whole world, and raising up the saints in holiness that was demonstrated constantly and consistently by love for neighbor. He was often cross and upset at officers and soldiers who claimed to be faithful to the principles of the Army but did little to further his postmillennial mission. Like Wesley before him, he was frequently frustrated that all Salvationists did not share his zeal, demonstrate his daily discipline, and forsake all for the salvation of the world. And he was not the easiest person to please on the motor car campaigns. As he grew older he was less patient with those around him and more demanding of those in whose homes he stayed during his travels. Some of his billets were delighted with the privilege of being a host to General Booth, while others felt like singing the doxology after he had left.

William Booth's Last Residence

The Army built a home for Booth at Hadley Wood in 1903. The Booths had moved to Hadley Wood in 1888, two years before Catherine's death, to ensure a more comfortable and quiet home for Catherine as she struggled with her cancer. William's new home, Rookstone, was built close to their previous home in Hadley Wood. There the lonely widower found refuge from his travels, for which his correspondence from various parts of the world during these last years frequently demonstrates his longing. This was a safe haven for the wanderer. It was a place of comfort for the preacher. It was a home of rest for the aging and somewhat failing General. "Old age brought him a relish for quiet and developed in him a taste for domestic tidiness."[1] He still missed Catherine, and loneliness often lingered in that house, especially when contrasted to the hectic life of earlier days when the Booth house was filled with children, servants, and Army officers, and the house served as both domicile and office.

That frenzied pace of the earlier days was now gone, but with a secretary in residence and with constant visits by staff officers, Booth kept up a daily routine of work interrupted only by his simple meals and his afternoon naps. He was energized by learning of the Army's work from frequent reports from Bramwell and from his occasional visits to International Headquarters. And he frequently became restless in his quiet home, and so prepared for his next motor campaign, his next public engagement in Britain, or his next visit to Salvationists in various parts of the world. There was a cycle of existence now for Booth, on the one hand wearied by his many travels and looking forward to peace and quiet in his home, and on the other hand bored by the routine of his home life and longing to get out and save the world from itself and for God.

William Booth's Eye Trouble

For a man of his age and disposition, and for a man often worn out by his worldwide travels and the many exigencies of leading an international movement, Booth was in fairly good health during these final years up until about 1909. But in a journal entry during his visit to Canada in March 1907, there is an ominous hint of trouble to come. He wrote, "My eyes failed me for reading my notes, so I plunged in anyhow, and Eadie [one of Booth's senior officers] reckons it was the best speech he ever heard me make of the kind."[2] By December 1908 it was determined that Booth would have to have surgery on his right eye. That surgery was performed on December 16, 1908, in his own home by Mr. Charles Higgens, Senior Consulting

Ophthalmic Surgeon at Guy's Hospital. The surgery was successful and Booth was cheered with a message of well wishes from Queen Alexandra.

For Booth, the surgery proved to be only a slight inconvenience. He soon resumed both his international travels as well as his motor car campaigns. However, in his writings he still makes frequent references to his bad eye. While away from Britain on February 12, 1909, he wrote to Bramwell, "I don't think you need have any anxiety about this place on my eye. If it does not get better I will consult Higgens."[3] But it evidently did not get better and a month later William had to admit to Bramwell that "my eye has been my chief anxiety. . . . Of course on my return the first thing that will require attention will be the examination by Mr. Higgens, and decide as to whether a further operation is to take place. My opinion is that the eye has no chance to do its best, because it does not get enough practice. I have to rush from one thing to another, mostly without glasses altogether."[4]

It was during his sixth motor car campaign that went into Wales that Booth's eye caused enough of a problem that he had to end the campaign and return to London. The second operation was performed on August 21, 1909, but with no success. Booth was now blind in one eye. He gave details of his affliction in a letter to an old Christian Mission friend, now Commissioner Elijah Cadman, written on September 13, 1909. The letter is important, not only because it provides a firsthand account of Booth's physical affliction but because it gives some insight into a rather indomitable spirit of this man now eighty years of age. Booth wrote:

My Dear Commissioner,

You will have gathered from reports in the Press and the descriptions in the "War Cry" something of the nature of the misfortune that has overtaken me with respect to my sight.

We have not thought it wise as yet to give any details to the public, or to our Officers and Soldiers in particular, of the extent of the injury suffered, but it seems desirable that you should have a little more exact information on the subject.

You will know that by the operation on my right eye, performed last December, the cataract or impediment to my vision was removed, and with it the lens in the eye was taken away. By artificial aid, however, I was able to read and write and see objects far and near with tolerable ease and correctness, and you will know that I was hoping by striving to accustom myself to spectacles to be able to see my congregations and the things passing around me without difficulty.

At the same time my left eye, on which a cataract was also forming, was of sufficient service to enable me to discern persons and things immediately around me, also to find my way about the house, and the road, or as far as that goes on to the platform, and to give me a general idea of the congregation before me.

Now, the sight of the eye on which the operation had been performed has been destroyed by a poison, so the Doctors say, injected by some small microbe, or fly, or dust, or something else which forced itself into the eye during my recent Motor Campaign,

It happened very suddenly. I had no knowledge of it on the morning of Tuesday, 17th August, while at night I found that the sight had gone from the eye altogether. The Doctors ascertained that an abscess was rapidly forming, which soon became so angry and alarming that for fear of injury to the brain it had to be cut out, which was done, destroying the power of vision. Its only utility now will be to carry an artificial mask, which they tell me will not, in a general way, be noticeable by the public.

The remaining eye, however, enables me to see surrounding objects, as I have said, quite as readily as I did before, and to write, although in a very bungling fashion.

Should the cataract grow worse there is still the possibility of having it removed, in which case I should be able to recover a reasonable measure of the power of sight, which I have so recently lost.

I hope you will be able to understand this hurried and imperfect description of my trouble and that it may be of service to you in speaking privately to those of my friends who may desire further information. I am sure that I shall have your continued sympathy and prayers.

It was a great trial to me after an effort to preserve my eyes extending over nine long months and in the full expectation of having its perfect use once more, to be so suddenly and completely deprived of it, and that in the midst of one of the most remarkable Campaigns of my life.

But, God has wonderfully sustained me. I have accepted the inevitable and thrown myself back on Him for support and comfort and the full assurance that He will use the trial for my good and to the good of the Army.

I believe He will fulfil my expectations and that He will not allow this or anything else in any way to interfere with the accomplishment of the Work he has given me to do.

I am still believing that I shall live to serve you, to serve the Army, to serve the World, to serve my Lord, and that He will give me wisdom, strength, and love needed for the fulfillment of my purpose, therefore, go on trusting and believing and regarding me as

Your affectionate General,
William Booth[5]

In spite of growing physical limitations caused not only by the loss of sight in one eye but also by the aches and pains of an elderly, weakened, and failing man, Booth continued his evangelistic work, beginning in early 1910 with visits to Holland, Germany, and Scandinavia. He was driven, to be sure, by his compassion for a needy and suffering world and by his desire to save that world. That dream was still part of his soul. But he was also driven by a less pure motive—a sense that he was indispensable to the welfare and the future of the Army. It was impossible for him to let go, although long ago he had named Bramwell as his successor. While constantly claiming that the Army was in God's hands, there were still times when he wondered how the Army would go on without him.

But his body was failing him. His correspondence from 1910 to 1912 is largely filled with references to his health—both good and bad—and especially his eyesight. On Monday, July 10, 1911, writing to Bramwell Booth from Berlin, he was especially optimistic about his general health. "My health continues remarkably good notwithstanding all the struggle I have passed through."[6] He also referred to his eyesight in that letter. "There is no probability of my submitting to an operation during 1911. My sight keeps better sooner than worse. I should think the likelihood is 18 months instead of earlier."[7]

By 1911 Booth was definitely wearing out. He himself mused "that the end might be drawing near."[8] He was occasionally losing consciousness, although never when he was in a public meeting. And he was troubled by his lapses in memory. Nevertheless, in spite of his failing health he was determined, upon returning to Britain from the Continent in 1911, to conduct one more motor car campaign—his seventh. And in 1912 he still continued his meetings abroad, leaving for Holland on February 23, 1912, and, after returning home for a few days leaving for Sweden. Upon returning home from Sweden, he never left Britain again. He was home to live out the remainder of his days and to die in August of that year. On April 10, 1912, he was eighty-three years of age, celebrating that evening with one thousand London officers in the Army's Clapton Congress Hall.

Tragedy interrupted Booth's life once more with the loss of the Army's friend, W. T. Stead. Booth had outlived nearly all of his old supporters, such as the Cory brothers and T. A. Denny. Booth was certainly not as close to Stead personally as Catherine and Bramwell had been, theirs being a bond that developed during their work together in the Purity Crusade and when Bramwell and Stead stood trial together.

William Booth distrusted Stead's less than orthodox religious inclinations. However, Stead's going down on the *Titanic* while on his way to the United States to speak at a peace conference troubled Booth greatly. Bramwell wrote to William, "I will write a column of appreciation [in *The War Cry*] in moderate terms, not claiming him as a Salvationist and yet speaking up for him as sincere and God-fearing and poor-loving, but I should like you to give me a brief comment to start my paper with."[9]

In the meantime, Booth's eyesight was getting worse. Something had to be done. The last time William Booth appeared in public was on May 9, 1912, in the Royal Albert Hall. An estimated ten thousand people attended that meeting in which Booth was saluted by Salvationists from many parts of the world. Of course, by this time his eyesight was nearly gone. He could see only shadows. And so he was told everything that was going on in the meeting. Booth was led to the podium when it was his time to address the audience. Standing fixed behind that podium must have been difficult for the evangelistic preacher who sometimes wandered on the platform when he spoke. He reviewed his life's work and humorously said to his audience, "I am going into dry-dock for repairs."[10] It was time for another eye operation.[11]

The surgery was performed on May 23, 1912, again by Mr. Higgens, assisted by Mr. Herbert Lightfoot Eason, Senior Ophthalmic Surgeon and Dean of the Medical School at Guy's Hospital, but this time in Booth's own home at Hadley Wood. Dr. Milne, the General's private physician, was also present. The operation was initially considered a success. His Majesty King George V sent a message from Buckingham Palace on May 24 wishing it so. The message read:

Buckingham Palace
24th May, 1912

General Booth
Hadley Wood

The King is anxious to be informed as to your condition this morning. His Majesty trusts that the operation you underwent yesterday was successful and that you are making satisfactory progress.

Stamfordham[12]

William Booth responded:

His Majesty the King
Buckingham Palace

I am deeply touched by your Majesty's kind inquiry. I am thankful to say that my surgeons inform me that the operation of yesterday has been successful, and that the eye is making satisfactory progress. I have consecrated my restored vision to the service of God and my fellowmen. With the assurance of grateful prayers for the highest welfare of your Majesty and the Queen,

William Booth[13]

But the optimism of the moment diminished in the following days. There was trouble ahead. Booth was blind. He received messages of condolence from far and wide, but one in particular was important to him and his answer demonstrates the quintessential Booth. Her Majesty Queen Alexandra wrote:

General Booth, Hadley Wood

Have heard with the greatest distress of the heavy and sad trial which has deprived you of the light of day, but feel sure that, with God's help, you will still continue the good and noble work which has been a blessing to the whole world.

Alexandra[14]

To which Booth responded:

Her Majesty Queen Alexandra
Marlborough House

I shall ever gratefully treasure the recollection of your Majesty's gracious sympathy with me in my loss. I am still resolved to continue my work for God and His Cause as zealously as in the past, and I pray that His continued goodness and comfort may rest upon your Majesty in the future.

William Booth[15]

The best account of those difficult days is in a letter from Bramwell Booth to his brother-in-law, Frederick Booth-Tucker—who was now serving back in India—written on May 31, 1912:

> We have indeed been overtaken by a calamity. The General's sight is injured I fear beyond recovery. We had two of the first men in Europe there—Higgins [sic] and a man named Eason who is the chief ophthalmic man of Guy's Hospital, and looked upon as one of the coming men in the world on these subjects. And notwithstanding all the precautions—many of which seemed to me to be extreme in their detail and precision—some poison must have entered the wound when it was made and the inflammation set up two days later proves, by the assistance of the analysts, to have been a purely septic result. It is hideous to think of, in fact one may almost say it is disgraceful. Higgins [sic] himself is very much bruised about it. He told me he had been in practice for 32 years and never had had such a case in his private practice and had only had one such case in the last 20 years in his Hospital work. . . .
>
> He has taken things well. I had the task of telling him yesterday morning at 9 o'clock that there was no hope. He made a very characteristic remark. After a short pause he said, "Well I have done all I could for God and the people with the help of my eyes, now I will do all I can for God and the people without my eyes. . . ."
>
> The General is making plans for artificial assistance in his writings and his coming Campaigns. What arrangements we shall make I do not know. You can imagine the difficulty in thinking things out.[16]

William Booth's Promotion to Glory

Thinking through and planning ways to help Booth with these new physical challenges proved difficult indeed. But Booth was determined to go on. He had a device made for his hand that would guide his hand across the page as he wrote. The first letter written after his blindness was to his daughter Eva.[17] On the one hand, Booth felt utterly helpless and alone; useless and disappointed. On the other hand, his optimism came through and he actually began making plans to visit America and Canada yet again, to the dismay of those around him, especially Bramwell. But Booth realized finally and fully that no further travels from Hadley Wood were going to take place. This was to be the place where he would await his own death. He had already entered into physical darkness, and now more than ever he longed to walk in the light of heaven. His work on earth was done. His thoughts were beginning to turn from time to eternity.

As with Catherine, so it was with William. Methodists died well, and the deathbed scenes of the Methodists were a source of inspiration to all the faithful. Very near his own passing, Booth matched Wesley's words, "The best of all is this—God is with us," with his own final pronouncement—"The promises of God are sure if you only believe." Then he entered into a coma.

The deathwatch around William's bed began.[18] Present were Bramwell and Florence Booth and two of their children, Commissioner Lucy Booth-Hellberg, and Colonel Theodore Kitching, a long-time confidant of William Booth[19] and some other officers. Sadly, "Ballington, Herbert, Katie and their families were absent. They were almost no longer part of the family, certainly they were no longer part of the family business."[20] On the very day Booth died, Bramwell wrote to his sister, Eva, in the United States describing his condition. "The first and foremost fact is, as you have already heard, that The General has again changed very much for the worse, and it looks as though we could not expect him to last many days—sometimes we feel like saying many hours. He had a short period of consciousness on Sunday morning and it may prove to have been the last. He could not say much as his speech has been very much affected since Saturday, but he spoke of himself and then referred to the promises of God saying in a very distinct and definite way, although in broken words, as I have described in 'The War Cry' which I enclose."[21] In that same letter Bramwell Booth mentioned a telegram that Evangeline had sent that was put into Booth's hands upon his dying. The telegram simply said, "Kiss him for me."[22] The very sad note in the letter is that it reveals still family animosity even at the hour of Booth's death. Bramwell Booth simply could not let the past go. He wrote, "While I have been dictating this has come in your telegram about Herbert. This is a great surprise to me. He said nothing in his recent [correspondence] with me which would lead me to think that he felt so deeply a desire to see The General as this would seem to indicate, and knowing all that has happened one naturally wonders whether there is behind this any ulterior thought. I hope not. However, I must leave it now."[23]

William Booth died on the evening of Tuesday, August 20, 1912. The public pronouncement came the next day: "The General has laid down his sword." His body was taken to Clapton Congress Hall and for three days sixty-five thousand people filed past his coffin. The memorial service was held in Olympia and thirty-five thousand people attended the service. On Wednesday, August 28, 1912, there was a march of thousands of Salvationists behind the casket of William Booth from the Army's International Headquarters past the Mansion House to Abney Park Cemetery. Booth was laid to rest beside his beloved Catherine. Bramwell Booth delivered the eulogy at the graveside.[24] "What matter, then, was here for tears? Booth's soldiers did not weep: they exulted."[25]

A few years earlier William Booth had written, "My arms are around the world and my heart is set upon its salvation."[26] Perhaps these words are the best measure of the man. For all his faults and shortcomings, of which he was often painfully aware, it is beyond question that he was deeply moved by the admonition of his Lord to love God and love his neighbor. There was, at his core, a love of God and of humanity. The testimony of his life demonstrated to all but the most skeptical that he was not a man to scheme, to pretend, to connive. He was forthrightly a believer in God the Father, Son, and Holy Spirit, and the Bible and his own experience spoke to his heart and motivated his actions. His life was ruled by his ambition to be a servant of that God whom he loved and whose cause he so forthrightly defended.

He served God and he served his generation. This is the legacy of William Booth.

EPILOGUE

Millions of people have followed in the footsteps of William Booth as both officers (ordained ministers) and soldiers (laypeople). All theology and all communities have a social context, and those committed to the ministry of The Salvation Army since it evolved from a struggling mission in 1878 have found their religious and social world enriched by the remarkable fellowship of like believers. William Booth's destiny became theirs also, and the continuing ministry of the Army today is a sign of faithfulness to the cause of Christ that moved William Booth at the time of his conversion to say that "God shall have all there is of William Booth."

History has demonstrated that the vision of William Booth, as it has been enfleshed by Salvationists around the world, has adorned both the world and the Church. Like their founder, Salvationists have at times demonstrated human frailties and weaknesses. Nevertheless, the endurance of the Army is a constant reminder that God uses his people in all their humanity to carry out his purposes. Another side of this story, of course, is that many of the men and women who have followed William Booth and sustained his Army have been people of remarkable strength, courage, and dignity, often in the face of extremely difficult and trying circumstances, and sometimes even in the face of death. The perseverance exemplified by Booth has become their perseverance, and still today there are extraordinary stories to be told of people faithful to the cause of Christ's kingdom through the ministry of The Salvation Army.

If Catherine Booth was correct that adaptability was the primary reason for the initial growth of the Army, so it may be said today that the continuing ability of the Army to minister in over one hundred countries around the world is a witness to that adaptability for the sake of the gospel. It goes without saying that the cultural context in which the

Army ministers today is far different from the world of William and Catherine Booth. And yet the motivation for ministry remains the same—to be obedient to the great commandment of the Lord to love God and love one's neighbor. This was the primary lesson taught by William Booth, always uppermost in his mind. This was his driving force as he attempted to serve his generation. And so it is today.

The chief legacy of William Booth is to be found wherever and whenever there are Salvationists around the world preaching the good news of the kingdom of God, and manifesting the compassion of their Lord to their neighbor—whether from pulpits in New Zealand, on the streets of Calcutta, in a hospital in Zambia, in various ministries in Finland, or in any of the thousands of ministries in many countries of the world. This is William Booth's final and lasting legacy, and the Army welcomes all who wish to embrace that legacy as their own.

NOTES

1. Beginnings: Life from 1829 to 1849

1. There are several biographies of William Booth, but many of them are now out of print. The best of the older biographies are the following: Charles T. Bateman, *Life of General Booth* (New York: Association Press, 1912); Harold Begbie, *The Life of General William Booth*, 2 Vols. (New York: The Macmillan Company, 1920); Frederick de Latour Booth-Tucker, *William Booth, The General of The Salvation Army* (New York: The Salvation Army Printing and Publishing House, 1898); Thomas F. Coates, *The Prophet of the Poor: The Life Story of General Booth* (London: Hodder and Stoughton, 1905); Richard Collier, *The General Next to God* (New York: E. P. Dutton and Co., 1965); St. John Ervine, *God's Soldier: General William Booth*, 2 Vols. (New York: The Macmillan Company, 1935); Jenty Fairbank, *William and Catherine Booth: God's Soldiers* (London: Salvationist Publishing and Supplies, Ltd., 1974); Alex M. Nicol, *General Booth and The Salvation Army* (London: Hebert and Daniel, 1911); G. S. Railton, *The Authoritative Life of General William Booth* (New York: The Reliance Trading Company, 1912); J. Evan Smith, *Booth the Beloved* (London: Oxford University Press, 1949); W. T. Stead, *General Booth* (London: Isbister and Company, 1891); and Harold C. Steele, *I Was a Stranger* (New York: Exposition Press, 1954). The best of the recent biographies are David Malcolm Bennett, *The General: William Booth*, 2 Vols. (Longwood, Florida: Xulon Press, 2003), and Roy Hattersley, *Blood and Fire: William and Catherine Booth and Their Salvation Army* (New York: Doubleday, 2000). For three interesting articles on William Booth see John A. Barker, "William Booth," *British Heritage*, 2:2 (February/March, 1981), pp. 46-55; Donaldson Grant, "General William Booth," *All the World* (March 1903), pp. 115-19; and G. Campbell Morgan, *Heroes of the Free Churches: William Booth, Founder of The Salvation Army* (London: The Epworth Press, 1935), 16 pp.

In his biography of William Booth, St. John Ervine gave the date of the death of William Booth as October 20, 1912 (see, for example, 2:810), but this was corrected in an errata sheet. In his biography Hattersley inexplicable follows St. John Ervine and gave the date as October 20, 1912 (see page 434). This error has been repeated in contemporary scholarship. For example, see Pamela J. Walker, *Pulling the Devil's Kingdom Down: The Salvation Army in Victorian Britain* (Berkeley, California: The University of California Press, 2001), p. 235.

2. Ervine, *God's Soldier: General William Booth*, 2:811-12.

3. *Who Was Who 1897–1915* (London: A & C Black, 1920), p. 54 wrongly records

William as the only son of a builder, a failure to recognize both the William from the first marriage and this son, Henry, who died at the age of two. Hattersley in *Blood and Fire: William and Catherine Booth and Their Salvation Army* also mentions William as the only son of Samuel and Mary (p. 13).

4. Begbie makes unsubstantiated remarks about Booth's "Jewish blood" and "Jewish features." He remarked that Mary Moss "was obviously of Jewish descent" (Harold Begbie, "Booth, William (1829–1912)," *Dictionary of National Biography 1912–1921* [Oxford: Oxford University Press, 1927], p. 50).

5. See the baptism certificate for the parish church of Sneinton in the county of Nottingham for April 12, 1829, where Samuel Booth is listed as "Gentleman" in the column identifying trade or profession. The baptismal entry is no. 694, p. 87 of the Register. It is interesting that, in the marriage certificate of William Booth and Catherine Mumford in 1855, Samuel Booth, although deceased by that time, was still listed as "Gentleman" in the column identifying the rank or profession of the father, although long before his death Samuel Booth's fortunes had fallen considerably, if not completely. The term, therefore, was more of a general term and not intended to convey a person of wealth or one belonging to the gentry.

6. Ervine, *God's Soldier: General William Booth*, 1:5.

7. Begbie, *The Life of General William Booth*, 1:23.

8. Ibid., 1:26.

9. See Railton, *The Authoritative Life of General William Booth*, p. 2.

10. Ibid., p. 3.

11. Begbie, *The Life of General William Booth*, 1:26-27. This is probably the most accurate and honest picture of William Booth's relationship with his mother in his early days. Booth-Tucker, the son-in-law of William and Catherine Booth and one who frequently romanticized the life of the Booths, wrote that "The mother, pure and tender as a breath from Heaven, was the guardian angel of her surviving boy. Mother and son idolized each other" (Booth-Tucker, *William Booth, The General of The Salvation Army*, p. 8). The truth is that, save for the company of his sisters, Booth's home life was rather lonely. Note also W. T. Stead's inaccurate portrayal of both father and mother: "If General Booth inherited from his father the genius for finance and his indomitable and resourceful mind, he owes to his mother that spirit of sympathy and of passionate affection which have been the chief secret of his spiritual power. His mother was a saintly woman of such blameless life that her son used to say that she was always a difficulty in the way of acceptance of the doctrine of the natural depravity of the human heart. She was everything to her only surviving son, and he was everything to her. It is the fashion to ascribe the unique position which is accorded to women in the Salvation Army to Mrs. Booth, the wife. Probably an equal share, at least, should be given to Mrs. Booth, the mother" (Stead, *General Booth*, p. 24).

12. Begbie, *The Life of General William Booth*, 1:27. Mary Moss Booth died on January 13, 1875, ironically the same death date as Samuel Booth's first wife. See William Booth, "My Mother," *All the World* (August 1893), pp. 81-85. In that article the date for the death of William's mother is incorrectly given as January 3, 1875.

13. The home of William Booth's birth is owned by The Salvation Army today.

14. Coates, *The Prophet of the Poor: The Life Story of General Booth*, p. 17.

15. Ibid.

16. The *Newark Advertiser*, Newark, Nottinghamshire, on May 16, 1962, records that the Church of St. Mary in Bleasby, Nottinghamshire, had a church school, "and among its pupils was William Booth." The biographies of William Booth do not mention this. See the William Booth File, The Salvation Army International Heritage Centre; London, England.

17. This shop was owned by Messers Dickemann and Knight, Ltd., 5, Poultry, Nottingham and William Booth also served in the branch shop situated at No. 4, Hockley. He was officially employed by Mr. John Knight. See the William Booth File, The Salvation Army International Heritage Centre; London, England.

18. Ervine, *God's Soldier: General William Booth*, 1:30.

19. Begbie, *The Life of General William Booth*, 1:41.

20. Begbie in *The Life of General William Booth* mistakenly records the date as 1842 (1:42).

21. Ibid., 1:44.

22. See William Booth, "The Days of Youth" *The War Cry* (April 10, 1909), p. 1.

23. John Wesley, "The Nature, Design, and General Rules of the United Societies in London, Bristol, Kingswood, and Newcastle upon Tyne," (1743) in Rupert E. Davies, ed. *The Works of John Wesley*, Vol. 9 (Nashville: Abingdon Press, 1989), pp. 69-70. For further description of the classes see Richard P. Heitzenrater, *Wesley and the People Called Methodists* (Nashville: Abingdon Press, 1995), pp. 118-19.

24. Ervine, *General William Booth*, 1:34-35.

25. See William Booth, "Will Sansom: A Memory of the General's Junior Solder Days," *The Young Soldier* (Christmas Number, December 25, 1889), p. 34.

26. Begbie, *The Life of General William Booth*, 1:60.

27. For an eyewitness account of this and other events of Booth in Nottingham, see "General Booth's Early Days by One Who Knew Him," in the William Booth File, The Salvation Army International Heritage Centre; London, England.

28. See J. E. Page, "William Booth's First Salvation Efforts," *The War Cry* (August 2, 1919), p. 10. For a description of Will Sansom's death and funeral, see Booth, "Will Sansom," p. 34.

29. Owen Chadwick, *The Victorian Church*, 2 Vols. (London: Adam and Charles Black, 1966), 1:334.

30. Ibid., 1:335.

31. William Booth, *In Darkest England and the Way Out* (London: Funk and Wagnalls, 1890), p. 1.

32. Stead, *General Booth*, p. 25.

33. Norman Murdoch, *Origins of The Salvation Army* (Knoxville: The University of Tennessee Press, 1994), p. 9. For an extended treatment of Chartism and the Church see H. U. Faulkner, *Chartism and the Churches: A Study in Democracy* (London: Frank Cass & Co. Ltd., 1970).

34. Wesley recorded in his *Journal*, "We went on in a lovely afternoon, and through a lovely country, to Nottingham. I preached to a numerous and well-behaved congregation. I love this people: There is something wonderfully pleasing, both in their spirit and in their behaviour." Elizabeth Jay, ed., *The Journal of John Wesley: A Selection* (New York: Oxford University Press, 1987), p. 233.

35. Begbie, *The Life of General William Booth*, 1:63.

36. In the 1840s James Caughey preached for the first time in England, and William Booth heard him. Philip D. Needham, speaking of the influence of the evangelist upon William Booth, states that "he learned much from this man that was to be of both theological and practical value in his future work among poor and simple people" (Philip D. Needham, "Redemption and Social Reformation: A Theological Study of William Booth and His Movement" [M.Th. thesis, Princeton Theological Seminary, 1967], p. 59). See also pp. 106-9; Begbie, *The Life of General William Booth*, 1:9, 61-62, 163, 284; Ervine, *God's Soldier: General William Booth*, 1:37, 74; and Murdoch, *Origins of The Salvation Army*, pp. 6-12.

Caughey influenced Booth in the use of revivalistic methods to win the masses for

Christ. However, the primary theological influence of James Caughey upon William Booth was in Caughey's teaching of the Wesleyan doctrine of holiness and the work of the Holy Spirit in the lives of believers. This is clear in an article in a Salvation Army publication entitled *The Conqueror* and published in July 1896. The article, however, incorrectly begins, "In view of the fact that the General was converted under the preaching of the late Rev. James Caughey, the following passage from the pen of this renowned evangelist becomes of almost historical interest" ("Dr. Adam Clarke and the General's Spiritual Father," *The Conqueror* 5 [July 1896], p. 306). Booth was converted two years before first hearing Caughey. See also Chadwick, *The Victorian Church,* 1:379, and "Holiness. Extracts from James Caughey," *The War Cry* (March 1880), pp. 1-2.

37. Murdoch, *Origins of The Salvation Army,* p. 12.

38. In his excellent biography of Charles Grandison Finney, Keith Hardman wrote that "an entire gamut of experiments promoting the perfection of humanity and the bringing of millennial bliss, unorthodox religious beliefs, new cults, and new political parties caused the area even then to be called a 'burnt' or 'burned-over district'" (Keith J. Hardman, *Charles Grandison Finney 1792–1875: Revivalist and Reformer* [Grand Rapids: Baker Book House, 1987], p. 146). It is possible that Lyman Beecher "in his published letters may have been particularly responsible for the expression gaining currency" (ibid., p. 25). Finney himself, later in his *Memoirs,* referred to this area as "a burnt district" (Garth M. Rosell and Richard A. G. Dupuis, eds. *The Memoirs of Charles Grandison Finney: The Complete Restored Text* [Grand Rapids: Zondervan Publishing House, 1989], p. 78, n. 24). One author rather ungraciously labeled this area as a "psychic highway" (Carl Cramer, *Listen for a Lonesome Drum: A York State Chronicle* [New York: McKay, 1950], p. 115, quoted in Hardman, *Charles Grandison Finney 1792–1875: Revivalist and Reformer,* p. 25).

39. Ervine, in *God's Soldier: General William Booth,* 1:47, incorrectly states that James Caughey had been banished from Nottingham in 1851 during a purge of the Connexion. Caughey had been sent out of England in 1847 and did not return until 1857. See Murdoch, *Origins of The Salvation Army,* p. 11, and Richard Carwardine, *Transatlantic Revivalism: Popular Evangelicalism in Britain and America, 1790–1865* (London: Greenwood Press, 1978), pp. 102, 175.

40. Murdoch, *Origins of The Salvation Army,* p. 8.

41. Carwardine, *Transatlantic Revivalism: Popular Evangelicalism in Britain and America, 1790–1865,* p. 118.

42. Murdoch, *Origins of The Salvation Army,* p. 11.

43. See the *Report of a Farewell Sermon Delivered in the Methodist New Connexion Chapel, Parliament Street, Nottingham, by the Rev. J. Caughey of America on the 12th of May, 1847* (Nottingham: R. Sutton, 1847) in The British Library.

2. A Follower of Wesley: Association with Methodism

1. For information on Dunn see Rowland C. Swift, *Lively People: Methodism in Nottingham 1740–1979* (Nottingham: University of Nottingham, 1982).

2. Begbie, *The Life of General William Booth,* 1:83.

3. Railton, *The Authoritative Life of General William Booth,* p. 18. See also Booth, "Will Sansom," *The Young Soldier,* p. 34.

4. Heitzenrater, *Wesley and the People Called Methodists,* p. 115.

5. For an insightful analysis of the complications involved in allowing lay preachers, see Kenneth J. Collins, *A Real Christian: The Life of John Wesley* (Nashville: Abingdon Press, 1999), pp. 97-99.

6. Ervine, *God's Soldier: General William Booth*, 1:41.

7. Begbie, *The Life of General William Booth*, 1:89.

8. Ibid., 1:90.

9. William Booth, "An Autobiographical Fragment: The General Relates Some Memories of His Early Days," *The Social Gazette* (November 11, 1905), p. 1.

10. Ibid.

11. Here the story of the Browns ends. There is no trace of either of them beyond this, and St. John Ervine, ever critical of the Begbie biography, challenges Begbie's assumption that Francis Brown was "the rich brother-in-law" of William Booth. There is no evidence for this, and the truth is that this Tunbridge hatter by trade was probably a shop assistant who made little of his life.

12. Railton, *The Authoritative Life of General William Booth*, pp. 27-28.

13. William Booth was listed in the March 30, 1851, census as "pawnbroker shopman." See the William Booth File, The Salvation Army International Heritage Centre; London, England.

14. Page 1. This letter is undated, but was written soon after William's arrival in London in the autumn of 1849, as he mentions in the opening line: "Safely arrived in London at last am I. . . ." The letter was addressed to "My Dear Friend," and was signed "Yours Affectionately." However, the recipient of the letter is unknown. This would in all probability be the first extant letter of Booth's after his move to London. However, Begbie refers to another letter and writes that that letter was "the oldest known of his letters" (*The Life of General William Booth*, 1:108). Begbie wrote that the letter was dated October 30, 1849, and that it was addressed to one John Savage in Nottingham, "one of the young men who had served as a disciple in the streets and slums of that city" (*The Life of General William Booth*, 1:108). Apparently Begbie is quoting from a different letter, written later. Hattersley in his *Blood and Fire: William and Catherine Booth and Their Salvation Army* confuses the issue by claiming that the letter quoted in this chapter was "the earliest letter to survive—undated, but beginning 'arrived safely in Nottingham at last' " (p. 34). Hattersley then quotes further from the first paragraph of the letter, but claims that "it was addressed to John Savage" (p. 34), whereas the letter from which Hattersley quotes is simply addressed "My Dear Friend." See the William Booth File, The Salvation Army International Heritage Centre; London, England.

15. Begbie, *The Life of General William Booth*, 1:100.

16. For a copy of these resolutions see the William Booth File, The Salvation Army International Heritage Centre; London, England.

17. Robert Hughes, *The Fatal Shore* (New York: Random House, Inc., 1986), p. 1.

18. In the March 30, 1851, census, Rabbits is listed as living on 1, Crosby Road near the Walworth Wesleyan Chapel. He is listed in the March 30, 1851, census as head shoemaker, employing 90 men and 85 women. Begbie in his *The Life of General William Booth* gives the name as E. J. Rabbits, and Booth-Tucker spells his name as Rabbitts in his biography of Catherine Booth entitled *The Life of Catherine Booth, The Mother of The Salvation Army*, 2 Vols. (New York: Fleming H. Revell Company, 1892). Earlier biographers of William Booth have conflicting opinions of the nature and intention of Mr. Rabbits. Begbie treats Rabbits rather contemptuously, writing about him as an "earnest if somewhat narrow-minded dissenter" (1:111), and as one who performed his office of helping William Booth at this time of his life "niggardly and half-heartedly" (ibid). St. John Ervine, ever correcting the inaccuracies in the Begbie biography, gives Rabbits more praise. He wrote that "Begbie allows his readers to infer that the boot manufacturer was a niggardly man who hoped to conduct the plan of salvation in terms of small nett cash, and was eager to obtain the services of a minister who would live like a Christian and a gentleman on a stipend suitable only for the needs of a Christian. Rabbits does not appear

to have been extravagant in his disbursement of money for ministers, but neither was he the niggard he has been proclaimed, and it is clear from evidence which either was not presented to Begbie or was ignored by him, that Rabbits was generous enough in the circumstances in which Booth found himself, and that his generosity was more extensive than Begbie seems to have known. The boot-manufacturer maintained friendly relations with the evangelist for many years, and was sufficiently under his influence to follow his guidance during the period of internal strife in the Methodist Church. These facts will appear later in this book, but it is well now to remove the aspersions which have been cast on the memory of a worthy, if not munificent, man" (1:49). See also Booth-Tucker's assessment of Rabbits in *The Life of Catherine Booth,* 1:80.

19. Ervine, *God's Soldier: General William Booth,* 1:50.

20. Begbie, *The Life of General William Booth,* 1:113. Begbie wrote that "Mr. Rabbits, in June, 1851, persuaded him to work among the Reformers, and later on the next year proceeded to settle the business of his entrance into the ministry" (1:112). However, on page 124 he lists Good Friday as April 10, the date of William Booth's birthday. However, Good Friday that year was April 9 and William Booth's birthday was on the Saturday, April 10. Hattersley in his *Blood and Fire: William and Catherine Booth and Their Salvation Army,* p. 41 also mistakenly gives that Friday of 1852 as Good Friday and April 10, William Booth's birthday. He also mistakenly states that this was his twenty-second birthday. It was his twenty-third birthday. Part of the reason for the confusion comes from William Booth himself. Bennett noted that "There is a tangle with dates in Booth's account at this point, which is rather surprising in this instance. He says that Good Friday that year fell on his birthday, so April 10, a date he should well remember, but the calendar stubbornly persists in making Good Friday that year the ninth" (Bennett, *The General: William Booth,* 1:79-80).

21. Chadwick, *The Victorian Church,* 1:5.

22. Ibid.

23. G. Kitson Clark, *The Making of Victorian England* (London: Methuen & Co. Ltd., 1962), p. 189.

24. G. M. Trevelyan, *History of England,* 3 Vols. (Garden City, New York: Doubleday and Company, Inc., 1952), 3:131.

25. For an excellent analysis of these three stages see Heitzenrater, *Wesley and the People Called Methodists.*

26. Henry Rack, *Reasonable Enthusiast: John Wesley and the Rise of Methodism* (Philadelphia: Trinity Press International, 1989), p. 409. Kenneth Collins also well underscores this in his *The Scripture Way of Salvation: The Heart of John Wesley's Theology* (Nashville: Abingdon Press, 1997). He wrote, "So, then, Wesley held not one but two aspects of his doctrine of salvation in tension: both process *and* instantaneousness. The former aspect depicts his 'catholic' emphasis and points to human cooperation with God as men and women are empowered by divine grace and are thereby *prepared* for the decisive gifts of salvation, that is, for justification and for initial and entire sanctification. The latter aspect, however, depicts his Protestant or 'evangelical' emphasis and points not to human cooperation, but to the sovereign activity of God and, therefore, to the sheer gratuity (favor) of grace. Again, the former aspect displays the ongoing growth and development that is a normal part of any vital spiritual life. The latter aspect displays not process but the crucial element of actualization or realization" (p. 99).

27. Ibid., pp. 203-4.

28. Rack, *Reasonable Enthusiast: John Wesley and the Rise of Methodism,* p. 390.

29. Heitzenrater, *Wesley and the People Called Methodists,* p. 220.

30. Ibid., p. 320.

31. Collins, *The Scripture Way of Salvation,* p. 153.

32. Heitzenrater, *Wesley and the People Called Methodists*, p. 312.

33. Chadwick, *The Victorian Church*, 1:386.

34. Booth-Tucker, *The Life of Catherine Booth*, 1:74. Booth repeated this claim on his sixtieth birthday. See Ervine, *God's Soldier: General William Booth*, 2:734.

35. Hattersley, *Blood and Fire: William and Catherine Booth and Their Salvation Army*, p. 2.

36. Begbie, *The Life of General William Booth*, 1:69.

37. Ibid., 1:70. Many members of the Booth family took exception to the Begbie biography because it seemed to denigrate Booth's biblical and theological convictions. For the most thorough criticism of the biography see "A Personal Letter from Commissioner Booth-Tucker to Commissioner Brengle Referring to Certain Difficulties in The Salvation Army," June, 1927, 9 pp. A copy of this letter is in my personal library.

3. Providential Meeting: William Booth and Catherine Mumford

1. There are several biographies of Catherine Booth. The following are four of the most important: Frederick de Latour Booth-Tucker, *The Life of Catherine Booth: The Mother of The Salvation Army*, 2 Vols. (New York: Revell, 1892). This biography was also put in an abridged edition by the same title, had three volumes (although considerably briefer than the original work), and was published by The Salvation Army in 1912. It was also put into a one-volume edition entitled *The Short Life of Catherine Booth, the Mother of The Salvation Army* (London: The Salvation Army, 1893). Other works on Catherine Booth include the following: Catherine Bramwell-Booth, *Catherine Booth: The Story of Her Loves* (London: Hodder and Stoughton, 1970); W. T. Stead, *Mrs. Booth of The Salvation Army* (London: James Nisbet and Co., 1900); and Roger J. Green, *Catherine Booth: A Biography of the Cofounder of The Salvation Army* (Grand Rapids: Baker Books, 1996).

2. Regarding the temperance movement Hattersley wrote that this was "a cause to which her father had remained devoted despite his estrangement from the Methodist Church" (*Blood and Fire: William and Catherine Booth and Their Salvation Army*, p. 43). This was not the case, a fact that often caused grief for Catherine and her mother.

3. Booth Papers, Mss. 64806, The British Library. See also W. T. Stead, *Mrs. Booth of The Salvation Army*, p. 22.

4. John Wesley, "A Call to Backsliders" in Albert C. Outler, ed., *The Works of John Wesley*, Vols. 1-4, Sermons (Nashville: Abingdon Press, 1986), 3:212.

5. For a discussion of total abstinence among the Methodists, see Rupert Davies, A. Raymond George, and Gordon Rupp, eds. *A History of the Methodist Church in Great Britain*, 4 Vols. (London: Epworth Press, 1978), 2:223-24, especially p. 224, n. 22.

6. "As a quite young girl, I early made up my mind as to certain qualifications, which I regarded as indispensable to the forming of my engagement. . . . Another resolution that I made was that I would never marry a man who was not a total abstainer, and this from conviction, and not merely to gratify me" (Stead, *Mrs. Booth of The Salvation Army*, pp. 57, 59).

7. See Begbie, *The Life of General William Booth*, 1:37, 232-33.

8. Coates, *The Prophet of the Poor: The Life Story of General Booth*, p. 18.

9. Begbie, *The Life of General William Booth*, 1:117. Catherine Booth eventually became a vegetarian and reared her children as vegetarians, although there were times

when the family digressed from vegetarianism. Likewise vegetarianism was encouraged in the followers of William and Catherine Booth in their religious societies. For two examples of this see William Booth, *Religion for Every Day* (London: The Salvationist Publishing and Supplies, n.d.), p. 106; and Bramwell Booth, "The Advantages of a Vegetarian Diet" (London: The London Vegetarian Society, n.d.). See also Lewis G. Regenstein, *Replenish the Earth: A History of Organized Religion's Treatment of Animals and Nature—Including the Bible's Message of Conservation and Kindness Toward Animals* (New York: Crossroad, 1991). The proper treatment of animals was also one of the stipulations for membership. See Catherine Bramwell-Booth, *Catherine Booth: The Story of Her Loves*, pp. 21-22.

10. Booth-Tucker, *The Life of Catherine Booth*, 1:26.

11. Rack, *Reasonable Enthusiast: John Wesley and the Rise of Methodism*, p. 241. See Catherine Booth's reflections on the importance of the class meeting in Booth-Tucker, *The Life of Catherine Booth*, 1:50-51.

12. Ibid., p. 35.

13. Ibid., p. 36.

14. Ibid., p. 37.

15. Ibid., pp. 38-39.

16. Roger J. Green, *Catherine Booth: A Biography of the Cofounder of The Salvation Army*, pp. 33-34.

17. Begbie, *The Life of General William Booth*, 1:124.

18. Chadwick, *The Victorian Church*, 1:379.

19. Booth-Tucker, *The Life of Catherine Booth*, 1:66-67. For a more balanced view of James Caughey and a brief description of his methods and influence on Catherine and William, see Murdoch, *Origins of The Salvation Army*, pp. 7-12. For an excellent treatment of Caughey see chapter 4 as well as other references in Carwardine, *Transatlantic Revivalism: Popular Evangelicalism in Britain and America, 1790–1865*, and John Kent, *Holding the Fort: Studies in Victorian Revivalism* (London: Epworth Press, 1978), pp. 77-87). For a treatment of Finney see Carwardine, chapter 5 and various references in Kent; see also the best biography of Charles Grandison Finney in Keith J. Hardman, *Charles Grandison Finney 1792–1875: Revivalist and Reformer*.

20. Carwardine, *Transatlantic Revivalism: Popular Evangelicalism in Britain and America, 1790–1865*, p. 131.

21. Begbie, *The Life of General William Booth*, 1:125.

22. Ibid., 1:127.

23. Booth Papers, Mss. 64799, The British Library.

24. It is clear that this is the date of their engagement. At least twice Catherine gives the wrong date in her letters. A year after their engagement she wrote, "We are one in all things; it will be twelve months on the 13th May since, bowed together at this sofa, we solemnly gave ourselves to each other and to God." And in 1857 she wrote the following to her parents: "It was Good Friday, April 10, the anniversary of our engagement" (Bramwell-Booth, *Catherine Booth: The Story of Her Loves*, pp. 69, 164). Murdoch in his dissertation entitled "The Salvation Army: An Anglo-American Revivalist Social Mission" (Ph.D. diss., University of Cincinnati, 1985), p. 96, n. 22 discusses this date. Murdoch is in error when in his endnote he states that "Ervine, 1, 57, for some reason cited May 5." A correction sheet inserted in Ervine clarifies that this was a misprint in the book and should have read May 15 instead of May 5. Ervine was correct in the date of the engagement. Murdoch does not include this discussion in his *Origins of The Salvation Army*.

25. Booth-Tucker, *The Life of Catherine Booth*, 1:98.

26. Bramwell-Booth, *Catherine Booth: The Story of Her Loves*, p. 73.

27. Hattersley in *Blood and Fire: William and Catherine Booth and Their Salvation Army,* p. 73 mistakenly gives June 17, 1855, as the date of the wedding.

28. David Thomas was a minister of note among the Congregationalists. From 1852 to 1858 he was the editor of a scholarly journal entitled *The Homilist,* and two pamphlets that he wrote were widely circulated among Congregationalists, the first entitled "The Unreasonableness of People in Relation to the Pulpit," reprinted from *The Homilist* (London, 1856); and "Journalism and the Pulpit," reprinted from *The Homilist* (London, 1857). Catherine had disagreed with Thomas over the issue of the equality of women with men, but she nevertheless admired Thomas. In a letter to William on March 17, 1853, she wrote, "I do like him; he is one of the nicest men I ever conversed with. . . . I really love him and his preaching gets better and better" (Booth Papers, Mss. 64799, The British Library).

4. Finding a Denominational Home: William Booth and New Connexion Methodism

1. Carolyn Ocheltree, "Wesleyan Methodist Perceptions of William Booth," *Methodist History* 28:4 (July 1990), pp. 264-65.

2. Chadwick, *The Victorian Church,* 1:385.

3. Ervine, *God's Soldier: General William Booth,* 1:61-62.

4. Ibid., 1:62-63.

5. Railton, *The Authoritative Life of General William Booth,* p. 31.

6. Begbie, *The Life of General William Booth,* 1:131-32. Begbie was quoting from "some autobiographical notes of a more or less fragmentary nature which were never published" (1:130). For the importance of Catherine Booth in this decision see Green, *Catherine Booth: A Biography of the Cofounder of The Salvation Army,* pp. 47-51.

7. See Nick Wardrop, "David 'Homilist' Thomas DD," *Friends of West Norwood Cemetery Online News* (May 2000), pp. 1-3 for an interesting article about David Thomas, who was appointed to the Stockwell New Chapel in 1844 and remained there until 1877. The nickname "Homilist" came from a scholarly periodical that David Thomas started in 1852.

8. Begbie, *The Life of General William Booth,* 1:132.

9. Collins, *A Real Christian: The Life of John Wesley,* p. 70.

10. Massie is the spelling given by Ervine, *God's Soldier: General William Booth,* 1:66 and 67. Booth-Tucker in *The Life of Catherine Booth,* 1:100 gives Massey as the spelling. Bennett in *The General: William Booth,* 1:111 and Hattersley in *Blood and Fire: William and Catherine Booth and Their Salvation Army,* p. 51 also give Massey as the correct spelling.

11. Bennett, *The General: William Booth,* 1:110.

12. Begbie, *The Life of General William Booth,* 1:134.

13. Railton, *The Authoritative Life of General William Booth,* p. 31.

14. Rack, *Reasonable Enthusiast: John Wesley and the Rise of Methodism,* pp. 312-13.

15. Ervine, *God's Soldier: General William Booth,* 1:69.

16. See the William Booth File, The Salvation Army International Heritage Centre; London, England. See also "How Congregationalism Lost General Booth," *The Review of Reviews* 3:13 (March 1891), p. 259; and H. G. Tibbutt, "The Cotton End Congregational Academy, 1840–74," *Transactions of the Congregational Historical Society* 18:3 (August 1958), pp. 103-4.

17. Letter from William to Catherine, probably March 14 or 15, 1853, quoted in Bennett, *The General: William Booth*, 1:123.

18. Hattersley, *Blood and Fire: William and Catherine Booth and Their Salvation Army*, p. 4.

19. Booth-Tucker, *The Life of Catherine Booth*, 1:105.

20. Begbie, *The Life of General William Booth*, 1:135.

21. Ervine, *God's Soldier: General William Booth*, 1:69-70.

22. Railton, *The Authoritative Life of General William Booth*, p. 32.

23. Hattersley, *Blood and Fire: William and Catherine Booth and Their Salvation Army*, p. 57.

24. William Booth was not in Spalding for eighteen months as St. John Ervine incorrectly asserts in his *God's Soldier: General William Booth*, 1:70. He was there only fifteen months, returning to London in February of 1854. St. John Ervine, absolutely intolerant of errors in previous biographies of William Booth, had his share of errors in his own biography.

25. Hattersley, *Blood and Fire: William and Catherine Booth and Their Salvation Army*, p. 71.

26. Ibid., p. 57.

27. Booth Papers, Mss. 64800, The British Library, letter written March 20, 1853.

28. Bennett, *The General: William Booth*, 1:130.

29. Booth Papers, Mss. 64801, The British Library.

30. See W. J. Townsend, *Life of Alexander Kilham* (London: J. C. Watts, n.d.); and John Blackwell, *Life of Reverend Alexander Kilham* (London: R. Groombridge, 1838).

31. Heitzenrater, *Wesley and the People Called Methodists*, pp. 316-17. Carolyn Ocheltree also notes that "This British Methodist denomination was begun in 1797. Its members had withdrawn from Wesleyan Methodism over the issue of laity rights. They also believed that Methodism should join with the nonconformist churches rather than with the Anglican establishment" ("Wesleyan Methodist Perceptions of William Booth," p. 265). The best article dealing with the formation of New Connexion Methodism is Victor A. Shepherd, "From New Connexion Methodism to William Booth," *Papers of the Canadian Methodist Historical Society*, Vol. 9 (1993), pp. 91-107. See also John T. Wilkinson, "The Rise of Other Methodist Traditions," in Davies, George, and Rupp, eds., *A History of the Methodist Church in Great Britain*, 2:280-94.

32. Ibid., 2:286.

33. Ervine, *God's Soldier: General William Booth*, 1:93.

34. For information on William Cooke see Henry Smith, *Sketches of Eminent New Connexion Methodist Ministers* (London: J. C. Watts, 1893), chapter 5.

35. Booth-Tucker, *The Life of Catherine Booth*, 1:153.

36. Booth Papers, Mss. 64801, The British Library. Church historian Owen Chadwick wrote, "Catherine had links with the Methodist New Connexion, and in 1854 persuaded him to join it" (Chadwick, *The Victorian Church*, 2:288). Precisely what those links were at this point is difficult to say. In his biography of Catherine Booth, Booth-Tucker states that Catherine wrote an article for the *Methodist New Connexion Magazine* and quotes this article at length. Robert Sandall gives the date as June 1855 in *The History of The Salvation Army*, 8 Vols. (Robert Sandall, vols. 1, 2, and 3; Arch Wiggins, vols. 4 and 5; Frederick Coutts, vols. 6 and 7; and Henry Gariepy, vol. 8 [London: Thomas Nelson, 1947–1986; Grand Rapids: William B. Eerdmans Company, 2000], 1:66. I have as yet been unable to locate this article in the *Methodist New Connexion Magazine*, although I have no reason to discount Booth-Tucker's or Sandall's reference to it. The article was reprinted many years later in *Harbor Lights* (September 1898), pp. 264-66.

37. Railton, *The Authoritative Life of General William Booth*, pp. 40-41.

38. Ervine, *God's Soldier: General William Booth*, 1:98.
39. Railton, *The Authoritative Life of General William Booth*, p. 41.
40. Ibid.
41. Begbie, *The Life of General William Booth*, 1:206-7.
42. See an account of Booth's ministry in this church in *Great the Heritage: History of the Methodist Church, Packington Street, London* in the William Booth File, The Salvation Army International Heritage Centre; London, England.
43. Bennett, *The General: William Booth*, 1:190.
44. Ibid., p. 204.
45. Ervine, *God's Soldier: General William Booth*, 1:116.
46. Ibid., 1:120.
47. Bennett, *The General: William Booth*, 1:376.
48. Ibid., 1:222.
49. Ibid., 1:118. For an extended treatment of matters of health with the Booths and The Salvation Army see Barbara Robinson, " 'Bodily Compassion': Values and Identity Formation in The Salvation Army, 1880–1900" (Ph.D. Dissertation, University of Ottawa, 1999).
50. Booth-Tucker, *The Life of Catherine Booth*, 1:117.
51. See Green, *Catherine Booth: A Biography of the Cofounder of The Salvation Army*, pp. 121-22. For a lengthy discussion about Catherine Booth's understanding of the equality of men and women, especially in ministry, see Roger J. Green, "Settled Views: Catherine Booth and Female Ministry," *Methodist History* 31 (April 1993), pp. 131-47; and Norman H. Murdoch, "Female Ministry in the Thought and Work of Catherine Booth," *Church History* 53 (Fall 1984), pp. 348-62.
52. Begbie, *The Life of General William Booth*, 1:236.

5. Difficult Decision: Leaving New Connexion Methodism

1. For extended treatments of hydropathy and homeopathy see Robinson, " 'Bodily Compassion': Values and Identity Formation in The Salvation Army, 1880–1900," chapter 2 entitled "Sectarian Systems: The Democratization of Care."
2. See Bennett, *The General: William Booth*, 1:300 and 2:346.
3. Ibid., 1:226.
4. For a biography on Bramwell Booth see Catherine Bramwell-Booth, *Bramwell Booth* (London: Rich and Cowan, 1933).
5. Green, *Catherine Booth: A Biography of the Cofounder of The Salvation Army*, pp. 81-82.
6. Murdoch, *Origins of The Salvation Army*, p. 11.
7. Members of the Hull Circuit where William Booth had preached heard about this decision, and in an emergency meeting in June of 1857 passed the following resolution: "That this meeting learns with deep and sincere regret that the Conference has decided to discontinue the evangelistic labours of the Rev. W. Booth and would urge upon them the necessity of reconsidering their decision, feeling assured that his withdrawal from work in which he appears to be specially and eminently qualified by the great head of the Church, and in which he has been so successful, will create much dissatisfaction in this Circuit where several through his instrumentality have been brought to a knowledge of the Truth. Should the Conference decide to discontinue the evangelistic labours of the

Rev. W. Booth during the coming year the Hull Circuit will be happy to avail itself of his services" (*The Methodist Conference Handbook, Hull 1938*, p. 106).

8. Begbie, *The Life of General William Booth*, 1:281.

9. Booth-Tucker, *The Life of Catherine Booth*, 1:298.

10. Ervine, *God's Soldier: General William Booth*, 1:212.

11. There is no biography of Ballington Booth.

12. Booth Papers, Mss. 64804, The British Library.

13. *The Methodist New Connexion Magazine* for the year 1858 recorded the following: "Several memorials were presented in favour of the Rev. W. Booth being again employed as an evangelist. It was, however, deemed advisable, at present, for our beloved brother, in accordance with his own wishes, to be appointed to a circuit" (Vol. 26, p. 332).

14. Booth Papers, Mss. 64804, The British Library.

15. Ibid., Catherine to her mother in a letter dated June 17, 1858.

16. *Methodism for 100 Years at Bethesda & Whitehall Road, 1836–1936*, p. 11, the William Booth File, The Salvation Army International Heritage Centre; London, England.

17. There are two biographies of Catherine Booth, the daughter: James Strahan, *The Maréchale* (New York: George H. Doran, 1921), and Carolyn Scott, *The Heavenly Witch: The Story of the Maréchale* (London: Hamish Hamilton, 1981).

18. The only biography about Emma Booth is that written by Frederick Booth-Tucker, *The Consul* (New York: Salvation Army, 1893).

19. Hattersley, *Blood and Fire: William and Catherine Booth and Their Salvation Army*, pp. 101-2.

20. Ibid.

21. Booth-Tucker, *The Life of Catherine Booth*, 1:371.

22. Ervine, *God's Soldier: General William Booth*, 1:227.

23. Green, *Catherine Booth: A Biography of the Cofounder of The Salvation Army*, p. 95.

24. For a discussion about the date of the letter see Green, *Catherine Booth: A Biography of the Cofounder of The Salvation Army*, chapter 5, footnote 2. Hattersley in *Blood and Fire: William and Catherine Booth and Their Salvation Army* correctly gives the date of this letter as 1853. Bennett in *The General: William Booth* holds to the date of 1855. See his discussion on pp. 279-80 of volume 1.

25. See ibid., p. 191. Hattersley in *Blood and Fire: William and Catherine Booth and Their Salvation Army* incorrectly gives the date of the pamphlet as 1862.

26. See Green, *Catherine Booth: A Biography of the Cofounder of The Salvation Army*, chapter 5, footnote 22 for a lengthy description of the various editions of this pamphlet.

27. See "Phoebe Palmer, 1807-1874" in Nancy A. Hardesty, *Great Women of Faith: The Strength and Influence of Christian Women* (Grand Rapids: Baker Book House, 1980), pp. 87-91; the section on Phoebe Palmer in chapter 7, "Trans-Atlantic Reform and Revivalism: Social Workers and Lay Evangelists," pp. 261-64 in Ruth A. Tucker and Walter Liefeld, *Daughters of the Church: Women and Ministry from New Testament Times to the Present* (Grand Rapids: Zondervan Publishing House, 1987). See also Harold E. Raser, *Phoebe Palmer: Her Life and Thought* (Lewiston, New York: Edwin Mellon Press, 1987). For two articles specifically on the influence of Phoebe Palmer on Catherine Booth see Lucille Sider Dayton and Donald W. Dayton, " 'Your Daughters Shall Prophesy': Feminism in the Holiness Movement," *Methodist History* 14 (January 1976), pp. 67-92; and Margaret McFadden, "The Ironies of Pentecostalism: Phoebe Palmer, World Evangelism, and Female Networks," *Methodist History* 31 (January 1993), pp. 63-75. See also Kate P. Crawford Galea, " 'Anchored Behind the Veil': Mystical Vision of a Possible Source of Authority in the Ministry of Phoebe Palmer," *Methodist History* 31 (July 1993),

pp. 236-47. See also P. J. Jarbo, *A Letter to Mrs. Palmer in Reference to Women Speaking in Public* (North Shields: Philipson and Hare, 1859) in The British Library.

28. Ibid. Walker, *Pulling the Devil's Kingdom Down: The Salvation Army in Victorian Britain*, pp. 23-24.

29. "Our Army Mother's First Sermon," *All the World* (June 1897), p. 245. See also "Our Army Mother's First Sermon," *Harbor Light* (July 1899), p. 223; Booth-Tucker, *The Life of Catherine Booth*, 1:358-63; Bramwell-Booth, *Catherine Booth: The Story of Her Loves*, pp. 184-87; Green, *Catherine Booth: A Biography of the Cofounder of The Salvation Army*, p. 135; Stead, *Mrs. Booth of The Salvation Army*, pp. 156-59.

30. Stead, *Mrs. Booth of The Salvation Army*, pp. 158-59. Catherine's reference to William encouraging her to do this ten years ago is indeed strange on two counts. First, she did not meet William until 1852, and second, she and William nearly broke their engagement over their controversy of the equality of women and men, and William became convinced on this subject only weeks before their marriage. William may eventually have been trying to get Catherine to preach, but he had certainly not been doing that for ten years.

31. Bramwell Booth, *Echoes and Memories* (London: Hodder and Stoughton, 1977), p. 56.

32. Begbie, *The Life of General William Booth*, 1:281.

33. Hattersley, *Blood and Fire: William and Catherine Booth and Their Salvation Army*, p. 103.

34. Ervine, *God's Soldier: General William Booth*, 1:233.

35. Hattersley, *Blood and Fire: William and Catherine Booth and Their Salvation Army*, p. 81.

36. For information on Stacey, see Smith, *Sketches of Eminent Methodist New Connexion Methodist Ministers*, chapter 5.

37. Booth-Tucker, *The Life of Catherine Booth*, 1:392. There is some difficulty knowing the precise date of this letter. Booth-Tucker gives the date as March 5, 1861. Ervine gives the date as March 15, 1861. Begbie does not make reference to this letter or to Stacey, strange omissions from a biography that was considered to be a definitive biography of William Booth, and given the length and the subject matter of the letter.

38. Booth-Tucker wrote that Booth received a rather curt answer to his letter, not from Stacey himself, who was ill, but from members of the Annual Committee. "Not a word of counsel, not a symptom of approval was conveyed, and it was manifest that the proposal would encounter from certain parties a vigorous an opposition as ever" (1:396). St. John Ervine was characteristically critical of Booth-Tucker on this point, and wrote that "Booth-Tucker, incurably sentimental and addicted to discovering the worst in the minds of those who do not instantly agree with him, complains that this letter contains 'not a word of counsel, not a symptom of approval,' but was manifestly antipathetic to Booth's appeal. As, however, he does not publish the letter, his readers are not able to agree or disagree with his interpretation" (1:234). As mentioned, Harold Begbie published neither the letter nor the response, which is inexplicable in that the letter to Stacey is such an important one and is preserved in its entirety in the Booth-Tucker biography of Catherine Booth. See Bennett, *The General: William Booth*, 1:286.

39. Green, *Catherine Booth: A Biography of the Cofounder of The Salvation Army*, pp. 108-9. However, see Col. Edmund C. Hoffman, "James Caughey and William Booth," *Officer Review* (January 1944): 32-37 for the final meeting of William Booth and James Caughey in America in 1886. Murdoch is correct that "Booth was Caughey's heir. Caughey convinced Booth that converting the masses was possible through scientific, calculated means. Revivals which were planned, advertised, and prayed for would succeed. From the time they met in 1846 to his death in 1912, Booth was consumed with

the idea of winning souls through mass meetings, house-to-house visitation, and personal witness. This was the legacy of James Caughey, who died in 1891 at age eighty-one, largely forgotten, despite his influence, not only on the Booths, but on all British evangelicalism" (Murdoch, *Origins of The Salvation Army*, p. 12).

40. Ervine, *God's Soldier: General William Booth*, 1:235.

41. The *Minutes of the Sixty-Fifth Annual Conference of the Methodist New Connexion Composed of Ministers and Lay Representatives Held at Liverpool on Monday, the Twentieth Day of May, Etc.* (London: William Cooke, 1861) demonstrate that William was officially appointed to Newcastle-Upon-Tyne for the following year.

42. Ibid., 1:244.

43. Hattersley, *Blood and Fire: William and Catherine Booth and Their Salvation Army*, p. 64.

44. Coates, *The Prophet of the Poor: The Life Story of General Booth*, pp. 51-52.

45. See a fuller treatment of this event in Green, *Catherine Booth: A Biography of the Cofounder of The Salvation Army*, pp. 110-13. William Townsend, a friend of the Booths, who may have been present at the 1861 Conference, evidently began this story (although his name is not listed as a delegate to that Conference). Townsend recorded that "Mrs. Booth, in the gallery of the church, greeted the statement of these proposals with the word 'Never!' and retired to the porch of the church, where she met her husband who was of like mind" (George Eayrs, *William John Townsend, D.D.* [London: Henry Hocks, 1916], pp. 47-48). Eayrs also records that "Mr. Townsend was their companion as they returned to the North of England, and discussed the situation with them" (p. 48). G. Packer, ed., *The Centenary of the Methodist New Connexion 1797–1897* (London: Geo. Burroughs, 1897) emphatically denies the sensational account of Booth's resignation and of Catherine crying out from the balcony (p. 137).

46. Booth Papers, Mss. 64805, The British Library. See Booth-Tucker, *The Life of Catherine Booth*, 1:417-18; Bramwell-Booth, *Catherine Booth: The Story of Her Loves*, p. 208; and Begbie, *The Life of General William Booth*, 1:287. All three authors quote from parts of the letter but omit Catherine's disdain for New Connexion Methodism.

47. Booth Papers, Mss. 64805, The British Library.

48. Ervine, *God's Soldier: General William Booth*, 1:243.

49. Murdoch, *Origins of The Salvation Army*, p. 35.

50. Green, *Catherine Booth: A Biography of the Cofounder of The Salvation Army*, p. 114.

51. Bennett, *The General: William Booth*, 1:300.

52. Murdoch, *Origins of The Salvation Army*, p. 35.

53. Booth, *Echoes and Memories*, p. 59.

54. Shepherd, "From New Connexion Methodist to William Booth," p. 98.

55. Green, *Catherine Booth: A Biography of the Cofounder of The Salvation Army*, p. 115.

56. Ervine, *God's Soldier: General William Booth*, 1:251.

57. Booth Papers, Mss. 64805, The British Library. See the *Minutes of the Sixty-Sixth Annual Conference of the Methodist New Connexion Composed of Ministers and Lay Representatives Held at Dudley on Monday, the Ninth Day of June, Etc.* (London: William Cooke, 1862). There is no mention in those minutes of the resignation of William Booth, and so it must have merely been accepted by the President of the Conference, in the *Minutes* listed as The Reverend T. W. Ridley of Staleybridge.

58. Ocheltree, "Wesleyan Methodist Perceptions of William Booth," p. 265.

59. Begbie, *The Life of General William Booth*, 1:291.

60. Ervine, *God's Soldier: General William Booth*, 1:256. St. John Ervine took these facts from a series of articles published in *The United Methodist* in March and April 1920.

61. Begbie, *The Life of General William Booth*, 1:289.

6. The Road to Freedom

1. Booth, *Echoes and Memories*, p. 56.
2. Rack, *Reasonable Enthusiast: John Wesley and the Rise of Methodism*, pp. 493-94. See also D. H. Luker, "Cornish Methodism, Revivalism, and Popular Belief 1780–1870," *Journal of Ecclesiastical History*, Vol. 37 (1986), pp. 603-19.
3. For an anonymous account of Booth's evangelistic work in Cornwall at this time see *The Revival at St. Ives, Cornwall* (London: George J. Stevenson, 1862) in the William Booth File, The Salvation Army International Heritage Centre; London, England.
4. William Booth to Mr. John Atkinson, November 18, 1861, the William Booth File, The Salvation Army International Heritage Centre; London, England.
5. *The Revival*, No. 123 (November 30, 1861), p. 132. For a fuller description of the St. Ives revival see the history of the St. Ives Fore Street Methodist Church.
6. *The Revival*, No. 152 (June 19, 1862), p. 231.
7. Ibid.
8. Although, as mentioned in the previous chapter, the acceptance of the resignation is not mentioned in the minutes of the New Connexion Methodist Annual Conference for 1862. Therefore, the President of the Conference must have formally accepted the resignation.
9. St. John Ervine made this claim. He wrote, "Six months later his name was altered to 'Herbert Howard,' although the alteration was not made soon enough to be officially effective" (Ervine, *God's Soldier: General William Booth*, 1:261).
10. For a biography of Herbert Booth see Ford C. Ottman, *Herbert Booth: A Biography* (Garden City, New York: Doubleday, Doran & Company, Inc., 1928).
11. Letter dated February 24, 1863, the William Booth File, The Salvation Army International Heritage Centre; London, England.
12. Ervine, *God's Soldier: General William Booth*, 1:263. Ervine adds that the ship "was wrecked off the island of Bermuda soon after it was christened!"
13. Hattersley, *Blood and Fire: William and Catherine Booth and Their Salvation Army*, p. 118.
14. P. W. Wilson, *General Evangeline Booth of The Salvation Army* (New York: Charles Scribner's Sons, 1948), p. 39.
15. Begbie, *The Life of General William Booth*, 1:304.
16. Hattersley, *Blood and Fire: William and Catherine Booth and Their Salvation Army*, p. 172.
17. Bennett, *The General: William Booth*, 1:370-71.
18. Ervine in *God's Soldier: General William Booth*, 1:269 incorrectly gives the date as May 19, 1864. Hattersley incorrectly spells her name as Marion (*Blood and Fire: William and Catherine Booth and Their Salvation Army*, p. 144). There is no biography of Marian.
19. Begbie, *The Life of General William Booth*, 1:307.
20. Ervine, *God's Soldier: General William Booth*, 1:269.
21. Wilson, *General Evangeline Booth of The Salvation Army*, p. 44. Arch Wiggins in *The History of The Salvation Army* (4:353) refers to Marian as "retarded." *The War Cry* article that recorded the death and funeral of Marian stated that "From early infancy the child developed a delicacy of health which persisted throughout life" ("Staff-Captain Marian Booth Goes to Heaven," *The War Cry* [January 16, 1937], p. 3). More recent literature does not clarify Marian's condition. For example, Pamela J. Walker in *Pulling the Devil's Kingdom Down: The Salvation Army in Victorian Britain* (p. 62) simply writes that "Only Marian, who was disabled in childhood, never assumed a leadership position."
22. Marian was ignored in public records of the Booths. For example, *Who Was Who*

1897–1915, p. 54 mentions only seven children of William and Catherine Booth. And Begbie, who in the biography of William Booth recorded the birth of Marian, inexplicably wrote the following in his article on William Booth in the *Dictionary of National Biography 1912–1921*, p. 51: "His wife, by whom he had three sons and four daughters, had died in 1890." And in his biography, while recounting an incident later in William Booth's life he records William sending kisses to his children, all mentioned by name with the exception of Marian, who, incidentally, lived until 1937 (2:402). William Booth was anxious that Marie was taken care of after his death. See "Voluntary Settlement Upon Miss Marie Booth and Others, Dated 22nd May 1912." A copy of this is in my personal files.

23. Ervine, *God's Soldier: General William Booth*, 1:270.

24. Green, *Catherine Booth: A Biography of the Cofounder of The Salvation Army*, p. 145.

25. Ervine, *God's Soldier: General William Booth*, 1:269.

26. Ibid., 1:276.

27. Ann Saunders, *The Art and Architecture of London: An Illustrated Guide* (Oxford: Phaidon Press Limited, 1984), p. 414.

28. Begbie, *The Life of General William Booth*, 1:310.

29. Ervine, *God's Soldier: General William Booth*, 1:277.

30. Murdoch, *Origins of The Salvation Army*, p. 38.

31. Wilson, *General Evangeline Booth of The Salvation Army*, p. 38.

32. Begbie, *The Life of General William Booth*, 1:320.

33. There are two biographies of Evangeline Booth: Wilson, *General Evangeline Booth of The Salvation Army*; and Margaret Troutt, *The General Was a Lady: The Story of Evangeline Booth* (Nashville: A. J. Holman Company, 1980).

34. Wilson, in *General Evangeline Booth of The Salvation Army*, states the following about the name for Evelyne:

> Naturally there arose the question what the child should be called. General Evangeline Booth remembers how Evangeline was the name chosen for her by her mother. But, it has to be added, that Catherine Booth had been reading *Uncle Tom's Cabin* and she decided that there should be another Little Eva, a joy in the home. Instructions to this effect were given to a proud father but on the register, for some reason, appeared the name, Evelyne, and apparently he really meant it for there is Evelyne in letters that he wrote many years later. However, Evelyne was never other than Eva in the home and on a day that she dimly remembers she was presented to a mouselike lady called Harriet Beecher Stowe, who unwittingly had been created her patron saint. For many years she remained Eva but in due course she came to the United States where she met the veteran, Francis Elizabeth Willard, founder of the Women's Christian Temperance Union, who had learned by experience that prestige is essential to a woman's responsibility if she is to hold her allotted place in the world. Francis Willard advised Eva Booth that she would be wise to assume the use of the full name, Evangeline, to which she was entitled. The suggestion was accepted. (p. 26)

Sometimes alternate spellings, Eveline or Evaline, were used. In any case, Evaline Cory Booth legally changed her name in a Deed Poll dated February 24, 1914. The spelling, Evaline, is what was used in that official Deed Poll. See the Evangeline Booth File, The Salvation Army International Heritage Centre; London, England.

35. The date of the birth of this child is disputed. Both Booth-Tucker and Begbie date the birth as 1867. St. John Ervine gives 1868 as the date and states this in a footnote: "the date of her birth is misstated by Booth-Tucker, who gives the year as 1867. Begbie follows him. Phillimore, in *Country Pedigrees*, gives both the day and the year incorrectly. According to him, Lucy was born on April 26, 1867" (1:294). Inexplicably Booth-Tucker

in a family tree on page 678 of volume 2 of his *The Life of Catherine Booth* gives 1868 as the date of birth. Bramwell-Booth in *Catherine Booth: The Story of Her Loves* gives April 28, 1868 (p. 206). There is no biography of Lucy Booth.

36. Wilson, *General Evangeline Booth of The Salvation Army*, p. 33.

7. The Beginning of a Mission

1. Murdoch, *Origins of The Salvation Army*, pp. 74-75.

2. See for example Ian J. Shaw, "Thomas Chalmers, David Nasmith, and the Origins of the City Mission Movement," *Evangelical Quarterly* 76:1 (2004), pp. 31-46; and Donald M. Lewis, *Lighten Their Darkness: The Evangelical Mission to Working-Class London, 1828–1860* (Westport, Connecticut: Greenwood Press, 1986). See also Bennett, *The General: William Booth*, 2:356.

3. Glenn K. Horridge, *The Salvation Army Origins and Early Days: 1865–1900* (Godalming, Surrey, England, 1993), pp. 10-11.

4. Bennett, *The General: William Booth*, 1:356.

5. Sandall, *The History of The Salvation Army*, 1:19-20.

6. Ervine, *God's Soldier: General William Booth*, 1:287.

7. Murdoch, *Origins of The Salvation Army*, p. 75.

8. Ervine, *God's Soldier: General William Booth*, 1:286.

9. Booth had proposed the establishment of a Christian Revival Association in *The Revival*. The East London Christian Revival Union was evidently the first name of that association, as attested in a ticket of membership for September 1865 within a month of the opening of the work in the dancing academy. The name was changed from these two early names to the East London Christian Revival Society, The East London Christian Mission, and finally in 1869 to The Christian Mission, reflecting the establishment of Christian Mission preaching stations beyond East London. The Christian Mission became The Salvation Army in 1878. There were several missions known as Christian Missions in various parts of London at that time, and thus it was appropriate that the first name that had any permanence was The East London Christian Mission, testifying to the particular location of this Christian Mission as opposed to other Christian Missions in London at the time.

10. Ervine, *God's Soldier: General William Booth*, 1:296.

11. Cyril Barnes, *With Booth in London* (London: The Salvation Army, 1986), pp. 21-22. There is confusion in the biographies about the time of the purchase of the Eastern Star, but apparently it was purchased soon after renting the Effingham Theater for Sunday evening services, which would mean that it was purchased sometime in the first half of 1867.

12. Jenty Fairbank, *Booth's Boots: Social Service Beginnings in The Salvation Army* (London: The Salvation Army International Headquarters, 1983), p. 3.

13. Ervine, *God's Soldier: General William Booth*, 1:295. However, the membership of these initial committees was more fluid than Ervine would lead one to believe. For a detailed account of the various committees see Sandall, *The History of The Salvation Army*, Vol. 1, Appendix C.

14. By 1870 the work of the Mission had expanded beyond East London, and so appropriately the name of the publication was changed to *The Christian Mission Magazine*. After the founding of The Salvation Army it bore the name *The Salvationist* for one year, 1879, and was changed in 1880 to *The War Cry*, the name still used today.

15. Christian Mission stationery from this time gives the postal address as 3, Gore Road, Victoria Park Road.

16. Barnes, *With Booth in London*, p. 27.

17. Sandall, *The History of The Salvation Army*, 1:144.

18. William Booth to William Stephenson Crow, April 17, 1872, the William Booth File, The Salvation Army International Heritage Centre; London, England. Crow acted as kind of a confidant for William Booth and the Booth correspondence to Crow during this time is voluminous, including correspondence about all kinds of personal matters. Crow had been with New Connexion Methodism at Gateshead where he became a friend of the Booths, followed Booth into The Christian Mission and became Booth's printer. He became the first printer of *The War Cry*, and was the person who coined the popular term "Hallelujah Lasses." He died in 1895 at the age of 71. See Colonel Sandall's "Interview with Mr. Booth Crow [the son of William Crow, named after William Booth] of Hatfield Road, Oaklands, St. Albans, 7th September, 1934," 4 pp. in the William Booth File, The Salvation Army International Heritage Centre; London, England.

19. Begbie, *The Life of General William Booth*, 1:355.

20. Begbie in his *The Life of General William Booth* gives the impression that Booth discharged this business rather hastily. He wrote that "In a moment of disappointment he abandoned the business altogether" (1:352). This was apparently not the case. Booth took care to examine the business, and was troubled with the many personnel issues caused by unreliable employees. For an interesting note on this program, including the title of "William Booth-Dining Rooms" for some of the feeding stations see Ervine, *God's Soldier: General William Booth*, 1:322.

21. Sandall, *The History of The Salvation Army*, 1:196.

22. In his book entitled *Blood and Fire: William and Catherine Booth and Their Salvation Army*, p. 190, Hattersley inexplicably wrote that "in Roger Green's *Catherine Booth* the date of the annual conference is given as 15-17 June 1870." He apparently ignored my endnote 27 on p. 312 where I wrote the following: "The first Conference was recorded as being held at The People's Mission Hall, 272 Whitechapel Road, London, from June 15-18, 1870. However, The Foundation Deed of 1875 is correct in listing November as the month when the first Conference was held. See Sandall, *The History of The Salvation Army*, 1:180" (Green, *Catherine Booth: A Biography of the Cofounder of The Salvation Army*, p. 312).

23. Ervine, *God's Soldier: General William Booth*, 1:310.

24. Murdoch, *Origins of The Salvation Army*, p. 86.

25. See Roger J. Green, "William Booth and Methodism," *Word & Deed: A Journal of Salvation Army Theology and Ministry* 6:2 (May 2004), pp. 23-38.

26. Ibid., p. 176.

27. Hattersley, *Blood and Fire: William and Catherine Booth and Their Salvation Army*, p. 220.

28. For the most thorough study of the doctrine of holiness and the Booths see John Pentecost, *William Booth and the Doctrine of Holiness* (1997). See Also Earl Robinson, "Wesleyan Distinctives in Salvation Army Theology," *Word & Deed: A Journal of Salvation Army Theology and Ministry* 6:2 (May 2004), pp. 5-21.

29. Adopted at the First General Conference of the Mission, held at Whitechapel, in November, 1870, pp. 16-17 of the Minutes. Note that the Conference Minute Book gives the date incorrectly as June 1870. The timing of these doctrines is an important issue. Murdoch wrote in his article entitled "Evangelical Sources of Salvation Army Doctrine," *Evangelical Quarterly* 87:3 (1987), pp. 235-44 that this article was not added until 1876 and that "This doctrinal addition reflected a growing Anglo-American interest in the doctrine of holiness, the doctrine that became the distinguishing theological mark of Booth's mission" (p. 241). However, the doctrine is in place in the *Doctrines and Rules of The Christian Mission, 1870*, which demonstrates that the doctrine of holiness was indeed

becoming central to the Booths' thinking before 1876. Murdoch is incorrect when he writes that "the Booths had slighted holiness teaching after Phoebe Palmer returned to America in 1863 but reembraced the doctrine in 1876. . . ." (Ibid., p. 242). He reiterated this position in his book entitled *Origins of The Salvation Army* when he wrote that "Only in 1875–76 did they adopt doctrines with a purely Wesleyan cast. Then the mission added an article which dealt with holiness and the perseverance of the saints" (p. 66). Pentecost wrote the following in his *William Booth and the Doctrine of Holiness* (p. 97): "Reviewing the evidence examined to this point, it is proposed that, far from indicating any lapse of interest in the doctrine of Sanctification/Holiness on the part of the Booths, the evidence strongly suggests a consistent and continuous preoccupation with the doctrine—at least over the decade 1861–1871. It is also proposed that the same evidence raises serious doubts about the validity of the claims made by both Murdoch and Kent [*Holding the Fort: Studies in Victorian Revivalism*], that a lapse of interest and/or pursuit of theological fashion were probable reasons for the 1865/66 omission of such a doctrinal statement."

30. It is true that the Conference of 1876 clarified the meaning of the doctrine of sanctification in this way: "Resolved that the following definitions of the doctrines numbered 9 and 10 in our list of Doctrines be printed and issued to all our members. . . .That is to say—We believe that after conversion there remains in the heart of a believer inclinations to evil or roots of bitterness, which, unless overpowered by Divine Grace, produce actual sin, but that these evil tendencies can be entirely taken away by the Spirit of God, and the whole heart thus cleansed from everything contrary to the will of God, or entirely sanctified, will then produce the fruits of the Spirit only. And we believe that persons thus entirely sanctified may by the power of God be kept unblameable and unreprovable before Him. Moved by Railton, Seconded by Garner" (*Minutes of the Conference of The Christian Mission, 1876*). But the doctrines themselves had been officially pronounced as Christian Mission doctrines previous to 1876.

31. William Booth, "Holiness. An Address at the Conference." *The Christian Mission Magazine* (August 1877), p. 194.

32. Ibid.

33. Ibid., p. 193.

34. William Booth, "The General's Address at the Wesleyan Conference," *The War Cry* (August 14, 1880), p. 1. See also Hattersley, *Blood and Fire: William and Catherine Booth and Their Salvation Army*, pp. 261-62.

35. Ibid., p. 216.

36. Norman H. Murdoch, "Wesleyan Influence on William and Catherine Booth," *Wesleyan Theological Journal* 20:2 (Fall 1985), p. 99. See also Murdoch, *Origins of The Salvation Army*, p. 31. This is a critical matter in identifying the Wesleyan heritage of the Booths, because some have argued that by their allegiance to the American revivalists their view of holiness was filtered through the Americans and thus was not consistently Wesleyan.

37. *Salvation Story: Salvationist Handbook of Doctrine* (London: The Salvation Army International Headquarters, 1998), pp. 130-31. See also Earl Robinson, "The History of Salvation Army Doctrine," *Word and Deed: A Journal of Salvation Army Theology and Ministry* 2:2 (May 2000), pp. 31-45. See also Murdoch, "Evangelical Sources of Salvation Army Doctrine," pp. 235-44. There he states that "The most likely primary source of Salvation Army doctrine is a list of nine doctrines adopted by the Evangelical Alliance in its first meeting in August-September 1846 at Freemason's Hall, Great Queen Street, London" (p. 235). However, in his book entitled *Origins of The Salvation Army* he tempers this by stating that "Although the Booths were Wesleyan-Arminian doctrinally, in 1865 they merged articles of faith from broad creeds of the Evangelical Alliance and the

Methodist New Connexion" (p. 65). Murdoch is correct that the Evangelical Alliance statement of faith held to nine doctrines.

38. There may have been some within the ranks of The Christian Mission who held to a doctrine of election and final perseverance, but the following resolution recorded in the *Minutes of The Christian Mission Conference* of 1873 settled the matter: "Resolved that no person shall be allowed to teach in The Christian Mission the doctrine of Final Perseverance apart from perseverance in holiness, or that the moral law was abolished, and that if any person after having been cautioned by the Superintendent continued to propagate this doctrine, they should not be allowed further to preach or speak in the Mission. Moved by Bramwell Booth. Seconded by Dowdle." The reason it is stated that the ninth doctrine was added at this time is because there was a rearrangement of doctrines in 1873–1874. What was previously doctrine nine (the doctrine on holiness) was made doctrine ten, and the ninth doctrine being discussed here was inserted. John Coutts in his book entitled *This We Believe: A Study of the Background and Meaning of Salvation Army Doctrines* (London: The Salvation Army International Headquarters, 1976) wrote, "But in 1870 the Conference of *The Christian Mission* accepted an eleven-point statement almost identical to the one in use in The Salvation Army today" (p. 99). However, in 1870 there were only ten doctrines, the final doctrine being added in 1873–1874.

39. Horridge, *The Salvation Army Origins and Early Days: 1865–1900*, p. 225.

40. The Salvation Army Act of 1980 again affirmed those eleven doctrines, and the clearest explanation of Army doctrines to date came with the publication in 1998 of *Salvation Story: Salvationist Handbook of Doctrine*.

41. The best biography of George Scott Railton is entitled *Soldier Saint* by Bernard Watson (London: Hodder and Stoughton, 1970). See also H. Benjamin Blackwell, *Ambassador Extraordinary* (London: Salvationist Publishing and Supplies, Ltd., 1944) and Eileen Douglas and Mildred Duff, *Commissioner Railton* (London: The Salvationist Publishing and Supplies, Ltd., 1920).

42. For two biographies of Elijah Cadman see H. Benjamin Blackwell, *Fighting Sweep: Elijah Cadman* (London: Salvationist Publishing and Supplies, Ltd., 1951) and Humphrey Wallis, *The Happy Warrior: The Life Story of Commissioner Elijah Cadman* (London: Salvationist Publishing and Supplies, Ltd., 1928). For James Dowdle see William Burrows, *Fiery Fiddler* (London: Salvationist Publishing and Supplies, Ltd., 1945), and George S. Railton, *Commissioner Dowdle: The Saved Railway Guard* (London: The Salvation Army, 1901). And for John Lawley see Minnie Linsday Carpenter, *Commissioner John Lawley* (London: Salvationist Publishing and Supplies, Ltd., 1924).

43. See Smith's autobiography entitled Rodney "Gypsy" Smith, *Gypsy Smith: His Life and Work* (New York: Fleming H. Revell, 1906).

44. Sandall, *The History of The Salvation Army*, 1:181.

45. Hattersley, *Blood and Fire: William and Catherine Booth and Their Salvation Army*, p. 214.

46. Begbie, *The Life of General William Booth*, 1:366. The issue of Bramwell's succession of William would later be problematic, but he did nevertheless succeed his father as the second General of The Salvation Army upon William's death in 1912. He remained General until 1929 when he was deposed from office for reasons of health and inability to continue in that office, and the succession of the office of General from that time on was by election by a High Council rather than by inheritance.

47. Ibid., 1:367-68.

48. Ibid., 1:372.

49. Green, *Catherine Booth: A Biography of the Cofounder of The Salvation Army*, pp. 166-67.

50. Ervine, *God's Soldier: General William Booth*, 1:317.

51. Horridge, *The Salvation Army Origins and Early Days: 1865–1900*, pp. 264-65.

52. The William Booth File, The Salvation Army International Heritage Centre; London, England.

53. Ibid.

8. The Evolution of a Mission and the Creation of an Army

1. Horridge, *The Salvation Arm Origins and Early Days: 1865–1900*, p. 33.

2. Bramwell Booth, *Echoes and Memories*, p. 60.

3. Rack, *Reasonable Enthusiast: John Wesley and the Rise of Methodism*, pp. 247-48.

4. Bramwell Booth, *Echoes and Memories*, p. 59.

5. J. Hampson, *Memoirs of John Wesley*, 3 vols. (London: 1791), 3:200-01, quoted in Rack, *Reasonable Enthusiast: John Wesley and the Rise of Methodism*, p. 541.

6. Green, *Catherine Booth: A Biography of the Cofounder of The Salvation Army*, p. 187.

7. Begbie, *The Life of General William Booth*, 1:374.

8. *The Christian Mission Magazine* (July 1877), p. 177.

9. See both of these letters in the William Booth File, The Salvation Army International Heritage Centre; London, England.

10. Watson, *Soldier Saint*, pp. 39-40.

11. Green, *Catherine Booth: A Biography of the Cofounder of The Salvation Army*, p. 188. See George S. Railton, *Heathen England and What to Do for It* (London: S. W. Partridge, 1877). There were several subsequent editions, and the fifth edition was entitled *Heathen England: Being a Description of the Utterly Godless Condition of the Vast Majority of the English Nation, and of the Establishment, Growth, System, and Success of The Army for Its Salvation Consisting of Working People Under the Generalship of William Booth* (London: International Headquarters, 1891).

12. Horridge, *The Salvation Army Origins and Early Days: 1865–1900*, p. 33.

13. Joel A. Carpenter, *Revive Us Again: The Reawakening of American Fundamentalism* (New York: Oxford University Press, 1997), p. 179.

14. Bennett, *The General: William Booth*, 2:91.

16. See Bramwell Booth, *Echoes and Memories*, p. 71.

17. For a more complete picture of the relationship of preaching the gospel and social ministry see Garth M. Rosell, "Charles Grandison Finney and the Rise of the Benevolent Empire" (Ph.D. Dissertation, University of Minnesota, 1971), and Roger J. Green, "Charles Grandison Finney: The Social Implications of His Ministry," *The Asbury Theological Journal* 48:2 (Fall 1993), pp. 5-26.

18. Begbie, *The Life of General William Booth*, 1:388.

19. Ibid., 1:389.

20. Minutes, First Conference of The Christian Mission, held in People's Mission Hall, 272 Whitechapel Road, London, June 15-17, 1870 [incorrect date given by the Conference Minute Book], microfilm collection, The Salvation Army International Heritage Centre; London, England.

21. Sandall, *The History of The Salvation Army*, 1:271.

22. Horridge, *The Salvation Army Origins and Early Days: 1865–1900*, p. 23.

23. Elijah Cadman File, The Salvation Army International Heritage Centre; London, England.

24. Pamela J. Walker, *Pulling the Devil's Kingdom Down: The Salvation Army in Victorian*

Britain, p. 56. Walker is not without criticism of how carefully the matter of the equality of women and men was worked out in The Christian Mission and The Salvation Army as these movements unfolded. However, the most insightful study and criticism of this matter can be seen in Andrew Mark Eason, *Women in God's Army: Gender and Equality in the Early Salvation Army* (Waterloo, Ontario, Canada: Wilfrid Laurier University Press, 2003). He sees more of an ambiguous heritage in The Christian Mission and The Salvation Army rather than a singularly consistent heritage. However a review of this book by Diane Winston well states the central problem with Eason's argument. She wrote, "Eason methodically makes his case, but his results beg the question—why does he see the glass half empty? Yes, Salvationists were products of their age, and their assumptions—shaped by theology and social theory—presupposed the doctrine of separate spheres. Yet, they belonged to the first modern Christian movement to envision an alternative. One might argue that, even as they clung to entrenched prejudices, Salvationists sought to fulfill the mandate of Galatians 3:28. Eason seems to think that they did not try hard enough; the historical record overwhelms the rhetorical pose. However, one could make the case that the Army mounted a significant challenge to nineteenth-century notions of women's roles, even when it failed to live up to its own promise. Through sheer numbers and public leadership (between 1887 and 1934, a Booth daughter or daughter-in-law headed the American Army), its example inspired women seeking ordination in other Protestant denominations" (Diane Winston, *Review of Women in God's Army: Gender and Equality in The Salvation Army* in *Church History: Studies in Christianity & Culture* 73:1 [The American Society of Church History, 2004], pp. 231-33).

For two excellent articles on women in ministry in The Salvation Army see Ann R. Higgenbotham, "Respectable Sinners: Salvation Army Rescue Work with Unmarried Mothers, 1884–1914," in Gail Malmgreen, ed. *Religion in the Lives of English Women, 1760–1930* (Bloomington: Indiana University Press, 1986); and Lynne Marks, "The 'Hallelujah Lasses': Working-Class Women in The Salvation Army in English Canada, 1882–1890," in Franca Iacovetta and Mariana Valverde, eds., *Gender Conflicts: New Essays in Women's History* (Toronto: University of Toronto Press, 1993). See also Lillian Taiz, *Hallelujah Lads & Lasses: Remaking the Salvation Army in America, 1880–1930* (Chapel Hill: The University of North Carolina Press, 2001).

25. William Cooke, *Christian Theology: Its Doctrines and Ordinances Explained and Defended* (London: Hamilton, Adams, and Co., 1879), p. 479.

26. John Pentecost, *William Booth and the Doctrine of Holiness*, p. 207.

27. William Booth, "Holiness. An Address at the Conference," p. 193.

28. See Sandall, *The History of The Salvation Army*, 1:228-30.

29. See Murdoch, *Origins of The Salvation Army*, p. 100.

30. Begbie, "Booth, William (1829–1912)," p. 51.

31. Bennett, *The General: William Booth*, 2:94.

32. Rack, *Reasonable Enthusiast: John Wesley and the Rise of Methodism*, p. 443.

33. Murdoch, *Origins of The Salvation Army*, p. 100. See also Horridge, *The Salvation Army Origins and Early Days: 1865–1900*, p. 45, where he identifies the twenty different facets of militarism that appealed to people and attracted members to the Army.

34. William Booth, "Our New Name," *The Salvationist* (January 1879), p. 1.

35. William Booth, "The Salvation Army," *The Salvationist* (February 1879), p. 29.

36. The analysis of Diane Winston regarding evangelicals in America being propelled by "postmillennial perfectionism" (p. 124) she also well applies to The Salvation Army in America. This may also be applied to the theology and ministry of William Booth and to British Salvationists as they led their Army and their crusade into the future. However, while Winston well explains the cultural and social foundations of postmillennial perfectionism, she does not deal with the biblical and theological background for that the-

ology. Therefore, she fails to make the close connection between Booth and The Salvation Army and their Evangelical and Wesleyan background on this and other matters. See Diane Winston, *Red-Hot and Righteous: The Urban Religion of The Salvation Army* (Cambridge, Massachusetts: Harvard University Press, 1999).

37. Begbie, *The Life of General William Booth*, 1:437.

38. Ibid., 1:438.

39. Ibid., 1:440.

40. Horridge, *The Salvation Army Origins and Early Days: 1865–1900*, pp. 99-100.

41. See Begbie, *The Life of General William Booth*, 1:379; and Bramwell Booth, *Echoes and Memories*, p. 71.

42. Heitzenrater, *Wesley and the People Called Methodists*, p. 132.

43. Horridge, *The Salvation Army Origins and Early Days: 1865–1900*, p. 92.

44. Ibid., p. 94.

45. Begbie, *The Life of General William Booth*, 2:3. See Bramwell Booth's reminiscence of John Bright in *Echoes and Memories*, pp. 141-42.

46. Horridge, *The Salvation Army Origins and Early Days: 1865–1900*, p. 110.

47. William Booth to William Crow, November 8, 1878, in the William Booth File, The Salvation Army International Heritage Centre; London, England.

48. Begbie, *The Life of General William Booth*, 1:437.

49. See Catherine Booth, "The Salvation Army and the Bishop of Carlisle," *The War Cry* (October 9, 1880), p. 1; (October 16, 1880), p. 2; (October 23, 1880), p. 1.

50. Catherine Booth, "The Salvation Army and the Bishop of Carlisle," (October 9, 1880), p. 1.

51. Green, *Catherine Booth: A Biography of the Cofounder of The Salvation Army*, pp. 213-14.

52. Booth's postmillennial theology is evident throughout his ministry. For three examples of this during three periods of his ministry see the following: his brief article entitled "The Conversion of the World" in the *East London Evangelist* (October 1, 1869), pp. 199-200; William Booth, "The War Spirit," *The General's Letters*, 1885 (London: The Salvation Army International Headquarters, 1890), p. 73; and William Booth, *To My Officers: A Letter from the General on his Eightieth Birthday* (London: The Salvation Army International Headquarters, 1909), 58 pp.

53. This is one of two letters in Appendix 7 of Horridge, *The Salvation Army Origins and Early Days: 1865–1900* entitled "Previously Unpublished Letters from George Scott Railton to Two Christian Mission Evangelists," p. 264. I have not found these two original letters.

54. William Booth to William Crow, December 19, 1878, in the William Booth File, The Salvation Army International Heritage Centre; London, England. This is the only instance that I know of where Booth referred to any office of General outside of his own office and title. What he referred to as "District Generals" became divisional commanders and held various ranks, including captain, but no other officer in Booth's day ever held the rank or title of General. That remains the case in The Salvation Army today. There is only one General who is the international leader of The Salvation Army, although upon retirement the General retains that title.

55. Carpenter, *Revive Us Again*, p. 235.

56. Ibid., p. 241.

57. Heitzenrater, *Wesley and the People Called Methodists*, p. 144.

58. Ibid., p. 146.

9. The Army in the Public Square

1. Barnes, *With Booth in London*, p. 34. While much is known about Henry Andrews because he became a Salvation Army officer, little is known of George Booth, affectionately called Georgie, the first of the two to be adopted. For Georgie see *The Christian Mission Magazine* (July 1877), p. 175, and *The Christian Mission Magazine* (November 1878), p. 305. In the first reference William referred to their nine children, and in the second reference Catherine did the same. See also Arch R. Wiggins, *T.H.K.: A Biography* (London: Salvationist Publishing and Supplies, 1956), pp. 22-23; and Jenty Fairbank, *Booth's Boots: the Beginnings of Salvation Army Social Work*, pp. 49-51 for the circumstances of Georgie coming into the Booth family. For two other interesting references see George Scott Railton, *Heathen England and What to Do for It*, p. 182, which makes reference to the Booths' four sons; and the letter from Catherine Booth to Herbert Booth, January 26, 1881, in the Catherine Booth File, The Salvation Army International Heritage Centre; London, England. Bennett claims that William Booth met Georgie in his 1902–1903 visit to America (*The General: William Booth*, 1:368).

2. Catherine Booth, *The Salvation Army in Relation to Church and State and Other Addresses* (London: International Headquarters, 1889), p. 30.

3. See Carolyn Ocheltree, "Wesleyan Methodist Perceptions of William Booth." See also Catherine Booth, *The Salvation Army in Relation to the Church and State and Other Addresses*.

4. Bennett, *The General: William Booth*, 2:151. For a record of Booth's address see William Booth, "The General's Address at the Wesleyan Conference," p. 1.

5. Bennett, *The General: William Booth*, 2:151.

6. See Henry Edward Manning, "The Salvation Army," *The Contemporary Review* 41 (August 1882), pp. 335-42. See also "Why Cardinal Manning Thinks the Army Valuable and Hopes for Good from It," *The War Cry* (September 7, 1882), p. 4.

7. This project proved to be a dismal failure. After the Army purchased the property, the original owners of the property took the Army to court on a technical matter. The Army relinquished its deed on the property in September of 1898. For a full account of this episode in Salvation Army history see Sandall, *The History of The Salvation Army*, 2:216-20.

8. Ibid., 2:139.

9. J. A. Atkinson, "The Salvation Army and the Church," *A Paper Read Before the Clergy and Lay Consultees of the Ardwick Rural Deanery, May 9, 1882*, 15 pp., in The British Library, pp. 12-13. See also James Augustus Atkinson, *The Salvation Army and the Church* (Manchester: John Heywood, 1882), 15 pp. in The British Library.

10. Begbie, *The Life of General William Booth*, 2:13.

11. Kenneth J. Collins, *A Real Christian: The Life of John Wesley* (Nashville: Abingdon Press, 1999), p. 142.

12. Norman H. Murdoch, "The Salvation Army and The Church of England, 1882–1883," *Historical Magazine of the Protestant Episcopal Church* 55 (March 1986), p. 34.

13. P. T. Marsh, *The Victorian Church in Decline: Archbishop Tait and the Church of England 1868–1882* (London: Routledge & Kegan Paul, 1969), p. 248.

14. Ervine, *God's Soldier: General William Booth*, 1:607.

15. Randall Davidson did not appreciate William Booth very much, but had high regard for Catherine Booth. It was his father who, after hearing Catherine Booth preach, is reported to have said, "If I am ever charged with a crime, don't bother to engage any of the great lawyers to defend me; get me that woman!" Davidson eventually became the

Archbishop of Canterbury. See George Bell, *Randall Davidson, Archbishop of Canterbury*, 2 Vols. (London: Oxford University Press, 1935).

16. However, it is evident from one letter written by Randall J. Davidson from Lambeth Palace in April of 1883 that the Army had not been forthcoming with all the necessary information for the deliberations. See Begbie, *The Life of General William Booth*, 2:18-19. The Army made reference to the conversation with the Anglican Church. For example, see "What the Bishops Say About Us," *The War Cry* (May 18, 1882), p. 4; "The Church Congress and The Salvation Army," *The War Cry* (October 14, 1882), p. 1; and "Notes of the Majors' Council," *The War Cry* (November 4, 1882), p. 3.

17. See especially the letter from Randall J. Davidson written from Lambeth Palace, S. E. on April 13, 1883, to William Booth in Begbie, *The Life of General William Booth*, 2:18.

18. Ervine, *The Life of General William Booth*, 1:610. Bramwell Booth in *Echoes and Memories* gives an assessment of each of the Anglican leaders involved in the negotiations, and writes the following about Davidson's feelings about Booth's autocratic control over the Army: "So far as Dr. Davidson was concerned, this was, I am afraid, from the beginning, fatal to the project" (p. 75).

19. Ervine, *The Life of General William Booth*, 1:610-11.

20. Randall T. Davidson, "The Methods of The Salvation Army," *The Contemporary Review* 41 (August 1882), p. 199.

21. See "Rules of The Christian Mission, 1870" in Sandall, *The History of The Salvation Army*, 1:275-77: "31 Baptisms (mode left to members. Discussion of the subject strictly forbidden. Not to be imposed upon any having conscientious scruples against it. No baptism by immersion at any station—if desired—to be administered elsewhere). . . . 34 The Lord's Supper (once a month unless two-thirds of the members of a society desire it oftener. Confined to holders of members' tickets or notes of admission. Unfermented wine only to be used)." For the most thorough treatment of the Booths and The Salvation Army on the sacraments see R. David Rightmire, *Sacraments and The Salvation Army: Pneumatological Foundations* (Metuchen, N. J.: Scarecrow Press, Inc., 1990).

22. "Baptism, therefore, was for William Booth a detail of symbolism, and he left it freely to his followers to decide whether they would be baptized or not; he felt no vital concern in the matter" (Begbie, *The Life of General William Booth*, 1:377).

23. Bennett, *The General: William Booth*, 2:197.

24. *The War Cry* (July 10, 1881), p. 3.

25. See *The War Cry* (March 27, 1880), p. 3 and *The War Cry* (March 31, 1881), p. 4.

26. See, for example, *The War Cry*, April 20, 1882.

27. Susie Swift, "The Conversion of Susan Swift," p. 4 in the Susie Swift File, The Salvation Army International Heritage Centre; London, England. It is parenthetically interesting to note that this Vassar graduate also found the intellectual life of International Headquarters highly stimulating. She wrote that "many highly educated men and women surround the leaders" (p. 4).

28. Begbie makes reference to a draft of a letter on the sacraments by George Scott Railton for Booth's consideration, but that letter is not available. See Begbie, *The Life of General William Booth*, 1:425-26.

29. Ervine, *God's Soldier: General William Booth*, 1:614.

30. William Booth, "The General's New Year Address to Officers," *The War Cry* (January 17, 1883), p. 2. Roland Robertson in his article entitled "The Salvation Army: The Persistence of Sectarianism" in Brian R. Wilson, ed., *Patterns of Sectarianism* (London: Heinemann Educational Books, 1967), pp. 49-105 is incorrect when he attributes this part of Booth's theology to institutional calculation alone. Booth's position on the sacraments was not, as Robertson affirms, a result of his desire to maintain the hierarchical organization and prevent sacramental power from falling into the hands and

under the control of lesser officers in the organizational hierarchy. Robertson writes that a denial of the place of the sacraments in the life of the Army was connected with the hierarchical structure of the Army, "for with so much power wielded by the officers, the temptation to interpose the latter as mediators between God and the Salvation soldier were very strong" (p. 66). Such an assumption is wrong for two reasons. First, it advances a high view of the sacraments and of sacramental power, a view that Booth never espoused. Second, it reduces Booth's theological decisions solely to organizational concerns, and that leads to a myopic view of Booth and his theology.

Robertson also incorrectly assumes that Booth's views of the sacraments constituted a kind of anti-sacramentalism. This is untrue. Booth was nonpracticing in his later theology but he was never anti-sacramental. He held that participation in the work of redemption, centered on Christ, was the one indispensable sign of the Church, and therefore did not view the sacraments as concomitant indispensable signs. But his sacramental theology was also rooted in his view of full salvation—holiness. As William Booth clarified his doctrine of holiness—both personal and corporate—he drew the implication that all of life was holy for the believer and for the Church. For example, he wrote, "nothing should be allowed in conversation that is contrary to sound doctrine" (William Booth, *Religion for Every Day* [London: Salvationist Publishing and Supplies, n.d.], p. 130). Thus the life of the individual believer and the life of the Church were sacred. Because of this, external ordinances of any kind were unnecessary to demonstrate periodically that which should be demonstrated continually and consistently.

31. Fred Cox, an aide to General Booth, in listing the duties of an aide, wryly said, "If the General says a thing is so, it is so—never mind what your own opinion may be on the matter!" (Fred Cox, *He Was There* [London: The Salvation Army, 1949], p. 39).

32. Begbie, *The Life of General William Booth*, 1:424-25. Begbie repeats this observation with various wording three more times in his biography of Booth.

33. Henry Edward Manning, "The Salvation Army," *The Contemporary Review* 41 (August 1882), pp. 338-41.

34. Henry S. Lunn, ed., "The Salvation Army and the Sacraments," *Review of the Churches*, Vol. 7, No. 2 (April 1895), p. 128.

35. Ibid.

36. Ibid. It is interesting that at the conclusion of the article, Lunn asked if the Army had passed its zenith. To give witness to the strength of the Army at that time, Booth responded, "Most emphatically not. . . . Perhaps the most striking illustration of the strength of the Army is to be found in the fact that last year we accepted 1,113 new cadets in Great Britain" (p. 131).

37. *The Doctrines and Disciplines of The Salvation Army, 1885* (London: The Salvation Army International Headquarters, 1885), p. 90. Not all editions of *The Doctrines and Disciplines of the Salvation Army* after 1883 contain this question. It was omitted in some editions, but left in others.

38. Ocheltree, "Wesleyan Methodist Perceptions of William Booth," p. 270.

39. Rightmire, *Sacraments and The Salvation Army: Pneumatological Foundations*, p. 196.

40. Editorial, "The Salvation Army," *The Methodist Times*, London (February 1885), p. 97, quoted in Ocheltree, "Wesleyan Methodist Perceptions of William Booth," p. 274.

41. Walker, *Pulling the Devil's Kingdom Down: The Salvation Army in Victorian Britain*, p. 119.

42. Green, *Catherine Booth: A Biography of the Cofounder of The Salvation Army*, p. 236.

43. See Edgar Rowan, *Wilson Carlile and the Church Army* (London: Hodder and Stoughton, 1905).

44. Bennett, *The General: William Booth*, 2:203.

45. For details of the intricacies of prostitution in Victorian England, and for some

accounting of the Army's work with prostitutes, see Edward J. Bristow, *Vice and Vigilance: Purity Movements in England Since 1700* (Dublin: Gill and Macmillan, 1977), and Judith R. Walkowitz, *Prostitution and Victorian Society: Women, Class, and the State* (Cambridge: Cambridge University Press, 1980).

46. Frederick Coutts, *Bread for My Neighbor: The Social Influence of William Booth* (London; Hodder and Stoughton, 1987), p. 47.

47. Green, *Catherine Booth: A Biography of the Cofounder of The Salvation Army*, p. 250.

48. Ann R. Higginbotham, "Respectable Sinners: Salvation Army Rescue Work with Unmarried Mothers, 1884–1914," p. 218.

49. See Josephine Butler's work entitled "A Grave Question (the system of officially organized prostitution) that Needs Answering by the Churches of Great Britain" (London: Dyer Bros., 1886), 7 pp. in The British Library. See also E. M. Turner, *Josephine Butler: Her Place in History* (London: The Association for Moral and Social Hygiene, n.d.); Josephine Butler, *Josephine Butler: An Autobiographical Memoir* (Bristol: Arrowsmith, 1911); and Mary Stacks, "Josephine Butler and the Moral Standards of Today," The Alison Neilans Memorial Lecture V, 21 February 1961 (London: The Association for Moral and Social Hygiene, 1961). See the letter from Josephine Butler to Florence Booth dated March 26, 1885, in the Florence Booth File, The Salvation Army International Heritage Centre; London, England. See also Catherine Booth, *The Iniquity of State Regulated Vice. A Speech Delivered at Exeter Hall, London, on Feb. 6th 1884* (London: Dyer Bros., 1884).

50. Bennett, *The General: William Booth*, 2:215,

51. W. T. Stead befriended the Booths, especially Catherine and Bramwell, became a champion of the Army's, and wrote voluminously on the Army. His biographies of William Booth and Catherine Booth are mentioned in the bibliographic essay. As well, see the following: his three articles on William Booth in Benjamin Waugh, *The Sunday Magazine* (London: Isbister and Company, 1891); W. T. Stead, "A Tribute to Mrs. Booth," *All the World* (November 1910), pp. 569-70; and W. T. Stead, "Interview with the General," *All the World* (July 1911), pp. 339-42. For articles about Stead see "Mr. W. T. Stead: Stalwart for Truth," *All the World* (May 1906), pp. 233-36; Bramwell Booth, "The Late W. T. Stead," *All the World* (June 1912), pp. 308-10; and the letter written from Bramwell to the General, March 24, 1909, p. 2 in the Bramwell Booth File, The Salvation Army International Heritage Centre; London, England. Bramwell wrote: "He is a wonderful fellow; he may yet do more for us than ever he has done in the past. It is not only his ability and his loyalty and his energy which are remarkable—though they are remarkable—but it is his courage. That was what attracted me to him at the very beginning, and you also. On certain lines, I consider he is unequalled in our day."

52. See Scott's "Is London more immoral than Paris or Brussels?" A letter reprinted from *The Sentinel* in The British Library; and *A State Iniquity: Its Rise, Extension and Overthrow* (London: Kegan Paul, 1890).

53. Richard Collier, *The General Next to God* (London: Collins, 1965), p. 124.

54. Stead succeeded John Morley as the editor of this paper when Morley became the Chief Secretary for Ireland.

55. See Josephine Butler's biography of Rebecca Jarrett entitled *Rebecca Jarrett* (London: Morgan and Scott, 1885), 59 pp. Rebecca Jarrett also wrote two autobiographies, the first handwritten when she was seventy-nine years old, and the other typescript. See the Rebecca Jarrett File, The Salvation Army International Heritage Centre; London, England. See also Pamela J. Walker's work on Rebecca Jarrett in *Pulling the Devil's Kingdom Down: The Salvation Army in Victorian Britain*, chapter 5 entitled "Authority and Transgression: The Lives of Maud Charlesworth, Effie Anthon, and Rebecca Jarrett."

56. See *The Maiden Tribute of Modern Babylon. Reprinted from the Pall Mall Gazette* (London: F. A. Roberts, n.d.), 31 pp.; George Scott Railton, *The Truth About the Armstrong Case and The Salvation Army* (London: The Salvation Army, n.d.), 23 pp. The Maiden Tribute Case File, The Salvation Army International Heritage Centre; London, England. Army publications followed this crusade extensively, as well as the trials that followed. For examples see the following: "Mrs. Booth on the Revelations Made by 'The Pall Mall Gazette.' A Meeting Convened by The Salvation Army in Prince's Hall," *The War Cry* (July 18, 1885), p. 1; that issue also contained a letter from William Booth on the same subject entitled "Giant Killing—Where are the Davids?" See also "Modern Babylon. The Protection of Young Girls. Salvation Army Meeting in the Prince's Hall, Piccadilly. Samuel Morley, Esq., M.P. in the Chair. Speeches by Mrs. Booth, Mrs. Josephine Butler, and Professor Stuart, M.P.," *The War Cry* (July 22, 1885), p. 1; "The Horrible Immorality of London. Salvation Army Indignation Mass Meeting at Exeter Hall," *The War Cry* (July 22, 1885), p. 1; "Immorality. The Recent Disclosures. Great Agitation Demonstration in the Free Trade Hall, Manchester," *The War Cry* (July 25, 1885), p. 1; "The Salvation Army's Petition to the Government," *The War Cry* (July 25, 1885), p. 1; William Booth's letter in the same edition entitled "Misery-Strippers," p. 1; "Protection of Young Girls. Great Mass Meeting of Women in Exeter Hall. Held by Mrs. Booth," *The War Cry* (July 29, 1885), p. 1; "The Recent Revelations. The General at the Albert Hall, Sheffield," *The War Cry* (July 29, 1885), p. 1; "Mrs. Josephine Butler on the Protection of Young Girls," *The War Cry* (July 29, 1885), p. 1; "The Horrible Immorality of London. Mass Meeting of Women at Exeter Hall. Speech by Mrs. Booth," *The War Cry* (August 1, 1885), p. 1; "The Tragedy of Modern Babylon. Great Meeting at Clapton Congress Hall. Second Letter from the Queen. Speeches by the General, Prof. Stuart, M.P., and Mrs. Booth," *The War Cry* (August 5, 1885), p. 1; "New National Scheme for the Deliverance of Unprotected Girls and the Rescue of the Fallen," *The War Cry* (August 8, 1885), pp. 1-2; and "Protection of Young Girls. Mrs. Booth at Portsmouth" in the same issue, p. 2; "Mrs. Josephine Butler on the Armstrong Case," *The War Cry* (October 7, 1885), p. 1; "A Call To Arms!" *The War Cry* (November 25, 1885), p. 1; "Petition to the Queen for the Release of Mr. Stead and Rebecca Jarrett," *The War Cry* (November 25, 1885), p. 1; "The Government Prosecution," *All the World* (October 1885), pp. 248-51; "God's Deliverance in the Armstrong Case," *All the World* (December 1885), pp. 296-98; and Alison Plowden, *The Case of Eliza Armstrong* (London: British Broadcasting Corporation, 1974).

57. Bennett, *The General: William Booth*, 2:227.

58. Begbie, *The Life of General William Booth*, 2:40.

59. Stead, *General Booth*, p. 94.

60. For Stead's involvement in the Purity Crusade see Victor Pierce Jones, *Saint or Sansationalist: The Story of W. T. Stead* (East Wittering, West Sussex, England: Gooday Publishers, 1988), chapters five and six.

61. Hattersley, *Blood and Fire: William and Catherine Booth and Their Salvation Army*, p. 323.

62. Ibid.

63. The petition was first announced in *The War Cry* (July 18, 1885), p. 1: "Special Notice! Protection of Young Girls." The notice read, "A PETITION TO THE HOUSE OF COMMONS for the above purpose will lie for Signature at the various Corps throughout the country, for the next few days. All Officers and Soldiers are earnestly desired to sign it and obtain as large a number of Signatures as possible, and forward the sheets, when full, to Headquarters, 101 Queen Victoria Street, E. C."

64. For Bramwell Booth's reflections on both the Purity Crusade and the trials that followed see *Echoes and Memories*, chapters 13 and 14.

65. Begbie, *The Life of General William Booth*, 2:49.

66. Begbie, "Booth, William (1829–1912)," p. 51.
67. Bennett, *The General: William Booth*, 2:238.
68. Ervine, *God's Soldier: General William Booth*, 2:627.

10. Turning Points

1. For information on Maud Charlesworth see Susan F. Welty, *Look Up and Hope! The Life of Maud Ballington Booth* (New York: Thomas Nelson, 1961). See also Pamela Walker's treatment of Maud Charlesworth in *Pulling the Devil's Kingdom Down: The Salvation Army in Victorian Britain*, chapter 5 entitled "Authority and Transgression: The Lives of Maud Charlesworth, Effie Anthon, and Rebecca Jarrett."

2. For information on Frederick St. George de Latour Booth-Tucker see the following: Frederick A. McKenzie, *Booth-Tucker: Sadhu and Saint* (London: Hodder & Stoughton, 1930); Madge Unsworth, *Bridging the Gap: Frederick Booth-Tucker of India* (London: Edinburgh House Press, 1943); and Harry Williams, *Booth-Tucker: William Booth's First Gentleman* (London: Hodder & Stoughton, 1980).

3. See Begbie, *The Life of General William*, 2:60. In his description of family life in the 1880s Begbie makes no mention of Marian Booth, a strange omission in that Marian lived until 1937.

4. Hattersley, *Blood and Fire: William and Catherine Booth and Their Salvation Army*, p. 406.

5. Edward H. McKinley, *Marching to Glory: The History of The Salvation Army in the United States, 1880–1992* (Grand Rapids: William B. Eerdmans Publishing Company, 1995), p. 1. See also R. J. Green, "Railton, George Scott (1849–1913) in Daniel G. Reid, ed., *Dictionary of Christianity in America* (Downers Grove, Illinois: InterVarsity Press, 1990), p. 972.

6. Sandall, *The History of The Salvation Army*, 2:260.

7. McKinley, *Marching to Glory*, p. 36.

8. Begbie, *The Life of General William Booth*, 2:74.

9. Barnes, *With Booth in London*, p. 41. Begbie in *The Life of General William Booth*, 2:84 mistakenly places the date for this move at 1889.

10. Sir James Paget was a famous surgical pathologist, widely published. See Stephen Paget, *Memoirs and Letters of Sir James Paget* (London: Longmans, 1903), 465 pp.

11. Railton, *The Authoritative Life of General William Booth*, p. 177.

12. Joseph Parker was a well-known preacher in London. He ministered at City Temple from 1869 to 1901. He wrote voluminously, and published commentaries and sermons.

13. See " 'Mrs. Booth to the Front Again' at Grand Celebration of the General's Sixtieth Birthday," *The War Cry* (April 20, 1889), p. 3.

14. See "Mrs. Booth at the City Temple," *The War Cry* (June 30, 1888), p. 9.

15. For example, in a letter written to Dr. Paton on December 19, 1889, from Clacton-on-Sea William Booth wrote, "On Sunday morning a remarkable change took place, and in the afternoon we thought she was dying, gathered around her bed and bade her farewell. It was a touching scene as she counseled us one by one and gave us her blessing. She talked like one inspired. To us all, however painful, it was like heaven on earth. Towards evening she rallied very remarkably, took a little refreshment, and although very prostrate there has been no return of the terrible anguish. . . ." The William Booth File, The Salvation Army International Heritage Centre; London, England.

16. Rack, *Reasonable Enthusiast: John Wesley and the Rise of Methodism*, p. 429.

17. Both Catherine Booth's illness, her promotion to glory and her funeral services

were reported in Army publications. Virtually the entire editions of *The War Cry* for October 11, October 18, and October 25, 1890, were devoted to Catherine Booth's death and funeral. For some examples of this see "Mrs. Booth's Condition," *All the World* (January 1890), p. 46; "Mrs. Booth's Condition," *All the World* (February 1890), pp. 91-92; "Mrs. Booth's Condition," *All the World* (May 1890), p. 235; William Booth, "Home at Last: To the Officers and Soldiers of The Salvation Army," *The War Cry* (October 11, 1890), p. 1; " 'Till the Resurrection Morning!" *The War Cry* (October 25, 1890), pp. 1-2; "Mrs. Booth's Funeral Services," *All the World* (November, 1890), pp. 538-40. Three of the most notable tributes to Catherine Booth were the following: "The Mother of The Salvation Army," *The Methodist Times* (October 9, 1890), p. 1; Dr. Joseph Parker, "A Tribute to Mrs. Booth," *The War Cry* (October 11, 1890), p. 8; and Josephine Butler, "Catherine Booth," *The Contemporary Review* (November 1890), pp. 639-54.

18. Hattersley, *Blood and Fire: William and Catherine Booth and Their Salvation Army*, p. 343.

19. Quoted in Begbie, *The Life of General William Booth*, 2:104.

20. William Booth, "Our New Name," p. 1.

21. William Booth, "The General's Address at the Wesleyan Conference," p. 1.

22. Begbie, *The Life of General William Booth*, 1:434.

23. Previous to this, in May of that year, a rescue home for women was opened in Glasgow, Scotland, but that home was evidently closed by March of 1884. Therefore, it is Australia that holds the distinction of beginning the sustained organized social work of The Salvation Army.

24. Hughes, *The Fatal Shore:Tthe Epic of Australia's Founding*, p.1.

25. Coutts, *Bread for my Neighbour: The Social Influence of William Booth*, p. 38.

26. H. J. Dyos and Michael Wolff, eds. *The Victorian City*, 2 Vols. (London: Routledge and Kegan Paul, 1973) 2:595.

27. William Booth, "The General's Address," *The War Cry* (January 1, 1887), p. 9.

28. Clark, *The Making of Victorian England*, p. 32.

29. The best and most comprehensive introduction to Charles Booth's work is Albert Fried and Richard M. Elman, eds., *Charles Booth's London: A Portrait of the Poor at the Turn of the Century, Drawn from His "Life and Labour of the People in London"* (New York: Random House, Inc., 1968).

30. Hattersley, *Blood and Fire: William and Catherine Booth and Their Salvation Army*, p. 353.

31. Ibid.

32. I am indebted to Kenneth G. Hodder for sharing his research on Frank Smith with me, research that he conducted while he was a student at Harvard University. The title of his research paper is "Report and Catalogue for Materials Obtained During Research on Frank Smith, M.P. and the B. B. C. Recording Archives" (September 1, 1978). See also E. I. Champness, *Frank Smith, M.P.: Pioneer and Modern Mystic* (London: The Whitefriars Press, Ltd., 1943). Smith resigned from the Army and channeled his energies into politics and journalism.

33. See *The Darkest England Social Scheme: A Brief Review of the First Year's Work* (London: International Headquarters, 1891), p. 158. When the deed was publicly executed it was stated that "A copy of the Trust Deed will be sent free to any person who may desire to obtain it" (p. 158).

34. Ervine, *God's Soldier: General William Booth*, 2:628.

35. John Kent, *Holding the Fort: Studies in Victorian Revivalism*, p. 335.

36. W. T. Stead, "Letter from W. T. Stead regarding authorship of 'In Darkest England,' " *The Star*, January 2, 1891.

37. " 'In Darkest England' Entirely the General's Own," *The War Cry* (January 10,

1891), p. 7. In his biography of Catherine Booth, Stead wrote that he helped Booth "as a kind of voluntary secretary and amanuensis in getting the MSS of 'Darkest England' into shape" (Stead, Mrs. *Booth of The Salvation Army*, p. 211).

38. Ibid. An essay in *The Victorian City* noted that during the 1889 London dock strike, "Support from institution representatives such as Canon Barnett, Stewart Headlam, William Booth, and Cardinal Manning served both to give a sense of direction to public feeling, and to consolidate the positions of the institutions on the East End." (2:595). In his essay on William Booth in the *Dictionary of National Biography*, 1912–1921, Harold Begbie wrote the following: "Deeper acquaintance with the problem he was so compulsively attacking led him to become a social reformer" ("Booth, William [1829–1912]," p. 52).

39. See "Mrs. Bramwell Booth with the Dockers' Wives and Children," *The War Cry* (September 11, 1889), p. 7; "The Salvation Army and the Strike," *The War Cry* (September 28, 1889), p. 2; "Ramblings in the East End," *The War Cry* (November 2, 1889), p. 2; and " '272' Becomes Food and Shelter Headquarters," *The War Cry* (November 9, 1889), p. 7.

40. Bennett, *The General: William Booth*, 2:300.

41. Ibid., 2:309.

42. Barbara Robinson, "The Wesleyan Foundation of Salvation Army Social Work and Action," *Word & Deed: A Journal of Salvation Army Theology and Ministry* 7:1 (November 2004), pp. 38-39.

43. William Booth, *In Darkest England and the Way Out*, p. 2.

44. Hattersley, *Blood and Fire: William and Catherine Booth and Their Salvation Army*, p. 377.

45. Tim Macquiban, "Soup and Salvation: Social Service as an Emerging Motif for the British Methodist Response to Poverty in the Late Nineteenth Century," *Methodist History* 39:1 (October 2000), p. 32,

46. William Booth, *In Darkest England and the Way Out*, p. 16.

47. One of the best expressions of the Army's social ministry being a reflection of the command of Jesus is found in a letter from William Booth to Bramwell Booth written on January 10, 1903. However, even with this biblical justification William still raises the question, "as to whether we get as much real benefit out of the time and labor and ability bestowed upon feeding the poor as we should do if spent in purely spiritual work is a very difficult question to answer" (p. 2). See The William Booth File, The Salvation Army International Heritage Centre; London, England. See also the letter from William Booth to Bramwell Booth, April 19, 1911, in the William Booth File, The Salvation Army International Heritage Centre; London, England.

48. See Donald Burke, "The Wesleyan View of Salvation and Social Involvement," pp. 11-32 in John D. Waldron, ed., *Creed and Deed: Toward a Christian Theology of Social Services in The Salvation Army* (Toronto: The Salvation Army, 1986).

49. Donald W. Dayton, " 'Good News to the Poor': The Methodist Experience After Wesley," chapter 4, pp. 87-88 in M. Douglas Meeks, ed., *The Portion of the Poor: Good News to the Poor in the Wesleyan Tradition* (Nashville: Kingswood Books, 1995).

50. Ibid., p. 243.

51. See Bernard Watson, *Soldier Saint*, especially chapter 17. In an undated letter from Bramwell Booth to Railton, Bramwell wrote, "When you say that you object to the 'placing of the Salvation work second to the Social' you only say what we all say" (p. 3). However, he then reprimands Railton for suggesting that even in the General's public meetings, the General makes the social more important than the spiritual. See the Bramwell Booth File, The Salvation Army International Heritage Centre; London, England. On July 9, 1894, ten senior officers in The Salvation Army addressed a letter to

"My Dear General" disagreeing with Railton's actions, recommending that some disciplinary action be taken against Railton, but allowing for the fact that "we cannot but think that Commissioner Railton would never have so acted, but for the physical and mental strain from which he is evidently suffering," and suggested that "you should order the Commissioner upon a lengthened furlough before coming to any final decision as to the future." The George Scott Railton File, The Salvation Army International Heritage Centre; London, England. It was inconceivable to these leaders that any disagreement with the Booth hierarchy, even that made by so faithful a follower as George Scott Railton, could be made apart from physical and mental strain.

52. Bennett, *The General: William Booth*, 2:306.

53. Stead, *Mrs. Booth of The Salvation Army*, p. 208.

54. Murdoch, *Origins of The Salvation Army*, p. 165.

55. Bramwell Booth's most poignant remarks about the Darkest England Scheme came in a newspaper interview after the became General upon the death of his father. See the *Daily News* and *Leader* (October 1912), p. 1.

56. Bennett, *The General: William Booth*, 2:316. Booth did thank Stead in the preface to *In Darkest England and the Way Out*, although even that acknowledgment was a bit backhanded in that he did not mention Stead by name, and made it clear to the reader that this man was "not in any way connected with The Salvation Army."

57. Murdoch, *Origins of The Salvation Army*, pp. 152-53. For some examples of Smith's writing see Frank Smith, "Salvation Socialism," *The War Cry* (December 25, 1889), pp. 17-24; Frank Smith, "The Battle-Cry of the Social Reform Wing," *All the World* (August 1890), pp. 355-58; Frank Smith, "'A Look at the 'Wing,'" *All the World* (October 1890), pp. 510-13; and Frank Smith, "Wanted, Samaritans!" *All the World* (December 1890), pp. 620-23.

58. In his *Origins of The Salvation Army* Murdoch mentioned that Suzie Forest Smith, an American and Vassar graduate who became a Salvation Army officer in 1889, "claims to have assisted with the writing of *In Darkest England and the Way Out* in 1890" (p. 156), but her claim has proved impossible to support from other writings. She did write an analysis of the Darkest England Scheme in 1891, which the British Library has erroneously attributed to her sister, Elizabeth Reeves Swift. See *The Darkest England Social Scheme: A Brief Review of the First Year's Work* (London: International Headquarters, 1891).

59. William Booth, "Salvation for Both Worlds," *All the World* (January 1889), p. 2.

60. Bennett, *The General: William Booth*, pp. 291-92.

61. For an excellent analysis of T. H. Huxley's attack upon Booth and his Darkest England Scheme see R. G. Moyles, Essay Six, "*The Times* of London, T. H. Huxley, and Booth's Social Panacea," pp. 117-36 in R. G. Moyles *The Salvation Army and the Public* (Edmonton: AGM Publications, 2000).

62. Needham, "Redemption and Social Reformation: A Theological Study of William Booth and His Movement," p. 80. Cardinal Manning, supporting Booth's plan, commended Booth for his analysis of the social plight of London in the last quarter of the nineteenth century, and for his encompassing social program which addressed itself to that plight. Manning's commendations were mixed with criticisms of some of the methods that Booth used to accomplish his goals. However, as early as 1882 in *The Contemporary Review* Manning wrote: "What, then, is the spiritual desolation of London? Let any man stand on the high northern ridge, which commands London from West to East, and ask himself: How many in this teeming, seething whirlpool of men have never been baptized? Have never been taught the Christian faith? Never set foot in a church? How many are living ignorantly in sin? How many with full knowledge are breaking the laws of God? What multitudes are blinded, or besotted, or maddened by drink? What sins

of every kind and dye, and beyond all count, are committed day and night? It would surely be within the truth to say that half of the population of London are practically without Christ and without God in the world. If this be so, then at once we can see how and why The Salvation Army exists." (Henry Edward Manning, "The Salvation Army," *The Contemporary Review* 41 [August 1882]: 342). See also Francis Power Cobb, "The Last Revival," *The Contemporary Review* 41 (August 1882): 183.

For further historical information on *In Darkest England and the Way Out* see the following: Commissioner Smith, "The Battle-Cry of the Social Reform Wing," *All the World* (August 1890), pp. 355-58; "A Look at the 'Wing,' " *All the World* (October 1890), pp. 510-13; Major Sowerby, " 'In Darkest England' Reviewed," *All the World* (December 1890), pp. 651-55; William Booth, " 'Darkest England' and Other Affairs," *The War Cry* (January 1891), p. 9; Frederick William Farrar, "Social Amelioration," *The War Cry* (May 1911), p. 2; and Swift, *The "Darkest England" Social Scheme: A Brief Review of the First Year's Work.*

For criticisms, both positive and negative, that were written by Booth's contemporaries see "An American View of 'Darkest England,'" *Review of Reviews* 4 (1891), p. 390; Archdeacon Farrar, "A Panegyric on The Salvation Army," *Review of Reviews* 3 (May 1891), p. 467; Thomas H. Huxley, *Evolution and Ethics*, 9 Vols. (New York: D. Appleton and Company, 1884); "In Darkest England and the Way Out: A Report of Progress with Criticisms and Comments," *Review of Reviews* 3 (January 1891), pp. 14-17; "In Darkest England: Progress Along the Way Out," *Review of Reviews* 3 (February 1891), pp. 160-61; C. S. Loch, Bernard Bosanquet, and Philip Dwyer, *Criticisms on "General" Booth's Social Scheme* (London: Swan Sonnenschein and Son, 1891); Francis Peek, "In Darkest England and the Way Out," *The Contemporary Review* 58 (December 1890), pp. 796-807; W. T. Stead, "The Book of the Year—In Darkest England," *Review of Reviews* 2 (July-December 1890), pp. 651-56; W. T. Stead, "The Darkest England Scheme," *Review of Reviews* 3 (January-June 1891), pp. 14-17; "The Darkest England Scheme: General Booth's Farm at Hadley," *Review of Reviews* 4 (November 1891), p. 594; and Arnold White, Francis Peek, and Frederick William Farrar, *Truth About The Salvation Army* (London: Simpkin, Marshall, Hamilton, Kent & Co., 1892).

The leader of the Social Gospel in America, Walter Rauschenbusch, in a trip to England in 1891, closely observed the work of The Salvation Army, visited the Army's International Headquarters, and heard William Booth speak. See Paul M. Minus, *Walter Rauschenbusch: American Reformer* (New York: MacMillan Publishing Company, 1988), p. 73.

For more recent criticisms see Herman Ausubel, "General Booth's Scheme of Social Salvation," *American Historical Review* 56 (April 1951), pp. 519-25. For two works that deal at length with various aspects of Booth's Scheme see the following: K. S. Inglis, *Churches and Working Classes in Victorian England* (Toronto: University of Toronto Press, 1963), and Norris Magnuson, *Salvation in the Slums: Evangelical Social Work, 1865–1920*, The American Theological Library Association Monograph Series, No. 10 (Metuchen, N. J.: The Scarecrow Press, 1977). See also Coutts, *Bread for My Neighbor*, chapters 6-13; Fairbank, *Booth's Boots*, chapter 11; Roger J. Green, "An Historical Salvation Army Perspective," pp. 43-81 in Waldron, ed., *Creed and Deed: Toward a Christian Theology of Social Services in The Salvation Army*; McKinley, *Marching to Glory*, pp. 70-72, 303; Murdoch, *Origins of The Salvation Army*, chapter 7; Needham, "Redemption and Social Reformation: A Theological Study of William Booth and His Movement," p. 165; and Christine Parkin, "The Salvation Army and Social Questions of the Day," pp. 103-18 in Michael Hill, ed., *A Sociological Yearbook of Religion in Britain* 5 (London: SCM Press, 1972).

63. Murdoch, *Origins of The Salvation Army*, p. 161.

64. I am indebted to Salvationists Graham Cook and Gordon Parkhill of Leigh-on-Sea for taking me on a tour of Hadleigh and explaining the work of The Salvation Army in that colony today.

65. For an analysis of the Army's social ministry in the United States, including the Farm Colonies in the United States, see Frederick Booth-Tucker, *The Salvation Army in America: Selected Reports, 1899–1903* (New York: Arno Press, 1972, Religion in America Series).

66. See Roger J. Green, "Theological Roots of *In Darkest England and the Way Out*," *Wesleyan Theological Journal* 25:1 (Spring 1990), pp. 83-105; and Norman H. Murdoch, "William Booth's *In Darkest England and the Way Out*: A Reappraisal," *Wesleyan Theological Journal* 25:1 (Spring 1990), pp. 106-16. The failure to connect the social ministry to Booth's theology is apparent in Hattersley's recent biography of the Booths. Gertrude Himmelfarb noted this in her review of Hattersley's book, "First Save the Body, Then the Soul," *The New York Times Book Review* (July 9, 2000), pp. 14-15. Himmelfard noted the following: "What did distinguish the Booths from most of the others was their linking of social and religious salvation. Today, when faith-based institutions are being proposed as the alleviation, if not the solution, of some social problems, we might reasonably look to the Booths for guidance and counsel. Yet here 'Blood and Fire' is disappointing, for there is little attempt to establish the connection, let alone a casual relationship, between their social and religious agendas. In the epilogue Hattersley intimates that perhaps there was none: 'It is not necessary to believe in instant sanctification—or in sanctification in any form—to admire and applaud their work of social redemption.' He means this in praise of his heroes, but it may be the most damning thing that can be said of them, for it deprives them of what might have been their best claim to our attention and to a place in the pantheon of eminent Victorians" (p. 15).

67. William Booth, *In Darkest England and the Way Out*, p. 257.

68. Ibid. See also pp. 35, 205, 264, 268.

69. Ibid., p. 45. See also pp. 104, 110, 218. Begbie claimed that "his social work was chiefly an excuse for getting at the souls of men" (Begbie, "Booth, William [1829–1912]," p. 51).

70. William Booth, *To My Officers: A Letter from the General on His Eightieth Birthday*, p. 44. See also pp. 19-20; Begbie, *The Life of General William Booth*, 2:113, 329, 331; Needham, "Redemption and Social Reformation: A Theological Study of William Booth and His Movement," pp. 74-76, 80, 83-84.

71. See William Booth, "the Millennium; or, the Ultimate Triumph of Salvation Army Principles," *All the World* (August 1890), pp. 337-43. See also William Booth, "My Idea of the Millennium," *The Review of Reviews* 2 (July-December, 1890), p. 130, and William Booth, "All Things New: A New Year's Message from the New World, *All the World* (January 1895), pp. 3-7.

72. John Coutts, *The Salvationists* (London: A. R. Mowbray and Company, Ltd., 1978), p. 142.

73. Chadwick, *The Victorian Church*, 2:297.

74. Macquiban, "Soup and Salvation: Social Service as an Emerging Motif for the British Methodist Response to Poverty in the Late Nineteenth Century," pp. 35-36. See also Inglis, *Churches and the Working Classes in Victorian England*, p. 211; and Magnuson, *Salvation in the Slums: Evangelical Social Work 1865–1920*, p. 173.

75. Begbie, *The Life of General William Booth*, 2:84.

76. Ervine, *God's Soldier: General William Booth*, 2:784.

77. "New General & His Plans," *Daily News and Leader* (October 1912), p. 1.

11. Three Who Left

1. In a letter dated April 25, 1892, from Bramwell Booth to "My Dear Commandant" giving the details of the broken engagement, Bramwell wrote that "all yesterday Lucy was

quite out of her senses. High brain fever" (p. 2). The Bramwell Booth File, The Salvation Army International Heritage Centre; London, England. In *The War Cry* (May 21, 1892), p. 9, Lucy Booth wrote a letter to the readers, thanking them for all their sympathy and prayers in her time of need and explaining that she had been called to India.

2. *The War Cry* (May 21, 1892) hinted that Lampard was mentally deranged, p. 9.

3. Ervine, *God's Soldier: General William Booth*, 2:752.

4. Bramwell Booth letter, April 25, 1892, p. 2. The Bramwell Booth File, The Salvation Army International Heritage Centre; London, England.

5. Ervine, *God's Soldier: General William Booth*, 2:752.

6. Ibid.

7. It was Ervine in *God's Soldier: General William Booth*, 2:753 who claimed that Lucy Booth met Emanuel Hellberg in India.

8. Ibid., 2:756.

9. Bennett, *The General: William Booth*, 2:342.

10. Begbie decided not to deal with these departures from the Army for two reasons, the first of which is patently untrue. He wrote, "We do not propose to refer to this domestic difficulty again, and we have purposely only glanced at it in this place because we feel, first, that the matter did not prove to be of great importance; and, second, because those chiefly concerned are still alive. But before leaving the subject we must say that, while we admire William Booth for his loyalty to his faith and to the discipline of The Salvation Army, we cannot fail to regret that he did not succeed in his efforts to discover a path to reconciliation." Begbie, *The Life of General William Booth*, 2:159.

11. See E. H. McKinley, "Booth, Ballington (1857–1940)" in Reid, ed., *Dictionary of Christianity in America*, pp. 173-74; and R. J. Green, "Booth, Maud Charlesworth (1865–1948)" in ibid., p. 175.

12. McKinley, *Marching to Glory*, p. 36.

13. Ibid., p. 95. For some interesting insights into Maud Booth's recollections of the early Salvation Army see her letter to Jason S. Joy, Esq., Twentieth Century-Fox Film Corp., Beverly Hills, California, March 18, 1940. Maud took her husband's first name as her own, and so signed the letter Maud Ballington Booth. The Ballington Booth File, The Salvation Army International Heritage Centre; London, England.

14. Wiggins, *The History of The Salvation Army*, 4:85.

15. *The Resignation of Commander and Mrs. Ballington Booth: The Correspondence Involved. Letters from the General, the Chief and the Commanders* (New York: The Salvation Army, 1896), pp. 4-5. The Ballington Booth File, The Salvation Army International Heritage Centre; London, England. Years later, in writing to his sister, Catherine, Ballington Booth reiterated their reasons for leaving the Army, and again criticized "the iron-clad government of a Movement that was constantly trying to ride down the convictions and consciences of its most faithful Officers, and always criticizing them. . . . Maud and I left the S. A. on principle. We did this because we had lost confidence in its government and in many of its methods. We could not serve where we did not believe in the righteousness or spirit of actions we were told to follow." Letter from Ballington Booth to Catherine Booth, August 3, 1934, p. 1. The Ballington Booth File, The Salvation Army International Heritage Centre; London, England.

16. Ibid., p. 4.

17. Letter from Josiah Strong to W. T. Stead, February 4, 1896, p. 1. The Ballington Booth File, The Salvation Army International Heritage Centre; London, England. The present relations between Great Britain and the United States referred to in the letter had to do with a border dispute in South America. Relations between Britain and the United States were strained.

18. Letter from William Booth to Bramwell Booth, January 25, 1898, p. 1. The

William Booth File, The Salvation Army International Heritage Centre; London, England.

19. Letter from Ballington Booth to Catherine Booth-Clibborn, October 15, 1896, p. 2. The Ballington Booth File, The Salvation Army International Heritage Centre; London, England.

20. William Booth to Catherine Booth-Clibborn, Marcy 13, 1896, p. 2. The William Booth File, The Salvation Army International Heritage Centre; London, England. See also the letter from William Booth to Ballington Booth dated March 6, 1903, after he had seen Ballington while on a trip to America. Even those many years later there was little reconciliation between father and son. William Booth wrote, "What deeps [sic] of sorrow were aroused in my breast by our melancholy interview yesterday. You did not appear to feel any regrets. I cannot but think you will someday. Perhaps our hearts may come together again then. I am sailing in the morning. How different things might have been, but I made up my mind before seeing you there should be no reproaches. I shall stand by my resolution. I shall go on praying for you all. It is at least some satisfaction to be able to do this. Believe me, Your sorrowful father, William Booth." The William Booth File, The Salvation Army International Heritage Centre; London, England.

21. As late as 1921 Evangeline Booth, then the national commander of The Salvation Army in America, complained that Ballington was calling himself simply General Booth and thereby confusing the public. Her animosity toward Ballington continued those many years later. See Letter from Evangeline Booth to Bramwell Booth, December 14, 1921, p. 4. The Evangeline Booth File, The Salvation Army International Heritage Centre; London, England.

22. See R. J. Green, "Booth-Tucker, Frederick St. George de Lautour (1853–1929)" and R. J. Green, "Booth-Tucker, Emma Moss (1860–1903)" in Reid, ed., *Dictionary of Christianity in America*, pp. 176-77.

23. See "Dowie, John Alexander (1847–1907)," in Reid, ed., *Dictionary of Christianity in America*, p. 365.

24. See the letter from Bramwell Booth to William Booth, March 7, 1907, p. 2. He wrote, "I have a note from Stead to-day in which he says, 'I have not heard anything from Clibborn but I think the end which you desire is nearer than it was when we met.' I take that to mean that he thinks Katie is more likely than she was to thoroughly disassociate herself from Clibborn." The William Booth File, The Salvation Army International Heritage Centre; London, England.

25. Letter from William Booth to Bramwell Booth [1902?], no page number. The William Booth File, The Salvation Army International Heritage Centre; London, England.

26. See *To Our Friends, Letter from Arthur Booth-Clibborn and Catherine Booth-Clibborn, Maréchale* to which were attached two letters "To our dear and honoured father-in-law, father and General." The Booth-Clibborn File, The Salvation Army International Heritage Centre; London, England. See also Percy Clibborn's letter of resignation to General Booth dated January 7, 1902. The Percy Clibborn File, The Salvation Army International Heritage Centre; London, England. In a letter dated December 22, 1935, to his sister-in-law, Catherine, Percy Clibborn speaks of Elizabeth Swift, an American and Vassar graduate and the wife of Commissioner Samuel Logan Brengle, as "the first spiritual child God gave to me, and during her first years we kept up a correspondence in which I was able to find the right counsel for her from time to time, and for which she often expressed her gratitude." The Percy Clibborn File, The Salvation Army International Heritage Centre; London, England.

27. The Booth-Clibborns left the Army over many doctrinal matters taught by Dowie that were at odds with Army doctrine. Faith healing has often been given as the main

cause for their leaving, but articles in *The War Cry* confirm that faith healing was practiced in the Army. See, for example, "Remarkable Answers to Prayer in Healing the Sick," *The War Cry* (February 25, 1885), p. 1; "Salvation Healing in Sheffield," *The War Cry* (March 11, 1885), p. 1; "Remarkable Case of Salvation Healing," *The War Cry* (March 14, 1885), p. 4; and "Faith Healing in Bristol," *The War Cry* (May 16, 1885), p. 4. However, as a result of the Booth-Clibborn resignation William Booth expressed some reservations about faith healing in his work entitled *Faith Healing—A Memorandum for the Use of The Salvation Army* (London: Salvation Army, 1902). Hattersley's opinion is that Catherine Booth belittled faith healing. Writing about the illness of Catherine, Hattersley stated that "There was no suggestion at least at the time, that Catherine either hoped for or anticipated divine intervention. Five years earlier, the Salvation Army—or at least some of its members—had dabbed in 'faith healing', without any recorded rebuke from the high command. In February 1885, Major Pearson had restored the hearing of two stone-deaf women from Hanley in the Potteries and gone on to confound his audience of thousands by successfully commanding a crippled woman to abandon her bath chair and walk. Unfortunately, three days later, he could not repeat the miracle, a failure he attributed to the presence of unbelievers in the hall. But Mrs. Booth had no time for such nonsense. She expected God and nature to allow her cancer to take its course. And she was perfectly prepared for their joint will to be done" (Hattersley, *Blood and Fire: William and Catherine Booth and Their Salvation Army*, p. 330).

28. Letter written June 8, 1937, from Catherine, p. 2. We do not know the recipient of this letter because the first page of the letter is missing. The Booth-Clibborn File, The Salvation Army International Heritage Centre; London, England.

29. Letter from Evangeline Booth to William Booth, March 10, 1905, p. 5. The Evangeline Booth File, The Salvation Army International Heritage Centre; London, England.

30. Scott, *The Heavenly Witch: The Story of the Maréchale*, p. 201.

31. Letter from Catherine Booth to Ballington Booth, November 11, 1927, p. 1. The Booth-Clibborn File, The Salvation Army International Heritage Centre; London, England.

32. Scott, *The Heavenly Witch: The Story of the Maréchale*, p. 217.

33. See Wiggins, *The History of The Salvation Army*, 4:363.

34. Ottman, *Herbert Booth: A Biography*, p. 214.

35. Wiggins, *The History of The Salvation Army*, 4:98.

36. Ottman, *Herbert Booth: A Biography*, pp. 189-90. See also Dean Rapp, "The British Salvation Army, the Early Film Industry and Urban Working-Class Adolescents, 1897–1918," *Twentieth Century British History* 7:2 (1996), pp.157-88.

37. Bennett in *The General: William Booth* wrote that "the letter had been released to the Australian press and published by them before the General had received his copy" (p. 358).

38. Letter written from Herbert and Cornelie Booth on February 3, 1902 to "Our Dear Father and General." A copy of this letter is in my personal files.

39. See Ottman, *Herbert Booth: A Biography*, p. 315; and the letter from Evangeline Booth to William Booth, September 2, 1902, in the Evangeline Booth File, The Salvation Army International Heritage Centre; London, England. Herbert Booth, in a three-page letter to his sister, Evangeline, dated October 22, 1910, reiterated his reasons for leaving the Army, and it is obvious by the letter that Herbert had not been reconciled with his father. "The only words that might reflect on my father which have escaped my lips have been spoken to friends in confidence when compelled to explain how it was that I, his son, and Cory his daughter [in-law], were left to the cold mercies of the world without such fatherly assistance as he might have rendered." Herbert Booth to

Evangeline Booth, October 22, 1910, p. 1, a copy in my personal file. Evangeline Booth then wrote to her brother, Bramwell, saying that the letter from Herbert "distressed me no little." Evangeline Booth to Bramwell Booth, November 1, 1910, p. 1, a copy in my personal file.

40. Ervine, *God's Soldier: General William Booth*, 2:766.

41. Letter from Catherine Booth to Ballington Booth, November 11, 1927, p. 2. The Booth-Clibborn File, The Salvation Army International Heritage Centre; London, England.

42. Ervine, *God's Soldier: General William Booth*, 2:767.

43. See the letter from William Booth to Bramwell Booth, November 12, 1903, p. 1. The William Booth File, The Salvation Army International Heritage Centre; London, England.

44. Ervine, *God's Soldier: General William Booth*, 2:769.

45. Wiggins in *The History of The Salvation Army* mistakenly gives Iowa as the state (4:361).

46. McKinley, *Marching to Glory*, p. 120.

47. See the five-page letter from Herbert Booth to Frederick Booth-Tucker, November 2, 1903, protesting this treatment at the hands of Booth-Tucker and Eva in the Herbert Booth File, The Salvation Army International Heritage Centre; London, England.

48. McKinley, *Marching to Glory*, p. 121.

49. Begbie, *The Life of General William Booth*, 2:282.

50. Bennett, *The General: William Booth*, 2:164.

51. See William Booth's letter to Bramwell after the death of Emma, November 12, 1903. The William Booth File, The Salvation Army International Heritage Centre; London, England.

52. Ervine, *God's Soldier: General William Booth*, 2:783.

12. International Evangelist

1. Begbie, *The Life of General William Booth*, 2:132.

2. At this juncture in Salvation Army history Bramwell Booth's powers increased considerably, one of the causes for the departure from the Army of his three siblings mentioned in the previous chapter. On August 16, 1895, in a twenty-nine-page letter to Bramwell William Booth laid down guidelines for his successor. The letter is a bit confusing because he says that at that point he had not selected his successor. However, on August 21, 1890, a legal document named Bramwell as his successor. See also Power of Attorney to Bramwell Booth, August 19, 1895, outlining all of Bramwell's duties and responsibilities in the William Booth File, The Salvation Army International Heritage Centre; London, England.

3. In 1889, in spite of Booth's attention to the social problems of the day, he took time to envision the missionary endeavor of the Army with the writing of *The Future of Mission and the Mission of the Future* (London: The Salvation Army, 1889). See the article by Paul du Plessis entitled "Echoes of Methodism in The Salvation Army's Commitment to World Mission," *Word & Deed: A Journal of Salvation Army Theology and Ministry* 7:1 (November 2004), pp. 5-16.

4. Begbie, *The Life of General William Booth*, 2:167. Booth's passion for preaching was recognized by other religious leaders. In a series of autobiographical Notes Cardinal Manning questioned the hindrances to the effectiveness of the Roman Catholic Church in England and wrote, "Why then do we not draw men as Spurgeon and 'General' Booth

or Hugh Price Hughes? I am afraid that there are two obvious reasons. We choose topics unwisely, and we are not on fire with the love of God of souls." Cardinal Manning, "Hindrances to the Spread of the Catholic Church in England," July 19, 1890 in *Latin Mass Society Newsletter* (August 2000).

5. Ibid., 2:169.

6. See William Booth, *Lessons of My Life. General Booth's 70th Birthday Speech, Delivered in the Sydney Town Hall, on Thursday Evening, April 11, 1899* (Sydney: William Brooks & Company, Printers, 1899), 16 pp.

7. Wiggins, *The History of The Salvation Army*, 4:152-53.

8. Chadwick, *The Victorian Church*, 1:5.

9. Diane Winston, *Red-Hot and Righteous: The Urban Religion of The Salvation Army*, p. 95.

10. See Diane Winston's review of Eason's book in *Church History*, Vol. 73, No. 1 (March 2004), pp. 231-33.

11. Walker, *Pulling the Devil's Kingdom Down: The Salvation Army in Victorian Britain*, p. 243.

12. William Booth, "The General's Address at the Wesleyan Conference," p. 1.

13. William Booth, "The May Meeting Address: Summary of the Year's History by the General," *The War Cry* (May 12, 1888), p. 10.

14. Winston, *Church History*, p. 233.

15. The two most concise works by William Booth on the subject of holiness were *Purity of Heart* and *A Ladder to Holiness*. Along with these works he wrote numerous articles on the doctrine and preached the doctrine often.

16. William Booth, "Christianity on Fire, No. IV," *The War Cry* (May 21, 1892), pp. 9-10. See also William Booth, *The General's Letters, 1885* (London: The Salvation Army, 1890), p. 35.

17. William Booth, *To My Officers: A Letter from the General on His Eightieth Birthday*, p. 33. The William Booth File, The Salvation Army International Heritage Centre; London, England.

18. William Booth, "Thou Christ of Burning, Cleansing Flame," *The Song Book of The Salvation Army* (Verona, N. J.: The Salvation Army National Headquarters, 1987), no. 203.

19. William Booth, *Purity of Heart* (London: The Salvation Army, 1902), pp. 71-72.

20. The evidence is overwhelming that those around Booth also shared much of his theology, including his postmillennial theology. There are innumerable examples of this, but the following with suffice: For Catherine Booth see the following: Catherine Booth, "The Holy Ghost," *All the World* (June 1900), pp. 339-42; Catherine Booth, "The Kingdom of Christ," *All the World* (August 1885), pp. 183-84; and Catherine Booth, *Popular Christianity* (London: Salvation Army Book Depot, 1887), p. 197; for Bramwell Booth see Bramwell Booth, "Salvation Army," *Encyclopedia of Religion and Ethics*, 12 Vols., James Hastings, ed. (New York: Charles Scribner's Sons, 1921), 11:151; for Evangeline Booth see Evangeline Booth, *Toward a Better World* (Garden City: Doubleday, Doran and Company, 1928), p. 241. Evangeline Booth wrote a song entitled "The World for God"; for Arthur Booth-Clibborn see Arthur Booth-Clibborn, "The Pentecostal Programme," *All the World* (June 1895), pp. 401-5; for John Lawley see John Lawley, "Down with the Gates!" *The War Cry* (November 1893), p. 12. For Elijah Cadman see Elijah Cadman, "The New Kingdom," *All the World* (July 1895), pp. 3-4. Roland Robertson's observation is correct—that during the history of The Salvation Army in Booth's lifetime, millennial teachings were important, and "from time to time the question of the millennium was viewed with some degree of urgency" (Robertson, "The Salvation Army: The Persistence of Sectarianism," p. 71).

21. James Black, *New Forms of Old Faith* (London, 1948), quoted in George Shepperson, "The Comparative Study of Millenarian Movements," *Millennial Dreams in Action*, Sylvia R. Thrupp, ed. (The Hague: Mouton, 1962), p. 44.

22. Donald W. Dayton, *Discovering an Evangelical Heritage* (New York: Harper and Row, Publishers, 1976), p. 125.

23. Ibid., p. 126.

24. William Booth, *The General's Letters*, 1885, p. 99. To understand the consistency of this message in Booth's ministry see the following as examples: William Booth, "Hints to Soul Winners," *The Christian Mission Magazine* (May 1875), pp. 124-26; William Booth, "Go!" *All the World* (November 1884), pp. 1-4; William Booth, "Memorial Challenge!" *The War Cry* (May 1911), p. 9; and William Booth, "Fifty Years' Salvation Service: Some of Its Lessons and Results. Interview with the General," *All the World* (July 1894), p. 7.

25. See William Booth, *The General's Letters*, 1885, p. 60.

26. Ibid., p. 22.

27. Ibid., pp. 142-45. Booth "believed that it was possible to bring men and women of every degree and temperament into the fold of The Salvation Army, and he even dared, in certain moments of enthusiasm, to think that he himself might live to accomplish this consummation" (Begbie, *The Life of General William Booth*, 2:252). See also pp. 251, 359, 402, 403. Shortly before his death in 1912 Booth said, "I am more confident than ever that Salvation is the only hope for the world. Were it not for Salvation and the Salvation of The Salvation Army, I should think that the probability was that the world was on its way to universal suicide" (ibid., 2:417).

28. See William Booth, "The Millennium; or the Ultimate Triumph of Salvation Army Principles," pp. 337-43.

29. Rack, *Reasonable Enthusiast: John Wesley and the Rise of Methodism*, p. 491.

30. Ibid., p. 382.

31. See the mentions of postmillennialism in Finney's theology in Hardman, *Charles Grandison Finney 1792–1875: Revivalist and Reformer*.

32. Horridge, *The Salvation Army Origins and Early Days: 1865–1900*, p. 178.

33. Ibid., p. 180.

34. Ibid., pp. 264-65.

35. See William Booth, *Proposal for a World University for the Cultivation of the Science of Humanity in Connection with The Salvation Army* in the William Booth File, The Salvation Army International Heritage Centre; London, England. It is interesting, as a personal note, that at the conclusion of the proposal he mentions the death of his daughter, Emma, who was very supportive of this idea, and in whom William Booth confided about this and other matters.

36. Sandall, *The History of The Salvation Army*, 2:69.

37. Ibid., 2:70.

38. Letter from William Booth to Bramwell Booth, February 10, 1893, p. 1. The William Booth File, The Salvation Army International Heritage Centre; London, England.

39. Letter from Evangeline Booth to Bramwell Booth, December 1, 1901, pp. 1-2. The Evangeline Booth File, The Salvation Army International Heritage Centre; London, England.

40. Letter from William Booth to Bramwell Booth, June 23, 1905, p. 4. The William Booth File, The Salvation Army International Heritage Centre; London, England.

41. Ibid.

42. William Booth, *Proposal for a World University*, p. 2.

43. See McKinley, *Marching to Glory*, p. 147. Evangeline Booth in 1916 tried to revive William Booth's idea of a University of Humanity, but was unable to do so even though Booth's original proposal called for one of the centers for the University being in New York.

44. Ervine, *God's Soldier: General William Booth*, 2:787.

45. Letter from William Booth to Bramwell Booth, [n.d.], p. 4. The William Booth File, The Salvation Army International Heritage Centre; London, England.

46. Letter from William Booth to Bramwell Booth, August 16, 1906, p. 1. The William Booth File, The Salvation Army International Heritage Centre; London, England.

47. It is little wonder that others, including Roman Catholics and sectarian groups, copied Booth's successful revivalistic methods to further their own causes. For an interesting article about this see Debra Campbell, "A Catholic Salvation Army: David Goldstein, Pioneer Lay Evangelist," *Church History*, Vol. 52, No. 3 (September 1993), pp. 322-32.

48. Letter from Fred R. Cox to John Mawle. The Fred Cox File, The Salvation Army International Heritage Centre; London, England.

49. F. Hayter Cox, *He Was There* (London: Salvationist Publishing and Supplies, Ltd., 1949), p. 48.

13. England Recognizes Her Son: Honors Bestowed upon William Booth

1. See, for examples, Douglas Bevan, *Startling Revelations: Eight Years' Experience in The Salvation Army in Liverpool* (Liverpool: D. Bevan, 1906); J. T. Cudmore, *The Doctrines of The Salvation Army and the Bible Compared; or Why I Left The Salvation Army* (Charlottetown P.E.I.: Cudmore Press, 1889); and J. J. R. Redstone, *An Ex-Captain's Experience of The Salvation Army* (London: Christian Commonwealth Publication Co., 1888). One of the strangest occurrences of an officer leaving the ranks was the case of one John Hugh Piggott, who left his Anglican priesthood to join the Army in 1884. He left after only five years, and joined an odd sect known as the Agapemonites, whose Temple of Love was in the neighborhood of the Army's Clapton Congress Hall. He soon proclaimed himself as the Messiah, to whom his followers, even his own wife, acquiesced. He had three children by a spiritual bride, Power, Glory, and Hallelujah, and for his immoral conduct was eventually expelled from the Church of England. For more information on Piggott and the Agapemonites see "False and Foolish Revelations," *The War Cry* (September 20, 1902), p. 8; and Donald McCormick, *Temple of Love* (London: Jarrolds Publishers, 1962). At times others, who had not been connected with the Army, vilified Booth and the Army. For example see "A Letter to William Booth, the 'General' of the So-Called 'Salvation Army,' " 7 pp. in The British Library.

2. See William Booth, *A Talk with Mr. Gladstone 1896* (London: The Salvation Army, 1897). This pamphlet also contains copies of letters from Gladstone to Booth. Note the very interesting references to Cardinal Manning on pp. 33-34 of that pamphlet.

3. Hattersley, *Blood and Fire: William and Catherine Booth and Their Salvation Army*, p. 424.

4. Letter from William Booth to Bramwell Booth, February 10, 1898, p. 5. The William Booth File, The Salvation Army International Heritage Centre; London, England.

5. This is the date given in Wiggins, *The History of The Salvation Army*, 4:257, and in Frederick Coutts, *No Discharge in This War* (New York: The Salvation Army, 1975), p.

125. Ervine gives the date as June 24, 1904, in *God's Soldier: General William Booth*, 2:786. Bennett gives the date as June 29, 1904, in *The General: William Booth*, 2:304.

6. Letter from William Booth to Bramwell Booth, May 7, 1910, pp. 1-2. The William Booth File, The Salvation Army International Heritage Centre; London, England.

7. Letter from William Booth to Bramwell Booth, May 8, 1910, pp. 1, 3. The William Booth File, The Salvation Army International Heritage Centre; London, England.

8. Begbie in *The Life of General William Booth* (2:322) mistakenly gives the date as November 2, 1905.

9. The Daily Graphic, Friday, October 27, 1905, p. 9.

10. *London's Roll of Fame: Being Records of Presentations of the Freedom of the City and Addresses of Welcome from the Corporation of London to Royal and other Distinguished Personages A.D. 1885–1959* (Printed by order of the Corporation under the direction of the library committee, 1959), p. 4. See the William Booth File, The Salvation Army International Heritage Centre; London, England.

11. Ibid.

12. Wiggins, *The History of The Salvation Army*, 5:231.

13. Ibid.

14. Ibid., 5:232.

15. Letter from William Booth to Bramwell Booth, May 6, 1907, p. 2. The William Booth File, The Salvation Army International Heritage Centre; London, England.

16. From the program for this service, *Encaenia, June 26, MCMVII, The Chancellor, The Right Hon. George Nathaniel Lord Curzon of Kedleston Presiding*. The William Booth File, The Salvation Army International Heritage Centre; London, England. See also the account of this ceremony in *The War Cry* (July 6, 1907), p. 3. Such a pity that Thomas Huxley, constantly an antagonist to Booth, was dead and could not see this recognition given to Booth.

17. Begbie, *The Life of General William Booth*, 2:400.

18. Ibid., 2:329.

19. Ervine, *God's Soldier: General William Booth*, 2:795.

14. Darkness and Light

1. Begbie, *The Life of General William Booth*, 2:269.

2. Ibid., 2:345.

3. Letter from William Booth to Bramwell Booth, February 12, 1909, p. 1. The William Booth File, The Salvation Army International Heritage Centre; London, England.

4. Letter from William Booth to Bramwell Booth, March 22, 1909, p. 3. The William Booth File, The Salvation Army International Heritage Centre; London, England.

5. Letter from William Booth to Elijah Cadman, September 13, 1909. The William Booth File, The Salvation Army International Heritage Centre; London, England.

6. Letter from William Booth to Bramwell Booth, July 10, 1911, p. 1. The William Booth File. The Salvation Army International Heritage Centre; London, England.

7. Ibid.

8. Entry in his journal in 1911, quoted in Begbie, *The Life of General William Booth*, 2:409.

9. Letter from Bramwell Booth to William Booth, April 18, 1912, p. 1. The Bramwell Booth File, The Salvation Army International Heritage Centre; London, England. See the eulogy to W. T. Stead by Bramwell Booth in *The War Cry* (April 27, 1912), p. 1.

10. "Festival of Thanksgiving: Enthusiastic Celebration of The General's 83rd

Birthday at the Royal Albert Hall, *The War Cry* (May 18, 1912), pp. 9-10. It has been commonly assumed that it was at this occasion in Royal Albert Hall that Booth uttered these words with which he is now popularly associated, even within The Salvation Army:

> While women weep as they do now, I'll fight;
> While little children go hungry as they do now, I'll fight;
> While men go to prison, in and out, in and out, as they do now, I'll fight;
> While there is a drunkard left, while there is a poor lost girl upon the streets,
> while there remains one dark soul without the light of God, I'll fight—I'll fight
> to the very end!

However, none of the records of Booth's speech on this occasion, including *The War Cry*, record those words as part of the speech. In fact there are several variations of that quotation, the first appearing in *All the World* in April, 1906. So, similar words are ascribed to William Booth even before his appearance in Royal Albert Hall in May of 1912. Begbie in his *Life of General William Booth* gives a version of the speech, but does not link those words with the this occasion. The speech certainly took on a life of its own after William Booth's death, and many years later some people who were present at Royal Albert Hall claimed that he said those words on that occasion. But most certainly *The War Cry* would have recorded those last stirring words of William Booth. In all likelihood these words were not uttered at Royal Albert Hall on May 9, 1912.

11. See "The General. Eye to be Operated On. Request for Prayer," *The War Cry* (May 18, 1912), p. 8; and "The General's Operation," *The War Cry* (June 1, 1912), pp. 9-10.

12. Ibid., p. 9.

13. Ibid.

14. *The War Cry* (June 22, 1912), p. 8.

15. Ibid.

16. Letter from Bramwell Booth to Frederick Booth-Tucker, May 31, 1912, pp. 1, 3, and 4. The Bramwell Booth File, The Salvation Army International Heritage Centre; London, England.

17. There is no date on this letter, but Evangeline Booth received the letter on June 27, 1912 and responded immediately. See a copy of the letter in the William Booth File, The Salvation Army International Heritage Centre; London, England.

18. The last days of Booth's life were described in detail in "The General's Illness: Letter from the Chief of the Staff to Officers, Soldiers and Friends," *The War Cry* (August 24, 1912), p. 9.

19. For more information about this officer see Wiggins, *THK: A Biography*.

20. Bennett, *The General: William Booth*, 2:409.

21. Letter from Bramwell Booth to Evangeline Booth, August 20, 1912, p. 1. The Evangeline Booth File, The Salvation Army International Heritage Centre; London, England.

22. See the Evangeline Booth File, The Salvation Army International Heritage Centre; London, England.

23. Letter from Bramwell Booth to Evangeline Booth, August 20, 1912, p. 4. The Bramwell Booth File, The Salvation Army International Heritage Centre; London, England. It is unfortunate that family rancor continued for years. For example see Herbert Booth's letter to Bramwell Booth dated January 20, 1914. In that letter Herbert Booth wrote, "I only know that I found Katie most desirous to make peace at the funeral [of William]. Of course she felt it awfully that she couldn't say a word at the grave but I don't think she and her splendid family were ever nearer the S. A. than they were that day as I told you. Now what object can you have in keeping all these old feuds alive and trying to keep us apart?" (p. 2). The Herbert Booth File, The Salvation Army International Heritage Centre; London, England.

24. The family feuds were still evident even at this occasion. Although present at the funeral, neither Herbert nor Catherine, William Booth's own son and daughter, were allowed to speak at the funeral. And Bramwell could not pass up the opportunity even in his eulogy to admonish his siblings who were present. He concluded by saying, "Be lovers of the Army—put it first. Anyway, if you cannot help it do not hurt it. Do not do anything which on your dying couch you will have need to regret when you think about this servant of Christ beside whose coffin you stand today." "The General. Address Delivered at the Graveside by His Son and Successor," *The War Cry,* (September 7, 1912), p. 2.

25. Ervine, God's Soldier: General William Booth, 2:812.

26. Referred to in a letter from Bramwell Booth to William Booth, September 25, 1907, p. 4. The William Booth File, The Salvation Army International Heritage Centre; London, England.

INDEX

Addie, Jack, 163

Agar, Louisa, 129

alcohol, 29, 38, 39, 40, 44, 47, 61, 94, 106, 119, 124, 168, 169

Alexandra, Queen, 6, 215, 221, 225, 229

All the World, 176

Andrews, Henry (adopted son of Catherine and William), 139

Anglican Church/Anglicanism. *See* Church of England

animals, 41, 101

Armstrong, Eliza, 153-55

Asbury, Francis, 44

Assembly Rooms, 108

atheists, 14

Atkinson, J. A., 141

Atkinson, John, 95

atonement, 56, 58

Auxiliaries, 186

Band Meeting, 79

baptism, 145-49, 202

Baptists, 29, 133

Bates, Josiah, 70

Begbie, Harold, 36, 44, 48, 91, 147, 180, 197, 220

Bell, [?], 33

benevolence, 128

Bennett, David Malcolm, 63, 98, 107, 127, 131, 140-41, 185

Benson, Edward White, 142

Bethesda Chapel, 79

Bible-Moths, 31

Biddulph, Sampson, 9

Billups, Mary Coutts, 101, 110, 111

Billups, Mr. and Mrs. J. E., 96, 110, 114

Binfield House Chapel, 37, 43, 47, 51-52, 55

Bitter Cry of Outcast London, The (Mearns), 172-73

Blind Beggar, 107, 108

Booth, Abraham, 57

Booth, Ann (sister of William), 6, 9; marriage of, 24

Booth, Ballington (son of William and Catherine), 18, 78, 160, 161, 186-90, 191, 194, 195, 196, 208, 231

Booth, Catherine (née Mumford; wife of William Booth), administrative duties of, 80-81, 112, 145, 161; childhood of, 38-43; children of, xiii, 2, 75, 95-99, 101-2, 119-20, 125, 159-62, 183-96; compassion of for animals, 41, 101; contributions of, xiii, 132; conversion of, 42; education of, 39-40; funeral and burial of, 165; health of, 40, 71-72, 75, 78, 99, 101, 102, 109-10, 111, 113, 161; illness and death of, 2, 5, 164-66; influences upon, xv; meeting, engagement, and marriage to William Booth, 37-50, 52-54; preaching ministry of, xv-xvi, 80-82, 91, 93-94, 95, 99, 100, 105, 108, 109-10, 126, 128-29, 153, 164-65, 172; and Purity Crusade, 153-57, 174, 215, 227

Booth, Catherine (Katie or Kate; daughter of Catherine and William), 79, 152, 190-92, 193, 194, 196, 231

Booth, Catherine (wife of son of Samuel, also named William, and first wife, Sarah), 7

Booth, Charles, 169, 171

Booth, Cornelie Ida Ernestine (née Schoch; wife of Herbert), 160-61, 192-94, 195

Booth, Emma (sister of William), 9, 49, 72, 79

Booth, Emma Moss (daughter of Catherine and William), 79, 160, 161-62, 190, death of, 194-96, 208

Booth, Evelyne (Eva, Evangeline) Cory (daughter of Catherine and William), 98-99, 101-2, 161, 190, 191, 193-94, 195, 196, 208-9

Booth, Florence (née Soper; wife of William Bramwell), 152-53, 159, 231

Booth(?), Gregory (cousin of William), 10, 11

Booth, Henry (brother of William), 6

Booth, Herbert Henry/Herbert Howard (son of Catherine and William), 96, 160-61, 192-94, 195, 196, 231

Booth, George (adopted son of Catherine and William), 139, 161

Booth, Lucy Milward (daughter of Catherine and William), 102, 161, 184-85, 231

Booth, Marian (Marie) Billups (daughter of Catherine and William), 98-99, 102, 161

Booth, Mary (née Moss; mother of William), 6-11, 72; death of, 8

Booth, Mary (sister of William), 6, 9, 72

Booth, Maude (née Charlesworth; wife of Ballington), 160, 186-90, 195

Booth, Samuel (father of William), 6-11; death of, 11

Booth, Sarah (née Lockitt; first wife of Samuel Booth), 6-7

Booth, William (son of Samuel and first wife Sarah), 6, 7

Booth, William (son of Samuel and Mary Booth; founder of The Salvation Army), abstinence of from alcohol, 40; in pawnbroking business, 10-11, 13, 14, 24, 26-27, 52; authoritarianism of, 63, 89, 114, 119, 121, 124-25, 137, 144, 184-96; as biblical man, 2; childhood of, 6-11; children of, xiii, 2, 75, 95-99, 101-2, 119-20, 125, 159-62, 183-96; compassion of for the poor, 10, 15, 36, 109, 111, 113-14, 168, 171, *see also* social ministries of; conversion experience of, 11-12, 17; death/funeral of, 5-6, 192, 230-32; depression of, 61, 97, 98, 99, 112-13; education of, 9, 10; as evangelist, xiii, 29-36, 51, 83, 87-88, 91, 93, 96, 109, 183, 205, 227; health of, 71-72, 75, 81-82, 97, 112, 212, 223-30; honors bestowed upon, 213-21; influences upon, xiv-xv; itinerancy of, 75-77, 100; last residence of, 223-24; leadership of, xiii-xiv, 52, 62-63, 118; legacy of, 33, 34, 232, 233-34; meeting, engagement, and marriage to Catherine Mumford, 37-51, 52-54; as monarchist, 17; motorcar campaigns of, 210-12, 223-27; moves to London, 25-29, 99-103; ordination of, 78; preaching (early), 13-14, 16, 22, 23-24, 27-29; preaching (return to), 183, 197-212; preaching (style), 95, 96; religion interest, 11-16; as Sabbatarian, 24-25; secret sin of, 12; six resolutions of, 27-28; social ministry of, 113-14, 157, 166-81. *See also* Salvation Army, The, social ministries of; theology of, 1, 18-19, 36, 130, 132, 148, 157, 176-81, 203-6; songs of, 100, 202-3; travels of, 162-63, 210-12; unemployment of, 25; unsubstantiated Jewish origin of, 7; vision of, xiii, 1, 18-19, 118, 126, 136, 176, 203-7, 223, 233

Booth, William Bramwell (son of William and Catherine), 75, 83, 89, 113, 119, 120, 125, 127, 129, 132, 133, 145,

152-56, 159-60, 166, 175, 180-81, 183-96, 198, 199, 208-9, 210, 214, 215, 216, 219, 224, 225, 227, 230, 231

Booth-Brown, Francis (husband of Anna), 24

Booth-Clibborn, Arthur S. (husband of Catherine the younger), 160, 190-92, 193

Booth-Hellberg, Emanuel Daniel (husband of Lucy), 161, 185

Booth-Tucker, Frederick (husband of Emma), 77, 80, 86, 87, 160, 190, 194-96, 230

Bosanquet, Bernard, 177

Bunting, Percy, 154

brass bands, 133

Bright, John, 134-35

British Banner, 56

Broad Street Wesleyan Chapel, 11, 13

Brown, Ann (née Booth), 24, 25

Brown, Antoinette, 82

Brown, Francis. *See* Booth-Brown, Francis

Bunot, Heléne, 139

"Burned-Over District," 17

Burns, John, 169

Butler, Josephine, 153, 155, 156

Cadman, Elijah, 118, 126, 129, 132, 198, 225

"Call to Backsliders, A" (John Wesley), 39

Calvin, John, 57

Calvinism, 33, 56-58, 105, 117

camp meetings, 16, 79

Campbell, John, 55-59

Carey, Henry, 11, 12

Carlile, Wilson, 151

Carlisle Cathedral, 6

Carnarvon, Lord, 154

Carpenter, Joel A., 127, 137

Carr, Staff-Captain, 165

Carter, William, 88

Carwardine, Richard, 17-18, 46

Caughey, James, xv, 16-19, 36, 45-48, 63, 76, 78, 81-82, 85, 88, 90, 93

Chadwick, Owen, 14-15, 29, 45, 52, 180

Charity Organization Society, 114, 171

Charlesworth, Maude. *See* Booth, Maude

Chartists, 14-16

Chase, Samuel, 105-6, 111

choir wars, xv

cholera, 27, 106, 113

Christian, The, 105

Christian Community, The, 107

Christian Mission, The, xv, 47, 63, 89, 101, 207-8, 209, 218, 220; 105-22; Committee/Council of 111, 124; constitution of, 114, 131; discipline in, 119, 125-26; doctrines of, 117-18, 127, 137; leadership of, 118; purpose of, 128; spirit of, 120; stations, 120, 123, 124, 125, 128, 131, 136; transition of to Salvation Army, 115, 118, 119, 122, 123-37, 166-67; women of, 128-29

Christian Mission of the Friends of Zion, 191

Christian Mission Magazine, 111, 121, 126, 130, 132

Christian Theology (Cooke), 68, 130

Church Army, 151

Church Growth movement, xiv

Church of England, 23, 29, 30, 44, 64, 117, 140-45

circus, 96

City Mission movement, 106

City Temple, 164-65

Civil War, 106

Clark, E., 177

Clark, G. Kitson, 29

Clemens, Samuel Langhorne, 219

Clibborn, Arthur S. *See* Booth-Cliburn, Arthur S.

Clibborn, Percy, 191

Coaklers, 134

Coates, 86

Coke, Thomas, 44

Coleridge, Lord, 134-35, 139

Collingridge, Eliza, 108, 118, 129

Collins, Kenneth J., 32, 33-34, 56

Combe, Madame, 154

Committee of the Evangelization Society, 110

Communion rail, 18, 22, 45, 60
Congregational Stockwell New Chapel, 49, 55
Congregational Union, 55, 56, 57, 59
Congregationalism, 29, 54-59, 133
conscience, social, 29-30
Contemporary Review, The, 141, 145
Coombs, Thomas B., 163
Cooke, William, 66, 68, 86, 130
Cooper, James Fenimore, 9
Cooper, Mr., 114
Cory, John, 96, 214, 227
Cory, Richard, 96, 214, 227
Cottrill, Elizabeth, 152
Coutts, John, 180
Cox, Adelaide, 152-53
Cox, Fred, 210-12
"Creeping for Jesus" meetings, 143
Crimean War, 131-32
Criminal Law Amendment Act, 156, 168
Crofts, Dr., 77, 85, 86-87, 89-90
Crow, William Stephenson, 121, 135, 136
Curzon, George Nathaniel Lord, 219

Dalhousie, Lord, 154
Darkest England Scheme, 175, 177-81, 197-98, 213, 220
"Darkest England" Trust Deed, 170
Darwin, Charles, 30
Davidson, Randall J., 142, 144, 145
Davis, Annie, 129, 132
daycare centers, 168
Dayton, Donald, 204
Deed Poll, 44, 118
deists, 14
Denny, T. A., 139, 214, 227
Dent, Anne, 11
Dent, Mr. and Mrs., 11
Diggle, Dr., 6
Dimsdale, Joseph Cockfield, 217
Discovering an Evangelical Heritage (Dayton), 204
dissenters, 14
Divine Sovereignty (Payne), 57
divinity, practical, 32
dock strike, 168, 169, 171

Doctrines and Disciplines of The Salvation Army, 1885, The, 148
Dowdle, James, 118, 132, 207
Dowie, John A., 190-91
Dunn, Samuel, 21-22, 23-24, 52, 55
Dwyer, Canon, 177
dyings, holy, 165, 231

Eadie, 211, 224
Eagle Tavern, 141
Eames, Francis, 10
Eason, Andrew, 200
Eason, Herbert Lightfoot, 228, 230
East London Christian Revival Society, 109, 115-16
East London Evangelist, 111
East London Special Services Committee, 88, 106, 107-8
Eastern Star, 110
Ebenezer Chapel, 65
Edinburgh World Missionary Conference, 127
Edward VII, 6, 215-17, 220
Effingham Theatre, 108, 110
election, doctrines of, 56, 58, 59
"Elevator," 168
emotionalism, 70-71, 94, 127-28
Ervine, St. John, 80, 86, 91, 98, 99, 109, 110, 121, 144, 146, 156, 180, 194
Evangelical Alliance, 117
Evangelical Alliance of the United States of America, The, 188-89
evangelicalism, xiv, 29-36, 127, 199
Everett, James, 52
evil, 116, 176, 179, 198, 202, 206

Fairbank, Jenty, 111
faith, justification by, 19, 31-34, 116, 130, 167, 201-7
fall, the, 39
Farrer, Archdeacon, 177
Fawcett, Millicent, 154
Fells, Honor, 108
Female Ministry (Catherine Booth), 100, 129, 150

Female Teaching (Catherine Booth), 81, 100, 150

Fillmer, William, 27

Finney, Charles Grandison, xv, 17, 18, 45, 57, 59, 63, 76, 79, 81-82, 128, 206

Flawn, James, 113, 114, 166, 208

Food-for-the-Millions, 113-14, 119, 156, 166

"Free Grace" (John Wesley), 56

Free Methodist Chapel, 96, 100

Freedom of the City award, 217-18, 219

Frost, John, 57

fundamentalism, 127

galvanism, 71

Garrick Theatre, 88, 108

"General's Address at the Wesleyan Conference, The" (William Booth), 116

"General's New Year Address to Officers, The" (William Booth), 146-47

George V, 6, 217, 228-29

George, Henry, 175

Gilton, P. T., 69, 70

Gladstone, William Ewart, 134, 155, 214

godliness, 128

Godly Club, 31

good works, 19, 31, 32, 111

Goodwin, Dr., 135

Goodwin, Harvey, 6

Gore, John, 108

government, church, 62

grace, God's, xv, 10, 31-32, 39, 56, 58, 116, 146, 149, 202, 206; falling from, 39; sacraments as means of, xvi, 149

Grecian Theater, 141

Greenbury, David, 14, 16, 90

Griffith, William, 52

"Grog-Sellers Dream, The," 44

Hadleigh Farm, 178

Haggard, H. Rider, 175

halfway house, 167

"Hallelujah Lasses," 129, 200, 201

Hammond, Edward, 88

Handbook of Doctrine, xiv

Harcourt, W., 134

Hart, Ernest, 154

Hattersley, Roy, 86, 97, 116, 119, 155, 169, 214

healing, divine, 127

heart, habits of, 28; holiness of, 31, 34, 35, 36, 105, 116, 118, 144, 167

Heathen England (Railton), 126-27

Heitzenrater, Richard P., 23, 33, 133

Hellberg, Emanuel Daniel. *See* Booth-Hellberg, Daniel

Herbert, Auberon, 154

Higginbotham, Ann R., 152-53

Higgins, Charles, 224-25, 228, 230

History of the Salvation Army, The (Wiggins), 186

Holiness Revival, xvi

Holiness Table, xvi

Home Guard, 131, 132

holiness, doctrine of, 32, 34, 47, 81, 116-17, 127, 130, 201-7; of heart, 31, 34, 35, 36, 105, 116, 118, 144, 167; justification by, 19; of life, 31, 35, 105, 148, 149

Holiness, Scriptural, xv

Holy Club, 31

Holz, Colonel, 186

Home Mission movement, 106-7

Home Missionary Society, 57, 59

homeopathy, 71

Horns Assembly Rooms, 108

Horridge, Glenn, 106-7, 117, 133-34, 207

How to Reach the Masses with the Gospel (William Booth), 118

Hugenots, 107

Hughes, Hugh Price, 154

Hughes, Robert, 28

Huxley, Thomas, 177, 213

hydropathy, 71, 72, 81, 97, 112

hymns, 22, 144

In Darkest Africa (Stanley), 177

In Darkest England and the Way Out (Booth), 154, 166, 169, 170-81, 206

Indian Mutiny, 131-32

International Doctrine Council, xvi

International Spiritual Life Commission, xvi

Jack, Besom, 14
Jackson, Lizzie, 129
Jarrett, Rebecca, 153-55
Jermy, James, 162, 163
justification. *See* faith, justification by

Kent, John, 170
Kilham, Alexander, 35, 64-65
kingdom of God, 202-7
Kipling, Rudyard, 219
Kitching, Theodore, 231
Knill, John, 5
Knollys, Lord, 215

Lamb, David C., 178, 198
Lampard, John, 184-85
Lawley, John, 118, 132, 210
levitation, 127, 133
life, holiness of, 31, 35, 105, 148, 149
Life and Labour of the People (Charles Booth), 169
life insurance, 72
Lightfoot, J. B., 139, 142
Limelight Department, 192-93
Loch, C. S., 177, 178
Lock, Louisa, 129
Lockitt, Sarah. *See* Booth, Sarah
Lord's Supper, 145-49
Love, Joseph, 85
love feasts, 16
Ludgate, Joe, 163
Lunn, Henry, 148

Macquiban, Tim, 172-73, 180
"Maiden Tribute of Modern Babylon, The" (Stead), 154
Mann, Tom, 169
Manning, Cardinal, 141, 147-48, 177, 214
Marsden, Isaac, 11
Mary, Queen, 6
Massey, James William, 57
Mawle, John, 211
Maxwell, [?], 33

McAll, John, 112
McKinley, Edward, 162, 163, 186
McKinley, William, 214
Mearns, Andrew, 172-73
mercy, God's, 39
mercy seat, xv, 94, 144, 152
merit, 32
Methodism, American, 44, 45; Booth's association with, 12, 18, 21-36; conflict/power struggles within, xv, 22, 34-35, 43-49; denominational, 16; formalism in, 16; founding of, 30-36; membership, 43; New Connexion, *See* New Connexion Methodism; preaching of in nineteenth century, 22, 23-24; Primitive, 35, 47, 79, 117, 118, 133; theology, 39
Methodist New Connexion, The. *See* New Connexion Methodism
Methodist New Connexion Magazine, 65
Midnight Movement for Fallen Women, 100, 153
Milburn, Mr., 214
Mile End Waste, xv, 108, 144, 146, 221
millennium, 203-6
"Millennium, The" (William Booth), 205-6
Milne, Dr., 228
Milward, Sarah. *See* Mumford, Sarah
Moody, Dwight L., 45, 160
Moodyism, 198
Moore, Thomas E., 163, 186
Morgan, R. C., 105-6, 111
Morgan, William, 31
Morley, Samuel, 109, 111, 139
motor cars, 210-12
Mourez, Madame, 155
mourner's bench, 18
Mumford, Catherine. *See* Booth, Catherine
Mumford, John, 37, 38-41, 49
Mumford, Sarah (née Milward), 37, 38-43, 72, 102, 112
"My God, I Am Thine" (Charles Wesley), 42
Murdoch, Norman, 17, 142

Neale, John B., 27
Needham, Philip, xiv
New Connexion Magazine, 70, 86
New Connexion Methodism, 22, 35, 51-74, 75-91, 117, 119, 120-21, 130
New East London Theatre, 110
New Itinerancy, The, 65
New Unionism, 169
Northern Star, 15

Ocheltree, Carolyn, 51-52, 90
O'Connor, Feargus, 15, 19
Origin of Species (Darwin), 30
Orr, J. Edwin, xv
Orson, Professor, 108
Oxford Movement, 142
Oxford University, 29, 30

Paget, James, 164
Paine, Tom, 14
Pall Mall Gazette, 153, 154, 156, 175
Palmer, Dr., 93-95
Palmer, Phoebe, xv, 17, 81, 82, 93-95
Parker, Joseph, 164
Payne, George, 57
People's Mission Hall, 112
Pearse, George, 88
Pentecost, John, 130
People's Charter, 14
perfectionism, 130, 206
Plymouth Brethren, 105
Poole, Richard, 63
postmillennialism, 203-6, 223
Pound, John, 217
preaching-houses, 111
preaching stations, 110-11, 123, 124, 128, 143, 166
predestination, 56, 57, 58
prisoners, 167, 186
Progress of Liberty Among the People Called Methodists, The (Kilham), 65
prostitution, 100, 106, 151-57, 168
Protestantism, 31-32, 199
Pulling the Devil's Kingdom Down (Walker), 81-82, 200-201

Purity Crusade, 151-57, 168, 174, 215, 227
Purity of Heart (William Booth), 201

Quakers, 133

Rabbits, Edward Harris, 28-29, 37, 43-44, 47, 49, 51, 53, 69, 85, 110, 214
Rack, Henry, 31-32, 41, 94, 165
Radcliffe, Reginald, 88
Railton, George Scott, 114, 118, 121, 126-27, 132, 136, 143, 145, 146, 162-63, 166, 174-75, 176, 195, 200, 207
Rawlinson Commission, 80
redemption, personal and social, 170-81; theology of, 1, 18-19, 34, 148, 157, 179, 201-6
Red-Hot and Righteous (Winston), 200
"Red(-Nose) Army, The," 134
Reed, Henry, 110, 113
Reformers, 43-49, 51-54, 59-60, 64
Reign of Grace (Abraham Booth), 57
repentance, 34, 39, 60, 116, 166, 167
Review of Reviews, 175
Revival, The, 105, 111
revivalism, 45, 47, 64, 66, 81, 88, 94-99, 117
Rhodes, Cecil, 178
Ridsdel, William, 132
Rightmire, David, 149
Robinson, Barbara, 172
Rodin, Auguste, 219
Roman Catholic Church, 141, 214
Roman Catholicism, 31-32
Roosevelt, Theodore, 214
"rough-music," 134

sacraments, 143, 145-51; as means of grace, xvi
Saint-Saëns, Charles Camille, 219
salvation. *See* redemption; sanctification
Salvation Army, The, in America, 162-63, 186-90; in Australia, 192-94; birth of, 130-32; bombing of International Headquarters, 3; in Canada, 163; conflict within, 183-96; corps of, 3, 206-7;

development/expansion of, xiii-xvi, 116, 141-42, 198-207, 233-34; doctrines of, 117, 118, 137, 148; ecclesiology of, xiv-xv, 140, 144-45; evolution of Christian Mission into, 115, 118, 119, 122, 123-37, 166-67; military language/imagery of, 126-27, 131-32, 136-37, 206-7; mission of, xiv, xvi, 132, 146, 166-67, 173-74, 175-76, 201-6; name of, 3, 130-32; opposition to, 133-36, 138-39; relationship with churches, 140-45; self-identification of, xiv; social ministries of, 151, 156-57, 166-81, 188, 197; songs of, 131; street marching of, 134-35; training in, 208-9; uniforms of, 131; women of, 129-30, 131, 143, 149-50, 199-201

Salvation Army Assurance Society, 174

"Salvation Army and the Church, The" (Atkinson), 141

Salvation Army Origins and Early Days, The (Horridge), 133-34

"Salvation for Both Worlds" (William Booth), 176

Salvation Story, 117

Salvationist, The, 132

Salvationists, The (Coutts), 180

sanctification, 22, 33-34, 36, 115-16, 130, 149, 201-6; corporate/institutional, 202

Sandall, 114

Sankey, [?], 160

Sansom, Will, 13-14, 22-23

Schoch, Cornelie Ida Ernestine. *See* Booth, Cornelie

science, 30

Scott, Carolyn, 192

Scott, Benjamin, 153

Scott, Walter, 9

"Scripture Way of Salvation, The" (John Wesley), 33

Scripture Way of Salvation, The (Collins), 33-34

Second Advent, 206

second awakening, xv

Second Coming, 204

sectarianism, 36

Shaftesbury, Lord, 154

"Sham Compassion and the Dying Love of Christ" (Catherine Booth), 172

Shirley, Amos, 162

Shirley, Annie, 162

Shirley, Eliza, 162

Shone, Mr., 94

Short, Jane, 101, 110, 111

sin, 116, 117, 130, 144, 198

"Skeleton Army," 134

Smedley, John, 81, 112

Smith, Amanda Berry, 82

Smith, Frank, 163, 169-70, 175, 177, 186

Smith, George, 57, 59

Smith, John, 16

Smith, Rodney "Gypsy," 118

Sneinton Anglican Church, St. Stephen's, 6

Social Reform Wing, 169-70, 171

Society of Friends, 190

Society for the Prevention of Cruelty to Children, 153

"Society for the Suppression of Street Parading, The," 134

"Soldiers of the Cross" (Herbert Booth), 192-93

songs, 100, 202-3. *See also* hymns

Soper, Florence. *See* Booth, Florence

spiritualism, 154

Spurgeon, C. H., 135, 154

St. James's Episcopal Church, 190

St. Paul's Cathedral, 14-15

Stabb, John, 106

Stacey, James, 84-85

Stanley, Henry Morton, 177

Star, The, 170

Stead, William Thomas, 15-16, 139, 150, 153-56, 170-71, 174, 175, 177, 189, 214, 227-28

Strong, Josiah, 188-89

Strong, T. Vezey, 5

Sturgess, Randolph, 198

Supererogation Men, 31

Swan, Annie, 152

Swift, Susie, 146

Tait, Archibald, 139, 141, 142, 143
tea, horehound, 72
Test Act, 30
theaters, 88, 108, 110, 141
Thomas, David, 49, 55, 72, 81, 145-46
Titanic, 154, 228
Tottenham Court Chapel, 56
Training Barracks, 208
traitors, 89, 120, 189-90
Tucker, Francis. *See* Booth-Tucker, Francis
Twain, Mark, 219
Tyerman, 120

"Unconverted Salvation Army," 134

vegetarianism, 71
Victoria, Queen, 215
Victorian Church, The (Chadwick), 180
Vine, 108
Volunteer Army, 131, 132
Volunteers of America, 190

Walker, Pamela J., 81-82, 129-30, 149-50, 200-201
Walworth Wesleyan Chapel, 28
War Cry, The, 135, 146-47, 148, 155, 161, 163, 168, 175, 184-85, 186, 189, 201, 202, 225, 228, 231
Watchman, 43
Waterford (retriever), 41
Watson, [?], 59
Watts, Isaac, 22
Waugh, Benjamin, 153
Webb, Beatrice, 175
Webb, Sidney, 175

Wedgwood, Arthur, 114
Wesley (Tyerman), 120
Wesley, Charles, 22, 23, 30, 31, 34, 35, 42, 83, 96, 133, 144
Wesley, John, 12, 23, 29, 30-36, 39, 41, 44-45, 56, 62, 64, 79, 83, 96, 114, 117, 124-25, 133, 137, 149, 163, 199, 201, 206, 213
Wesley, Susanna, 97
Wesley Banner, 22
Wesleyan Times, 43
Westcott, B. F., 142
White, Arnold, 175
white-slave trade, 151-57
Whitefield, George, 23, 56, 79, 83, 96, 133, 213
Wiggins, Arch, 186, 198-99
Wilberforce, Canon, 154
Wilkinson, Canon, 142
will, freedom of, 39
Winston, Diane, 200, 201
women, alcoholic, 168; equality with men, 72-73, 81, 129, 150, 200; preaching/ministries of, xv-xvi, 73, 80-82, 91, 93-94, 95, 105, 117, 127, 128-30, 131, 143, 149-50, 199-201; shelter for, 168; working mothers, 168
Women in God's Army (Eason), 200
Women's Social Services, 152-53
workshops, sheltered, 168
World Methodist Council, xvi
World University of Humanity, 207-10
Wright, Philip James, 76, 77, 85

Zionites, 190-91